The Financial Crisis Reconsidered

The Financial Crisis Reconsidered

The Mercantilist Origin of Secular Stagnation and Boom-Bust Cycles

Daniel Aronoff

palgrave
macmillan

THE FINANCIAL CRISIS RECONSIDERED

First published 2016 by
PALGRAVE MACMILLAN

Palgrave Macmillan in the UK is an imprint of Macmillan Publishers Limited, registered in England, company number 785998, of Houndmills, Basingstoke, Hampshire, RG21 6XS.

Palgrave Macmillan in the US is a division of Nature America, Inc., One New York Plaza, Suite 4500, New York, NY 10004-1562.

Palgrave Macmillan is the global academic imprint of the above companies and has companies and representatives throughout the world.

Hardback ISBN: 978–1–137–55368–3
E-PUB ISBN: 978–1–137–54788–0
E-PDF ISBN: 978–1–137–54789–7
DOI: 10.1057/9781137547897

Distribution in the UK, Europe and the rest of the world is by Palgrave Macmillan®, a division of Macmillan Publishers Limited, registered in England, company number 785998, of Houndmills, Basingstoke, Hampshire RG21 6XS.

Library of Congress Cataloging-in-Publication Data

Aronoff, Daniel, 1961– author.
The financial crisis reconsidered : the mercantilist origin of secular stagnation and boom-bust cycles / Daniel Aronoff.
pages cm
Includes bibliographical references and index.
ISBN 978–1–137–55368–3 (hardback : alk. paper)
1. Global Financial Crisis, 2008–2009. 2. Financial crises. 3. Business cycles. 4. Mercantile system. I. Title.

HB37172008 .A76 2015
330.9′0511—dc23 2015027275

A catalogue record for the book is available from the British Library.

Contents

Figures and Tables

Figures

Tables

Preface

This book attempts to explain the broad features of the US housing boom of the 2000s, the subsequent financial crisis and the slow recovery that followed. Every acre of this territory has been surveyed by the most eminent contemporary economists, historians, and journalists. The reader must be provided a good reason to spend her time and attention (and money) on yet another tome on the subject. In this preface I shall attempt to pique her interest.

Disagreement with the "Conventional Wisdom"

In this book I present and substantiate a hypothesis that the mercantilist policies of China and other Southeast Asian countries created a capital flow bonanza[1] in the United States that set off an unsustainable housing boom, which was followed by a catastrophic financial crisis from which the United States has still not fully recovered, seven years after the event. Many of the conclusions I reach in this book differ from commonly held views on the housing boom, the financial crisis and its aftermath (relevant sections are in parenthesis).

- Most people believe the housing boom was primarily caused by a reckless increase in financial sector and household leverage and a decline in loan underwriting standards—I disagree (part I).
- Most people believe reckless lending during the housing boom was perpetrated by unscrupulous bankers—I disagree (part II).
- Most people believe that housing investors, lenders, and borrowers were motivated by irrational beliefs during the boom—I disagree (part II).
- Most people believe policymakers should have acted to slow the credit expansion during the housing boom—I harbor some doubts (part II).
- Few people (if any) see the current account deficit and income concentration as essentially similar phenomena in terms of impact on the US economy—I propose a theory that explains why they are similar and why they cause secular stagnation and boom-bust cycles (part III).
- Many people (particularly policymakers) believe it was prudent for the government to shield bank bondholders from loss and banks from bankruptcy during the financial crisis—I disagree (part IV).

- Some people believe that fiscal and monetary stimulus will speed the recovery from recession—I harbor some doubts (part V).
- Most people think banks should be subject to tighter regulation—I disagree (part VI).

Evidently, I disagree with a lot of what has been written, but this book is more than just an exercise in debunking conventional wisdom. I hold a particular view, or set of views, of the causes of the events discussed here, and I largely formed my views by piecing together insights and evidence from a number of authors and data sources. This book offers a coherent interpretation of the causes of the events at issue. It is an attempt to solve the jigsaw puzzle in a different way than has been done so far. The individual pieces may be familiar and uncontroversial, but the overall composition is new and will likely be controversial to some people.

Elements of the Jigsaw Puzzle

What follows are the people and the ideas I have drawn on to construct the explanation of the US housing boom and the financial crisis that is the subject of this book.

- Martin Wolf of the *Financial Times* has been a crucial influence in two respects. He has, through his books and newspaper columns over the past decade, emphasized the growing importance of trade and capital flows on the US economy. He also suggested to me that I read the pre-Keynesian underconsumption theorists, which led me to Malthus, from whom I got the concept of Accumulation (which is a form of underconsumption).[2] The two most important ideas in this book are that the current account deficit was the underlying cause of the US housing boom and that structural underconsumption—generated by offshore mercantilists and top income earners—is the cause of secular stagnation.[3] Mr. Wolf led me to both of them. The reader should also understand that when I disagree with Mr. Wolf on policy, I choose to wrestle with his position out of respect for the substance of his argument.
- Carmen Reinhardt, Vincent Reinhardt, and Kenneth Rogoff established the empirical linkage between capital flow bonanzas and financial crises. Their work and the work of some others convinced me that the capital flow bonanza (which was a mirror image of the current account deficit during the housing boom) was the catalyst for the US housing boom. I was not an easy convert. I had been taught that the home country benefits when foreign countries accumulate home country money without the intention of spending it. When that happens the home country receives real stuff in exchange for a claim on its resources that the foreign country does not exercise.[4] On that reasoning, I initially viewed the US current account deficit with China as an unmitigated benefit to the United States. We received

goods from China of greater value than we gave them in return, and we were able to maintain full employment. What is wrong with that? When I first read a paper by the two Reinhardts, which asserted "[capital flow] bonanzas are no blessing for advanced or emerging market economies,"[5] I was unmoved. But as I took in what they had to say, and the vast store of data they assembled to back it up (especially in the book *This Time Is Different: Eight Centuries of Financial Folly*[6]), I became convinced, and I now fully embrace their proposition.

- The Dissenting Statement of Keith Hennessey, Douglas Holtz-Eakin, and Bill Thomas to the conclusion reached by the *Financial Inquiry Commission* of the US Congress shaped my view of the causes of the housing boom and the financial crisis. In many respects, this book is an extension and elaboration of their position.
- Ben Bernanke raised an early warning of the danger of the trade and financial imbalances in 2005, and he explained that the US current account deficit was caused by the actions of foreigners, not the US government or US residents. His "global savings glut" generated the capital flow bonanza that lies at the center of my explanation of the housing boom. Bernanke made some egregious wrong calls on the eve of the financial crisis, and his policy of quantitative easing in the years that followed it may have been a big mistake. But when the crisis hit he was the right man, at the right time, in the right job. He is a leading student of monetary policy in the Great Depression, and he acted as if he knew exactly what to do, which was essentially the opposite of what the Fed did in the early 1930s. It worked. I think it counts as an instance where a single person made a difference to the unfolding of history. Bernanke is also an intellectually honest, lucid, and clear writer and one can do no better than to read his speeches from 2008 to 2013 to gain an understanding of the financial crisis and its aftermath. That is what I did.
- My reading of John Maynard Keynes and F. A. Hayek has influenced my thinking about the housing boom and the financial crisis, but not for any of the reasons most often cited in connection with either of them. They each thought very deeply about epistemology; how people gain economically relevant knowledge; how they form expectations of the future; how they act on their knowledge; and how those actions shape economic outcomes in different institutional settings. In many respects their epistemological approaches and concerns are complementary. Crudely, Keynes enquired into what we can and cannot know about the future while Hayek explored the same questions in relation to our knowledge of our surroundings.[7] Hayek is celebrated for showing how the price system increases wealth when prices guide decisions. It does so by enabling a division and utilization of knowledge that is dispersed among individuals. Yet, I think one of the ways in which the housing boom got out of hand was that people, acting on price signals, failed to recognize when prices had become distorted by the capital flow bonanza and the opacity of subprime mortgage security

structures. The fact that relevant information was not reflected in market prices misled people into making bad decisions.

Many authors invoke animal spirits as a cloak for irrational decision-making. But Keynes's concept of animal spirits is not the same thing as irrationality. Animal spirits are part of our response to the epistemological limitations of our knowledge of the future. The influence of animal spirits on decision-making is affected by the institutional structure of the economy. In particular, Keynes explained how animal spirits have a greater impact on securities prices in markets where securities can be traded, compared to environments where the opportunity to retrade is restricted. During the housing boom there was an acceleration in the growth of financing through traded assets—securitizations that occurred in the so-called shadow banking sector—versus traditional "hold to maturity" bank financing. Almost all subprime mortgages were financed by securitizations. This structural shift increased the influence of animal spirits on mortgage values and housing prices. Keynes is a deep well, and I draw insight from his writings on liquidity and his proposal for governing world trade.

- After the financial crisis hit, there was a scramble to map out the hitherto uncharted territory of shadow banking, which is where financing, money dealing, and the issuance of money-like liabilities take place outside of the commercial banking sector.[8] Much of finance had moved there, and much of the trouble that precipitated the financial crisis appears to have emanated from there. To understand how the capital flow bonanza worked its way into the US economy, one needs to trace its impact through the shadow banking sector. Tobias Adrian, Hyun Song Shin, and Zoltan Poszar have gone further than any others I am aware of in fleshing out the plumbing of the sector and identifying the motivations and the interactions of its various elements. Their studies make it possible to work out the channels through which the capital flow bonanza was transmitted into the housing boom.
- Ricardo Caballero and Emanuel Fahri developed the concept of the safe asset shortage and explained how an increase in offshore demand for safe assets incentivized the creation of pseudo-safe assets out of subprime mortgages. In so doing, they identified an important pathway by which the capital flow bonanza transmitted into the housing boom.
- Irving Fisher's long neglected concept of debt-deflation is now recognized as central to explaining the extended length and depth of the recession that followed the financial crisis. However, there is a difference between the situation after the financial crisis and the situation Fisher wrote about. Fisher described how deflating goods prices would cause the economy to enter a vicious circle of increasing real debt payments and declining consumption. In the recent crisis the Fed averted goods price deflation but asset prices spiraled downward. Ben Bernanke illuminated how asset price deflation can act as both an amplifier and an independent cause of economic contraction. John Geanakoplos and Anna Fostel's theory of the leverage cycle provides a good description of how the debt overhang on

banks and households caused by deflating asset prices triggered a contraction in lending. Atif Mian and Amer Sufi have documented that the debt overhang caused consumer spending to contract in the aftermath of the financial crisis.

- Christopher Foote and his colleagues brought forth evidence that undermines many popular explanations of the subprime housing boom. Anyone who attempts to explain the boom must grapple with their findings. Foote and his colleagues, along with Mian and Sufi, also provide the most detailed profile of spatiotemporal patterns and borrower characteristics involving subprime mortgages that I am aware of.
- Thomas Piketty and Emmanuel Saez have documented the increase in US income concentration in recent decades. I identify income concentration and current account deficits as primary sources of Accumulation, and I argue that Accumulation was the root cause of the secular stagnation and volatility that has plagued the US economy since the late 1990s.

A Preview of the Composition

This book is divided into six sections. Here is a brief description of the topics covered in each.

In Part I, I explain how the large US current account deficit was both a necessary condition and the most important contributory cause of the US housing boom. In the absence of a current account deficit, a nascent housing boom would have triggered competition for scarce resources. The result would have been an increase in interest rates and inflation, which would have quashed the housing boom at an early stage.

In Part II, I explore the channels through which the US current account deficit generated the housing boom. I show that the large purchases of US government guaranteed debt by China's central bank, and the crowding out from government debt markets and low interest rates those purchases caused, compressed the profits and impaired the solvency of one set of institutions; life insurers defined benefit pension plans and banks, which compelled them to reach for yield and undertake riskier investments. The large purchases of US government guaranteed debt by China's central bank created a shortage of assets for another set of institutions; investors seeking safe liquid holdings such as money market funds. Subprime securities with investment grade tranches were manufactured to solve problems for both sets of institutions. Subprime securities—which were highly leveraged—increased yields for the former and their use in repo trades increased the liquidity available to the latter set of institutions. I argue that the behavior that generated the housing boom was not manifestly irrational and that any attempt to prick the housing boom would have caused a large increase in unemployment.

In Part III, I present a theory of Accumulation, which is in essence the idea that any portion of saving that is not intended to be spent later on—which I call "Accumulation"—will cause deflationary pressure, increase unemployment, and slow growth. I argue that the growth in Accumulation in recent decades lies behind the secular stagnation the United States has experienced since the late 1990s. The excess saving can also induce a credit boom that is destined to end in a crisis of overproduction. I explain how the mercantilist generated current account deficit and increased income concentration were sources of Accumulation that were present during the housing boom.

In Part IV, I examine the unfolding of the financial crisis and the Fed's policy response. I explore the channels through which a collapse in the price of subprime mortgage backed securities—caused by unexpectedly large defaults—metastasized into a collapse of credit and securities prices throughout the economy. I then explain how the Fed averted a catastrophe and quelled the panic by flooding the economy with liquidity. I question the necessity for, and the motives behind, the bailout of bank creditors that took place during the financial crisis. I explain why it is more important to ensure that financial intermediaries maintain adequate capital than that they maintain adequate liquidity.

In Part V, I explain how the decline in asset values during the financial crisis created an overhang of debt on banks and household borrowers, which trapped the economy in a prolonged "balance sheet" recession. The debt overhang rendered banks undercapitalized, which limited their ability to expand credit and forced households to use their cash flow to pay down debt, rather than to spend. The contraction of credit and the application of income to pay down debt muted the effectiveness of monetary and fiscal policy. It did so by limiting the amount by which private sector spending would increase in response to stimulus from either source.

In Part VI, I recommend policy frameworks to escape the balance sheet recession; to reduce the probability of a recurrence of financial crisis, and to reverse Accumulation, which is the underlying cause of the financial crisis and the balance sheet recession that followed.

Some readers might wonder why I limit analysis of the international dimension of the financial crisis to the US current account deficit and capital flow bonanza. I recognize there were other linkages between events that took place in the United States and other countries, particularly in Europe, that are not addressed in this book. But to include that aspect would have far exceeded the scope of what can be covered in one book, particularly at the level of detail of the present analysis.

Acknowledgments

I wish to acknowledge and thank Mark Serrahn for commenting on an early draft (and for preparing many of the figures and tables in this book) and Dr. Phillip Huxley for intensively commenting on a near final draft (at least it was until he reviewed it!). I made substantial revisions in response to both reviews. I embarked on writing a book on this topic without any definite prospect of publication, without any timeline, and with only the encouragement of my family. Once my children, Chloe, Joseph, Giselle, and Lila Aronoff, became aware of what I was doing, they pressed me to keep at it and would not allow me to quit (which I wanted to do on several occasions). My wife Nancy usually tolerated with equanimity the endless hours I spent reading and drafting, zombie-like in front of my computer, as havoc sometimes reigned throughout our home. A time came when my daughter Gigi Aronoff, age 13, put her foot down and insisted that I wrap it up and find a publisher. I complied, and this book is the result.

PART I

The Current Account Deficit and the US Housing Boom: Establishing the Connections

In part I, present corroborating evidence showing that the unprecedentedly large US current account deficit was both a necessary condition and the most important contributory cause of the US housing boom that extended from approximately 2003 to 2007.

Chapter 1 recounts China's emergence as a major trading nation by the late twentieth century and the motivation behind its policy of running trade surpluses. Chapter 2 reviews both historical and contemporary studies of the causal factors that lie behind the recurring pattern of credit-fueled booms followed by financial crises, and shows the US current account deficit to have been an important cause of the US housing boom. Chapter 3 shows that the US current account deficit during the housing boom was generated by the mercantilist policies of foreign governments, particularly Southeast Asia and China. Chapter 4 presents a logical demonstration that the United States required a current account deficit in order to have sustained a boom of a large magnitude such as the housing boom.

CHAPTER 1

The Metamorphosis of China's Trade Policy

Let China sleep; when she awakes she will shake the world.

—Napoleon Bonaparte

Well, you can just stop and think of what could happen if anybody with a decent system of government got control of the mainland. Good God... they will be the leaders of the world.

—Richard Nixon[1]

Part I of this book analyzes the forces that generated the US housing boom of the 2000s. The most important causal element, it shall be argued, was China's trade surplus with the United States. Therefore, I begin with a brief account of China's emergence at the turn of the twenty-first century as the greatest trading nation on earth and the propagator of a large trade imbalance with the United States.

China's Traditional Aversion to Trade

China was not historically a trading nation. During the four millennia in which the Middle Kingdom was culturally and politically ascendant in Asia, it was economically self-sufficient. Its trade primarily consisted in the emperor's receipt of gifts from the surrounding Barbarian peoples, as part of their annual pilgrimage to Kowtow before the Sun King. By the eighteenth century, the advances in navigation, shipbuilding, and weaponry that enabled Europe to explore and dominate much of the world led to the opening up of seaborne trade routes to China. In 1760, the Qing Dynasty responded by restricting European trade to the port of Canton ("Guangzhou"), a city located on the tributary to the Pearl River Delta. There, trade and foreign residency was limited to five months of the year, and foreign traders were required to deal solely through a small number of licensed Chinese Hong merchants. In 1793, the British sent an embassy under the command of George Macartney "loaded with expensive gifts designed to show the finest aspects of British manufacturing technology"[2] intended to entice China into broadening trade and diplomatic relations with Britain. The Qianlong emperor rebuffed the overture, explaining that China needed nothing from other countries, and sent an edict to King George III stating, "We have never valued ingenious articles, nor do we have the slightest need of your country's manufacturers."[3] Then followed several decades of respite from foreign pressure to open trade, not, as many in China probably believed, because King George was awed into submission by the emperor's rebuke, but rather because the Napoleonic Wars commanded the attention and consumed the resources of Europe. Soon after the end of war in 1815, the British returned and resumed their efforts to open trade with China.

By 1836, a constellation of pressures, most notably a Chinese crackdown on the importation of opium, which was the major commodity imported into China by British traders at that time, escalated into a conflict that resulted in a Chinese ban on foreign trade and a blockade of the foreign "factories" in Guangzhou. The British responded by dispatching a naval fleet that blockaded China's major ports, disrupted traffic and communications along its major river and canal routes, and occupied portions of Guangzhou and Shanghai. The Chinese capitulated, and in 1842 the first Opium War ended with the Treaty of Nanjing. The treaty required that China pay indemnities to Britain; it exempted Britain from the traditional formalities required of foreigners in communications with the emperor's court; it disbanded the Canton Cohong trade monopoly and opened several additional ports to trade, and it required China to hand over Hong Kong to Britain. The Treaty of Nanjing marked the worst reversal of fortune in Chinese history. It coincided with, and accelerated, a weakening of Imperial control that ushered in an era of violence, rebellion, and instability in China.

The weakening of Imperial control enabled foreigners to become involved in internal Chinese affairs for the first time; in the mid-1850s Western powers provided assistance to the emperor in quashing the Taiping's attempted seizure of Shanghai. During that time the British occupied Guangzhou, exiled a high Chinese official who was not to their liking, and forced the Chinese into a new treaty—the Treaty of Tianjin of 1858—that contained additional terms more favorable to Britain. Of particular importance was the concession that permitted permanent residence of a British ambassador in Peking ("Beijing"). Never before in Chinese history had non-Chinese persons been allowed to reside in the capital. It was, in the context of Chinese history and culture, an epic humiliation. When the Chinese balked at some of the treaty terms, the British marched on Beijing and burnt to the ground the emperor's Summer Palace, which was located in a nearby suburb.

For China, the century that followed the Opium Wars began the unraveling of an order that had been in more or less continuous existence for four thousand years. The Middle Kingdom disintegrated into a period of internal turmoil, culminating in the abdication of the Qing emperor in 1912, succeeded by a brief era of soaring hopes and flourishing culture that soon descended into fractious bloody contests among warlords. China's disintegration attracted the attention of foreign opportunists, which reached a crescendo with the brutal Japanese invasion in 1937.

The founding of the People's Republic of China in 1949 marked the end of its century long political disintegration (though not an end to the violence and suffering inflicted on its people). Chairman Mao was convinced that the Confucian foundation of Chinese polity and society, which for millennia had underpinned its supremacy, was unsuited to the modern world. The insularity of Confucianism made China incapable of adopting new technology, modes of organization and thought that he deemed necessary for China to defend itself, and successfully compete with industrialized nations. On the basis of that analysis, Mao set out to obliterate all vestiges of traditional Chinese culture and to remold society in accordance with Marxist precepts, which he regarded as the vanguard of modernism. On one matter, however, Mao's interpretation of Marxism was fully in accord with traditional Chinese practice and the recently wounded pride of many Chinese people; it was that China should cut off trade with foreigners. The Marxist reason was that Western imperialists like Britain and the United States desired trade as a means to exploit Chinese labor and to provide a market for the overproduction of goods manufactured by the toil of exploited Western proletarians. The traumas and humiliations suffered at the hands of foreigners over the prior century fed a desire to expel from China any foreign influence or involvement. Therefore, for understandable reasons, China positioned itself in the second half of the twentieth century, as regards trade and involvement with the outside world, in the same insular position it had occupied for millennia prior to the encroachment by Western powers that began in the eighteenth century.

It is from this long historical perspective that China's rise, over a mere two decades, to become the world's greatest trading nation, ought to be considered. In light of its past, the recent growth of China's trade is nothing short of miraculous, and one should not be surprised to find that China's historical experience has influenced the manner in which it conducts its trade and that it will likely affect the way it responds to the growing pressures from its foreign trading partners to modify its behavior.

Reform and Opening—the 1980s

By the Third Plenum of the Chinese Communist Party (CCP) in 1978, two years after Mao's death, Deng Xiaoping solidified his position as the leader of China and began to introduce market reforms into the Chinese economy. The initial reforms involved agriculture. During the Mao era, each province aimed to attain self-sufficiency in food production and formed centrally controlled collectives to achieve the goal. One of Deng's key protégés, Zhao Ziyang, who became premier and then general secretary of the CCP in the 1980s, realized this system involved three layers of inefficiency. First, he recognized that the drive for self-sufficiency prevented China's regions from specializing in the cultivation of crops and livestock for which they held a comparative advantage, and that specialization would have enabled them to reap the benefits of that advantage by trading with other regions in China for product in which those other regions possessed a comparative advantage. Second, he understood that collectivization damped the incentive to work, and deprived farmers of the authority to make decisions about what to plant, even though her superior knowledge of local circumstances equipped the individual farmer to make more informed decisions concerning the property she cultivated. Third, the collectivized organization of agriculture meant that bargaining among committees of central planners, rather than market prices, guided resource allocation and perpetually resulted in surpluses of some perishable commodities and shortages of others. The reforms dealt with each of these issues by allowing individual farmers to make their own decisions about crop cultivation, to retain a portion of their profits, and to pay for inputs and sell outputs at prices formed in a market, rather than as dictated by the government. Here is how Zhao described the effects of the agricultural reforms:

> The rural areas experienced a prosperity, in large part because we resolved the issue of "those who farm will have land" by implementing a "rural land contract" policy. The old system where farmers were employees of a production team, had changed; farmers began to plant for themselves. The rural energy that was unleashed in those years was magical, beyond what anyone could have imagined. A problem thought to be unsolvable had worked itself out in just a few years' time.[4]

Another part of Deng's reform agenda, opening trade with foreigners, met with stiff internal resistance and was slow to get off the ground. Zhao, as usual, understood better than most of his contemporaries that trade with other countries conferred the same benefits as trade among the internal provinces of China:

> Only under the conditions of an open-door policy could we take advantage of what we had, and trade for what we needed. Each place and each society has its strengths; even poor regions have their advantages, such as cheap labor. That is a great advantage in international competition... I now realize that if a nation is closed, is not integrated into the international market, or does not take advantage of international trade, then it will fall behind and modernization will be impossible.[5]

What Zhao and Deng (and Deng's other protégée Hu Youbang) were advocating was a veritable revolution in Chinese policy; it went against China's traditional aversion to trade by seemingly embracing the source of China's recent humiliations. Its most powerful opponent was Deng's co-elder Chen Yun, who had been in charge of economic policy under Mao. Chen, and many others, saw the opening of trade as an abandonment of Marxist principles and argued that it would be impossible for China to gain any benefits from trade with capitalist countries in pursuit of "surplus profits."[6] Underlying the opposition to trade was the fear of reopening the wounds of the past; Zhao reported that

> it was not easy for China to carry out the Reform and Open-Door Policy. Whenever there were issues involving relationships with foreigners, people were fearful. And there were many accusations made against reformers: people were afraid of being exploited, having our sovereignty undermined, or suffering an insult to our nation.[7]

Zhao countered (in his memoirs) with a powerful rebuke worthy of Adam Smith:

> China had closed its doors for many years in the name of independence and self-reliance, but in fact it was a self-imposed isolation. The purpose of implementing

> an open-door policy was to conduct foreign trade, to trade for what we needed. Some people felt ashamed about the idea of importing. What was there to feel ashamed about? It wasn't begging! It was a mutual exchange, which was also a form of self-reliance. The issue has caused us to make costly mistakes. This was a close-minded mentality, a failure to understand how to make use of one's own strengths.[8]

As part of its trade policy, China carved out space for private enterprise and competition in export industries while barring state owned enterprises ("SOEs") from the sector. In fits and starts, beginning with the designation of three rural villages as "special economic zones" (two of them located on the Pearl River Delta near Guangzhou), China began its ascent to the pinnacle of world trade. As Zhao stated: "At the time, I had doubts. Could it really be that easy? It now appears that it indeed was not all that difficult. The key was to embrace openness.[9]"

No region of China has benefitted more from trade that Guangzhou, the location of the early British trade and source of conflict that led to the Opium Wars. Its port is the second busiest in China and fourth busiest in the world. It population has grown to become the second largest with the second highest per capita income on the Chinese mainland.

Finally, Deng's reforms enabled private enterprise to flourish in the less regulated rural areas, away from the large cities which were dominated by urban political machines. Economist Yasheng Huang has documented the dramatic proliferation of new entrepreneurial rural enterprises and their contribution to raising incomes in rural areas that occurred in the 1980s.[10] Professor Huang has demonstrated that the 1980s was the decade in which China experienced the greatest advance in median household incomes and poverty reduction, with growth balanced between the sectors of its economy, including rural and urban areas, without being overly dependent on exports or FDI.

Policy after Tiananmen—the 1990s

Zhao was purged after he refused to order Chinese troops to fire upon the student demonstrators in Tiananmen Square in 1989. He lived out his remaining years under permanent house arrest. Chinese economic policy underwent a significant change after Tiananmen, as Deng pulled back on many of the freedoms previously granted to domestic enterprise. The government clamped down on the free market reforms in rural areas, bolstered the role of monopoly SOEs in the domestic economy, and reasserted government control over banking. At the same time, however, China increased its commitment to trade, which Deng endorsed with his famous "Southern Tour" of port cities in 1992. Yasheng Huang described the change in Chinese economic policy this way;

> The prevailing economic policy in the 1990's was to favor the urban areas over the rural areas and to favor foreign capitalists—FDI—over indigenous capitalists. The cumulative effect of all these policies was a dramatic change in the balance

> of power between the two China's—the rural China that is more capitalistic and market- driven and the urban China that is more state-controlled. In the 1990's the balance tilted decisively in favor of the urban China.[11]

China became a mixed economy. The state dominated certain industries. Factor markets for agriculture and industrial goods—steel, power generation, transportation infrastructure, and land—and banking remained heavily regulated by the state and/or monopolized by SOEs. The state limited investment options for individual savers to residential real estate and bank deposits. Money flowing into real estate became a primary source for funding local governments, which were able to confiscate land from peasants and lease to property developers. Interest paid on bank deposits were set at very low levels, and banks were directed to lend to SOEs at low interest rates and to invest in government bonds. The SOEs did not distribute dividends to the state, but rather reinvested earnings in new projects (why they did not distribute dividends is a matter of ongoing speculation). The result of state domination was to divert savings and SOE profits into investment in infrastructure, to promote real estate development, and to reduce factor prices for the rest of the economy, which provided a subsidy to producers.

Consumer goods markets and export industries operated with far less state regulation and SOE involvement. Low factor prices and low labor costs encouraged production, but the lack of credit—which was channeled to SOEs—required nonstate firms to finance investment with retained earnings. The combination of profitable growth opportunities and limited credit resulted in an extremely high private corporate savings rate. The limitation on shareholder distributions also damped consumer demand, which encouraged the flow of investment toward export industries.

Social insurance spending—for education and healthcare—was reduced, which caused households to increase precautionary savings. The State reduced its expenditure on social benefits while SOEs, who offered some level of benefits, rationalized operations, and shed workers. Nonstate firms possessed a significant bargaining advantage over the massive wave of rural labor moving to the port cities in search of employment and did not find it necessary to offer fringe benefits to attract employees. The poor bargaining position of rural workers was partially caused by the post-Tiananmen discouragement of rural entrepreneurship, which suppressed rural incomes.

The post-Tiananmen economic policy reshaped the balance between sectors of the Chinese economy. Exports, infrastructure, and real estate development became the engines of China's economic growth, and they were financed by dramatic increases in both corporate and household savings and FDI. Consumer goods industries lagged due to the extremely high rate of saving.[12]

During the 1990s savings, as a proportion of GDP, grew in all sectors: household, business, and government. In 2000 China's savings rate of 37 percent of GDP was the highest ever recorded for a country. Notwithstanding China's breakneck GDP growth rate, which averaged above 10 percent from 2000 to 2007,[13] the domestic economy could not profitably invest all of its growing pool of savings. The rate of return on domestic investment in China became very low. China's economy continued to grow, but its growth had become unbalanced

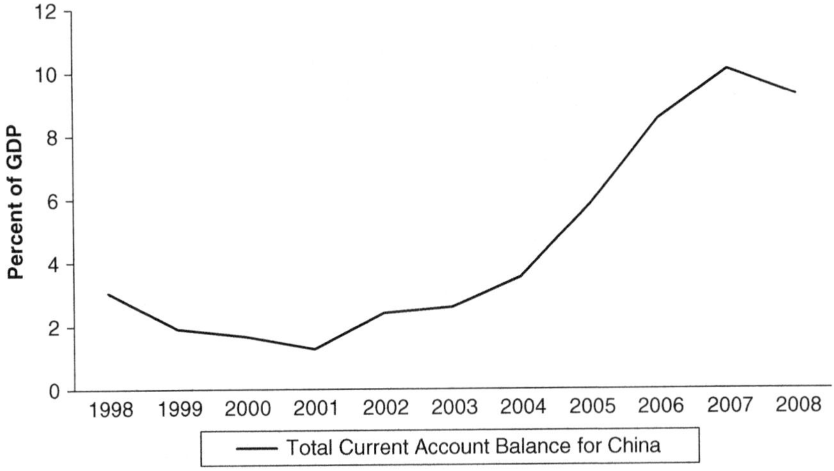

Figure 1.1 Total current account balance for China, 1998–2008.
Source: OECD.

between sectors; heavy in basic industries, construction, and real estate and underweight in consumer goods and social infrastructure. Ben Bernanke pointed out that China's return on investment had been declining into the early 2000s

> from 1990 to 2001, fixed investment as a share of GDP in China averaged about 33 percent, and the economy grew at an annual rate of 10 percent. Between 2001 and 2005, fixed investment's share of GDP rose to about 40 percent, but the economy's average growth rate remained about the same, suggesting a lower return to the more recent investment.[14]

The conjuncture of a low return on domestic investment (resultant from the low rate of consumption relative to GDP) and excessive saving created a policy dilemma by the early 2000s. If the savings were not invested, the economy would contract, but if domestic investment continued to grow at it prior trend, there was a risk of massive defaults and bankruptcies. Market opportunities directed investment toward the export sector, where savings could be profitability employed. The increase in the share of investment directed to exports was the fundamental force that propelled China into current account surplus (figure 1.1).

Manufacturer to the World—the 2000s

In 1994 China devalued and pegged the renminbi (RMB) to the dollar at an exchange rate that was below the market determined exchange rate in order to improve the competitiveness of its exports (figure 1.2).

Also in the 1990s, China began to subsidize its exports. For example, China's corporate income tax rate from 1991 to 2008 was 30 percent, but firms located in special economic and coastal development zones could reduce their tax rate

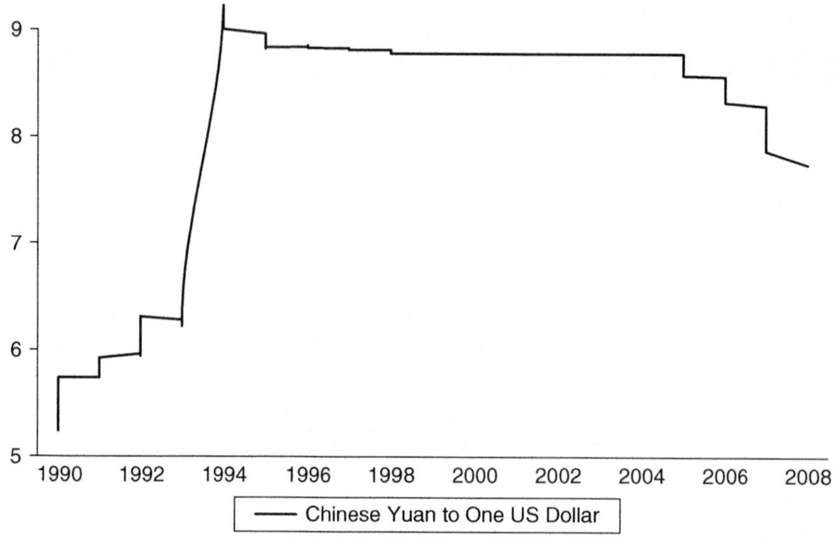

Figure 1.2 China/US foreign exchange rate, 1990–2008.
Source: Board of Governors of the Federal Reserve System.

to 10 percent if they exported over 70 percent of their output.[15] It has been estimated that China's export subsidies in the 2000s were around 1.5 percent of GDP.[16] At the same time, the discouragement of imports was a cornerstone of China's economic policy.[17] China's export promotion and import restriction policies generated large current account surpluses with the United States and EU, offset to some extent by net imports of raw materials and energy from commodity exporters required for its economic expansion. China's current account surplus was amplified in 2005, when the Chinese government implemented policies to slow the growth of domestic investment. From 2005 to 2008 (when policy reversed in response to the collapse in exports caused by the financial crisis) the growing gap between saving and investment was reflected in a widening of China's current account surplus (figures 1.2 and 1.3).[18]

A watershed event for China was its entry into the World Trade Organization (WTO) in 2001. WTO membership facilitated exports by lowering barriers to sales of Chinese goods into other countries. In addition to its own export promotion policies and the benefits of WTO membership, another factor that contributed to Chinese exports may have been the flow of saving from China into the United States. This possibility arises from the evolving nature of supply chains. The reasoning is as follows: first, China's savings outflow caused US interest rates to decline (as I shall explain in the next chapter). Second, supply chains for manufactured goods have become highly globalized, meaning that intermediate products move through different countries in the steps from basic materials to final product, where the location of each stage relates to some advantage in cost or quality.[19] Third, the transport of intermediate product between locations takes time (and money[20]), which implies that the time to produce a good increases with the number of separate locations for intermediate

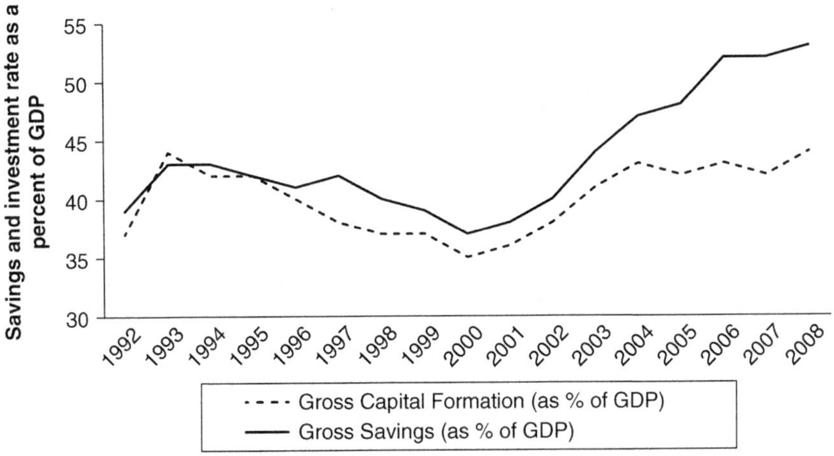

Figure 1.3 Saving and investment in China, 1992–2008.
Source: World Bank.

production. This gives rise to a tradeoff between the advantages of location specialization versus the cost of financing a production process that takes more time as the number of separate locations increases. As interest rates decline, the penalty for transporting intermediate goods between locations declines, which will cause supply chains to spread out geographically.[21] It does so because lower interest rates imply a lower time cost of money. Therefore, China's savings flow into the United States may have caused, by lowering interest rates, an increase in offshore production from the US, much of which gravitated to China.[22]

In the 2000s, China managed to avoid the contractionary effects of oversaving at least in part by exporting a sizeable proportion of its output and its excess saving abroad. China's external trade grew steadily since the early 1980s, but in the 2000s trade, and exports in particular, morphed into gargantuan proportions. In 2000 China's export/GDP ratio was around 23 percent, which was actually below the world average export/GDP ratio of around 25 percent. By 2007 China's export/GDP ratio increased to over 38.4 percent, compared to a world average of just under 29 percent.[23] By the end of the 2000s China had become the largest exporter in the world.

It is a supreme irony that China's reemergence as a great economic power has been intertwined with, and dependent on, a veritable addiction to trade; and not just trade per se, but export penetration into the same Western developed countries who so traumatically forced their exports into China in the nineteenth century. It is a reversal of China's experience over the previous four thousand years. Trade has propelled China to unprecedented heights, but the sheer volume of its exports, which have saturated world markets, implies that trade cannot be the growth engine for China in the future. This has been recognized by China's leadership. Former president Hu Jintao described China's reliance on investment in infrastructure, high domestic saving, and extreme export dependence as "unbalanced, uncoordinated, and unsustainable."[24]

How China will adjust, and whether it will continue to achieve a high rate of growth, is an unresolved question. It is generally agreed that the key is for China's rate of consumption to increase. But there is much controversy over how, and whether, this can come about. The future of China's economy hinges on the answer, but it is a question that lies beyond the scope of this book.

Understanding an Important Concept: Mercantilism

A fundamental contention of this book is that the origins of the US housing boom and the financial crisis that followed arose, in large part, from the mercantilist policies of China and other Southeast Asian countries. Consequently, it is vital that the reader understand what I mean by the phrase "mercantilism."

Mercantilism

In *The Wealth of Nations*, Adam Smith defined the policy of using government intervention to run trade surpluses as "mercantilism."

> The encouragements of exportation, and the discouragement of importation, are the two great engines by which the mercantile system proposes to enrich every country... Its ultimate object [is] ... to enrich the country by an advantageous balance of trade.[25]

Therefore, any policy that has as its primary goal to run a current account surplus for the home economy is "mercantilist." In chapter 3 I shall explain how the trade policies of Southeast Asian countries in response to the Asian financial crisis of 1997, and of China during the 2000s, were mercantilist.

China's Trade Policy and the US Housing Boom

After its entry into the WTO, China's exports to the United States took off, as did its bilateral trade surplus and its accumulation of dollar reserves. Export of goods to the United States rose from $100 billion in 2000 to $320 billion in 2007; China's bilateral trade surplus with the United States increased dramatically, and its estimated holdings of US securities rose from under $100 billion in 2000 to over $1 trillion in 2008 (figure 1.4).[26]

China's emergence as the leading trading nation is unique and unexpected given its long and deep historical aversion to trade. In light of that history, it may yet prove impermanent. In any event, it is quite understandable why China would be less trusting of the vagaries of an unfettered market, and therefore more prone to intervene to control its trade, than the United States. The United States has long perceived trade as advantageous, and the promotion of economic integration through institutions such as the WTO has been a centerpiece of it

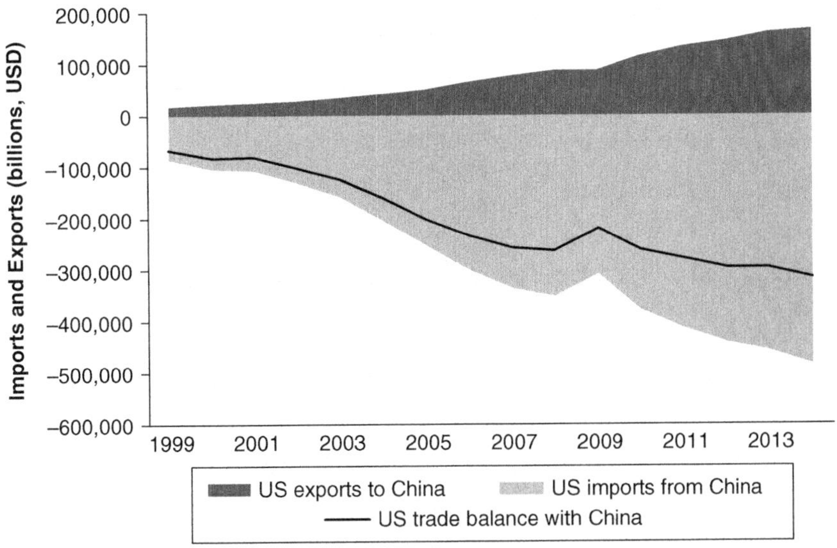

Figure 1.4 US China bilateral trade in goods, 1999–2014.
Source: US Bureau of Economic Analysis.

foreign policy since World War II. China, on the other hand, was deeply traumatized when it was forced to open itself to trade in the nineteenth century. This divergence in past experience with trade has given rise to sometimes incongruent reactions to contemporary trade issues. China is much more dependent on trade for its prosperity than is the United States, and as I shall argue in this book, the United States was injured by the trade imbalances that emerged in the 2000s. Yet, China's attitude toward trade remains more ambivalent than that of the United States.

Ultimately, I think the US attitude is the correct one. The law of comparative advantage, so brilliantly expounded by Zhao Ziyang, suggests that China's emergence as a trading nation has improved the living standards not only of its own people, but also of those with whom it trades. Yet, the massive bilateral trade imbalance generated by China's trade policies, and the reinvestment of its dollar reserves into the US economy, created a new force at work inside the United States, which propagated imbalances throughout the US economy. China avoided a deflationary contraction in the 2000s in large part by exporting a sizeable portion of its output and its excess savings to the United States; this was bound to have a profound impact on the US economy. The first part of this book is a study of the channels by which the trade imbalance perpetrated by China made possible the US housing boom from 2003 to 2007.

CHAPTER 2

The Current Account Deficit and the Housing Boom

It ain't what you don't know that gets you into trouble. It's what you know for sure that just ain't so.

—Mark Twain

Did Leverage Maketh the Boom?

There is a near consensus among financial journalists, economists, and policy-makers that the US housing boom—which started just after the turn of the millennium and ended by mid-2007[1]—and the financial crisis that followed were caused by loose monetary policy and negligent financial regulation, aided and abetted by avarice and dishonesty among bankers and their borrowers.[2] Many people believe that these errant practices enabled reckless financial leverage, easy credit, and fraud to proliferate, which generated an unsustainable boom that, because of its unstable foundation, was destined to end in a calamitous crisis. That was the core conclusion of the Financial Inquiry Commission appointed by the US Congress to investigate the causes of the crisis.[3] "We conclude a combination of excessive borrowing, risky investments and lack of transparency put the financial system on a collision course with crisis."[4]

Considerable evidence supports this view. Mortgage lending grew rapidly during the housing boom and was accompanied by an unprecedented run up in home prices. From 2000 to 2008, residential mortgage liabilities more than doubled and the volume of subprime and Alt-A mortgages, which were ground zero for the crisis, grew by 800 percent (figure 2.1).[5]

Between 2000 and the peak of the housing boom in mid-2006, home prices more than doubled, while the consumer price index (CPI) increased by less than 20 percent. In 2005 alone, real home prices increased by more than 12 percent compared to a 2 percent increase in real gross domestic product (GDP) (figure 2.2).

During the same period, the leverage of broker-dealers (often referred to as "investment banks") rose from around 20X at the beginning of the housing boom, to over 40X at the peak in 2007 (see figure 2.3). Meanwhile, US

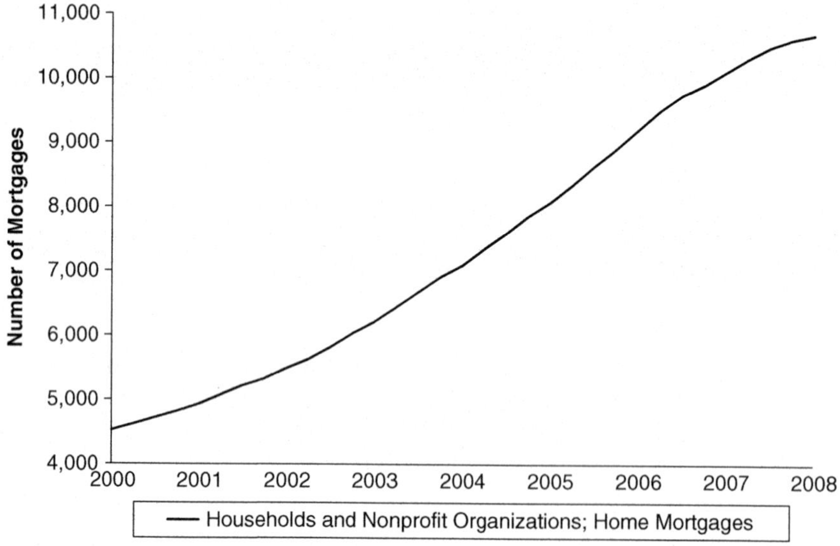

Figure 2.1 Home mortgage liability levels, 2000–2008.
Source: Board of Governors of the Federal Reserve System.

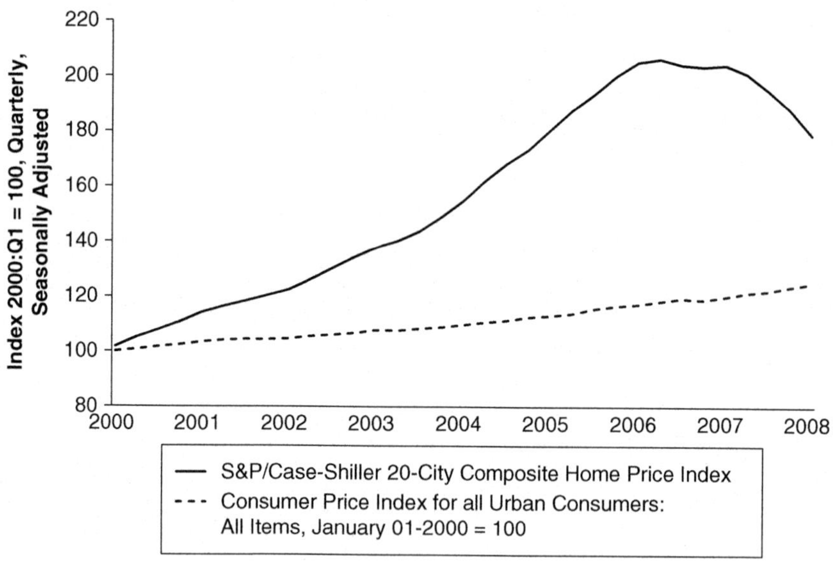

Figure 2.2 Home price and CPI growth, 2000–2008.
Source: S&P Case Shiller and US Bureau of Labor Statistics.

commercial banks, which operated under stricter on-balance sheet leverage limits, evaded the constraint by expanding off-balance sheet financing to underwrite the asset backed securities (ABS) into which they sold a significant portion of the mortgage, credit card, and other debt they originated (see figure 7.2).

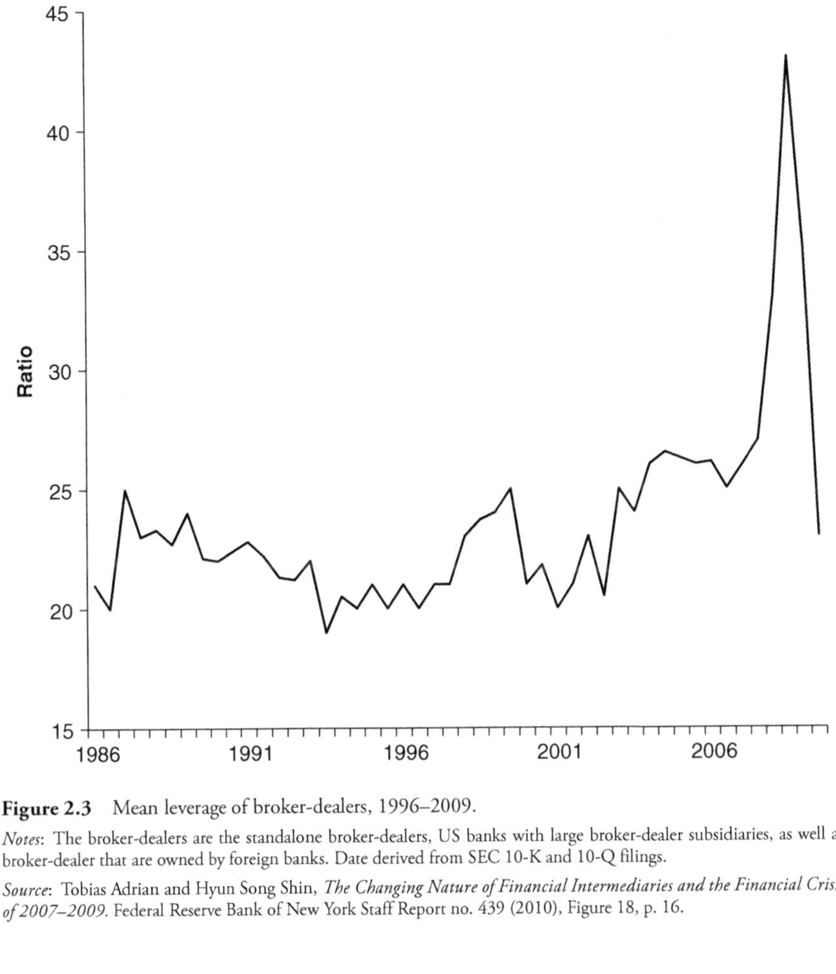

Figure 2.3 Mean leverage of broker-dealers, 1996–2009.

Notes: The broker-dealers are the standalone broker-dealers, US banks with large broker-dealer subsidiaries, as well as broker-dealer that are owned by foreign banks. Date derived from SEC 10-K and 10-Q filings.

Source: Tobias Adrian and Hyun Song Shin, *The Changing Nature of Financial Intermediaries and the Financial Crisis of 2007–2009*. Federal Reserve Bank of New York Staff Report no. 439 (2010), Figure 18, p. 16.

The coincident explosion in financial intermediary and household leverage, and the run up in real home prices prior to the financial crisis reflected a situation where mortgage investors, lenders, and households had taken on an extraordinary amount of debt to support overvalued residential real estate. When home values began to decline, mortgage defaults soared. The collapse in the performance and ratings of subprime mortgage securities forced financial intermediaries and institutional investors, who held the bulk of subprime mortgage securities, to write down the value of their mortgage holdings, which rendered many of the largest US financial institutions insolvent. These facts lend substantial credence to the hypothesis that the primary cause of the housing boom and the financial crisis that followed was a domestic credit boom gone too far.

The belief that the financial crisis was caused by the credit explosion that preceded it found its way into popular discourse, with attribution of moral culpability placed on borrowers and lenders, depending upon political leanings. One variant of this view blames the financial crisis on the moral failings of those who borrowed recklessly during the boom. Rick Santelli, a financial reporter at the network *CNBC*, became something of a folk hero to millions when, on February 19, 2009, he vented against the idea of providing taxpayer relief to homeowners who had imprudently borrowed in order to live beyond their means:

> This is America! (turns around to address pit traders) How many of you people want to pay for your neighbors' mortgage that has an extra bathroom and can't pay their bills? Raise their hand. (traders boo; Santelli turns around to face CNBC camera) President Obama, are you listening?[6]

Another variation on this theme places blame on predatory bankers, who allegedly seduced unsuspecting homeowners to take on debt they could not afford and then received a bailout from the federal government when their loans turned sour. Frank Rich, a *New York Times* columnist, expressed frustration from the other side of the aisle, so to speak:

> Americans must be told the full story of how Wall Street gamed and inflated the housing bubble, made out like bandits, and then left millions of households in ruin . . . Why was our money used to make these high-flying gamblers whole while ordinary Americans received no such beneficence?[7]

The common thread running through both populist reactions is the conviction that the increase in household borrowing that accompanied the boom, reflected a growing decadence among US homeowners and banks—that an outbreak of profligacy and irresponsibility, aided and abetted by Wall Street's alchemic profusion of new temptations and possibilities to borrow, caused the calamity. Subprime mortgages enabled millions to achieve the American dream of home ownership, albeit by living beyond their means, and the massive wave of home equity borrowing enabled people who already owned their homes to live in larger homes or to treat their homes as cash registers to support enlarged spending habits. Many assert that the overleveraging made possible by lax regulation and loose monetary policy enabled a flourishing of latent avarice among bankers and immoderation among their borrowers. The political right rails against the fecklessness of defaulted mortgage borrowers, and the left against the guile of bankers.

A compelling and highly regarded explanation for the decline in risk aversion that underlay all of the alleged key drivers of the boom (easy money, absentee financial oversight, leverage, loose underwriting standards, and spendthrift habits) is often associated with the writings of economist Hyman Minsky. It attributes these policy and behavior shifts to a complacency over risk brought on by nearly two decades of relatively crisis-free economic growth that preceded the financial crisis, popularly referred to as the "Great Moderation." During this period, an implicit Fed guaranty to reduce interest rates whenever asset prices precipitously declined cast a safety net that placed a floor on losses.[8] This socialization of investment risk acquired the epithet "The Greenspan Put,"[9] named after Alan Greenspan, chairman of the Fed from 1987 to 2006. According to this Minskyan view, regulators, lenders, and borrowers gradually ceased to worry about, or to hedge, the possibility that asset prices could plunge deeply. Borrowers became more willing to increase their leverage, banks became more eager to increase profit by shrinking their capital cushions, and by lending to riskier prospects, while regulators looked the other way.

During the housing boom, banks and broker-dealers employed a sophisticated mathematical methodology for calculating risk called Value at Risk (VaR),[10] which appeared to confirm that economic conditions had become more stable, and that loan default risks had receded. VaR models estimate the decline in the prices of assets in a bank's portfolio, and therefrom the net worth of the bank, that will occur in an adverse, low probability event. It provides an answer to the question, "what is the expected decline in the value of such and such an asset if its price plunges below a level that can only occur with a very small probability?" Or, alternatively, "by how much would the value of our portfolio decline if a market crash occurs, one that will only occur X% of the time?" To generate an answer to those questions, the actual history of asset prices are fed into the VaR model and the more recent prices are treated as more informative, since they are presumed to reflect contemporary circumstances.

The methodology of VaR implies that if asset price volatility has declined (more particularly, if the estimated lower tail of the probability distribution of asset prices has become thinner), asset prices will not plunge too deeply, even in

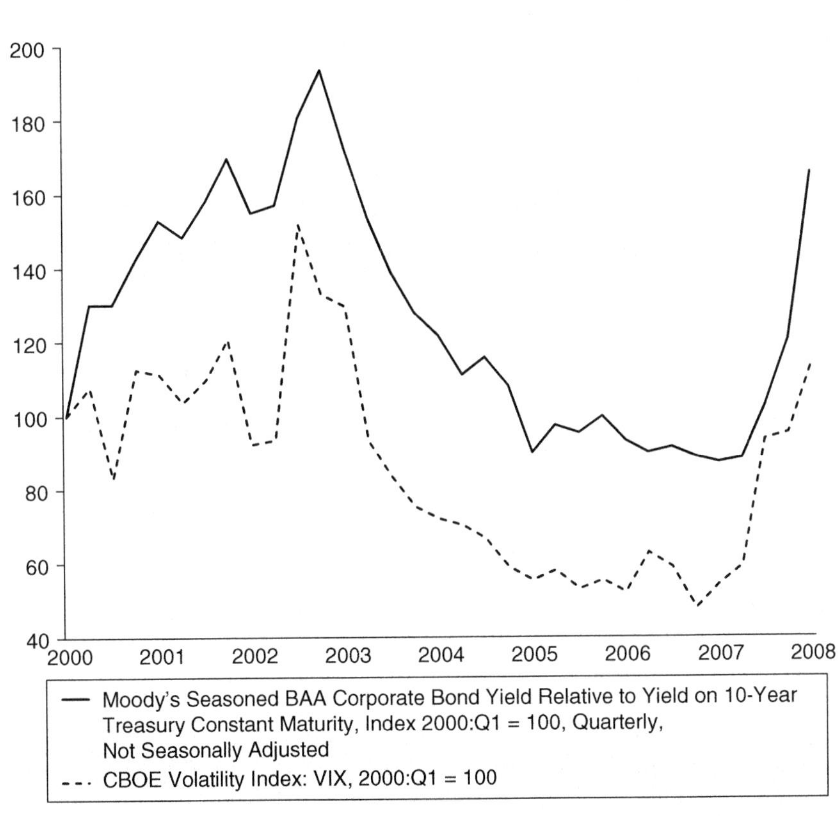

Figure 2.4 BAA corporate bond yield relative to yield on ten-year treasury, 2000–2008.

Source: Moody's and CBOE.

low probability, adverse circumstances. VaR risk measurements compressed during the Great Moderation, since the Greenspan Put prevented steep declines in asset prices. During the housing boom, implied volatility as measured by the VIX equity index and risk bond yield spreads declined precipitously (figure 2.4).[11] VIX and risk yields are key inputs into VaR models, since they are measures of different dimensions of market risk. The decline in those risk measures provide support for the Minskyan view that credit expansion—both the amount of leverage and the scope of assets financed—were fueled by a decline in perceived risk.

Economists John Geanakoplos and Ana Fostel developed a theory, called the "leverage cycle," that adds to Minsky's insight that leverage tends to expand during quiescent periods.[12] The leverage cycle theory predicts that leverage and credit are strongly procyclical. They expand in periods of low volatility because lenders, who are not very concerned about the risk of large declines in collateral values when volatility is low, will be willing to increase the leverage offered on loans. This in turn increases funds available to speculators, who can use their borrowing capacity to bid up asset prices. The bidding up of asset prices reduces losses, which begets more leverage.

Studies Linking Leverage to Booms and Financial Crises

Economists Oscar Jordà, Moritz Schularick, and Alan Taylor assembled an historical database on economic variables for 14 developed countries from 1870 to 2008 to examine the predictive value of credit, money, current account balance, and other macroeconomic indicators on subsequent financial crisis. They show that financial sector leverage has increased considerably since the end of World War II, and that credit growth has become the most powerful predictor of financial crises. The most robust result of their study is that above-trend growth in domestic bank credit increases the probability of a subsequent financial crisis occurring within 5 years. Their results provide key empirical support for the consensus view, by establishing that, among developed countries over the past century, domestic credit expansion has become the most reliable predictor of a future financial crisis.[13]

> We test one element of the credit view argument—associated with Minsky, Kindleberger, and others—that financial crises can be seen as "credit booms gone wrong"...Lagged credit growth turns out to be highly significant as a predictor of financial crises, but the addition of *any* of the other variables adds very little explanatory power.[14]

In another study focused on the underlying forces driving bank credit, Oscar Jordà, Moritz Schularick, and Alan Taylor hone in on the role of housing booms in generating financial crises.[15] Using a dataset on bank balances sheets covering 17 developed economies since 1870, they document that the increase in the bank credit/GDP ratio over time has been caused almost exclusively by the growth of mortgage credit. Since 1900, the share of mortgage loans in bank balance sheets has doubled, from about 30 percent in 1900, to about 60 percent in 2014. As a consequence, fluctuations in the volume of credit have become increasingly driven by mortgage lending. Jordà et al. show that, among components of domestic credit, mortgage lending has become the most potent predictor of subsequent financial crisis.[16] In another study, they also found some evidence that an increase in mortgage lending and house prices, relative to trend, increase the probability of a financial crisis occurring within 5 years.[17]

Economist John Geanakoplos and his collaborators were able to answer the question of how housing prices would have behaved had leverage not increased during the housing boom.[18] Their results provide the most persuasive evidence linking the housing boom (and subsequent bust) to increased leverage. Using detailed individual mortgage loan performance and home sales data on Washington DC area households, Geanakoplos et al. developed a model that related home prices to mortgage interest rates and loan leverage levels. When they inputted the time-path of average loan rates and leverage levels that occurred from 1997 to 2009, their model generated a time-path of average home prices that matched what actually occurred during that period. When they simulated the path of home prices under varying counterfactual paths for mortgage interest rates and mortgage leverage levels, they found that holding interest rates constant at their 1997 levels hardly affect the path of home prices at all, but when leverage (measured as the Loan-to-Value ratio) is held constant at the 1997 level, the housing boom and the bust that followed virtually disappear.[19] Geanakoplos et al. concluded that "leverage, not interest rates, seems to be the important factor driving the 1997–2010 boom and bust."

The evidence cited here establishes an empirical linkage running from mortgage lending volume and leverage—of lenders, borrowers, and loan collateral—to an increased risk of financial crisis. It lends empirical support to the conventional view that the US financial crisis was caused by a reckless expansion in credit and increase in leverage. But there is other evidence that points in a different direction.

An Intriguing Observation

Figure 2.5 shows that increases in household leverage and home price appreciation were positively correlated in all developed countries during the period of the US housing boom, which accords with Geanakoplos's conclusion that the rise in leverage caused home prices to increase. It is notable, however, that the United States was a middling performer in terms of its rate of growth of home price and leverage. Britain (UK) was ahead of the United States in both categories, and yet the former did not experience a housing crash, as the latter did. What differentiates the United States from Britain is that the volume of home construction was significantly higher in the United States, in relation to the size of its economy. For countries represented in figure 2.5, the volume of home construction is a better predictor of subsequent house price collapse than is the growth in leverage or home prices. The United States, Spain, and Ireland experienced the largest volumes of home construction relative to GDP during the period of the housing boom and suffered the largest declines in home prices during the financial crisis.

The housing booms in the United States, Spain, and Ireland all ended with a huge inventory of vacant homes and barren subdivisions. By contrast, in the

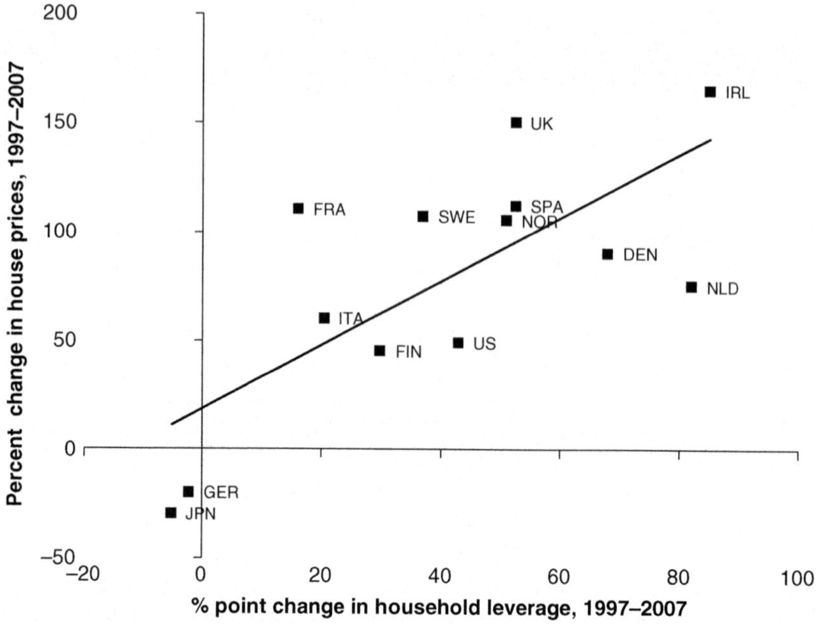

Figure 2.5 Household leverage versus household price change, 1997–2007.
Source: Reuven Glick and Kevin J. Lansing, *FRBSF Economic Letter Federal Reserve Bank of San Francisco*, January 11, 2010.

Britain which suffered as much as did the United States from the financial crisis, home prices did not fall and home vacancies did not rise during the crisis. The importance of home construction as a precursor to house price collapse suggests construction volume was at least as important a causal factor of the housing boom and subsequent bust as were credit expansion and leverage. This gives rise to an interesting question. The United States, Spain, and Ireland were near full employment at the onset of their housing booms and both private and government spending increased during the housing boom. So, where did they get the money to build all those houses? That seems a question worth looking into. It will be seen that the answer provides the key to understanding the ultimate cause of the US housing boom.

Questioning the Conventional Wisdom

The conventional wisdom, in all of its variations, misses an important destabilizing force at work during the boom; one that is not directly related to banks or borrowers or credit expansion per se. It is the unprecedented growth in the US current account deficit, which ballooned from approximately 1.5 percent in mid-1996 (at the onset of the Asian financial crisis) to well over 6 percent in mid-2006 (at the peak of the housing boom). It was the largest external deficit, as a percentage of GDP, in US history (figure 2.6). It stands to reason (but is not, in and of itself, proof) that something so momentous must have affected the economy in a significant way. An alternative view, expressed by

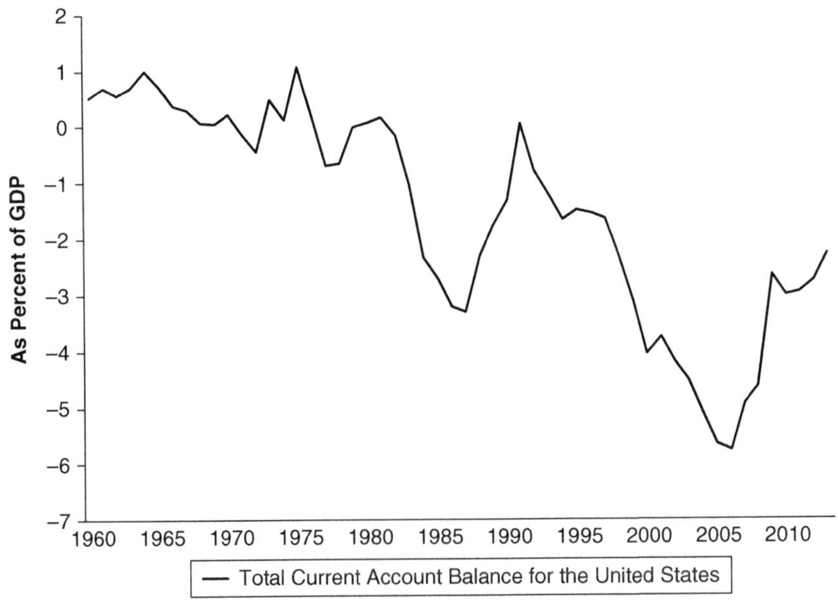

Figure 2.6 Total current account balance for the United States, 1960–2014.
Source: Board of governors of the federal reserve system.

three of the dissenters to the conclusions of the Congressional Financial Inquiry Commission, is that the pattern of global capital flows—and by implication US trade imbalances—precipitated the housing boom and the subsequent financial crisis. This alternative hypothesis does not deny the existence or negate the importance of financial excesses or complacency over risk in promoting the boom and abetting instability; but it recognizes that those forces alone could not have generated the boom that occurred.

Understanding two important concepts: the "current account deficit" and the "capital flow bonanza"

A fundamental contention of this book is that the housing boom required a large and growing negative current account balance. This important concept will be used throughout the book. The current account balance of a home country is an accumulation of net liabilities issued by foreign countries to the home country over some interval of time arising from three types of transactions.[20]

(i) the trade balance—which is the net amount of money or other financial claims received from foreigners as payment for goods and services. It is exports minus imports of goods and services.

(ii) the investment balance—which is the net amount of money received from foreigners arising from income on cross-border assets and debt in existence at the beginning of the period, and

(iii) net transfers—which is net amount of money received by the home country from foreign countries that does not have to be repaid. It is comprised of donations, aid, and remittances to family members.

$$\text{Current Account Balance} = \text{Trade Balance} + \text{Investment Balance} + \text{Net transfers} \qquad (2.1)$$

The current account balance measures the net saving of the home country. A negative current account balance is called a "current account deficit." A current account deficit indicates that the home country is spending more than it earns; that its net savings rate is negative. It implies an increase in the liabilities of the home country to foreign countries over the time interval. Between two countries, if one is running a current account deficit, the other must have a current account surplus of identical magnitude.

Current account and trade deficits are related. The trade deficit component is the net flow of real resources from foreign countries into the home country, which is paid for by the transfer of financial liabilities from the home country to foreign countries. The current account deficit is a flow of net liabilities incurred by the home country to foreign countries arising from cross-border payments for goods, services, profits, interest and transfers. There is no necessity for foreign countries to use the net liabilities accrued from the home country to invest in the home country. During the gold standard era, for instance, the central banks of surplus countries would often accumulate gold inflows from deficit countries without spending them. In our era of fiat currencies, a country running a current account surplus accumulates reserves of home country money, typically in the form of reserve balances of the central bank of the home country. It is conceivable that the country running a current account surplus could hold onto its accumulated home country money (or reserves) without investing it into the home country.

During the housing boom, when the United States ran a bilateral current account deficit with China, Chinese entities received a net transfer of dollar denominated bank deposits from US entities, as proceeds from sales of goods to the United States. Chinese recipients exchanged the dollar deposits they received into bank deposits denominated in their domestic currency, the RMB, by transferring their dollar deposits to the Chinese central bank, the Peoples Bank of China (PBOC), which stood ready to accept dollar bank deposits in exchange for RMB bank deposits at a fixed exchange rate that overvalued the dollar.[21] The PBOC received a transfer of reserves at the US Fed from the bank where the transferred dollar deposit was initially held, and it issued an RMB reserve in exchange for an RMB deposit of equivalent value, at a Chinese bank. It then completed the transaction by transferring the RMB deposit to the Chinese entity that initiated the transaction.

At the end of this chain of transactions, the Chinese money supply (which includes bank deposits) and reserves had each increased, respectively, by an amount equal to its current account surplus.[22] The US economy, which transferred the deposit and the reserve into China, experienced a decline in its reserves and money supply, respectively, equal to its current account deficit.[23] The Chinese entities that converted dollars to RMB received a windfall, since the PBOC overpaid for their dollar deposits. The PBOC suffered a decline in wealth, since it acquired dollar reserves that were worth less than the RMB reserves it issued to create the deposit required to complete the transaction. If the matter ended there, the US bilateral current account deficit with China would have caused a monetary contraction in the United States and a monetary expansion in China.

The PBOC, however, did not sit on US Fed reserves (which, as explained earlier, it could have). Instead, it invested almost all of its dollar reserves into US government-guaranteed debt, which involved a reverse flow of reserves back into the US economy.[24] The PBOC transferred its dollar reserves to US banks, who then issued deposits to the PBOC (or its representative), and the deposits were used to purchase US debt. As a result, the PBOC invested into the United States, directly or indirectly, an amount of money that was roughly equal to the United States' bilateral current account deficit with China.

In this book, I define a "capital flow bonanza" as the reinvestment into a country running a large current account deficit (over several percentage points of GDP) of monies from its trading partners that is roughly equal to its current account deficit. In other words, a capital flow bonanza is an inflow of foreign investment equal to the size of a country's current account deficit, when the deficit is large.[25]

The US capital flow bonanza meant there was little net transfer of central bank reserves between the United States and China, and therefore little direct monetary impact on the United States from its bilateral current account deficit with China.

While the capital flow bonanza neutralized the impact the current account deficit would otherwise have had on the US money supply, it altered important relationships inside the US economy. The PBOC had no intention of spending on US goods, since doing so would cause a shift in demand for tradable goods toward the United States and away from China, which was contrary to China's policy goals. Therefore, while the capital flow bonanza meant the income earned by China from its current account surplus with the United States remained inside the United States, it implied, as a first order effect, a shift toward less consumption and more saving in the United States. The reduction in demand required an investment boom to bring the economy to full employment and the increased saving caused a decline in interest rates and an expansion in credit that made fertile ground for such a boom to occur. I explain this in chapters 4 and 7.

Finally, the RMB bank deposits created in the process of converting dollars into RMB at a fixed exchange rate added to the Chinese money supply and was potentially inflationary. In chapter 4 I will explain how the PBOC dealt with that issue by causing an offsetting contraction in the Chinese money supply.

As I explain in detail in chapter 7, the current account deficit accommodated the housing boom in two complementary and linked ways: (i) it enabled the US economy to spend more than it produced (the resources acquired by the home economy from foreigners); and (ii) it provided an increase in the pool of domestic saving that fueled credit growth. The housing boom, and in particular the dramatic increase in home construction and consumer spending that was enabled by home equity extractions, could not have progressed very far without the large and growing current account deficit. It is a striking fact that in 2006, at the zenith of the housing boom, the gross issuance of subprime and Alt-A mortgage in dollar volume nearly matched the current account deficit.[26] In this book, I shall demonstrate that it was no mere coincidence, which is consistent with the view expressed by the dissenting minority on the Financial Crisis Inquiry Commission.

> Starting in the late 1990's, China, other large developing countries and the big oil-producing nations built up large capital surpluses. They loaned these savings to the United States and Europe, causing interest rates to fall. Credit spreads narrowed, meaning that the cost of borrowing to finance risky investments declined. A credit bubble formed in the United States and Europe, the most notable manifestation of which was increased investment in high-risk mortgages.[27]

The empirical literature on the causes of booms and banking crises in general, and the US housing boom in particular, which is discussed below, supports the view that the US current account deficit was a factor in causing the boom and crisis that followed. The three dissenters were correct. Leverage, by itself, did *not* maketh the boom; the boom required a large current account deficit.

Studies Linking Current Account Deficits to Booms and Financial Crises

Historical Studies Linking Current Account Deficits to Financial Crises

The start of the financial crisis is commonly identified as the collapse of two Bear Stearns sponsored hedge funds in July of 2007, which coincided with a nosedive in the value of subprime mortgage asset-backed securities (ABS).[28] The crisis reached a crescendo in the fall of 2008, with the collapse in the value of subprime mortgage debt[29] and the debt of Fannie Mae and Freddie Mac (which elicited a [reaffirmation of] government guaranty of GSE debt), the bankruptcy of Lehman Brothers, the takeover of AIG, and the enactment of the TARP legislation and emergency liquidity measures by the Fed. This identification of the recent financial crisis is consistent with the definition used by economists Carmen Reinhardt and Kenneth Rogoff in their book *This Time Is Different* (Reinhardt and Rogoff), which surveyed the history of financial crises over the past eight centuries. They defined a "banking [or financial] crisis," inter alia, as "the closure, merging, takeover, or large-scale government assistance of an important financial institution (or group of institutions) that marks the start of a string of similar outcomes for other financial institutions."[30] Reinhardt and Rogoff is the most comprehensive compilation ever assembled of historical information and analysis of factors leading up to financial crises, the character of crises, and their aftermath.

It is unsurprising to find, as do both Jorda et al. and Reinhardt and Rogoff, that financial crises are usually preceded by credit booms.[31] After all, a financial crisis is an event where deterioration in loan quality jeopardizes the solvency of banks. It does so on the asset side through defaults, and on the liability side through withdrawals of short-term funding induced by fears over credit quality.[32] Banks are highly leveraged institutions, and they usually fund expansions in credit by increasing their liabilities (rather than increasing their equity funding), which implies an increase in leverage during the credit boom.[33] As a bank increases its leverage, a smaller percentage decline in the value of its assets can render it insolvent. Therefore, the very nature of a credit-fueled boom increases the risk of a financial crisis when the boom ends.

Although financial crises are usually preceded by credit booms, it is important to note that booms do not *require* an expansion in credit. The difference is that when a boom occurs without an expansion in credit, the crash that follows may not precipitate a banking crisis. The US dotcom boom of the late 1990s, which preceded the housing boom, was not accompanied by excessive credit growth, and there was no financial crisis after its collapse. I shall explore in chapter 4 the idea that, while a credit boom is a vital precursor to a financial crisis, it is neither a necessary nor a sufficient component of a boom.

Reinhardt and Rogoff document a coincidence of financial crises and surges in international capital mobility. In particular, capital flow bonanzas are historically very often associated with financial crises, though not as frequently as are credit expansions.[34] According to Reinhardt and Rogoff, "The probability of a banking crisis conditional on a capital flow bonanza is higher than the unconditional probability."[35] While it is obvious why financial crises are often preceded by credit expansions, the coincidence of capital flow bonanzas and financial crises is a more striking—because less obvious—pattern. The historical record cited by Reinhardt and Rogoff shows that financial crises typically follow a recurring combination of factors: current account deficits, increases in asset prices, debt buildups, and capital flow bonanzas.

> The literature on financial crises suggests that markedly rising asset prices, slowing real economic activity, large current account deficits, and sustained debt buildups (whether public, private or both) are important precursors to financial crises.

> Sustained capital inflows have been particularly strong markers for financial crises, at least in the post-1970 period of greater financial liberalization.[36]

Reinhardt and Rogoff identify the coincidence of these factors in the boom that preceded the US financial crisis:

> The US financial crisis of the late 2000's was firmly rooted in the bubble in the real estate market fuelled by sustained massive increases in housing prices, a massive influx of cheap foreign capital resulting from record trade balance and current account deficits, and an increasingly permissive regulatory policy that helped propel the dynamic between these factors.[37]

Financial liberalization magnifies the potential for trade imbalances to precipitate credit booms by increasing the potential size of capital flow bonanzas, which can finance a credit boom. Figure 2.7 displays the coincidence of international capital mobility with financial crises. The first period of financial liberalization, from the late 1800s to the 1930s, was marked by an increase in both capital mobility and financial crises. This was followed by the post–World War II Bretton Woods era, which lasted into the early 1970s, in which capital flows were restricted and financial crises were rare. In the late 1970s financial liberalization once again was marked by a dramatic increase in both capital mobility and financial crises. It is important to note, however, that large capital flows do not imply that there are capital flow bonanzas. I will show in chapter 4 that US international capital flows vastly exceeded the size of its capital flow bonanza in the 2000s. One point of contention among economists is whether the level of overall capital flows was more destabilizing to the United States than its capital flow bonanza. I argue in chapter 4 that the capital flow bonanza was the crucial

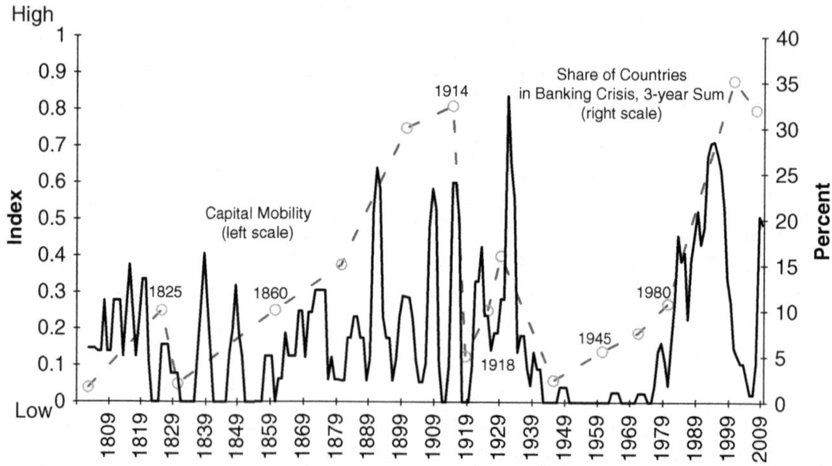

Figure 2.7 Capital mobility and the incidence of banking crises, 1800–2008.

Source: Carmen Reinhardt and Kenneth Rogoff, *This Time Is Different: Eight Centuries of Financial Folly* (Princeton University Press, 2009), Figure 10.1, p. 156.

causal factor. But either way, the evidence points to external capital flows as being an important cause of the housing boom.

Reinhardt and Rogoff's documentation of the striking historical association of capital flow bonanzas with booms and financial crises, along with the presence of a large and growing US capital flow bonanza (and overall gross external capital flows) during the housing boom, casts some doubt on the conventional view that domestic credit expansion alone was the dominant cause of the housing boom and subsequent financial crisis.

Historical studies of financial crises have the strength of analyzing a large set of macroeconomic data, from which recurring patterns can sometimes be discovered. Indeed, the fundamental point made by Reinhardt and Rogoff is that some recurring features of financial crises are so prevalent that they most likely reflect elements of commonality that hold across time and space: A financial crisis that occurred several hundred years ago in a far-off land shares certain features with the US financial crises of the early twenty-first century. Yet, a potential limitation of the comparative historical approach arises from the effects of technological and institutional change during the course of the past two centuries which may have created novel features of contemporary crises that were not factors in crises of the distant past. The possibility that innovation has given rise to unique economic relationships underscores the importance of studying the most recent financial crisis separately from past occurrences.[38]

An Event Study Linking Capital Flow Bonanzas and Leverage during the Housing Boom

An empirical investigation into the causes of the buildup of credit and leverage in OECD countries during the period of the early twenty-first century US (and peripheral European[39]) housing boom corroborates the link between capital flow bonanzas and credit booms. Economists Ouarda Merrouche and Erlend Nier (Merrouche and Nier)[40] tested three potential causes of the increase in leverage that some, but not all, OECD economies experienced in the early to mid-2000s: loose monetary policy, lax bank supervision, and capital flow bonanzas. They measured the impact of each potential causal factor on several indicators of leverage and financial fragility, including the ratio of bank credit to deposits—which captures the dependence of banks on wholesale funding, which is less stable than deposit funding—the ratio of financial sector credit to deposits; the ratio of bank credit to GDP; household sector leverage and house price inflation. They also investigated the channels that linked the causal factors to leverage. Their results show capital flow bonanzas to have been a key driver of compressed maturity spreads, increased leverage and house price appreciation.[41]

First, capital flow bonanzas caused a compression in maturity spreads. The mechanism by which this occurred was that capital inflows were invested in long-term, ultra-safe, government-guaranteed securities, which depressed their yields and compressed the spreads between short- and long-term interest rates (the "maturity spread"). The reduction in maturity spreads compressed the profit margins on bank lending because banks borrow short and lend long term. As a consequence, the net interest margin of US commercial bank lending declined by a quarter during the housing boom (see figure 7.9). Banks attempted to recoup lost profits by increasing wholesale borrowing to fund an expansion in lending. Between 2000 and 2008, US commercial bank credit increased from 47 percent to 62 percent of GDP, and the ratio of bank credit to deposits increased from 77.5 percent in 2000 to 83 percent at the height of the housing boom in 2006.[42] This indicates an increased reliance upon wholesale funding. US banks also increased off balance sheet guarantees to support asset backed securities they originated, which grew by $1.3 trillion from 2001 to 2008 (see figure 7.2).

Second, the increase in credit generated by the capital flow bonanza was channeled into home mortgage lending, which fueled an increase in house prices. This pathway, which was documented by Jordà et al.,[43] establishes a link between the current account deficit and the housing boom (figure 2.8).

Third, the increase in bank leverage (measured by the loan to deposit ratio) and the increase in household sector leverage reduced the margin by which a decline in loan collateral and asset values could render banks and homeowners insolvent.[44] This occurred because the leverage of a bank or household is measured by the percentage of the value of its assets that remains after deducting its debt, which is the net-worth-to-asset ratio: the higher is the leverage, the lower will be the net-worth-to-asset ratio. During the housing boom asset values rose,

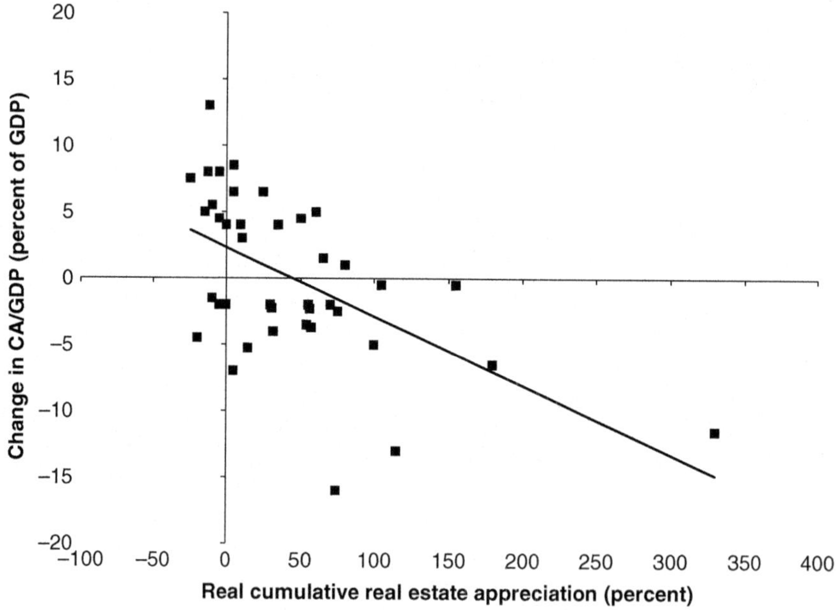

Figure 2.8 Real estate appreciation and change in current account, 2000–2006.

Source: Maurice Obstfeld and Kenneth Rogoff, *Global Imbalances and the Financial Crisis: Products of Common Causes Asia and the Global Financial Crisis*, ed. Reuven Glick and Mark M. Spiegel (Federal Reserve Bank of San Francisco, 2009), Figure 16, p. 155, available at http://www.frbsf.org/economic-research/events/2009/october/asia-global-financial-crisis/Conference_volume.pdf.

but the increase in leverage meant that net worth as a percentage of asset values declined. As a result, it required a smaller percentage decline in asset values to render banks and households insolvent.

Finally, Merrouche and Nier found no correlation linking either lax regulation or loose monetary policy to increases in any of their measures of leverage or financial fragility, which implies that domestic government policy was not responsible for the expansion of credit. Merrouche and Nier summarized their results as follows:

> We find that cross-country differences in net capital inflows can account for differences between countries in the build-up of financial imbalances, as measured by the ratio of banking-sector credit to core deposits. By contrast, we do not find that differences in the monetary-policy stance had an effect on the build-up of financial imbalances when capital flows are accounted for.[45]
>
> Overall, our findings lend strong support to the conjecture that *"[c]apital flows provided the fuel which the developed world's inadequately designed and regulated financial system then ignited to produce the firestorm that engulfed us all"* (King 2010).[46]

The Effect of Offshore Purchases on the Yield on US Debt

In another study, economists Frank and Veronica Warnock ("Warnock") provide direct evidence of the depressive effect of capital inflows on US interest rates. They showed that offshore purchases of US government securities caused a reduction in the yields on those securities.[47] They estimate that in the early 2000s foreign purchasers were pushing down treasury yields by a significant amount.[48]

> If foreign governments did not accumulate U.S. government bonds over the twelve months ending in May 2005, our model suggests that the ten year treasury yield would have been roughly 80 basis points higher, if instead they reduced holdings by the same magnitude of their accumulation, the impact would be doubled... US mortgage rates are also depressed by the foreign inflows.[49]

Warnock also found, pace Merrouche and Nier, that foreign capital inflows compressed the maturity spread.

Figure 2.9 shows that Southeast Asian purchases of treasuries spiked upward in the mid-1990s, around the onset of the Asian financial crisis, and again in the early 2000s, at the onset of the housing boom. During the latter period, east Asian purchasers were dominated by China. Warnock's study ended in 2005, while Chinese purchases of treasuries was significantly higher in 2006 and 2007. It is therefore likely that China caused an even larger decline in treasury yields at the height of the housing boom in 2006/7.[50]

A study of the long-term effect of foreign holdings of US treasuries on treasury yields undertaken by economists at the US Fed found that Chinese purchases of treasuries had a significant effect on US interest rates.

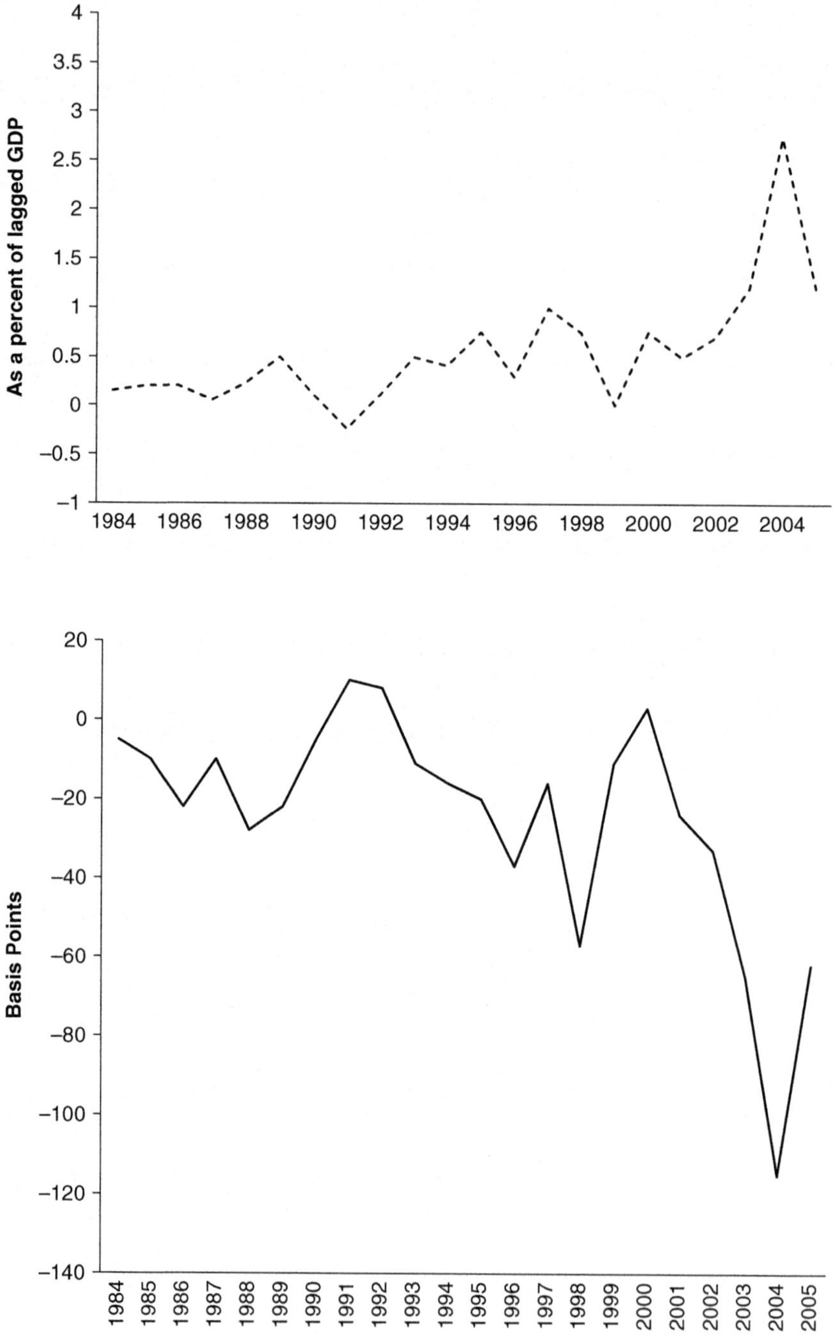

Figure 2.9 (a) Southeast Asian and other flows into US government bonds, 1984–2005 (b) Southeast Asian and other flows on ten-year treasury yield, 1984–2005.

Source: Figure 2.9 is a smoothed version of Francis E. Warnock and Veronica Cacdac Warnock, "International Capital Flows and US Interest Rates," *Journal of International Money and Finance*, Vol. 28 (2009): 903–919, Figure 5, p. 917. Note that each line represents a different estimator.

> Between 1995 and 2010 China acquired roughly $1.1 trillion in U.S. Treasury notes and bonds. A literal interpretation of our long-run estimates suggests that if China had not accumulated any foreign exchange reserves during this period, and therefore not acquired these $1.1 trillion in Treasuries, all else equal, the 5-year Treasury yield would have been roughly 2 percentage points higher by 2010.[51]

These studies probably underestimate the extent to which Chinese investment in US debt reduced long-term US interest rates during the housing boom, since the majority of PBOC holdings of US securities prior to the financial crisis was in long-term government sponsored enterprise (GSE) debt.

The Link between Interest Rates and the Housing Boom

Economists Oscar Jordà, Moritz Schularick, and Alan Taylor assembled a historical dataset of mortgage lending and house prices in 18 developed economies from the late 1800s to 2012 to explore the impact that exogenous changes in interest rates have on the volume of mortgage lending, home prices, and the probability of financial crisis.[52] In their work, "exogenous" refers to changes in interest rates that emanate from outside the home economy. The effect of offshore purchases on treasury yields identified by Warnock and the Fed economists fits their definition of an exogenous change in interest rates.

Jordà et al. shows that a linkage exists connecting an exogenous decline in interest rates to subsequent increases in mortgage loans/GDP and house price/income ratios, relative to trend.[53] Their results show that a 1 percent decline in short-term interest rates generates an approximate 2.5 percent mean increase in the mortgage loans/GDP ratio within 4 years. These findings provide evidence of the linkage between capital inflows, declines in domestic interest rates (albeit their results pertain to short-term rates, whereas the other cited studies pertained to long-term rates), and increased mortgage lending.

Reconciling the Evidence

The studies of Reinhardt and Rogoff, Merrouche and Nier, Warnock, the Fed, and Jordà et al.[54] provide evidence of a strong linkage between capital flow bonanzas and the key financial conditions of low interest rates, high leverage, and soaring home prices that accompanied the housing boom. These studies compel us to look beyond the conventional view that leverage, credit expansion, loose monetary policy, and lax regulation within the US economy, unaided by other factors, caused the boom.

It is necessary to evaluate how the evidence presented in this section stacks up against the evidence presented earlier, which showed a strong correlation between domestic credit expansion, home price appreciation, and financial crises. They are not incompatible. The evidence linking domestic credit expansion to the housing boom leaves open the question of the underlying cause of the credit expansion. The evidence linking the capital flow bonanza to the boom provides the answer to that question. The capital flow bonanza caused the expansion in credit that flowed through the US financial sector into housing.

That is why any acceptable explanation of the housing boom and the financial crises must take on board the central importance of the capital flow bonanza. The growth in the current account deficit was an indispensible causal factor. Economists Maurice Obstfeld and Kenneth Rogoff, who have both been chief economists at the International Moentary Fund (IMF), succinctly summarized the effects of the capital flow bonanza:

> The role of the US net external deficit, in our view, was to enable a constellation of interest rates and asset prices consistent with apparently low inflation but simultaneously conducive to housing appreciation, lax mortgage lending practices, overall credit expansion, and strong incentives toward high leverage and regulatory arbitrage. These market dynamics created a vicious circle in which the expectation of ongoing housing appreciation fed mortgage credit expansion, which in turn pushed housing prices higher... all the while, the US current account deficit widened.[55]

The evidence provided so far establishes correlations between the current account deficit and the housing boom, but there is a lot left to be explained concerning the details of the transmission mechanism connecting the capital flow bonanza to the housing boom. I address the transmission mechanism in chapter 7.

Misreading the Evidence during the Boom

There were at least three important misconceptions concerning the nature of US industry and financial markets that may have contributed to the benign view most people (including this author) had of the capital flow bonanza.

Misreading US Corporate Profits

One misconception involved a misunderstanding of the source of the growth in profits of US corporations during the period of the housing boom. As figure 2.10 shows, profits of US corporations rose steeply from 2002 onward.

Historian Niall Ferguson and economist Mortiz Schularick proposed a theory—which they called "Chimerica"—that attributed the rise in profits to the entry of Chinese labor into the global workforce.[56] The explanation goes as follows. The increase in the global workforce had the effect of reducing the capital-to-labor ratio, which, according to economic theory, should have caused an improvement in the return on capital investment everywhere—including the United States. This follows from the well-supported observation that capital is subject to declining marginal productivity; a lower amount of capital per worker implies a higher level of output per unit of capital. At the same time, the entry of Chinese labor into the global workforce pushed down wages, which increased the share of revenue that went to profits. The combination of higher capital productivity and lower labor costs boosted profits.

The problem with the Chimerica theory is that it is inconsistent with the decline in capital investment in the US tradeable manufacturing sector that took place during the period. One would expect an increase in the productivity of capital to have elicited an increase in investment. In addition, the claim

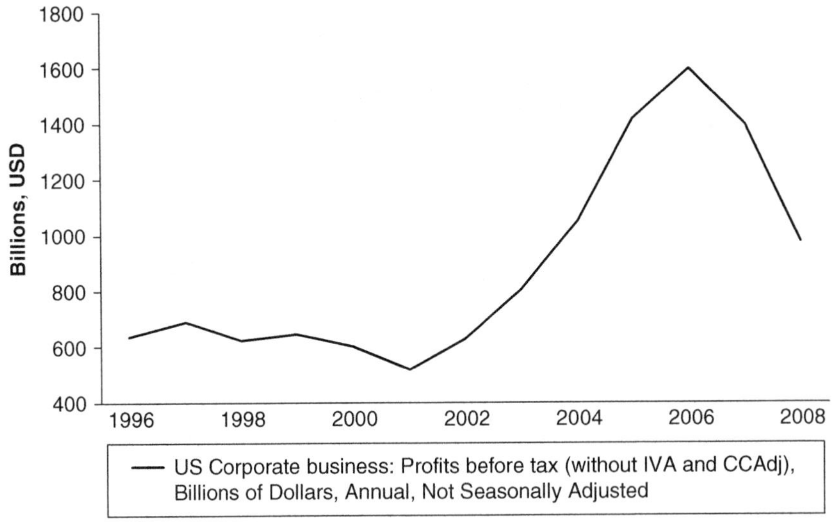

Figure 2.10 US corporate business: profits before tax, 1996–2008.
Source: US Bureau of Economic Analysis.

that capital had become more productive was at odds with the data showing a decline in US productivity growth. Alas, Chimerica was based on flawed logic. Capital is not easily moveable, so the capital-to-labor ratio for the combined US and Chinese workforce was a meaningless statistical artifact. The capital-to-labor ratio in the United States had not changed, and therefore the entry of Chinese labor into the global workforce did not improve the return on capital in the United States. Meanwhile, the low skill level in China limited the productivity of capital there. Improving capital efficiency was not part of the story of increased corporate profits in the 2000s.

Ferguson and Schularick were nevertheless right to attribute the rise in profits of US corporations to the increase in trade with Asia. The source of increased profits was the shift by US companies to outsource the assembly of manufactured goods to China, where labor costs were lower. The lower production costs boosted profits of US companies. But, if anything, the shift in production offshore reduced investment prospects inside the United States.[57]

Misreading US Capital Market Efficiency

In the years prior to the financial crisis the IMF expressed the view that the United States was an exception to the long-standing pattern linking capital flow bonanzas and credit expansions to financial crises.[58] The argument was that "this time was different" because the United States was uniquely stable. The reasoning went as follows.

Savings accumulating in the fast growing but politically unstable countries of Asia and OPEC flowed into the United States primarily for two reasons. One reason was that the stable legal, regulatory, monetary policymaking and financial institutions of the United States made it a more secure place in which to hold assets. The other reason was that Asian and OPEC capital markets were not sufficiently developed to offer savers a wide choice of liquid investments. Crucially (and fortuitously), it was argued, the United States was able to absorb the capital flow bonanza without any risk of financial disruption due to its stability, and the depth and liquidity of its financial markets. The IMF recognized that the inflow of Asian and OPEC savings into the United States constituted a capital flow bonanza, but it reasoned that the same factors that made the United States an attractive place in which to invest also ensured that the heightened capital inflow would not cause disruption.

While the perception of the stability of US institutions and property rights was accurate, subsequent events disproved the notion that US financial markets could absorb a large capital inflow without causing disruption. Reinhardt and Rogoff point out that the idea that rich countries possess unique financial stability is a perennial illusion.

> Historical experience already shows that rich countries are not as "special" as some cheerleaders had been arguing, both when it comes to managing capital inflows and especially when it comes to banking crises... Surprisingly, not only are the frequency and duration of banking crises similar across developed countries and middle-income countries; so too are quantitative measures of both the run-up to and the fallout from such crises.[59]

In addition to lacking empirical support, the IMF view was conceptually flawed. The IMF assumed that the US capital market could absorb the capital flow bonanza because it was large and efficient. Yet, an efficient US financial system would have channeled savings into the most profitable investments, ensuring that the risk-adjusted rate of return on the marginal investment equaled the applicable market interest rate. In that case, few opportunities to earn investment returns that exceeded prevailing interest rates would remain unexploited. However, during the housing boom in the mid-2000s, US interest rates were near historic lows and US productivity growth was declining (see figures 3.1 and 3.2), implying there was little room for additional profitable investment. Therefore, a large capital flow bonanza that increased domestic US investment was likely to push down returns to very low levels, which implies some of the additional debt would likely end in default. The IMF was apparently wedded to the notion that only good things happen in efficient markets. The IMF wrongly interpreted the low interest rates and risk spreads in the United States as evidence of market stability, when in fact they implied precisely the opposite. According to Reinhardt and Rogoff:

> One can argue that it was precisely the huge capital inflow from abroad that fueled the asset price inflation and low interest rate spreads that ultimately masked risks from both regulators and rating agencies... Capital inflows pushed up borrowing and asset prices while reducing spreads on all sorts of risky assets, leading the International Monetary Fund to conclude in April 2007... that risks to the global economy had become extremely low and that, for the moment, there were no great worries.[60]

Reinhardt and Rogoff maintain that the illusion of US economic exceptionalism bred a complacency that paved the path to crisis.

> The US conceit that its financial and regulatory system could withstand massive capital inflows on a sustained basis without any problems arguably laid the foundations for the global financial crisis of the late 2000's.[61]

Misreading the Decline in US Manufacturing

The US manufacturing sector was a prime beneficiary of the IT revolution; the amount of labor input necessary to produce a unit of output had been on the decline long before the current account deficit began to grow. It was argued by many at the time that the offshoring of production in manufacturing had at best a second-order impact on US employment. It was thought that if the products purchased from abroad were manufactured in the United States, it would be done primarily by machines, not people.

This view was flawed; off-shoring caused large US job losses. US manufacturing was undergoing a significant decline in competitiveness as the current account deficit soared. Relative unit labor costs in US industry compared to China surged around the turn of the millennium, which caused a shift in new plant investment in tradable labor-intensive manufacturing industries to China. As a result, the most internationally exposed US industries hemorrhaged jobs and ceded domestic market share to lower cost Chinese competitors. Economist Doug Campbell concluded his study of US/China relative unit labor costs around the turn of the millennium as follows:

> The shock to trade in the early 2000's was large enough to explain at least close to two-thirds of the decline in American manufacturing employment in this period, and perhaps substantially more if input-output linkages are taken into account. The job losses were potentially large enough to have had a macro-economic impact.[62]

Economist David Autor and his colleagues documented a direct linkage between Chinese imports and manufacturing job losses in the communities where US production had taken place:

> Rising imports cause higher unemployment, lower labor force participation, and reduced wages in local labor markets that house import-competing manufacturing industries... import competition explains one-quarter of the contemporaneous aggregate decline in US manufacturing employment.[63]

The implosion of US manufacturing employment should have raised some concerned questions about the sustainability of the boom. Instead, the attainment of full employment in the United States—achieved by offsetting the jobs lost in manufacturing with employment in the real estate and finance sectors—and the historic eradication of poverty in China offered an appealingly powerful vindication of the idea that free international trade generated bountiful benefits for all participants. Proponents of globalization did not usually acknowledge that China subsidized exports restricted imports and intervened in the currency market in order to promote its exports, which were rank violations of the principle of free trade.

Conclusion

In this chapter I have presented evidence suggesting that the growth of the current account deficit and the accompanying capital flow bonanza was a crucial underlying cause of the US housing boom. This leaves open the question of what caused the growth in the current account deficit. I explore that question in the next chapter.

CHAPTER 3

Mercantilism and the Current Account Deficit

> Why was the United States, a mature economy, the recipient of net capital inflows that rose to as much as 6 percent of its gross domestic product prior to the financial crisis?
>
> —Ben Bernanke[1]

> What then accounts for the rapid increase in the U.S. current account deficit? My own preferred explanation focuses on what I see as the emergence of a global saving glut in the past eight to ten years.
>
> —Ben Bernanke[2]

In the last chapter, I presented evidence linking the current account deficit to the US housing boom, which raises the question of what drove the increase in the current account deficit. In this chapter, I explore the cause of the growth of the current account deficit and the accompanying capital flow bonanza during the US housing boom. There are several candidate explanations: perhaps the United States needed the offshore savings to augment its deficient domestic savings. Perhaps foreign investors presumed the United States to be a safer place to invest their savings than elsewhere. Perhaps they supposed the United States to have unexploited prospects for earning high returns. Or perhaps something else motivated offshore investors to pile into US securities. This is a crucial matter, since it is necessary to identify the forces that generated the US current account deficit in order to understand the housing boom. To set the stage for consideration of this question, I review some of the key macroeconomic conditions that prevailed during the housing boom.

The Two Phases of Global Imbalances

In an address in 2005, future US Fed chairman Ben Bernanke famously attributed the ultimate cause of the growing US current account deficit and low interest rates to a "global saving glut," by which he meant the rise of saving in

Southeast Asia, China, and OPEC, rather than a rise in global savings overall.[3] Mr. Bernanke divided the evolution of global imbalances into two phases. In the first phase, from roughly 1997 to 2000, an increase in Asian accumulation of dollar assets—brought on in reaction to the Asian financial crisis—interacted with an enthusiasm over US investment prospects, notably in so-called dot-coms, which was accompanied by a surge in US productivity, to generate an investment boom. Bernanke stated that "equity prices played a key equilibrating role in international financial markets . . . fueling large appreciations in stock prices and in the value of the dollar."[4] The centrality of equities to the dot-com boom underscores that a capital flow bonanza does not always cause an expansion of credit or leverage. No significant increase in credit or leverage accompanied the equity-fueled dot-com boom. The surge in US productivity meant that perceived rates of return on US investment were elevated, which prevented real interest rates from declining, even as the capital flow bonanza grew.

In the second phase identified by Bernanke, from 2000 to 2005, however, US productivity growth and real interest rates declined while offshore savings continued to flow into US fixed income securities (figures 3.1 and 3.2).[5] Obstfeld and Rogoff noted that, since a capital flow bonanza was present during both phases, the decline in US interest rates during the second phase could not be attributed to the savings inflow. They focused on the change in productivity growth between the two phases as the source of variation in interest rates: "an end to the sharp productivity boom of the 1990's, rather than the global saving glut of the 2000's, is a much more likely explanation of the general level of low real interest rates"[6] that took hold after 2000.

The conjuncture of low interest rates and the concentration of foreign investment in long-term US government fixed income securities, rather than equities, underscores that during the housing boom, offshore investors into the United States were unlikely to have been attracted by the prospect of earning high returns. The relative dearth of productive investment prospects is reflected by the curious fact

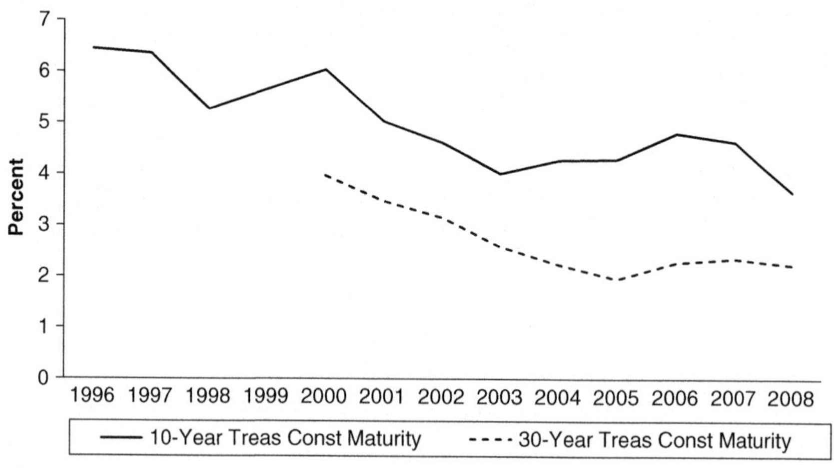

Figure 3.1 10-/30-year treasury constant maturity rate, 1996–2008.

Source: Board of Governors of the Federal Reserve System.

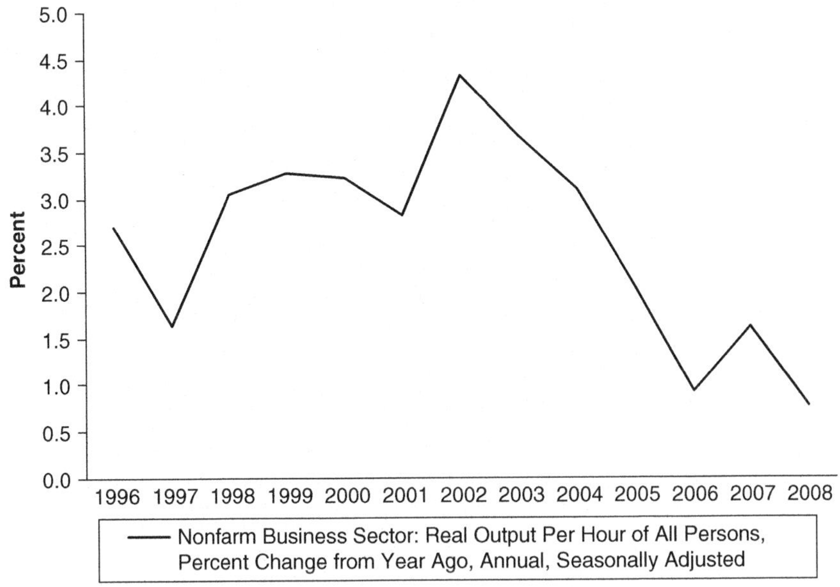

Figure 3.2 US productivity growth, 1996–2008.
Source: US Bureau of Labor Statistics.

that corporate investment remained flat even as corporate profits surged. As discussed in chapter 2, the reason increased profits failed to elicit increased investment is that the profits were generated by shifting production to lower cost Chinese labor, which, in and of itself, reduced the need for US investment.[7] The fact that capital inflows surged at a time when US interest rates and productivity growth were low and declining is a puzzle that must be solved in order to understand the source of the capital flow bonanza during the housing boom. What was it that prompted foreigners to pile into US securities when the returns on offer were so low?

Did Low US Saving Cause the Current Account Deficit to Grow?

There is a popular notion that the profligacy of the US government created a dependency on foreign borrowing to finance its deficits. There have been many historical occurrences of the so-called twin-deficits where current account and government deficits rise in tandem. In the 1980s, for example, the US experienced its largest peacetime government deficit and its largest current account deficit (up to that time). At the time, many believed that increased government borrowing demand caused the current account deficit.

However, to ironically paraphrase Reinhardt and Rogoff, this time really was different. Figure 3.3 shows the time-path of the twin deficits. It shows that the current account deficit began to accelerate at the time of the Asian financial crisis (in July 1997) right on through to the end of the housing boom, in 2007. Yet, just as the current account deficit took off, the government budget went into surplus, and stayed there for several years. Then again, in 2004, as the current account

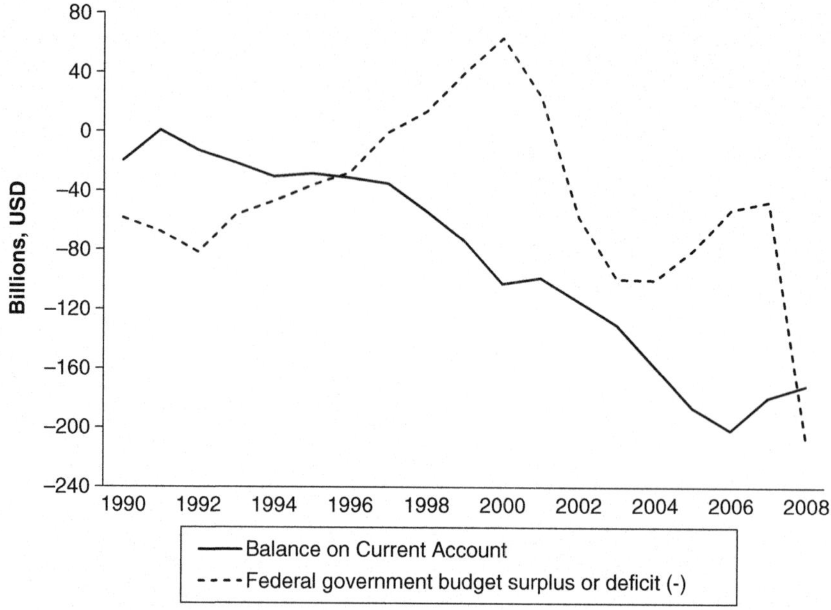

Figure 3.3 Balance on current account and Federal government budget, 1990–2008.
Source: US Bureau of Economic Analysis.

deficit accelerated toward its historic peak, the government deficit began to shrink. It does not take a sophisticated econometric analysis to show that the behavior of the two deficits were unrelated during this time period.[8] The conjuncture of the reduction in US military spending after the first Gulf War and steady economic growth (the so-called Great Moderation) of the 1990s sent the US budget into surplus by the late 1990s. The 2001 recession and the Bush tax cuts reversed the surplus. The current account deficit, on the other hand, was driven by the desire of Southeast Asian countries, China, and OPEC to accumulate dollar assets (as I shall explain later). Its downward descent was paused briefly in 2001 because the US recession caused a decline in imports (which reduced the US trade deficit). Therefore, it cannot be maintained that government borrowing precipitated the growth in the current account deficit in the decade following the late 1990s.

One might wonder if the profligacy of the US private sector required it to borrow from abroad. Figure 3.3 shows the current account deficit was larger than the government budget deficit from 1997 to the end of 2007, which means the US private sector was a net borrower throughout the period. That is so because the portion of the capital flow bonanza that exceeded the US government deficit had to be matched by private sector borrowing. Another way to phrase this is that saving in the US private sector was declining—and had become negative. The private sector is comprised of corporations and households. The corporate saving rate became positive from the late 1990s onward. Thus, the surplus savings of the capital flow bonanza had to have been matched by increased borrowings by the household sector.[9] Indeed, households were borrowing an increasing amount to finance their consumption (see figure 2.1). One reason household spending (relative to income) might have increased is that household net worth was rising (see figure 7.10). It is well documented that an increase in wealth—especially housing wealth—tends to elicit a decline in household saving (out of current income).[10] Therefore, in order to know what caused household borrowing to rise, one must know what caused asset prices to rise.

This question takes us back to the two phases of global imbalances. In the late 1990s asset values were driven up by increases in productivity and enthusiasm over the prospects of the Internet, neither of which were directly related to the current account deficit. Nevertheless, causality is difficult to disentangle during that period since US households increased their borrowing just as foreigners—especially Southeast Asian countries—began to increase their current account deficits with the United States (which I shall explain later on in this chapter). In the 2000s, the decline in productivity growth makes it more likely that asset values were driven up by the current account deficit. During that period the capital flow bonanza facilitated an increase in home values by pushing down interest rates and triggering a loosening of mortgage underwriting standards. Therefore, the increase in asset values that fueled the increase in household borrowing during the housing boom was a consequence of, and not a cause of, the growing current account deficit.

Did a Safe Asset Shortage Cause the Capital Flow Bonanza?

Economist Ricardo Caballero has proposed an intriguing answer to the question of what motivated foreign investors to pile into US securities, even as real interest rates plummeted. Consistent with the first part of the IMF view cited in chapter 2, Caballero believes the root cause of global imbalances was the conjuncture of the dramatic increase of the wealth of Asian and OPEC countries and their relatively undeveloped financial markets, which included inadequate legal protection of property rights. These are the countries that generated the capital flow bonanza into the United States.[11] Asian and OPEC wealth-holders, he argues, desired safe havens in which to invest their savings, and the United States was the most attractive venue. The US current account deficit thus generated was a by-product of the search for safe assets.

> I believe the root imbalance was not the global imbalance but a safe-assets imbalance: The entire world, including foreign central banks and investors, as well as many U.S. financial institutions, had an insatiable demand for safe debt instruments which put an enormous pressure on the U.S. financial system and its incentives.[12]

Caballero has argued that the demand for safe and liquid assets—in excess of the supply of investment grade corporate and US government-guaranteed debt—promoted the growth of ABS, in particular subprime mortgage-backed securities that began to proliferate in the early 2000s.[13] However, there was a risk that the demand for safe assets could exceed the ability of the private sector to generate safe income streams. The dearth of profitable investment prospects in the United States, due to declining productivity growth, gave rise to the dilemma pointed out in chapter 2. On the other hand, its superior legal system and market liquidity made the United States attractive to investors looking for safety, while, on the other hand, the low return prospects made further investment (or lending of any type) quite risky. Caballero points out, moreover, that while subprime mortgage ABS may have carried a low probability of default, they contained a potentially fatal flaw: Their safety arose from the fact that they bundled together mortgages spread throughout the country. Local housing markets historically did not tend to decline in synch; there had not been a national downturn in home prices since the Great Depression. The perceived low probability of a synchronized national housing downturn enabled the investment grade rated senior cash flow ABS tranches—which were sold to investors—to be cushioned by a very thin junior tranche. This feature made the ABS profitable to the sponsors (the banks and broker-dealers who created the ABS), who were usually required to retain the junior tranche. A downturn in a single local housing market would not be a large enough event to reduce the cash flow of the senior tranches of a portfolio of mortgages that spanned all local housing markets. Yet, the thinness of the junior tranche meant that even a mild synchronized downturn in the national housing market could cause a decline in cash flows of the senior tranches.

> From a systemic point of view, this new found source of AAA assets was much riskier than the traditional single-name highly rated bonds... for a given unconditional probability of default, a highly rated tranche made of lower quality underlying assets will tend to default, in fact it can only default, during a systemic event. This means that, even if correctly rated as AAA, the correlation between these complex assets distress and systemic distress is much higher than for simpler single-name bonds.[14]

Not only would AAA subprime ABS tranches fail in a systemic downturn, the concentration of their ownership in the leveraged financial sector would amplify their distress through the financial system. Banks, GSEs, pension funds, hedge funds, and insurance companies retained the lion's share of subprime ABS exposure, including the junior tranches (a matter that is explored in chapter 7).

> The systemic fragility of these instruments became a source of systemic risk in itself once a significant share of them was kept within the financial system rather than sold to final investors. Banks and their SIVs, attracted by the high return and low capital requirement combination provided by the senior and super-senior tranches of structured products, kept them on their books and, once satiated, began to pass their (perceived) infinitesimal risk onto the monolines and insurance companies (AIG, in particular). Through this process, the core of the financial system became interconnected in increasingly complex ways and vulnerable to a systemic event.[15]

Caballero is correct that investors from the countries of Southeast Asia and China were seeking safe assets to hold, but it is curious that those countries invested most of their current account surpluses in just one type of security; US government-guaranteed debt. The primary investors in the new, AAA subprime ABS created during the housing boom were not foreigners; they were mostly US institutions.[16] Emerging economy investors crowded out other investors in government-guaranteed securities, forcing them into other investments. These displaced investors became the ones who demanded the production of synthetic "safe" assets. As I shall explain in chapter 7, that is one channel through which the capital flow bonanza promoted subprime mortgage securitizations.

However, there remains a question of why Asian investors were so concentrated in US government-guaranteed debt; why didn't they partake their share of the newly created AAA securities? Even if the primary motivation of these investors was to place their savings in a safe haven, investment theory predicts they would diversify their holdings within the United States. I think proponents of the safe asset shortage view have inadvertently bundled together two dimensions of the perceived safety of US investments, which are really separate and distinct. One dimension is that the United States offers legal protection and liquidity to foreign investors. The other dimension is that, within the United States, investors have a choice among many different types of assets, with varying risk/return profiles. Asian investors did not diversify their holdings of US assets. A study by economist Frank Warnock and his collaborators revealed that the portfolios of foreign investors in US markets are more heavily weighted in highly rated bonds than are the portfolios of US investors abroad.[17] Warnock et al. showed that the comparative risk aversion of foreign investment into the United States accounts for a significant portion of their lower returns relative to US investments abroad. While it is possible that offshore investors into the United States desired to offset the extreme precariousness of their holdings abroad by going "full Monty," accumulating the safest but lowest return US securities, it does at least raise a question

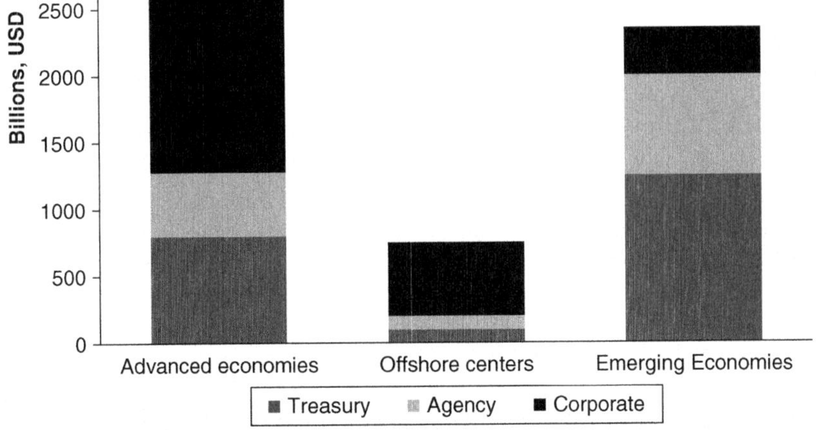

Figure 3.4 Foreign holdings of US securities, 2007.

Source: Gian Maria Milesi-Ferretti, Francesco Strobbe, and Natalia Tamirisa, "Bilateral Financial Linkages and Global Imbalances: A View on the Eve of the Financial Crisis" (IMF Working Paper 10/257, 2010), Figure 1, p. 30.

about their extreme risk aversion, particularly when their portfolio concentration forced down yields on US government debt. Presumably, many of those investors would have diversified a portion of their holdings into other assets—even if only into higher yielding AAA securities like the newly created AAA securitized assets—as the returns on government securities plummeted. Yet, Asian investors did not diversify their US portfolios in response to the decline in treasury yields.

The motives of Asian investors can be discerned by looking at who was doing the investing. For those countries driving the capital flow bonanza, it was not the private sector. As I shall explain, the increase in the capital flow bonanza during the housing boom was generated primarily by China's central bank, the PBOC, and OPEC. The PBOC was not looking to invest in the United States as an alternative to risky domestic securities. It does not appear the PBOC was motivated by a shortage of safe assets at home. Rather, Chinese policy forced it to accumulate dollars in order to maintain a pegged exchange rate. To earn interest on its accumulation of dollars, it needed to invest in dollar assets. China's State Administration of Foreign Exchange (SAFE) mandated that the PBOC's foreign exchange reserves be invested to optimize "security, liquidity, and increases in value, among which security is the primary principle."[18] The way to accomplish that goal was to invest exclusively in US government-guaranteed debt.

Asian Mercantilism and OPEC: The Sources of the US Current Account Deficit in the 2000s

The Asian Financial Crisis of 1997

The buildup of the US current account deficit, from the onset of the Asian financial crisis in July 1997, to the onset of the US financial crisis in 2008, was a product of its bilateral current account deficits with Southeast Asia, China, and OPEC (see figure 3.6).[19]

The buildup of the bilateral deficits began in July of 1997, when Southeast Asian countries (which did not include China) experienced an abrupt reversal of offshore capital inflows. All of a sudden, foreign investors rushed to liquidate their investments in those countries. The countries of Southeast Asia were in a vulnerable position, because much of the foreign investment in their countries was comprised of short-term liabilities of domestic banks and corporations, and virtually all of it was denominated in dollars—the international reserve and transactions currency. Economist Guillermo Calvo described the phenomenon of an abrupt reversal of offshore capital inflows by panicked offshore investors as a "sudden stop."

The sudden stop of capital inflows to Southeast Asia forced domestic debtors to deplete their dollar reserves and to exchange local currency into dollars, in order to pay off their debts. This caused depreciation in the value of the local currency relative to the dollar. The depreciation, in turn, increased the domestic currency value of the debt, and forced debtors to liquidate assets in order to raise dollars to pay the debt. Fire sale liquidation created a vicious circle of loan defaults, asset price contraction and further depreciation. This downward spiral is called a "debt-deflation," a phenomenon about which I shall have more to say later on in this book in the context of the US financial crisis. It placed the afflicted countries in a difficult predicament: their currencies had collapsed, their economies were contracting, and domestic borrowers were defaulting on their international debt obligations. This bankrupted many and made it very difficult for the survivors to regain the confidence of international lenders. Those countries wanted to do whatever they could to avoid such jeopardy in the future. They implemented reforms to reduce the risk of a sudden stop. A crucial part of the approach was to build a cushion of dollar reserves. A cushion would provide means to pay off dollar denominated debt in a panicked situation. The existence of the cushion would help discourage the panic from occurring at all, by making investors confident that the country possessed a reserve of dollar assets sufficient to meet its foreign currency obligations.

In order to build dollar reserves, Southeast Asian countries needed to run a current account surplus with the United States; only by selling more products into the United States (by value) than they imported from the United States could they accumulate reserve dollars in excess of dollar claims. In reaction to the trauma of the Asian financial crisis, many of the countries of Southeast Asia became mercantilists (see the definition of "mercantilism" in chapter 1).

Excess Saving in China and Excess Revenues in OPEC

In the early 2000s China began to run large current account surpluses with the United States, and by the mid-2000s OPEC began to run large surpluses.

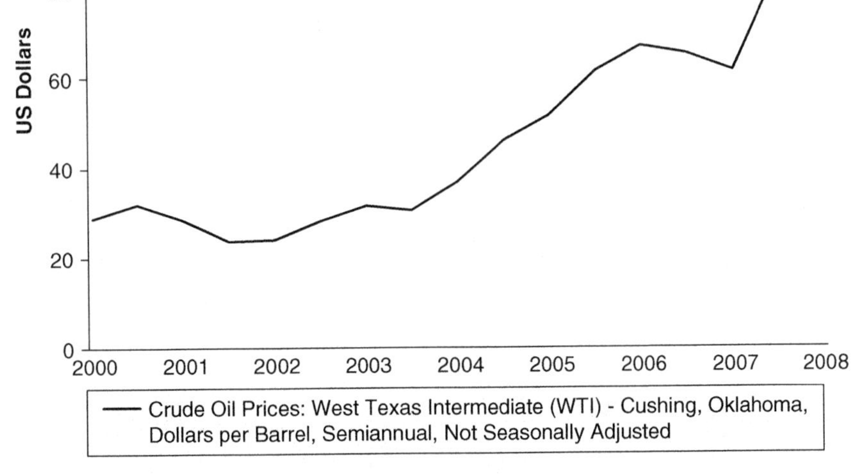

Figure 3.5 Crude oil prices, 2000–2008.

Source: US Energy Information Administration.

China's current account surplus was mercantilist, but the motives that generated it differed from its neighbors. China emerged unscathed by the Asian financial crisis, since it had a closed capital account that precluded any foreign "hot money" (short-term debt) investment, and it allowed only a limited amount of domestic borrowing in foreign currencies. Because China had no significant borrowing or short-term investment from foreigners, there was no capital inflow to "stop." As was explained in chapter 1, China ran large current account surpluses with the United States and Europe as part of a deliberate policy of promoting of the growth of its export industries.[20] The PBOC followed its mandate to accumulated dollar reserves in order to maintain its fixed exchange rate with the dollar.

OPEC accumulated dollar reserves for yet a different reason. OPEC's bilateral trade surplus with the United States grew exponentially in the mid-2000s driven by an upward spike in the price of oil, from around \$30/barrel in January 2004, to nearly \$100/barrel in January 2008 (figure 3.5).

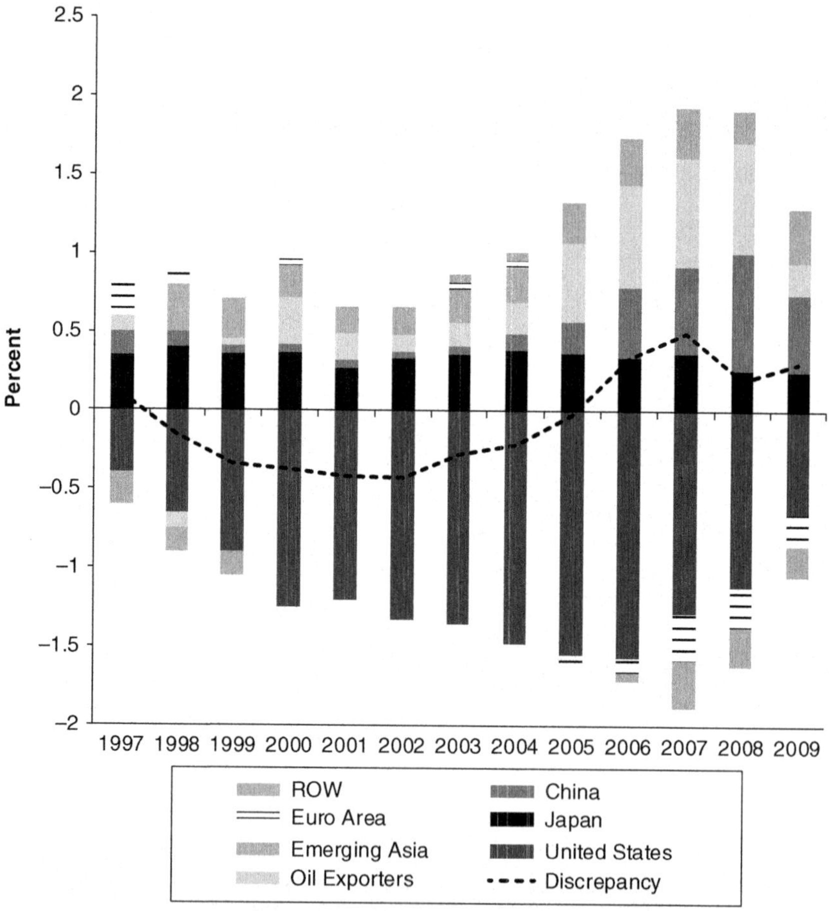

Figure 3.6 Global imbalances (in percent of world GDP), 1997–2009.

Source: Gian Maria Milesi-Ferretti, Francesco Strobbe, and Natalia Tamirisa, *Bilateral Financial Linkages and Global Imbalances: A View on the Eve of the Financial Crisis* (IMF Working Paper 10/257, 2010), Figure 4, p. 33.

OPEC nations accumulated a large trade surplus because their comparatively small domestic economies could not generate spending sufficient to match the inflow of revenue from oil sales. OPEC had an incentive to help maintain the value of the dollar, as it quoted the oil price, and received payment, in dollars. While OPEC probably would have invested a significant portion of its foreign reserves in dollar assets in any event, the incentive to support the value of the dollar likely added to the concentration of investment in dollar assets. Figure 3.6 shows that global imbalances from the onset of the Asian financial crisis to the 2008 US financial crisis were dominated by the surpluses of Southeast Asia, China, and OPEC and the matching US deficit.

How Did China Maintain Its Current Account Surplus?

I have argued that the capital flow bonanza was an integral part of the housing boom and the subsequent financial crisis, and that China was the most important source of the US capital flow bonanza during that period. I now explain how China managed to counteract the market adjustments that would ordinarily have acted to eliminate its trade imbalance with the United States.

The Chinese government promoted its trade surplus with the United States by subsidizing exports discouraging imports and fixing its exchange rate with the dollar. The PBOC posted the rate of exchange at which it stood willing to purchase as many dollars (or dollar bank deposits) as necessary to maintain its fixed RMB/dollar exchange rate.[21] From 1994 to mid-2005, China pegged the RMB to the dollar at around 8.28 yuan (the base unit of the RMB) per dollar, after which it adopted a managed peg system that allowed the RMB to gradually appreciate. By mid-2008 the RMB had appreciated by 18.7 percent, to 6.83 yuan (see figure 1.2).[22] The PBOC was required to purchase dollars at the exchange rate its government set. Since China ran large current account surpluses with the United States, this policy resulted in a massive accumulation of dollar reserves by the PBOC, as Chinese companies exchanged their excess dollar bank deposits for RMB bank deposits needed to pay taxes, wages, and domestic suppliers.

From the beginning of 2003 through the beginning of 2008, China's cumulative trade surplus with the United States was $1.24 trillion,[23] and its officially reported cumulative purchase of US debt was $914 billion.[24] Since most experts believe China's actual official holdings of US debt exceed the reported figure, it is reasonable to conjecture that China nearly matched its trade surplus with holdings of US debt. China invested most of its US holdings in Treasuries and GSE debt; in 2008, 87 percent of its reported US securities holdings were in Treasury and GSE debt.[25] A report by the US Congressional Research Service stated:

> China's policy of intervening in currency markets to limit the appreciation of its currency against the dollar (and other currencies) and large current account surpluses have made it the world's largest and fastest growing holder of foreign exchange reserves, especially dollar-denominated assets.[26]

Chinese central bank intervention blocked the market adjustment process that would have rebalanced trade in its absence. It did so by intervening in the currency market to maintain a fixed exchange rate, and by sterilizing the impact of the accumulation of dollar reserves on its domestic money supply In the absence of either one of these interventions, the trade imbalance would have contracted. If the PBOC had not stood ready to exchange dollars for RMB at a fixed exchange rate that overvalued the dollar, Chinese exporters would have been required to exchange their excess dollars for RMB in the foreign exchange market, and the excess supply of dollars would have forced down the exchange price of dollars. As the dollar depreciated, US tradable goods manufacturers would have become more competitive, resulting in a shift in expenditure on tradable goods away from Chinese and toward the US manufacturers. This process would have continued until trade rebalanced. Alternatively, given the fixed exchange rate, in the absence of intervention in the domestic money market, the exchange of dollars for RMB would have significantly increased the Chinese money supply and likely triggered inflation. The resultant increase in prices of Chinese tradable goods would have conferred a competitive advantage on US tradable goods manufacturers and set in motion a reduction of China's surplus until trade rebalanced. In the event, the PBOC successfully offset the inflationary pressure and thereby blocked that avenue for rebalancing trade.[27] Obstfeld and Rogoff summed up the logic:

> Had the natural "Humean" [named after David Hume] international adjustment process been allowed to function earlier on, rather than a combination of undervaluation and expenditure compression policies, the dollar would have been weaker in real effective terms, there would have been more upward pressure on world interest rates, and the US external deficit would likely have been smaller.[28]

The only other avenue for adjustment to reduce the trade imbalance would have been for the US Fed to force deflation by contracting the money supply, in order to reduce the price of its tradable goods relative to China. But deflation would have been a potentially calamitous course for the US economy, resulting in a contraction that would far outweigh any benefit it received from rebalancing trade.[29]

Looking at the matter in somewhat more detail, it can be seen that the PBOC was able to thwart the market adjustment process by (1) fixing the RMB exchange rate at price at which China ran a large bilateral current account surplus with the United States. It did this by agreeing to exchange dollar bank deposits accumulated by Chinese exporters for RMB bank deposits at a fixed price. Without some offsetting adjustment, this policy would have caused the domestic money supply to increase, as the PBOC paid out RMB deposits in exchange for the flood of dollar deposits it received. The increase in money supply would have set in motion a market adjustment by causing domestic price inflation, which would have eroded the competitiveness of Chinese exports and caused the current account to adjust toward balance. Therefore, in order to prevent this adjustment and to maintain domestic price stability, the PBOC (2) sterilized the increase in RMB supply. It accomplished this through two mechanisms: by issuing bonds to remove RMB from the market (PBOC Bills), and by increasing the reserve requirements on Chinese banks in order to reduce the money multiplier (see figure 3.7).

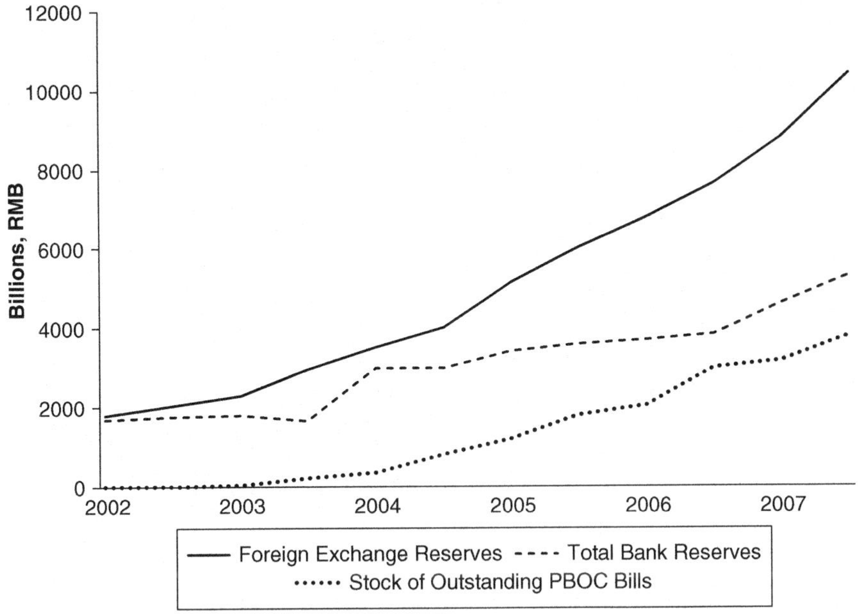

Figure 3.7 China's stocks of bank reserves, forex reserves, and PBOC bills, 2002–2008.
Source: Eswar S. Prasad, "Is the Chinese Growth Miracle Built to Last?" *China Economic Review*, Vol. 20, (2009): 103–123, 117, Figure 13.

The sterilization was sufficient to offset the increase in money supply that would otherwise have been induced by the intervention required to fix the RMB exchange value with the dollar.[30] The primary purchasers of the PBOC bills were state-owned banks, who funded their purchases with low cost deposits from captive savers, who were offered few alternatives in China's repressed financial system. As evidence of the effectiveness of these interventionist policies in containing inflation, the PBOC's foreign reserves increased twelve-fold, from 1,000 billion yuan to around 12,000 billion yuan, while its monetary base increased only three-fold and its average annual inflation rate remained below 3 percent in the period 1997–2008 (figure 3.8).

To summarize, the saving inflows during the US housing boom did not occur in response to high return investment opportunities in the United States. If that were so, an elevated rate of return on investment would likely have prevented US real interest rates from declining after the turn of the millennium. During the housing boom—in contrast to the dot-com boom that preceded it—both productivity growth and real interest rates declined. The capital flow bonanza from Southeast Asia, OPEC, and China was primarily invested in the lowest yielding securities, US government-guaranteed debt, and pushed down the yields on those securities by a considerable amount. The capital flow bonanza into the United States came not from the private sector, but from entities controlled by foreign governments. This suggests that the primary cause of the capital flow bonanza during the housing boom originated from government policies aimed

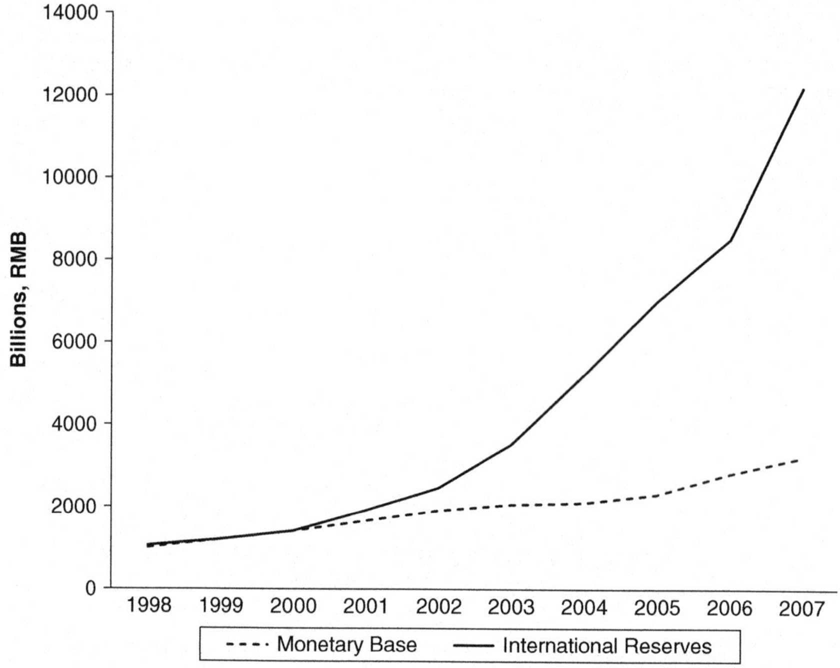

Figure 3.8 China's monetary base and international reserves, 1998–2007.

Source: Maurice Obstfeld and Kenneth Rogoff, "Global Imbalances and the Financial Crisis: Products of Common Causes," paper delivered at FRBSF Asia Economic Policy Conference, October 18–20, 2009, p. 140 Figure 5.

at promoting exports (China) or accumulating buffer stocks of foreign exchange (Southeast Asia) and as a by-product of the rise in the price of oil (OPEC).

Why Didn't Dollar Depreciation Reduce the US Current Account Deficit?

Southeast Asia and China undervalued their currencies relative to the dollar in order to run a current account surplus with the United States. OPEC ran a surplus with the United States for structural reasons. What of the rest of the world? The United States ran balanced trade with everyone else, and this is puzzling because the official US trade weighted real exchange rate with the rest of the world was declining sharply during the housing boom—the dollar was getting cheaper (figure 3.9). It raises the question of why did not the United States run trade surpluses with the rest of the world?

Economist Gian Maria Milesi-Ferretti has pondered this question and determined that the official statistics overstate the dollar's depreciation in the 2000s.[31] He identifies several reasons for this. One is that the United States shifted an enormous amount of trade to low-cost developing countries, principally China and India, while the official Federal Reserve measure only partially accounts for the reduction in import costs implied by the shift. This caused a significant

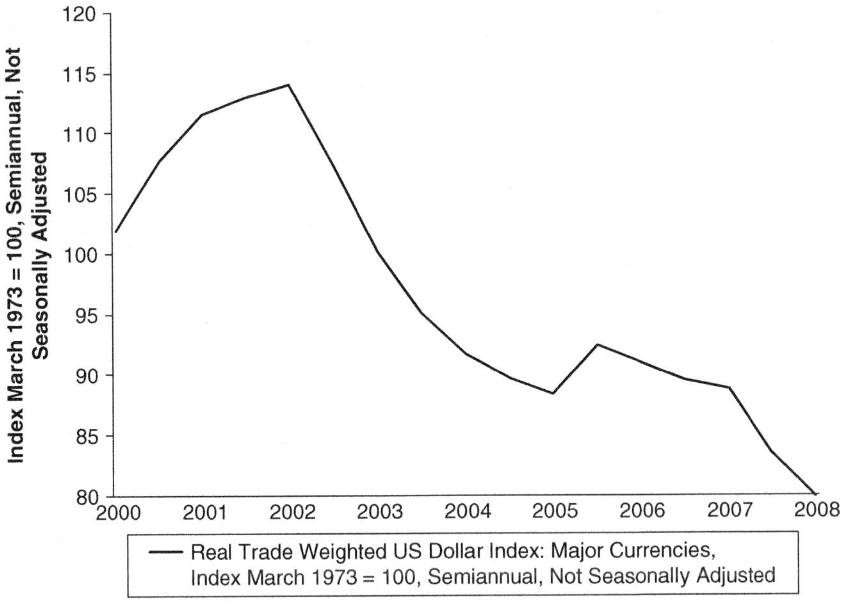

Figure 3.9 Real trade weighted US dollar index: major currencies, 2000–2008.
Source: Board of Governors of the Federal Reserve System.

underestimation of the true trade weighted dollar exchange rate in the 2000s.[32] Another reason is that the spike in oil prices weakened the US terms of trade and, due to the inelastic demand for oil, increased US imports, which added to the current account deficit. An additional possible reason has to do with a delay in the response of trade patterns to changes in relative prices. Economist Doug Campbell has documented an asymmetry in the response of US exports to changes in real exchange rates: namely, when the dollar appreciates, as it did in the late 1990s to early 2000s, export growth declines to a much greater extent than the rate at which exports increase after depreciation. In sum, the apparent "puzzle" of why the United States did not run trade surpluses with countries against whose currencies the dollar had depreciated may not be so puzzling after all.

Conclusion

So far in this book I have provided empirical evidence linking the current account deficit to the US housing boom and I have shown that the current account deficit was generated by policies of foreign governments. These facts imply the current account deficit was an independent cause of the housing boom.[33] In the next chapter I demonstrate on logical grounds that the current account deficit was a necessary condition for a housing boom to have occurred.

CHAPTER 4

The Current Account Deficit: A Necessary Condition for the Housing Boom

Nature is pleased with simplicity.

—Isaac Newton[1]

In the last two chapters I reviewed empirical evidence showing a chain of causation running from offshore mercantilism to the growing US current account deficit, and from the current account deficit to the US housing boom. The evidence points to Southeast Asian, OPEC and Chinese mercantilism as the primary underlying cause of the growth of the US current account deficit and the housing boom. In this chapter, I provide another reason for linking the current account deficit to the housing boom by explaining why, given spending patterns in the United States, the ballooning US current account deficit was a necessary condition, in the absence of which the 2003–2007 US housing boom could not have occurred.

While it is often noted that an increase in financial sector and household leverage accompanied the dramatic increase in home construction and home mortgage lending,[2] it will be shown that the expansion in credit, by itself cannot, given that spending increased throughout the US economy, account for the sustained and sizeable boom in housing construction and consumer spending that occurred during the housing boom. Moreover, the absence of any increase in leverage during the dot-com boom, which preceded the housing boom, refutes the notion that an increase in financial sector leverage is either a necessary or a sufficient condition for a boom to occur on general.

As a matter of simple logic, the US economy could not have sustained the increase in aggregate demand, nor could it have maintained low interest rates and price stability, as it experienced from 2003 to 2007, without running a large current account deficit. This holds true independently of the leverage or recklessness of its financial institutions and households, or the policy of its central bank. In order to present the argument I regrettably must utilize some simple algebra to keep track of the relationship between a few economic variables. However, if I have written as clearly as I intend, there should be sufficient explanation to enable those not inclined to follow the mathematics to fully grasp the argument.

The Salient Facts of the Housing boom

The US housing boom involved massive increases in residential mortgage lending, home prices, and home building. Figure 2.1 shows that mortgage lending doubled. Figure 2.2 shows that, from 2000 to 2006, the leading measure of US home prices, the Case Shiller HPI, more than doubled. During that period annual new single family home starts increased by more than a third and annual home construction spending almost doubled.[3] The share of residential construction in GDP increased from just over 3 percent to just under 5 percent (at its 2005 peak) and the share of residential construction in total gross domestic investment increased from 17 percent to 24 percent (figure 4.1).[4] After the housing boom took off in 2003, the US economy rapidly moved toward full employment (figure 4.2). Finally, the sum of all categories of US spending—consumption, investment, and government—grew larger and increased faster than US GDP (figure 4.3).

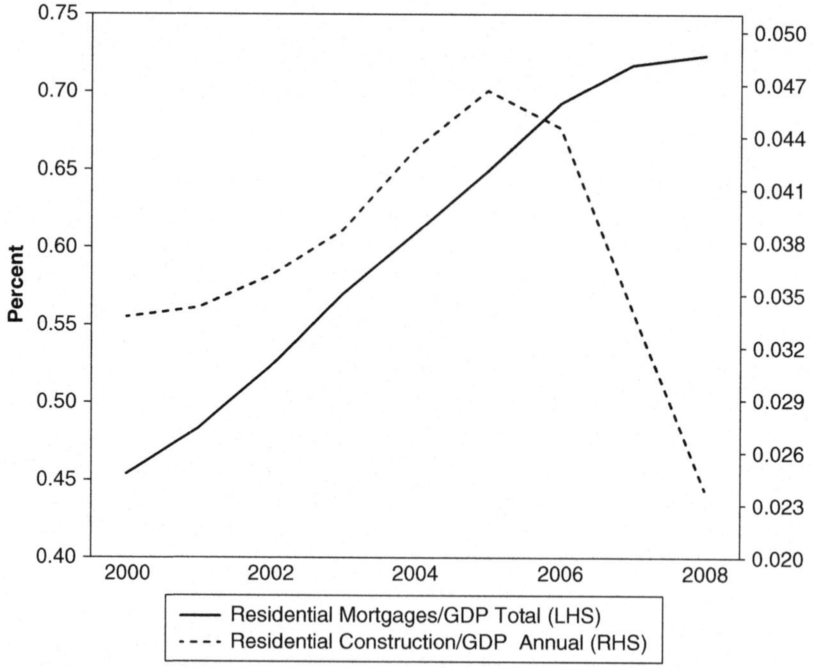

Figure 4.1 Residential construction and mortgages as percent of GDP, 2000–2008.
Source: Board of Governors of the Federal Reserve System and US Census Bureau.

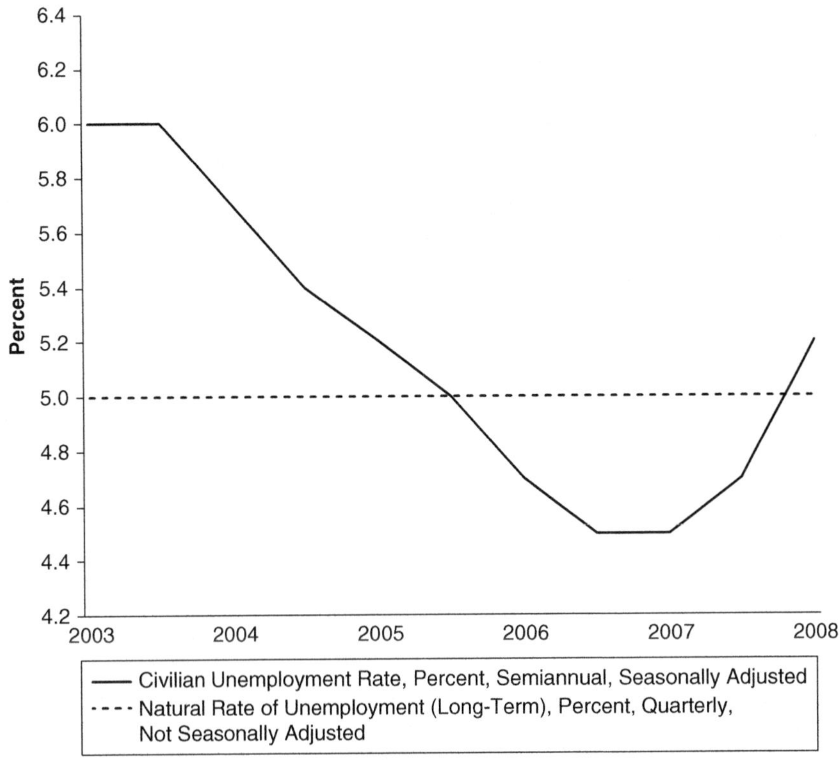

Figure 4.2 US unemployment, natural rate, 2003–2008.
Source: US Bureau of Labor Statistics and US Congressional Budget Office.

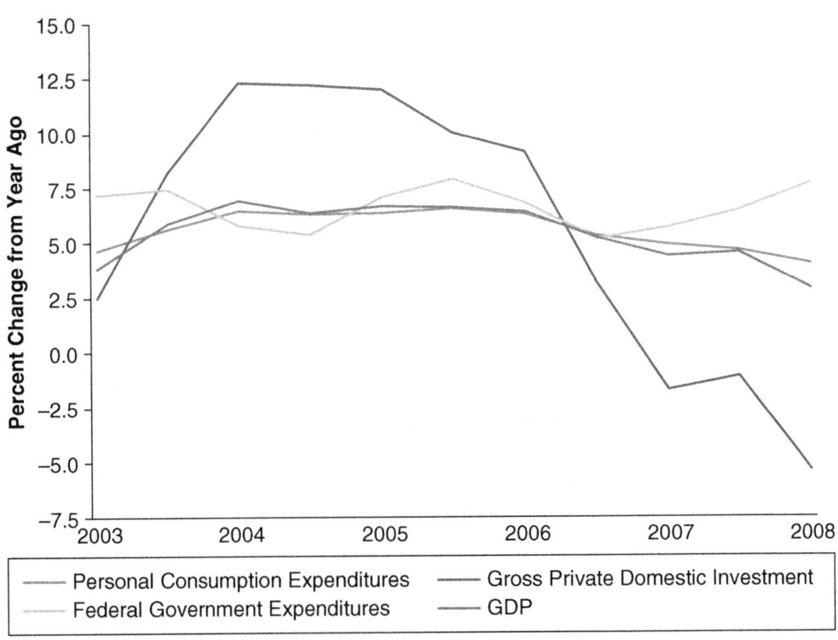

Figure 4.3 Expenditure growth, 2003–2008.
Source: US Bureau of Economic Analysis.

What Has Tobin's "Q" Got to Do with the US Housing Boom?

I make the assumption that home price increases spurred home construction during the housing boom. This assumption is crucial to understanding the housing boom because it is one of the channels through which the effects of the boom was transmitted into the US economy (the other channel was the increase in borrowings collateralized by existing homes).

One might ask the question, "Is it possible for the price of some asset to blow up without an accompanying expansion of investment?" Well, yes it is. The Mona Lisa, if offered for sale, would probably fetch a pretty penny, and might even spark a mania that could drive up its price to an astounding height. However, it would not lead to more investment as there is just one Mona Lisa and it is unique. A more relevant example is British housing. In the discussion of figure 2.5 I mentioned that UK home prices rose further than US house prices in the early 2000s, and that UK home construction did not increase by very much. That is because it was much more difficult to obtain permission to build a new home in the Britain than in most of the United States. So, UK homes were like Mona Lisas during the housing boom. But most things are not like Mona Lisas (or British homes). Most assets are reproducible, and there will be an incentive to invest to produce more of the asset as its price increases. In the case of housing, labor assembles various components (like wood, shingles, pipe, bricks, etc.) on a plot of land. The sum of all these inputs, plus the profit the developer requires to build the home, is the cost to produce the home. The purchaser of the home pays a single price for the finished product—the fully assembled house and the lot on which it is situated. The ratio between the final product and the sum of the input costs is Tobin's "Q," named after the Nobel Prize–winning economist James Tobin, who developed the concept.

Whenever Tobin's "Q" for homes exceeds 1, the construction of a new home will earn the builder an extranormal profit. For this reason, a flood of new home construction will usually occur whenever the gap between home prices and input costs becomes large. During the housing boom home prices soared while inflation for everything else remained low, which meant Tobin's "Q" for homes grew quite large. That is what connected the home price increases that occurred during the housing boom to the increase in home construction. That is what Tobin's "Q" has got to do with the housing boom.[5]

The US Current Account Deficit and the US Housing Boom

The Algebra of National Income Accounting

In an open economy such as the United States, some individuals and firms (I shall refer to them collectively as "agents") purchase foreign made goods, and some foreigners purchase US made goods. In order to measure US national income, one has to subtract from total expenditure by US agents on final goods, services, transfers and investments that portion they spend on imported goods, services, transfers, and investments (including payments to foreigners arising from their US investments). These are "imports" (M). Then, one has to add the amount that foreigners spend on US produced goods, services, transfers, and investments (including payments to US agents arising from their foreign investments). These are "exports" (X).[6] The result is US income, which is expressed by the variable Y, which is the value of income earned by US agents from the sale of final goods and services, divided by an index of the domestic price level (often called "real income"). Real income is the same as the value of output produced by US agents. Economists sometimes refer to income and output interchangeably, and I will adhere to this convention. The following identity[7] relates US real income (Y)[8] to its components of expenditure; consumption (C); investment (which includes home construction) (I); US government spending (G)[9]; exports (X); and imports (M)[10]:

$$Y \equiv (C + I + G) + (X - M), \tag{4.1}$$

where $(C + I + G)$ represents expenditure on US produced goods by US agents (called home economy "absorption") and $(X - M)$ is the current account balance. A positive current account balance means exports exceed imports and the US economy is running a current account surplus, while a negative value means imports exceed exports and the US economy is running a current account deficit.

Yf stands for the level of income earned when the US economy is fully employing its productive resources, including labor. The concept of full employment allows some flexibility. For example, the US economy could temporarily operate above its long run capacity if people agreed to work longer hours than is customary or by utilizing facilities and equipment more intensively (and deferring downtime for maintenance) than their long run sustainable rate. Yf is the maximum level of output sustainable for a long time. Yf can be changed over time by the creation or destruction of plant, natural resources, human skills, and shifts in the size of the labor force and by changes in the nature of social customs and institutions and regulations.

There are some useful insights about the economy that can be gleaned from identity (4.1). One is that, with balanced current account ($X - M = 0$), if spending on US economy goods—the sum of the variables on the right-hand side—exceeds what the US economy can produce at full employment, something has to give because the economy cannot operate above Yf indefinitely. Typically, "what gives" is prices. When the demand for goods and services exceed their supply, producers and retailers will encounter opportunities to enhance revenue by raising prices—and increases in their input costs may compel them to do so. If producers anticipate that prices will soon rise, they may even raise their prices before facing excess demand, which could spur inflation at less than full employment. This phenomenon, known as "stagflation," occurred in the United States in the 1970s.[11]

Another insight is that, since US output is by definition the income earned by US agents, a current account deficit means that total spending by US agents exceeds their income. Therefore, in order to achieve full employment while running a current account deficit ($X - M < 0$), US agents must spend in excess of their income, since $Yf < C + I + G$. Finally, a current account deficit makes it possible for US spending to exceed US income without creating inflationary pressure, because additional resources are being imported from abroad to meet the excess demand for goods.

Although I shall maintain that the large and growing US current account deficit was a necessary condition for the housing boom to have occurred, it was the configuration of US spending that made it so; in general, a current account deficit is neither a necessary nor a sufficient condition for booms. It is important to grasp this point in order to understand the dynamic that drove the US housing boom. It will help to state formally the relationship between real income and its component uses:

$$Y \equiv C + S + T, \tag{4.2}$$

where (again) C is consumption, S represents home economy saving, and T is taxes collected by government. Identity (4.1) and (4.2) represent two different ways of accounting for national income; identity (4.1) expresses spending by US agents in accordance with the final categories their money is ultimately spent on, whereas identity (4.2) expresses the same spending according to where US agents initially spend the money they earn. So, for example, (4.1) includes the amount government spends (G), whereas (4.2) shows what US agents pay to the government out of their income: (T) and a portion of (S). Note that the left-hand side of each identity is the same Y, which represents the real income earned by US agents. Combining the right-hand sides of (4.1) and (4.2) and then rearranging the terms yields the identity.

$$(S - I) + (T - G) \equiv (X - M). \tag{4.3}$$

Identity (4.3) shows that the current account balance is equal to the sum of the excess of private saving over investment (which includes home construction) and the excess of taxes over government spending (net public saving). The three variables in parentheses are the sectoral financial balances, which is a concept I will take up in the discussion on fiscal policy in chapter 13. Identity (4.3) shows that the sum of financial outflows from the private sector ($S - I$), government ($T - G$), and the foreign sector ($M - X$) must always equal zero. It provides a useful perspective for understanding the relationship between booms and current account deficits.

A Current Account Deficit Is neither a Necessary nor a Sufficient Condition for a Boom to Occur in General

Identity (4.3) shows that, even in the absence of a current account deficit, a high level of investment is supportable if the rate of saving is high. In fact, an economy with a high rate of saving can support a high level of investment while running a current account *surplus* ($X - M > 0$). This implies that an economy does not need to spend more than it earns to have an investment boom; it can finance the boom if has a high savings rate.[12] There have been notable instances where high saving economies ran current account surpluses and supported investment booms at the same time. Japan ran surpluses while undergoing a real estate boom in the 1980s; the Asian countries involved in the Asian financial crisis of 1997 had previously experienced large surpluses and real estate booms; and China has been undergoing a massive investment boom—in real estate and basic industries—while running a large current account surplus for the past quarter century.[13] All of these countries had extremely high savings rates by historical standards.[14] China in the 2000s had the highest savings rate ever recorded for a country.[15]

Another circumstance where an economy could sustain a protracted investment boom without a current account deficit is if it is initially operating below full employment, in which event there will be idle resources available for deployment in a booming sector. It is less common to find instances where this has occurred, since the booming sector will usually take up the slack and push the economy to full employment. Yet, one can make an argument that China fit that bill from the beginning of its economic rise in the 1980s to at least the late 2000s, as its huge reserve of "underemployed" rural labor was transitioned to more productive occupations in urban centers. The possibility of financing an investment boom over a period of years out of domestic savings, without needing to run a current account deficit to finance the boom, demonstrates that a current account deficit is not a necessary condition for a boom to occur.

That a current account deficit is not, by itself, a sufficient condition to cause a boom should be obvious as well. The deficit creates a hole in demand; by definition US agents purchase more from abroad than from home when the United States runs a current account deficit. The hole in demand can be filled if its trading partners recycle the current account deficit into the US economy via a capital flow bonanza. However, there is no iron law that says trading partners will do so, and if they do not, the current account deficit will induce a deflationary monetary contraction. Even with a capital flow bonanza, it is not assured that the US economy will always fill the hole. If it does not do so, it will still spend in excess of its income, which is the defining attribute of a current account deficit, but will operate below full employment. A good example of this is the economies of the United States and the European periphery in the aftermath of the financial crisis; they were mired in deep recession, operating well below full employment, while running sizeable (albeit shrinking) current account deficits.

Yet the Current Account Deficit Was a Necessary Condition for the US Housing Boom to Have Occurred

Soon after the housing boom took off in 2003, the US economy was operating near full employment, so there was very little slack in the US economy available to finance a boom. At the same time, private saving did not rise and the US government deficit abated somewhat, but did not turn to surplus (see figure 3.3). Identity (4.1) shows us that if home economy expenditure $(C + I + G)$ increases in an economy initially operating at full employment with a current account deficit—which it did during the housing boom—then the current account balance $(X - M)$ must become more negative. This follows from the facts that home economy output cannot exceed Yf for a protracted period, and that all components of US expenditure increased during the housing boom.

In terms of identity (4.3), the first term $(S - I)$ became more negative as investment (home construction) rose during the boom and saving decreased (due to increased consumption spending); the second term $(T - G)$ remained negative, as tax rates were reduced (offset somewhat by increased income) and spending on the Iraq War increased (offset somewhat by reductions in social insurance payments after the 2001 recession ended). This implies that the third term $(X-M)$, which is the current account balance, must have become more negative during the housing boom. Since the United States was already running a current account deficit prior to the commencement of the boom, the current account deficit had to increase further to accommodate the increase in home construction and the home equity g financed increase in consumer expenditure.

To underscore this insight, let us consider how differently matters would have evolved if the current account deficit had not increased. In that case, the only way the housing boom could have proceeded would have been if either private savings increased by an amount equal to the increase in home construction, or if some other component of investment declined, so that the term $(S-I)$ would not have decreased.[16] Neither of these things occurred, and it would have been quite strange if they did. During the boom, private incomes increased, due to the effects of full employment in improving the bargaining position of workers; and private wealth increased, due to the bidding up of asset prices. An environment where income and wealth are increasing is one in which consumption and investment are likely to be on the rise, as they were. Under these circumstances, if the housing boom got going without an increase in the current account deficit the increase in home construction would have bid up the prices of land, labor, and materials used to construct and furnish homes, and the increased borrowing demand from homebuilders and homeowners would have bid up interest rates and consumer goods prices. Prices and interest rates would have risen until the increases discouraged a sufficient number of purchasers and borrowers throughout the economy to bring demand in line with the productive capacity of the US economy. In the absence of a current account deficit, the competition for scarce goods, labor, and financing would have tempered the size of the housing boom.

The US economy needed to draw additional resources from abroad to accommodate the increased spending during the housing boom. The current account deficit enabled the US economy to spend more than it earned by expanding available resources beyond what the United States could produce, through the importation of goods from abroad. The current account deficit made possible a noninflationary increase in home construction and spending while the United States was operating at full employment. Between 2000 and 2007, the US annual current account deficit grew by nearly $600 billion, a threefold increase. As a percentage of GDP, the current account deficit grew from 1.5 percent in 1996 to just below 7 percent in the final quarter of 2006.[17] In the absence of a current account deficit, the bubble would have burst at an early stage because with balanced current account US consumption and investment spending could not have exceeded full employment output for a protracted period. This constraint is unyielding; it holds regardless of the amount of credit or leverage in the US economy: It can be demonstrated by setting the current account balance $(X-M)$ in identity (4.1) to 0. Identity (4.1') shows that, with balanced trade, home economy expenditure $(C+I+G)$ cannot exceed the income earned from home economy production (Y). The two must always be equal:

$$Y = C + I + G. \tag{4.1'}$$

To summarize the argument so far: The US housing boom lasted for four–five years during most of which time the US economy, according to conventional measures, was fully employed. The sum of all categories of spending were increasing faster than GDP and inflation was negligible. It is quite simply impossible that such a lengthy and large boom could have taken place in the absence of a current account deficit. This relatively simple point has been missed by most analysts and has not factored prominently in the policy discussions and response to the subsequent financial crisis.

Most analyses of the housing boom, and the financial crisis that followed, has focused on leverage and other elements of financial structure as causal factors. I do not doubt the importance of such matters in explaining the genesis of the boom and the character of the crisis; I shall have something to say about these matters myself in the remaining chapters of this book. The point about the current account deficit, however, is that in its absence, the boom would have ended much earlier, probably before serious dislocations in the housing and financial markets had developed. The geometric increase in the current account deficit relaxed a natural systemic constraint on the boom, a fact that policymakers should consider, but have not so far, in responding to the crisis. *A central aim of this book is to drive home the simple fact that the US housing boom could not have taken place without an accompanying current account deficit.*

Leverage Was Not a Necessary Condition for the US Housing Boom

I have shown that the current account deficit was necessary for the housing boom to have occurred, and therefore that credit expansion was not alone sufficient to have generated the boom. But is it possible to maintain that an excessive expansion of credit and leverage was a necessary condition for the US housing boom? During the boom, both financial and household sector leverage exploded. Financial institutions expanded their balance sheets by increasing their liabilities and leverage. Broker-dealer leverage increased dramatically, from 20X equity in 2000 to over 40X equity in 2007 (see figure 2.3), US commercial banks issued $1.3 trillion of off balance sheet securitizations,[18] and residential mortgage liabilities more than doubled (see figure 2.1). Moreover, as I discuss in chapter 7, the impact of the capital flow bonanza (which was the mirror image of the US current account deficit during the housing boom) was channeled into the US economy by increasing leverage in the household sector. While I think it is reasonable to argue that, because homes were primarily financed by debt prior to the boom, increased borrowing was the only channel by which a "housing" boom could have occurred. But it cannot be maintained that an increase in leverage is a necessary condition for booms in general. The nature of the first bubble to surface after the rise in the US current account deficit in the late 1990s underscores this point. The dot-com boom of the late 1990s was an investment boom that was not accompanied by any increase in leverage. Therefore, increased leverage is neither a necessary nor a sufficient condition to sustain a lengthy boom. Where leverage does make a difference, as I shall explain later on, is in the aftermath of the crash. When absent, as in the dot-com boom, the economy recovers at a "normal" pace. When it is present, as it was in the housing boom, the resulting debt overhang can propel the economy into a debt-deflation spiral and a protracted and deep recession.

Did Gross Capital Flows Contribute to the US Housing Boom?

The capital flow bonanza is a net flow calculated by subtracting US gross capital outflow from US gross capital inflow (capital flow in – capital flow out). During the housing boom, gross capital flows were an order of magnitude larger than the "net" capital flow bonanza. Look again at figure 2.7. It displays a coincidence of banking crises and global capital flows. It shows that international capital mobility was very low for decades after World War II, and began to surge in the 1980s, reaching a postwar peak in the early 2000s. It shows that financial crises also began to surge after the 1980s. Capital mobility is not the same thing as capital flow bonanzas, however. It is possible, for example, that two countries can have large capital flows that offset each other, so that the current account is balanced.

Economists Claudio Borio and Piti Disyatit of the Bank for International Settlements have shown that the explosion in gross capital flows, which coincided with the liberalization of international capital markets that began in the 1980s, has promoted the formation of an integrated global market for credit and a highly elastic international supply of credit.[19] In 2006, when the US capital flow bonanza peaked at over 6 percent of GDP, total gross international capital

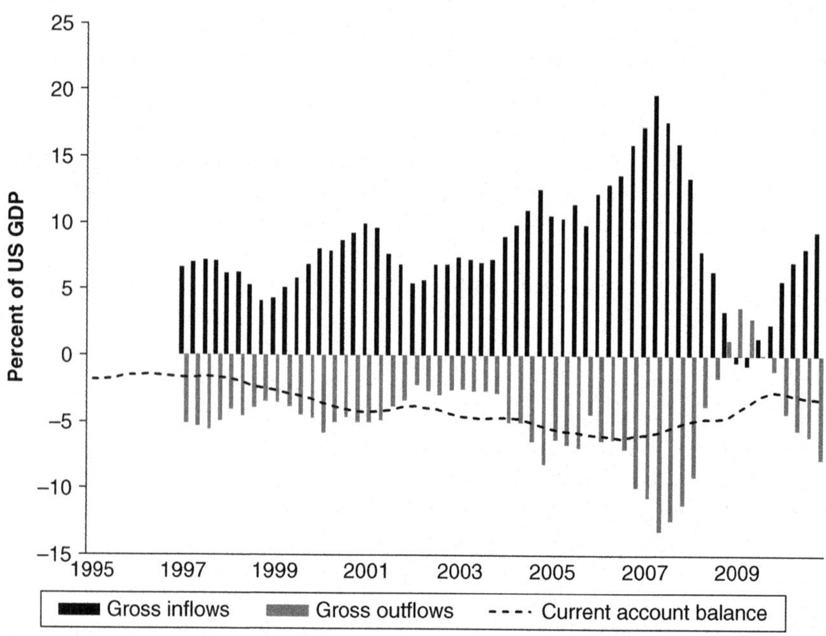

Figure 4.4 Gross capital flows and current accounts, 1995–2010.

Source: Claudio Borio and Piti Disyatit, "Global Imbalances and the Financial Crisis: Link or No Link?" Bank for International Settlements Working Paper No 346, May 2011, Graph 6, p. 14.

flows into, and out of, the United States were around 24 percent of US GDP. This underscores the magnitude of gross international capital flows (figure 4.4).[20]

These observations have led some economists to conjecture that gross capital flows exerted a major influence on interest rates and credit market conditions in the United States (and elsewhere) in the 2000s.[21] Former US Federal Reserve chairman Ben Bernanke and his colleagues identified an intriguing phenomenon. Gross capital inflows from Europe, with whom the United States maintained a balanced trade, dwarfed gross capital inflows from China during the housing boom. However, unlike the case with China, the United States sent a roughly equal amount of capital back to Europe. In aggregate, a massive amount of capital essentially took a round trip between the United States and Europe (figure 4.5).[22]

European banks were engaging in an arbitrage trade. They borrowed money from US money market funds at very low rates (they were the largest borrowers from those funds) and invested the sums in US subprime mortgages and other US ABS for somewhat higher returns. Some German Landesbanks were major investors in subprime mortgage securities, and eventually suffered large losses from the collapse in subprime ABS. Figure 7.5 shows foreign banks held 12 percent of subprime mortgage exposure at the time of the financial crisis. It is an interesting question as to why European banks engaged in the trade. It has been suggested that the answer might have something to do with the fact that regulatory constraints on European banks were loosened after the adoption of the Euro, which enabled them to expand the geographic scope of their operations.[23]

The question pertinent to the present enquiry is whether the gross capital flows generated by European banks contributed to the housing boom. The fact that some European banks were major investors in subprime ABS shows they

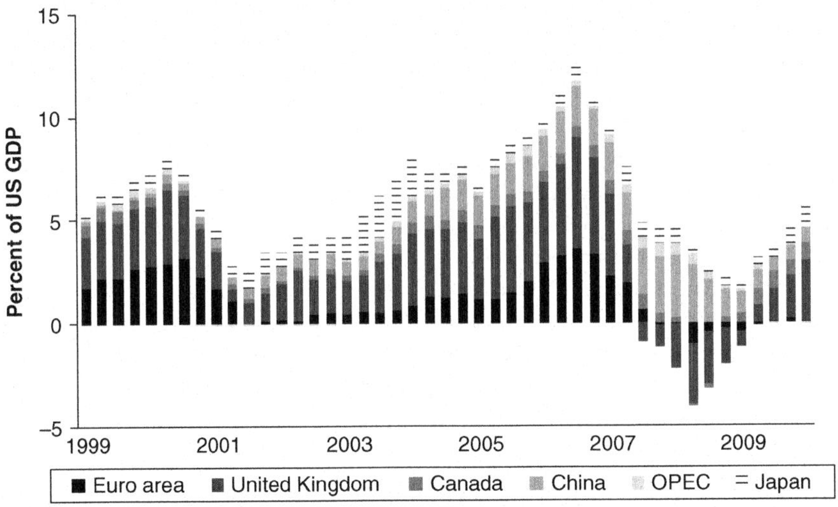

Figure 4.5 Gross capital flows by region, 1995–2010.

Source: Claudio Borio and Piti Disyatit, "Global Imbalances and the Financial Crisis: Link or No Link?" Bank for International Settlements Working Paper No 346, May 2011, Graph 6, p. 14 (lower left graph).

indirectly added to the demand for subprime mortgages. Economist Hyun Song Shin maintains that European banks exerted a decisive influence on credit markets in the United States during the housing boom;

> The gross capital flows into the US in the form of lending by European banks via the shadow banking system will have played a pivotal role in influencing credit conditions in the US in the run-up to the subprime crisis. However, since the Eurozone has a roughly balanced current account while the UK is actually a deficit country, their collective net capital flows vis-à-vis the US do not reflect the influence of the their banks in setting overall credit conditions in the US.[24]

Nevertheless, in balancing the inflows of US money market funding with the outflows of investing in US securitizations, European banks did not expand the resources available to the US economy. That could only have occurred if the United States had run a sizeable current account deficit with Europe, which it did not do. So, while the frenetic to-ing and fro-ing of capital between the United States and Europe might have tilted the composition of US investment toward housing and increased the volume of credit in the United States, it could not have added to the potential for a sustainable boom. In the absence of the current account deficit, US resource constraints would have snuffed out the housing boom at an early stage.

Did the Current Account Deficit Cause the US Housing Boom?

The increase in US financial sector leverage and the explosion in homeowner debt may have contributed to, and reflected, an underestimation of risk that fueled the frenzy of lending, leverage, and spending during the housing boom. However, the underlying, indispensable factor that enabled spending to expand after reaching full employment was the growth of the current account deficit. It was a necessary condition for a long-lasting boom to occur. Yet there remains the question of whether the current account deficit was an active agent in promoting the boom.

I will show that the current account deficit contributed to the housing boom as an independent causal factor. First, as was explained in the last chapter, forces internal to the United States did not generate the current account deficit. Rather, China (principally) engineered it as part of its policy to promote its exports to the United States. Second, the effect of China's mercantilist policy was to flood the US capital markets with a capital flow bonanza that lowered interest rates, flattened the yield curve, and reduced risk premiums. In the next four chapters, I explore the ways in which these changes affected the US economy and promoted the housing boom. The first step, which I undertake in the next chapter, is to review alternative explanations that have been proposed to account for the housing boom.

PART II

The Capital Flow Bonanza, the Credit Explosion, and the US Housing Boom: Channels of Transmission

In part II, I explain the channels through which the US current account deficit generated the housing boom.

Chapter 5 is a review of the most coherent explanations that have been proposed to account for the specific factors that caused a surge in the financing of subprime mortgages. I find them to be enlightening, but not fully convincing. Chapter 6 is an attempt to show how the subprime mortgage boom could plausibly have arisen from rational decision-making, which is contrary to the conventional opinion that investors in subprime mortgage securities were imbued with "irrational exuberance." Chapter 7 is an attempt to trace out in detail the way in which the capital flow bonanza interacted with the institutional structure of US financial intermediaries to generate an appetite for investment in risky securities, and subprime mortgages in particular. It also explains the motives of households who signed up for subprime mortgage loans. Chapter 8 revisits the policy decisions made by the Fed during the housing boom and challenges the popular notion that the Fed should have pricked the housing boom at an early stage (assuming it had the power to do so).

CHAPTER 5

A Review of Explanations for the Housing Boom

Failures, repeated failures, are finger posts on the road to achievement. One fails forward toward success.

—Charles Kettering

Basic Subprime Facts

Subprime lending played a key role in the housing boom. Subprime mortgage lending entailed increased risk compared to traditional "prime" mortgage lending, but also offered the prospect to the lender of earning an elevated return. The typical subprime borrower had a FICO[1] score (a measure of borrower creditworthiness) below 660, had delinquent debt repayment in the previous 12–24 months, or had filed for bankruptcy in the past few years. By comparison, traditional prime mortgage borrowers had FICO scores above 700 and no derogatory credit histories.[2]

The growth in subprime and Alt-A[3] lending in the first half of the 2000s was stupendous. From 2000 to 2007 the dollar volume of residential mortgages overall doubled in size,[4] while subprime and Alt-A mortgages grew by 800 percent.[5] The share of subprime and Alt-A mortgages, as a percentage of total residential mortgage backed securities (MBS) issued, increased from 11.2 percent in 2000, to a peak of 39.4 percent in 2006.[6] As a result of this growth, subprime and Alt-A mortgages, as a percentage of all residential mortgage securities outstanding, increased from 4 percent in 2000 to 25 percent in 2007. In addition, the proportion of "risky" conventional mortgages (those that "conformed" to the Government Sponsored Enterprise [GSE] standards) increased from 22.6 percent in 2001 to a peak of 49.9 percent in 2004.[7] The vast majority of subprime mortgages were securitized: by 2006 over 80 percent of subprime originations became part of tradable asset backed securities (ABS). The cash flow from subprime ABS was divided into tranches. Oftentimes tranches from different ABS were assembled into securities called "collateralized debt obligations" (CDO).[8] In total there were approximately $1.8 trillion of subprime ABS and $640 billion of subprime CDO issued from the turn of the century to 2008.[9] Subprime mortgage defaults skyrocketed at the end of the housing boom; the proportion of subprime mortgages in default increased from 5 percent in mid-2005 to over 21 percent in mid-2008. By comparison, only 4.5 percent of overall securitized residential mortgages (including subprime) were in default in mid-2008 (figure 5.1).[10]

As the issuance of subprime mortgages propelled ever upward, so did the associated leverage of the loans (the loan to collateral value ratio) and the leverage of the borrowers (the borrower's overall debt-to-assets ratio). Figure 5.2, which is from a study of subprime loans issued in the state of Massachusetts by economist Christopher Foote and his colleagues at the Federal Reserve Bank of Boston (Foote), displays this phenomenon.

The performance of subprime mortgage originations deteriorated during the course of the housing boom; 93 percent of subprime mortgage backed securities rated AAA at issuance in 2006 were eventually downgraded to junk status.[11] The key questions that must be answered in order to understand the housing boom are: "who invested in subprime securities," "what motivated them—and their borrowers—to do it," and "why did they perform so badly"?

Before providing my proposed answer in chapters 6 and 7, I will review several prevalent explanations of the housing boom—all of which provide some illumination—and discuss their shortcomings. The first three explanations attribute causality to the structure of the financial sector. The fourth explanation attributes the mispricing of mortgage securities to "irrational exuberance."

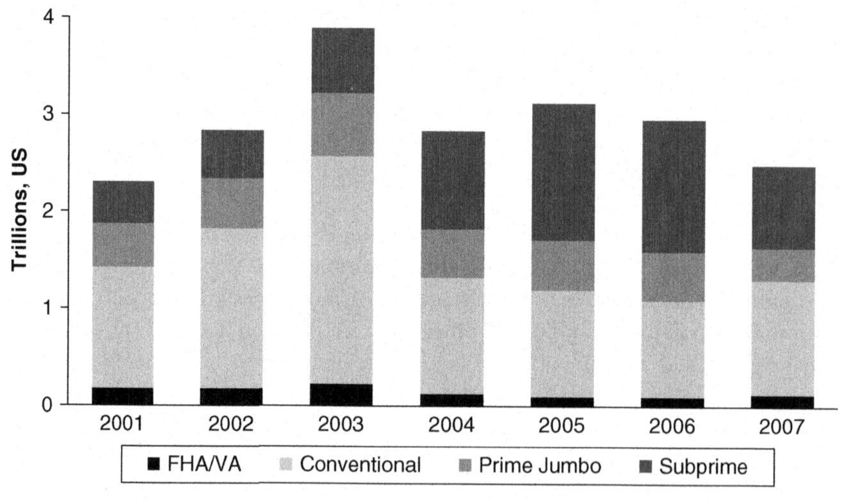

Figure 5.1 Mortgage origination by type, 2001–2007.

Notes: The original entries for subprime, Alt-A, and Home Equity are combined here into subprime. Note that there are variations of risk within the category of Conventional (i.e., conforming) mortgages, and the share of high risk conforming loans increased as the housing boom progressed. According to the most reliable estimate, the proportion of conventional mortgage loans that were "high risk" increased from 22.6 percent in 2001 to a peak of 49.9 percent in 2004. See Dwight Jaffee and John M. Quigley, "United States," Chapter 8 in *Housing and the Financial Crisis*, ed. Edward L. Glaeser and Todd Sinai, National Bureau of Economic Research, 2013, Table 8.3 p. 376.

Source: Gerald P. Dwyer and Paula Tkac, "The Financial Crisis in Fixed Income Markets," Federal Reserve Bank of Atlanta Working Paper, 2009 20, Figure 3.

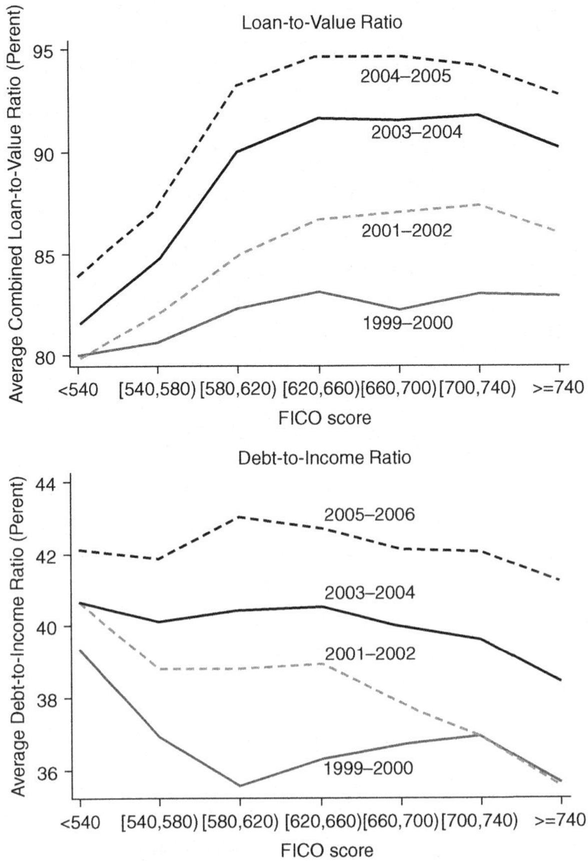

Figure 5.2 MA LTV DTI subprime, 1999–2006.

Source: Christopher Foote et al., "Subprime Facts: What (We Think) We Know about the Subprime Crisis and What We Don't," Federal Reserve Bank of Boston, Public Policy Discussion Papers No. 08–2, 2008, Figure 9, p. 30.

Conventional Explanations of the Causes of the Housing Boom

Asymmetric Information—Originate to Distribute

A popular explanation for the increase in risky mortgage lending during the housing boom posits that the "originate to distribute" model of mortgage issuance enabled, perhaps even encouraged, originators and sponsors (it is often unclear which of these two distinct players critics have in mind) to misrepresent the quality of their mortgages to investors.[12] "Originate to distribute" occurs when originators sell mortgages they have issued to securitizers,[13] who aggregate groups of mortgages, then divide the income stream from the aggregation into tranches, package the tranches into securities, and sell them to investors.[14] This explanation assumes that originators and securitizers had no "skin in the game," and therefore had no incentive to pay attention to the risks of the loans they originated, since they retained no investment in the loans. There are two key premises that underlie the view that investors were victimized by withheld information: one is that originators, who dealt directly with borrowers, knew more than investors about their prospects and could withhold information from investors in order to induce investors to overpay for the securities. The second is that investors were not cognizant of the risk arising from asymmetric information either because they were naïve, or because the "originate to distribute" practice was so new that investors lacked the experience to understand the potential for sponsors to withhold information. Neither of these premises withstands scrutiny.

The first premise, that mortgage originators possessed information about the true risk of their loans that investors did not have, implies originators "knew" things about their borrowers that was not communicated in the data transmitted to investors in the mortgage securities. According to this view, as mortgage securitizations took off in the 2000s, originators took the opportunity to expand their issuance of loans, by lending to borrowers they recognized as poor risks, but whom outsiders could not, and sold off the poor quality mortgages into the pools from which overpriced mortgage securities were constructed. Yet it is not clear that issuers had any informational advantage at all. The idea that originators possessed superior information about borrowers evokes an image of George Bailey, the small-town banker in the movie *It's a Wonderful Life*. George Bailey knew his borrowers personally; he knew their families and their employers. He knew stuff about them that no other banker could possibly know, which enabled him to assess their character and prospects for repayment more accurately than could an outsider with information limited to the borrower's credit score, loan repayment history, and other quantifiable data. Crucially, George Bailey got to decide, on the basis of his superior but unquantifiable information, which loans to make. Lending did not work that way during the housing boom. The vast majority of mortgages issued during the housing boom were originated by behemoth institutions issuing billions of dollars of residential mortgages annually. Countrywide, JP Morgan and Wells Fargo did not empower their loan officers to issue mortgages based on "character" assessments. Loans issued by those institutions had to meet quantifiable criteria. There was no way for organizations operating at that scale to qualify borrowers on any other basis. Therefore, the only opportunity for large originators to misrepresent would have been to withhold some portion of quantified data from investors. I am not aware of any evidence unearthed so far that would suggest this occurred on a widespread basis.

Consider one of the most notorious mortgage securities scandals, the 2007 Abacus deal, in which Goldman Sachs aggregated a collection of subprime mortgage securities and sold the resultant CDO to two large financial institutions. Unbeknownst to the buyers, Goldman allowed hedge fund manager John Paulson, to whom Goldman sold a short position, to participate in the selection of mortgage backed securities that made up Abacus.[15] Paulson made a fortune on the deal and Goldman earned a hefty fee. The buyers lost their shirts. Abacus became a poster child for the view that the ubiquity of asymmetric information—where one side of a transaction possesses knowledge of the traded good that the other side lacks—created incentives for mortgage originators and intermediaries to sell overpriced securities to unsuspecting investors. Yet a closer look at Abacus challenges this notion. The buyers were ABN AMRO, a mammoth

Dutch multinational bank, and IKB, a large German lender. Both were experienced and sophisticated investors in mortgage securities, each holding multibillion dollar portfolios. The Abacus offer documents disclosed information sufficient to enable the investors to obtain the origination information and delinquency status of every individual mortgage loan in the deal.[16] The investors had access to the same information as Paulson. As Foote et al. wrote: "To make an obvious point, many Wall Street investors who lost money were seasoned financial professionals, a group generally not known for being overly trusting of those on the other side of high stakes deals."[17] The second premise, the idea that the "originate to distribute" model was some sort of financial innovation, was not true. Mortgage backed securities had been traded in large volume for decades prior to the recent housing boom.[18] The securities that were assembled out of ABS, with derivative payoff structures, may or may not be counted as a new innovation (it is matter that is under debate) and their performance when underlying mortgage defaults spiked may not have been properly understood by many investors. Yet, this is not an issue of asymmetric information, since the legal structure of the securities was known by both seller and buyer.

Finally, the asymmetric information theory is undermined by the fact that mortgage market insiders, those firms who supposedly had an informational edge, suffered the greatest losses on mortgage securities when the market crashed. Commercial banks and broker-dealers took on large exposures to subprime mortgage securities through warehousing of loans, issuance of guarantees of sponsored securitizations, and retention of unrated junior tranches of mortgage securities (the so-called toxic waste). Table 5.1 shows Merrill Lynch's subprime exposure in 2007. Merrill was one of the largest players involved in creating subprime mortgage securities. Notably, the "Residuals" held by Merrill were the junior/first loss portion of the subprime securities it issued; Merrill retained the riskiest portion of subprime securities, as well as other exposures. Merrill's portfolio was typical of the large originators and sponsors.

Table 5.2 ranks the 20 biggest losers during the financial crisis. They are all large financial institutions with a great deal of experience in trading mortgage

Table 5.1 Merrill Lynch 2007 AR—residential mortgage

	Net Exposure as of Dec. 29, 2007 (in \$ millions)	*Net Losses for the Year ended Dec. 28, 2007 (in \$ millions)*
US subprime		
Warehouse lending	137	(31)
Whole loans	994	(1,243)
Residuals	855	(1,582)
Residential MBS	723	(332)
Total US subprime	*2,709*	*(3,188)*
US Alt-A	2,687	(542)
US prime	28,189	N/A
Non-US	9,582	(465)
Mortgage service rights	389	N/A
Total	*43,556*	*(4,195)*

Source: Merrill Lynch Annual Report 2007, p. 357.

Table 5.2 Mortgage related losses to financial institutions from the subprime crisis—June 18, 2008

	Institution	*Loss ($ billions)*		*Institution*	*Loss ($ billions)*
1	Citigroup	42.9	11	Washington Mutual	9.1
2	UBS	38.2	12	Credit Agricole	8.3
3	Merrill Lynch	37.1	13	Lehman Brothers	8.2
4	HSBC	19.5	14	Deutsche Bank	7.6
5	IKB Deutsche	15.9	15	Wachovia	7.0
6	Royal Bank of Scotland	15.2	16	HBOS	7.0
7	Bank of America	15.1	17	Bayerische Landesbank	6.7
8	Morgan Stanley	14.1	18	Fortis	6.6
9	JPMorgan Chase	9.8	19	Canadian Imperial (CIBC)	6.5
10	Credit Suisse	9.6	20	Barclays	6.3

Note: Foote selected a date prior to the Lehman Bankruptcy to avoid contamination from the wider financial crisis.

Source: Christopher L. Foote, Kristopher S. Gerardi, and Paul S. Willen, *United States Ex Post United States Federal Reserve Bank of Boston Public Policy Discussion Papers* No. 12–2, July 20, 2012, Table 4, p. 60. The information is from Bloomberg.

securities. Six of the top 10—Citigroup, Merrill Lynch, HSBC, Bank of America, Morgan Stanley, and JP Morgan—not only securitized subprime mortgages, they actually owned companies that originated them.[19] Moreover, many of the managers of these institutions lost a considerable portion of their wealth during the crash. Lehman executives, who owned a third of the equity in their firm, forfeited the entire value of their holdings. Richard Fuld and James Cayenne, the chairmen of, respectively, Lehman and Bear Stearns, lost over a billion dollars each when their firms went under.

The concentration of subprime mortgage losses in the financial sector casts serious doubt on the claim that the "originate to distribute" model created perverse incentives for "insiders" to pump up fees by selling shoddy and fraudulent mortgages to unsuspecting and naïve "outsiders." Rather, the "perversity" that needs to be explained is why those supposedly "in the know" took such an enormous gamble on the housing market.[20]

Moral Hazard

Another prevalent view, which has informed much of the postcrisis reform of banking regulation, is that the implicit government guarantee of the unsecured debt of the GSEs and large banks made bondholders indifferent to the risks taken on, and malfeasance engaged in, by managers of these institutions.[21] Large banks, broker-dealers, and GSEs were major players in the subprime mortgage market in all phases—as originators, underwriters of securitized asset pools, and as investors in subprime mortgage securities. The price of their debt was based on an implicit government guarantee, which decoupled the risk from the underlying performance of the issuer of the debt. It is possible to imagine scenarios where managers might have reacted by increasing risk in order to earn higher profit, but there are also scenarios where this would not occur. Those who link the bank and GSE borrowing subsidy to the housing boom argue that managers of those institutions had an incentive to aim for higher returns by taking on more risk than noninsured bondholders would have allowed them to do.[22] They argue that banks and GSE managers were attracted to subprime mortgage ABS, because they paid a higher interest rate than equivalently rated securitizations comprised of traditional prime loans. The temptation to reach for yield may have been particularly enticing in banking, where profits from loans are booked at the time of issuance, rather than at the time of repayment.

The problem with the moral hazard hypothesis has to do with timing rather than incentives. The implicit government guarantee of GSE and "to-big-to-fail" bank debt predated the subprime boom by many years. Therefore, while it may help to explain the eagerness of these institutions to participate, it does not help to explain why the boom occurred in the first place. A caveat to this rejection of the moral hazard view is that there is some plausibility in the idea that the deregulation unchained bank managers to do things they were not previously allowed to do. For example, the Basle II capital rules, published in 2004 and informally followed by bank regulators, allowed banks to develop their own risk weights on asset classes, which opened the door to increased risk taking by managers in the years that followed. Yet, the subsidence of volatility during the period and the investment grade ratings conferred on the senior tranches of subprime mortgage securities make it appear quite reasonable for mangers to have allocated investment in subprime securities. How were they to know that the market, and the ratings agencies, had got it grievously wrong?

GSE Securitizations

A number of economists[23] have argued that the Community Reinvestment Act (CRA), first passed by the US Congress in 1977, and modified on several occasions thereafter, incentivized banks and GSEs to increase risky mortgage lending. An econometric study by a group of University of Chicago economists demonstrated that the CRA did increase risky mortgage lending.[24] In a recent book, economists Charles Calomiris and Steven Haber[25] explain how the CRA led the GSEs to create a market for risky mortgage securities in the 1990s, which, they explain, pioneered the market for subprime mortgage securities. Although the GSEs held a small percentage of subprime mortgage debt (8 percent according to table 7.1), Calomiris and Haber claim the GSEs were perceived by investors as buyers of last resort, who would acquire any amount of subprime debt that others were reluctant to hold. By providing subprime investors with an implicit option to sell their securities without suffering too great a loss, the GSEs were a de facto insurer to market participants. This magnified their influence on the market for subprime mortgage debt to an extent that greatly exceeded their direct share of holdings of subprime securities. According to this hypothesis, the trigger for the collapse in the price of subprime securities occurred when the market realized, sometime in 2008, that the GSEs were insolvent and would be incapable of absorbing a large volume of additional subprime debt.

The argument that the CRA and the GSEs contributed to risky mortgage lending is intriguing, but, as before, the timing is off as an explanation for the subprime mortgage boom. These incentives were around for many years before the boom. Moreover, the GSEs' primary influence in the mortgage securities market lies in their originations (on which they issue guarantees) more than in their direct holdings of mortgage securities. In 2000 the GSEs held under 30 percent of outstanding residential mortgage securities, while they had originated around 70 percent of those securities.[26] The GSEs were late entrants into the high risk mortgage loan business. Until 2007, their originations and acquisitions of high risk conforming[27] loans—while large due to the absolute size of the GSE portfolios—both as a percentage of their overall originations and mortgage purchases, and as a percentage of total conforming loan issuance, lagged the market.[28] This finding led economists Dwight Jaffee and John Quigley to conclude that "the GSE's were not leading the market for high risk lending as the subprime boom took off."[29] The Financial Inquiry Commission noted that the GSEs also lagged the market in purchases of non-conforming subprime mortgage securities. The commission concluded, "[The GSEs] followed rather than led Wall Street and other lenders in the rush for fool's gold."[30] It does not seem plausible that a laggard could have driven the explosion in subprime lending.

Irrational Exuberance

Perhaps the most prevalent view of the cause of the housing boom is that realistic projections of housing demand and price were swept aside by investors amid a mania for mortgage securities. The hypothesis is that "irrational exuberance" sent the housing market on a rising trajectory, fueled by a credit expansion that lifted prices and seemingly validated the unsustainable optimism. This explanation has the patina of plausibility, since home prices did rise to an unsustainable level and then ultimately crashed. Yet, the idea that irrationality can account for the boom requires an explanation for how the unsupportable optimism took hold.[31] Moreover, several facts undermine this view.

First, the increase in home prices of 52 percent from 2003 to 2007 was not unprecedented, even in recent history. Home prices rose by a considerably higher percentage from 1975 to 1980 (though there was significant price inflation during those years) and by a considerable, though lesser, percentage from 1995 to 2000 (see figure 5.3).[32] In neither of those episodes did prices subsequently crash. So, the historical record did not irresistibly compel any rational person to conclude that large home price increases were unsustainable. Another reason market participants may have discounted fears of sustainability is that it is very difficult to predict future trends based on past patterns. In the recent past, a highly regarded prediction of impending housing collapse turned out wrong. In 1989 two Harvard economists, observing that the Baby Boom generation was passing its peak household formation years, which is the key driver of housing demand, made the compelling prediction that housing demand would slump for the next two decades (until the "Baby Echo" generation entered its household formation peak). The authors stated, "If the historical relation between housing demand and housing prices continues into the future, real housing prices will fall substantially over the next two decades."[33] We now know that housing demand soared during the following two decades, but that was due to an

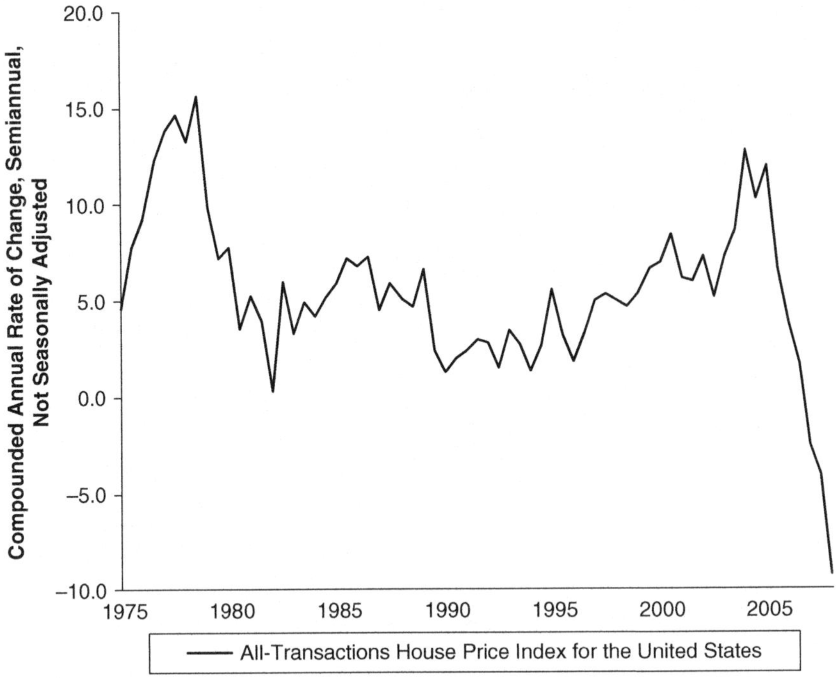

Figure 5.3 House price index rate of change, 1975–2009.
Source: US Federal Housing Finance Agency.

unanticipated change in a demographic pattern; baby boomers suddenly began to form households at older ages in the 1990s.

Second, the temporal pattern of subprime lending does not support the idea that subprime mortgage lending, driven by overoptimism, caused home price appreciation. The evidence suggests that lending neither caused, nor reacted to, home price increases in a very close manner. The spike in home prices commenced *before* the spike in subprime lending, so there was no reason for lenders to believe rising home values were being driven by the splurge in subprime lending, which might have prompted concern that credit fueled price increases would unwind as lending tapered off at some future time (see figure 5.4).

Third, the geographic pattern of subprime lending casts doubt on the idea that mortgage lending was solely motivated by exuberance over home price appreciation. Mortgage lending was expanding throughout the country, including in cities that experienced little home price growth. Economists Atif Mian and Amir Sufi (Mian and Sufi)[34] provide evidence that subprime mortgage lending increased by as much in cities with relatively low home price appreciation as in those that experienced high home price appreciation. Their findings show that credit expansion was not tied to, and did not uniformly cause, high levels of price appreciation. Their results undermine the idea that bullishness over home price increases was the sole motivation for subprime lending. If that were the case, there would not have been aggressive lending in cities where home prices did not rise substantially.

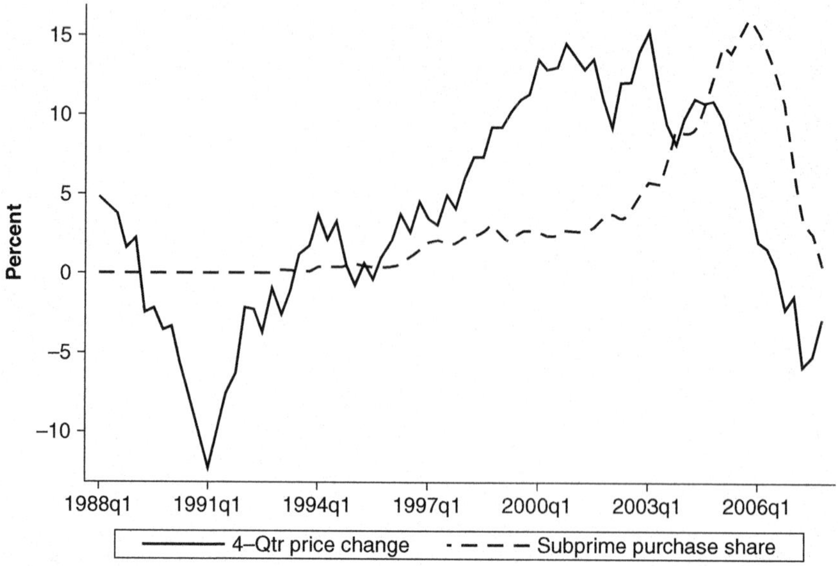

Figure 5.4 HPI and subprime lending MA, 1988–2007.

Source: Christopher Foote, et al., *Subprime Facts: What (We Think) We Know about the Subprime Crisis and What We Don't*, Federal Reserve Bank of Boston, Public Policy Discussion Papers No. 08–2, 2008, Figure 16, p. 49.

> If the housing bubble caused credit expansion, then we would observe a credit expansion to marginal borrowers *only in cities that experienced a housing bubble*... However, the evidence refutes [this] prediction... It proves that the house-price bubble was not driving the growth in mortgage credit.[35]

While subprime lending entailed more risk than prime mortgage lending, lenders charged higher interest rates as compensation for the greater risk. Lenders earned about 3 percent, or around 60 percent higher rate than what they could earn on a prime home mortgage loan.[36] The question is whether these higher rates adequately compensated for the increased risk of lending to less creditworthy borrowers. It does not seem so now, but we have the unfair advantage of hindsight.

Yet there was a troubling aspect of subprime lending that ought to have raised some eyebrows at the time. Mian and Sufi show that housing investment was being channeled into an unpromising direction during the housing boom; a majority of subprime loans were issued to borrowers who were experiencing relatively declining income growth:

> The behavior of lenders from 2002 to 2005 produced a very unusual statistical pattern: mortgage—credit growth and income growth became negatively correlated. That is, areas with lower income growth received more mortgage credit.[37]

Therefore, subprime lending involved not only increased risk due to the lower creditworthiness of its borrowers, but also increased risk due to their deteriorating relative earnings trend.[38] Unfortunately, Mian and Sufi does not delve into the reasons for this pattern of lending, but instead skirt the issue by invoking the deus ex machina of irrational behavior. They conclude, on the basis of the ex-post evidence of mispricing of risk in lending to borrowers with deteriorating credit, often in locations with little price appreciation, that the expansion in subprime lending involved "irrational behavioral tendencies."[39]

As far as Mian and Sufi is concerned, that is the end of further inquiry. Their conclusion—which is shared by many other economists and commentators—is unsatisfactory in no small part because their finding that subprime lending flourished in areas of low price appreciation, to households with declining relative earnings prospects, implies a more serious deviation from apparently sensible behavior than that associated with enthusiasm over self-validating price increases. To attribute that pattern to irrational behavior, and to treat it as if it were beyond explanation, implies that mortgage underwriting and mortgage security pricing had become completely random, and for no apparent rhyme or reason. That is not an acceptable point at which to curtail further inquiry.

Finally, I address the charge that there was a basic flaw in the design of subprime mortgages. A significant and much criticized form of subprime lending was the adjustable rate mortgage (ARM) loan.[40] An ARM loan charged a certain interest rate in the first couple of years, but then "adjusted" to a higher rate after that time. Many commentators have alleged that the typical borrower who obtained ARM loans was able to afford the initial payments, but could not afford to make the higher payments that followed. This makes the decision to take on the loan to seem reckless. On its face, it does appear that ARM loans were designed to pump up lending volumes. The asymmetric information argument outlined earlier assumes that originators had an incentive to make such "toxic" loans because they were collecting origination fees and selling the loan—and the attendant risk—into an ABS financed by a hopelessly naïve investor (never mind that ABS investors were sophisticated financial institutions and who often received guarantees from the originators). In response to this perceived abuse, critics have called for reform requiring lenders to retain some portion of ownership in the loans they originate and to make more explicit disclosure of risks to borrowers (notwithstanding that loan originators during the housing boom retained a larger portion of loans than the Dodd-Frank regulation would have required of them).[41]

However, there is another side to this story. Prior to the collapse of the subprime mortgage market in 2007, a person who took on an ARM loan and made the required payments during the initial lower interest rate period would usually become eligible for either a prime loan or a new ARM loan. Many people refinanced their original ARM loans prior to the date of adjustment in rate in just this way. Moreover, Foote showed that the spread between the initial ARM rates and the reset rates were not that great; on average they narrowed from 3.2 percent in 2004 to 0.5 percent in 2007.[42] Foote also showed that there was no correlation between mortgage defaults and ARM resets; ARM resets did not trigger a spike in defaults.[43] Therefore, it was not irrational for a borrower to take on an ARM loan, or for an investor to purchase the mortgage loan, even when both parties knew the probability of default was higher at the reset rate.

Conclusion

In this chapter I reviewed the leading explanations of the US housing boom and concluded that, while each one sheds some light on the phenomena, none of them are able to account for the boom in a convincing way. That leaves open three choices in the search for an explanation: call the behavior "irrational" and move on; develop a customized "behavioral" theory; or search for another explanation rooted in rational behavior. In the following two chapters I proceed with the latter approach. I will attempt to demonstrate that the housing boom was the unintended consequence of rational decisions made in a particular cognitive and institutional environment. In the next chapter, I attempt to explain the ecologically rational foundation of decision-making during the housing boom.

CHAPTER 6

Decision-Making during the Housing Boom

> Market forces generate euphorias and panics.
>
> —Martin Wolf[1]

> The crowd of mankind are directed in their establishments and measures, by the circumstances in which they are placed... and nations stumble upon establishments, which are indeed the result of human action, but not the execution of any human design.
>
> —Adam Ferguson[2]

Describing Behavior during the Housing Boom

Do people pursue their self-interest? The discipline of economics is founded upon the belief that they do. Adam Smith laid down the fundamental premise thus:

> It is not from the benevolence of the butcher, the brewer, or the baker, that we expect our dinner, but from their regard to their own interest. We address ourselves, not to their humanity, but to their self-love, and never talk to them of our own necessities but of their advantages.[3]

This "Smithian" premise seems at odds with behavior during the housing boom, where so many homebuilders, bankers, mortgage borrowers, and investors lost vast sums of money in a speculative frenzy that drove up home prices and home construction to levels that, in retrospect at least, appear to have been recognizably unsustainable. It is reminiscent of notorious speculative excesses of the past, like the South Sea Bubble of the early 1700s, where the share price of a British chartered monopoly company rose to a spectacular height and took in the leading investors of the day before collapsing; or the Dutch "tulip mania" of 1637, where some single tulip bulbs sold for more than ten times the annual income of a skilled craftsman. One might conclude that people went a little nuts during the housing boom.

The view that human nature has an emotional side that can cause behavior to deviate from rational self-interest is embodied in a literature on the seducing effects of greed, fear, and crowd psychology. Freud once wrote that "the ego is not master in his own house"[4]; men are swayed by drives and emotions contrary to what Adam Smith referred to as "their own interest" far more often than a simplistic interpretation of the Smithian premise would seem to imply.[5]

Yet, the idea that people deviated from their normal behavior during the housing boom is undermined by the evidence showing a recurring (though loosely correlated) pattern of boom followed by bust throughout history. In chapter 2 I summarized findings obtained by Reinhardt and Rogoff,[6] and Jorda et al.,[7] which document the existence of a pattern linking above trend credit and asset price growth and capital flow bonanzas to subsequent financial crises across numerous countries spanning many years. The existence of a recurring pattern suggests the behavior that generates that pattern must be normal in the sense that it is not a product of a unique deviation from the way people usually behave. Moreover, unless it is maintained that people become predictably irrational on a regular, periodic basis, and do not learn from their mistakes, it makes no sense to presume decision-making during episodic booms is irrational. Another way of stating this is that people make mistakes and do stupid things all the time, but there is no convincing reason to believe the incidence of recognizably errant behavior clusters in some predictable fashion. Therefore, rather than trying to divine why people became irrational during the housing boom, as some authors have done,[8] I will try and work out how the boom could have arisen from the interaction of decisions and actions of people who were rationally pursuing their self-interest from their own perspective.

The Four Situations for Decision-Making during the Housing Boom

Ecological Rationality

To explain the behavior that generated the housing boom I proceed on the assumption that the actors involved behaved rationally. But in order to understand why people made their choices, it is necessary to take account of salient difficulties and constraints they faced. The key is to recognize that what constitutes rational decision-making is situational or what some authors call "ecological."[9] Different situations will elicit different rules of decision-making. During the housing boom many agents found themselves involved in multiple situations, which sometimes overlapped. This means some people were affected by more than one set of constraints and conflicting information.[10]

There were four fundamentally different situations that meaningfully affected decision-makers during the housing boom. The reactions to these situations determined the course of the boom. In this chapter I describe the four situations and the types of decision-making engendered by each. In the next chapter I describe how the capital flow bonanza triggered an interaction between these various decision-making processes to generate the housing boom.

Four Decision-Making Situations

The four types of decision-makers and situations that affected decision-making during the housing boom were:

1. Institutional investors, who inherited commitments for future payouts that required them to achieve a minimum yield on their investments; and banks, who by custom and regulation lent money on longer terms than they borrowed. I call this group "contractually constrained institutions."
2. Agents who had never experienced a boom of long duration and great magnitude that was generated by a capital flow bonanza. I call this group "experience constrained agents."
3. Investors, lenders, and borrowers who by and large arranged their portfolios on the assumption that the yields and underwriting standards of residential mortgage backed securities and mortgage loans were sustainable. I call this group "informationally constrained agents."
4. Investors and money managers who invested and traded marketable mortgage and other securities and in so doing were required to make guesses about the future. I call this group "uncertainty constrained investors."

Contractually Constrained Institutions

The decline in long-term interest rates in the early 2000s pushed the contractually constrained group toward insolvency. It did so, first, by reducing the achievable yield on safe investments. This made it impossible for those investors that needed to meet long-term payout commitments to achieve their required returns by investing safely. These included life insurers and defined benefit pension plans. Low yields on safe investments also threatened money managers, such as long-only bond funds and hedge funds, with an exit of investors (many of whom were life insurers and pension plans). The decline in long-term interest rates squeezed profit margins for commercial banks, who borrowed short to lend long. The rational response for these investors, because it was a requirement for survival, was to "reach for yield" to retain the prospect of solvency. In order to boost yields this group chose to increase leverage. They did so by borrowing; by entering into derivatives contracts and by shifting asset allocations toward riskier investments, such as subprime mortgage securities.[11]

Experience Constrained Agents—Vernon Smith

It is commonly recognized that people are shaped by their upbringing, education, and experiences, which are limited. It is, perhaps, less commonly recognized (and explicitly ignored in most economic theory, which assumes individuals perform complex mathematical calculations involving preference functions that span possible choices each time they make a decision) that the scarcest resource of our brain is attention. The brain has limited capacity. As a result, it developed, as an evolutionary adaptation, the facility to economize on attention by delegating a substantial amount of decision-making to heuristics that operate outside the purview of consciousness.[12]

When confronted with a novel circumstance that calls for decision-making, the brain will search its database for analogous situations for which it has already developed a response. This is normally an economical and reliable way to reach decisions. Nobel Prize–winning economist Vernon Smith wrote:

> The challenge of any unfamiliar action or problem appears first to trigger a search by the brain to bring to the conscious mind what one knows that is related to the decision context. Context triggers autobiographic experiential memory.[13]

However, this manner of processing information can lead to bad decisions when the brain's database does not include appropriate analogues. The danger is that the mind will match up the novel event with a past experience that superficially appears to be similar, but is not.

I argue in this book that the housing boom was caused by an unprecedented increase in the US current account deficit (and the associated capital flow bonanza),[14] which, for many people affected by it, was a novel event. In addition, as I shall explain later on, the dramatic increase in subprime mortgages and the shift from bank-based financing to market financing fundamentally altered the behavior of the housing market in a way that was not recognized at the time. From the standpoint of participants in the housing market, however, it looked like a typical housing boom, which was not novel at all. Residential construction has long been the most cyclical sector of the economy. Someone who thought they were experiencing a "typical" cyclical surge in home construction would be inclined to believe that feedback mechanisms in the economy (or at the Fed) would temper the boom before it got too far out of hand. It was not the first time—even in recent history—that home prices had risen (see figure 5.3). They would also assume, as had long been the case, that home prices would not significantly decline after the boom ended. To predict that home prices would collapse would be to forecast the occurrence of an unprecedented event—which might have appeared unreasonable at the time.

Experience constrained homebuyers and lenders were insufficiently concerned about the downside risks of subprime mortgages because they had never before experienced anything like it. The problem was that they did not recognize the uniqueness of what was taking place. Instead, they drew from the database of their memory and knowledge of past events, an analogy that appeared to be similar, but was deeply misleading.

Informationally Constrained Agents—Hayek

During the housing boom, presumably many agents acted on the belief that elevated home prices were sustainable without intending to speculate on housing. Nevertheless, they did. Lenders retained subprime mortgage exposure, dropped underwriting standards and massively increased the risk of loss in their portfolios. Homeowners increased their mortgage borrowing. Investors piled into AAA rated ABS backed by subprime mortgages. It is important to understand how this came about.

Nobel Prize–winning economist F. A. Hayek's writings shed some light on this matter. Hayek emphasized the limitations on knowledge of events that lie far afield from the comparatively small slice of the world of which an individual can be cognizant (which he called "local knowledge").

> The peculiar character of the problem of a rational economic order is determined precisely by the fact that the knowledge of the circumstances of which we must make use never exists in concentrated or integrated form, but solely as the dispersed bits of incomplete and frequently contradictory knowledge which all the separate individuals possess . . . it is a problem of the utilization of knowledge not given to anyone in its totality.[15]

According to Hayek, people act on the institutional incentives and knowledge of those things that lie within their limited cognitive purview,[16] which include the market prices they encounter. Prices transmit, in coded form, knowledge from elsewhere in the economy. The price system overcomes the problem of informational constraints by aggregating information that is dispersed throughout society.

> The marvel is that in a case like that of a scarcity of one raw material, without an order being issued, without more than perhaps a handful of people knowing the cause, tens of thousands of people whose identity could not be ascertained by months of investigation, are made to use the material or its products more sparingly; i.e., they move in the right direction . . . Through [the price system] not only a division of labor but also a coordinated utilization of resources based on an equally divided knowledge has become possible.[17]

The "marvel" of the price system, however, suggests a source of instability. In a market economy people have little choice but to rely upon the prices they encounter in making decisions about how to allocate their resources. Hayek explains the reason why it is rational for them to do so. The allocation of resources by prices enables the division of labor and knowledge to which we owe our high standard of living. But if for some reason prices are distorted, and do not accurately aggregate information about the underlying conditions of supply, demand, and risk throughout the economy, reliance on prices can lead to decisions that unknowingly add to risk and push the economy off of a sustainable path.

Hayek's trade cycle theory traced the effect a distortion in prices had in causing people to misallocate resources. He conjectured that precipitous declines in interest rates—when generated by deviations from their "natural rate"[18]—would trigger an expansion of borrowing, since the lowered discount rate would increase the projected profitability of capital investment projects.[19] But because the lower rates were produced by an unsustainable distortion, and would eventually be forced back up, many of the new projects would have to be abandoned mid-stream later on when interest rates corrected. It is worth quoting Hayek's description of his approach in his own words:

> The point of real interest to Trade Cycle theory is the existence of certain deviations in individual price relations occurring because changes in the volume of money appear at certain individual points; deviations, that is, away from the

> position which is necessary to maintain the whole system in equilibrium. Every disturbance of the equilibrium of prices leads necessarily to shifts in the structure of production... The nature of the changes in the composition of the existing stock of goods, which are effected through such monetary changes, depends of course on the point at which the money is injected into the economic system.[20]

What is germane to this analysis is not Hayek's specific model, however, but rather his insight that disturbances to prices can cause rational decision-makers to allocate their resources in ways that unintentionally add to risk for themselves and for the entire economy.

One need only to reflect that the PBOC's injection of its dollars into the market for long-term government-guaranteed debt is akin to a change "in the volume of money... at certain individual points" to appreciate Hayek's relevance to understanding the housing boom. In chapter 2 I cited evidence that foreign capital inflows pushed down interest rates, and in chapter 7 I will explain how it caused a compression in risk spreads. Hayek's insight that we have no choice but to use market prices in making decisions enables us to understand why it is that agents did not, by and large, question the sustainability of the lower rates and risk spreads. These distortions caused lenders and investors to underestimate the risks involved in subprime lending and homeowners to overestimate the increase in the value of their homes. I shall explain in the next chapter how the altered credit conditions and perceptions of home values interacted with the institutional structure of contractually constrained investors to induce rational decisions that led to a "shift in the structure of production" that marked the housing boom.

An example illustrates how market prices led banks and borrowers astray during the housing boom. A lesson learned during the S&L crisis of the early 1990s was that it turned out many of the loss-making real estate loans were issued without adequate valuation of the underlying collateral. Sometimes lenders obtained appraisals that relied upon inappropriate comparison transactions that were allegedly selected to inflate value in order to justify loans they wished to make regardless of collateral value, and sometimes there was no appraisal at all. To ensure that type of abuse did not occur in the future, regulations were enacted requiring banks to obtain appraisals on real estate loans that utilized, inter alia, comparable market transaction data to justify conclusions of value.[21] The new appraisal requirements were a rational response to the abuse that was uncovered. There is no better basis for determining the value of a home than to compare the prices at which nearby homes of similar size and quality have recently sold. For this reason, regulators, investors, and lenders placed confidence in the appraisals. But there was no way for this methodology to detect when home prices began to rise above a sustainable level. In fact, it reinforced the upward movement in prices, since the last transaction price became input into the next appraisal and validated an upward trend in prices. In this instance, which was a major factor in generating the housing boom, participants used their local knowledge of market prices to make decisions that turned out be much riskier than they intended to make. Economist Andrew Haldane believes the economy has evolved from a complex adaptive system, to a complex "system of systems." He described the global economic and financial systems as "a nested set of sub-systems, each one themselves a complex web."[22] This is precisely the line along which Hayek argued a decentralized market economy would evolve. It reflects an ever expanding division of labor and knowledge, accompanied by a contraction in the range of knowledge of the overall economic environment possessed by any individual.

The complexity and opacity of subprime securities is an example of how the increasing division of knowledge and specialization of functions in the economy can propagate risk. In chapter 5 I explained that subprime ABS investors had access to full information on the characteristics of the credit history of the borrowers and loans that comprised subprime securities. But until the introduction of the ABX.HE indices of subprime mortgages in early 2006, there was no aggregate information about subprime securities prices. Very few people knew what the market price for the various subprime ABS were. And even after the introduction of the ABX.HE, there still was no information on the location of subprime mortgage risk exposure among sectors and institutions in the economy. Economist Gary Gorton described the problem thus:

> What is the loss of information? The information problem is that the location and extent of the... subprime risk is unknown to anyone. It is very hard to determine the location of the risk, partly because the chain of interlinked securities, which does not allow the final resting place of the risk to be determined. But also, because of derivatives it is even harder: negative basis trades moved CDO risk and credit derivatives created additional long exposure to subprime mortgages. Determining the extent of the risk is also difficult because the effects on expected losses depend on house prices... Simulating the effects of that through the chain of interlinked securities is basically impossible.[23]

I do not think the fact that individuals had limited knowledge of the details of risk exposures by institution posed an economic problem. As Hayek taught, the advantage of the price system is that it allows us to operate on limited knowledge. The problem was that the risks were not registering in market prices. There was no market feedback mechanism that caused the price of securities issued by the financial institutions who were most exposed to subprime risk, to be discounted. There is perhaps a deeper paradox here. The increasing division of knowledge and specialization enabled by the price system increases our dependence on market prices in guiding decisions, while at the same time the increased complexity enabled by the price system can degrade the informational content of prices and lead people astray.

Uncertainty Constrained Investors—Keynes

The foregoing shows that many investors and mortgage borrowers had good reasons to accommodate the housing boom. Yet, a satisfactory explanation must account for the nagging question of why investors who possessed specialized knowledge of the market for housing mortgage securities failed to pull back earlier. They observed the expansion in lending to low credit borrowers with relatively declining prospects, often in locations that were not experiencing home price appreciation.[24] They knew that mortgage lending had expanded to an unprecedented level (figure 2.1). It is a striking feature of the housing boom that sophisticated and experienced financial institutions appeared to be apathetic to these developments, even though, in Hayek's phraseology, it was part of their "local knowledge."[25] An example of this indifference was a 2005 Lehman Brothers study, which was distributed to investors, noting that BBB rated subprime ABS bonds required average home price appreciation of 5–8 percent for the life of the underlying loan—which meant decades—to avoid default.[26] There had never before been a sustained home price increase of that magnitude. Why did it not cause investors to pull back from housing securities? To address this question I turn to J. M. Keynes, an accomplished mathematician who made an important contribution to the theory of probability.

The Illusion of Risk in the Presence of Uncertainty

One of Keynes's most profound insights is to point out that there are classes of processes, uncertain processes, whose outcomes are unpredictable because it is impossible to calculate a probability of their occurrence. It is impossible to do so because there are often innumerable possibilities or possible outcomes that exceed our powers of imagination.[27] For such processes, "our existing knowledge does not provide a sufficient basis for a calculated mathematical expectation."[28] This problem becomes greater, the further out into the future we try to predict, because the passage of time allows for more causal influences to impact events which generates a greater variety of possible outcomes.[29] As a result, according to Keynes, people are compelled to rely on rules of thumb that ignore uncertainty in guiding future oriented decisions involving uncertain processes, like stock and bond investments.[30] Keynes did not maintain that people assumed certainty in their knowledge of the future—which would be literally insane—but that they coped by thinking about the future in terms of risk, which involves assigning calculable probabilities to finite enumerable possible future outcomes. Risk creates an illusion that the vagaries of the "dark forces of time and ignorance," which is how Keynes described the future, can be described with mathematical precision. It is an illusion, because risk is incommensurable with the concept of uncertainty.

> It would be foolish, in forming our expectations, to attach great weight to matters which are very uncertain. It is reasonable, therefore, to be guided to a considerable degree by the facts about which we feel somewhat confident... the facts of the existing situation enter, in a sense disproportionately, into the formation of our long-term expectations; our usual practice being to take the existing situation and to project it into the future, modified only to the extent that we have more or less definite reasons for expecting a change.[31]

Keynes wrote that passage in 1937, yet it accurately describes how financial institutions behaved during the housing boom nearly 60 years later. The VaR methodology I discussed in chapter 2 involves utilizing recent market price behavior to construct a probability distribution of future asset values. Broker-dealers used VaR models to manage their balance sheets. During the housing boom, when VaR models predicted a low risk of large asset price declines (because there had been no large declines during the preceding "great moderation"), broker-dealers massively increased their leverage in the belief that they could increase profits without increasing risk (see figure 6.1).[32]

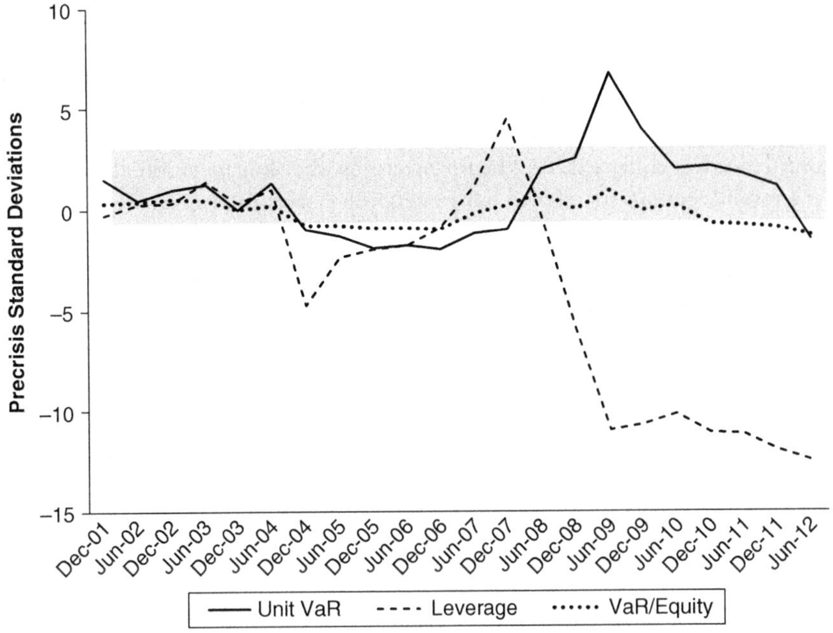

Figure 6.1 Broker-dealer leverage and VaR, 2001–2012.

Source: Tobias Adrian and Hyun Song Shin, "Financial Intermediary Leverage and Value—at- Risk," Federal Reserve Bank of New York Staff Reports, Number 338, 2012, Figure 5, p. 12.

Animal Spirits—Definition

Keynes believed people were aware of the omnipresence of uncertainty, even though they often suppressed the knowledge. He conjectured that people employed two additional approaches, besides projecting on the basis of recent performance, to cope with uncertain processes. One additional approach is to condition our belief in our risk forecasts by the degree of confidence we place in our projections.

> The state of long-term expectation, upon which our decisions are based, does not solely depend, therefore, on the most probable forecast we can make. It also depends on the *confidence* with which we make this forecast... If we expect large changes but are very uncertain as to what precise form these changes will take, then our confidence will be weak.[33]

The other additional approach is to condition our beliefs by the sway of human emotion, which he called "animal spirits."

> A large proportion of our positive activities depend on spontaneous optimism rather than on a mathematical expectation... Most, probably, of our decisions to do something positive, the full consequences of which will be drawn out over many days to come, can only be taken as a result of animal spirits—of a spontaneous urge to action rather than inaction, and not as the outcome of a weighted average of quantitative benefits multiplied by quantitative probabilities.[34]

Animal spirits and confidence is not the same thing. Animal spirits operate independently of risk. Spontaneous urges to action or inaction are not tied down by mathematical projections. Yet, the concepts are closely related. One would expect projected outcomes to rise, and perceptions of risk to fall, when animal spirits surge. It is difficult to imagine animal spirits being buoyant when confidence has collapsed, or when projections of risk have markedly increased. As a result, economists refer to both phenomena as animal spirits. I shall follow the convention in this book.

The Shift to Market Financing and the Amplification of Animal Spirits—Theory

The setting in which Keynes wrote about investor behavior was an organized financial exchange where securities are priced and traded continuously. Keynes contrasted the financial exchanges with the circumstance of a closely held business, where the firm is funded by its managers and close associates. Investors in a closely held firm have the advantage (relative to investors in financial exchanges) of more local knowledge, in Hayek's sense, and therefore face less uncertainty concerning the future prospects of the firm. However, investors in closely held firms have the disadvantage of having to make irreversible investments, since they rarely have opportunities to sell their holdings. The irreversibility of their investments limits their liquidity and their ability to diversify their holdings. The attraction of liquidity and diversification to investors are, according to Keynes, the underlying reason why financing shifted toward financial exchanges. Yet, along with increased liquidity and diversification came increased uncertainty, since investors in financial exchanges have greater cognitive distance from the firms they invest in, compared to the managers of the firms. The financing that occurs on financial exchanges is commonly called "market financing."

Keynes skipped over an important institution that arose alongside the organized financial exchange. It was the bank. Banks—or at least good banks—have local knowledge of their borrowers and make long-term loans that are not easily traded. But banks are funded by deposits, shares, and loans from people who desire liquidity and diversification. So, banks are sort of an intermediate solution to the tradeoff between the advantages of local knowledge, diversification, and liquidity. I shall call the financing that occurs through banks "bank financing." Most financing in the United States from the late nineteenth century onward was either market or bank financing. During the housing boom a preexisting shift from bank to market financing accelerated and virtually all subprime mortgages were financed with market-financed ABS (see figures 6.2 and 6.3). The fact that during the housing boom the share of market financing, which included subprime mortgages, was rising, makes Keynes's analysis of behavior in financial exchanges highly relevant to understanding the US housing boom.

Keynes explained that the price of securities in a financial exchange, where securities are traded and "marked to market" on a continuous basis is formed by consensus. One might think this applies to any market where trading occurs. In this respect, the market for toothpaste reaches a consensus valuation, which is the price at which the good is traded. But that is not what Keynes meant. In

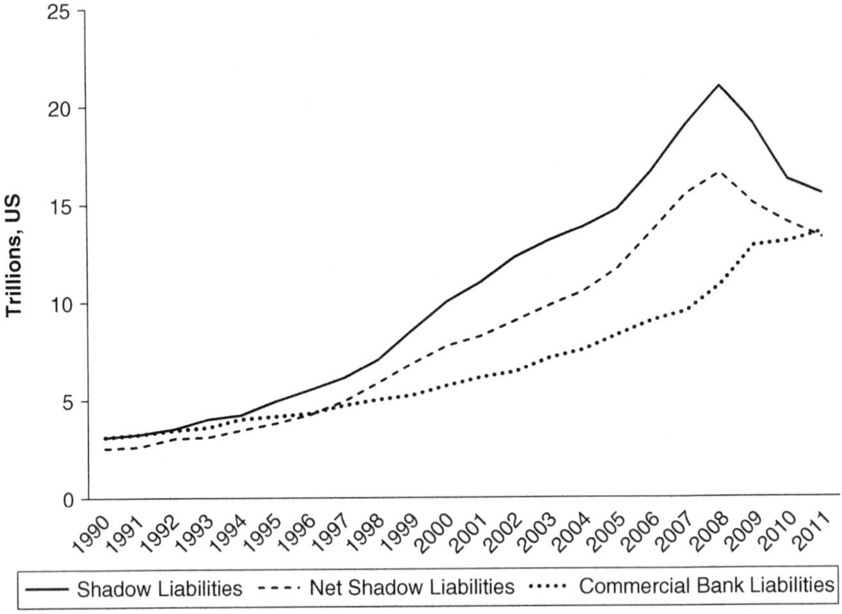

Figure 6.2 Shadow bank, commercial bank liabilities, 1990–2011.

Source: Zoltan Pozsar, Tobias Adrian, Adam Ashcraft, and Hayley Boesky, "Shadow Banking," Federal Reserve Bank of New York Staff Report no. 458, 2012, Figure 1, p. 8.

the toothpaste market, each buyer has her independent valuation of the product, and makes her buying decision on that basis alone. In a financial exchange, by contrast, the security has no value to its buyer except for her forecast of what someone else will be willing to purchase it for in the future. Speculation is an inherently social activity in the sense that it involves trying to figure out the views that others have, or will have in the future, of a security; knowing that each other person is forming her view by going through the same evaluation. The two signal features of financial exchanges are the cognitive distance that increases uncertainty over the future performance of the firms that issue securities, and liquidity, which makes investors speculators. These features tend to drive investors away from forming their valuation based on their perceptions of the prospects of the issuers and toward speculation over what other speculators will pay for the security. That is why animal spirits hold great sway in financial exchanges. Here's how Keynes described it:

> Most [investors] are, in fact, largely concerned, not with making superior long-term forecasts of the probable yield of an investment over its whole life, but with foreseeing changes in the conventional basis of valuation a short time ahead of the general public. They are concerned, not with what an investment is really worth to a man who buys it "for keeps," but with what the market will value it at, under the influence of mass psychology, three months or a year hence. Moreover, this behaviour is not the outcome of a wrong-headed propensity. It is an inevitable result of an investment market organised along the lines described.[35]

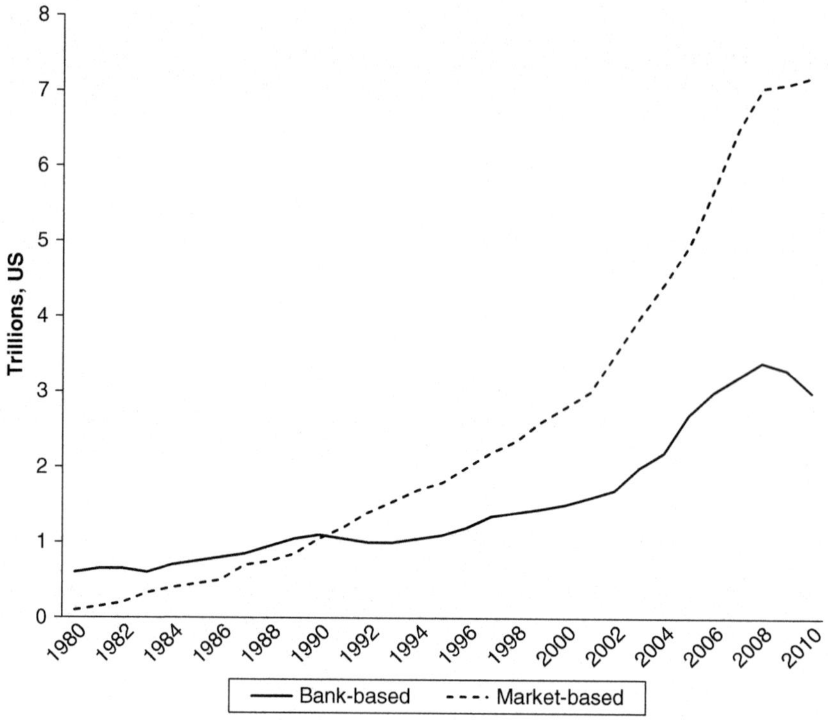

Figure 6.3 Market-based, bank-based holdings of home mortgages, 1980–2010.

Source: Tobias Adrian and Hyun Song Shin, "The Changing Nature of Financial Intermediation and the Financial Crisis of 2007–2009," Federal Reserve Bank of New York Staff Report no. 439, 2010, Figure 4, p. 3. US Flow of Funds, Federal Reserve.

Some commentators have interpreted Keynes to be arguing that behavior in financial exchanges is prone to be irrational, but his thinking is not as simple as that. For Keynes, the proneness to herd-like investment behavior is not a manifestation of irrationality, but rather arises from our ignorance of the future. The ubiquity of uncertainty literally forces us to leap into the unknown when making investment decisions.

> By "uncertain" knowledge... I do not mean merely to distinguish what is known for certain from what is merely probable. The game of roulette is not subject, in this sense, to uncertainty... the expectation of life is only slightly uncertain. Even the weather is only modestly uncertain. The sense in which I am using the term is that in which the prospect of a European war is uncertain, or the price of copper and the rate of interest twenty years hence, or the obsolescence of a new invention... About these matters there is no scientific basis on which to form any calculable probability whatever. *We simply do not know.*[36]

And when doing that, there is nothing irrational about averting our eyes from the abyss and tagging along with our fellows. "Nevertheless, the necessity for action and for decision compels us to as practical men to do our best to overlook this awkward fact."[37] Keynes identified four additional features of financial exchanges that subject securities prices to the herd-like influence of animal spirits. First, the tribe of money managers, who dominate the market, tend to cluster in close physical and cognitive proximity, so that gossip and knowledge circulates quickly among them. Second, their activities require making guesses about the future prices of financial assets, which is intrinsically uncertain. This implies there is a limited "objective" basis in forming opinions about the future path of securities prices. Third, their clients tend to shift their savings away from those managers whose performance lags behind the average, in favor of those whose performance at least equals the average among professional money managers. Fourth, the net worth of the financial intermediaries is measured almost continuously by the prices at which their assets trade during the day. Therefore, the clients of money managers are able to assess at short intervals the relative performance of their investments. This places enormous pressure on money managers to keep pace with the herd on a continuous basis, which limits the scope for contrarian investment strategies.

Uncertainty makes it extremely difficult for an investor, regardless of talent, to systematically outperform the average. Therefore, alpha performance is rarely a viable strategy.[38] The professional investor can, however, avoid lagging behind the average; she can do this by pursuing an investment strategy that replicates the consensus opinion, which requires investing with the herd. The herd-like nature and influence of animal spirits in financial exchanges, and its potential to shift independently of changes in objective facts, is, according to Keynes, a primary, ineradicable source of economic instability. The reason is that the state of animal spirits in the financial market influences the price of securities, which, via Tobin's Q, determines the volume of investment.[39]

While Keynes offered a compelling description of the market structure that created fertile ground for herd-like investment behavior, he did not identify any fundamental determinants of that behavior. He did not explain what might cause animal spirits to rise and fall. I alluded in chapter 2 to one of Keynes's acolytes, an economist named Hyman Minsky, who described a scenario where animal spirits will soar. Minsky reasoned that investors are prone to become overly complacent about risk after a long period of low volatility, where growth has been steady and default rates have been low.[40] The Great Moderation, which began in the early 1990s, was just such a period. Growth was steady, stock prices rose, while inflation and bond yields declined, and the Federal Reserve under Chairman Alan Greenspan endeavored to socialize investment risk by cutting interest rates savagely whenever securities prices began to fall.[41] This response became known as the "Greenspan Put." Minsky's analysis connects the decline in volatility and risk spreads to the financial excesses of the housing boom.

More recently, economists John Geanakoplos and Ana Fostel have formalized Minsky's insight into a theory the call the "leverage cycle."[42] The leverage cycle, which I introduced in chapter 2, is a theory that links leverage to asset prices. The basic idea is that asset values are driven by optimistic speculators. The more money they can obtain the more assets they will bid on, which will drive up price. Higher leverage means speculators can borrow more against assets, which enables them to purchase more assets with a given amount of equity capital.

Leverage limits are set by investors, who wish to make a profit from lending, but who are concerned about protecting against the risk of loss. Repayment is at risk when the value of the asset drops below the loan amount. Therefore, the lower is leverage, the lower will be the risk of loss. But the risk of loss at any given level of leverage is conditioned by volatility: the lower the perceived probability of a given amount of decline in price, the less is the risk of loss at any given level of leverage. Therefore, leverage will rise when volatility falls, and as leverage rises, speculators will drive up asset prices. The process, once under way, is self-reinforcing.[43]

The idea behind Minsky's theory and the leverage cycle resonates throughout psychology, literature, popular culture, and even the Bible ("the prosperity of fools shall destroy them": Proverbs 1:32), and seems to fit the circumstances of the 2000s quite compellingly: we got burned, at least in part, for the age old reason that we had grown too complacent for too long.[44] The shift to market financing created the potential for speculative excess and the preceding great moderation created the psychological preconditions that allowed those excesses to flourish.

The Shift to Market Financing and the Amplification of Animal Spirits—Experimental Evidence

There is a crucial difference in the underwriting analysis a bank intending to hold a loan to maturity will undertake, and the underwriting analysis an investor in a tradable security will undertake. This difference underscores the significance of the shift in loan financing from bank based to market based. When a bank underwrites a group of mortgage loans it intends to hold to maturity, it addresses the likelihood of default during the life of the loans and the expected resale value of the homes. When an investor underwrites a mortgage-backed security derived from the same group of homes, she addresses the likelihood of changes in market value of the security (not the underlying homes) over whatever time horizon she intends to hold the security. In a perfect market, both exercises should yield identical valuations. In theory, the value of the ABS should incorporate anticipations of the performance of the underlying mortgages through termination, since each successive buyer of the ABS will be looking to future performance of the security over some interval, until the termination of all the underlying mortgage loans. The final holder of the security will need to address the probability of underlying loan payoff at termination (and the resale value of the homes); the penultimate security holder will need to address the likelihood of default on underlying loans during the interval over which she intends to hold the security, and the price the final holder will pay (which will equal her valuation) and so forth. A familiar (to economists) process of backward induction issues the result that the initial investor will place the same value on the ABS as would the bank holding it to maturity.

Theory and reality differ markedly in this instance and Keynes's analysis explains why these two underwriting procedures may result in different valuations from time to time, and why the valuations of ABS will be more volatile than held to maturity loans.[45] What generates the difference is that the investor can retrade the security. She speculates on the path of market price of the security over time, which creates the opportunity for animal spirits to impact the price of the security. A hold to maturity loan, by contrast, cannot be retraded after it has been originated,[46] so there is less scope for speculation to impact the price of the loan after it has been issued.[47] This is a fundamental insight which explains why animal spirits affect securities prices and are more prone to influence loans packaged into tradable securities than loans held to maturity by banks. It is one of the many reasons that Keynes's writings are as relevant today as they were 80 years ago.

Keynes's insight has been reinforced by more recent work by economists in theoretical models that assume, contra Keynes, that the future path of securities prices can be described in probabilistic terms, but incorporate Keynes's insight that securities prices are determined not only by investors' private beliefs about future payoffs, but also their beliefs about other investors' beliefs, and higher-order beliefs. This perspective is captured by Keynes's metaphor of financial exchanges as beauty contests:

> Professional investment may be likened to those newspaper competitions in which the competitors have to pick out the six prettiest faces from a hundred photographs, the prize being awarded to the competitor whose choice most nearly corresponds to the average preferences of the competitors as a whole; so that each competitor has to pick, not those faces which he himself finds prettiest, but those which he thinks likeliest to catch the fancy of the other competitors, all of whom are looking at the problem from the same point of view. It is not a case of choosing those which, to the best of one's judgment, are really the prettiest, nor even those which average opinion genuinely thinks the prettiest. We have reached the third degree where we devote our intelligences to anticipating what average opinion expects the average opinion to be. And there are some, I believe, who practise the fourth, fifth and higher degrees.[48]

Keynes's concept of uncertainty captures this phenomena. Economists Franklin Allen, Stephen Morris, and Hyun Song Shin developed a risk-based model of securities pricing in which securities are longer lived than risk-adverse investors. In the model there are two types of information about securities: public information that every investor has access to, and private information that may differ between investors, which makes it difficult to discern what other investors are thinking. Since most investors will wish to sell off their holdings before the security has reached its termination (because securities are longer-lived than investors), investors will base their trading on their anticipations of the price at which they will be able to sell off their holdings to other investors.[49] This indeterminacy will cause market price to deviate from fundamental value.

The difference in market pricing behavior between loans held to maturity by banks and loans traded in the market has been borne out in the laboratory by economist Vernon Smith and his collaborators (V Smith).[50] V Smith demonstrated the difference in experiments where subjects were given endowments of money and a commodity that paid a different dividend to each subject. The subjects were allowed to trade the commodities with each other—and negotiate prices—over several periods. Nobody knew the dividend payment to other subjects, and therefore did not know the equilibrium market price. In one scenario

(scenario 1) a subject was not allowed to resell a commodity it had purchased. In scenario 2, subjects were allowed to retrade. Scenario 1 is analogous to a "hold to maturity" situation, while scenario 2 is analogous to a speculative financial market, such as the shadow banking sector. In scenario 1, traded prices converged rapidly to the equilibrium.[51] In scenario 2, traded prices took longer to converge to the equilibrium price and the dispersion of traded prices was much higher than in scenario 1. In addition, there was a significant amount of "speculative" trading in scenario 2. Many subjects retraded an acquired commodity at a later period, and many buyers paid in excess of their private payoff in early periods, which can only be accounted for as pure speculation.[52]

These results show that prices in traded securities markets are more volatile than in markets where participants acquire assets to consume or hold to maturity, and that what drives the difference is the activity of speculation where equilibrium price is unknown. This is similar to the distinction Keynes attempted to explain. It is not exactly the same, since Keynes was concerned with the uncertainty engendered by the potential for novel events to emerge in the future, whereas the parameters in the experiment do not change over time.[53] The fundamental insight, however, is the same. It is that pricing behavior is affected by the institutional context in which trade takes place. Another aspect of the experimental results, that prices converge toward the equilibrium over time, shows that experience with a security tends to reduce its volatility. This may help to explain why the dot-com boom and the housing boom involved securities—Internet start-ups and subprime mortgages—that had limited prior exposure to the market.

Another notable result of the V Smith experiment is that the same subjects generated very different pricing patterns when placed in different trading environments. It cannot be said that subjects in scenario 1—where prices converge more quickly to equilibrium—were more "rational" than were subjects in scenario 2, since the pricing behavior in both experiments were generated by the very same individuals! This result has relevance in the ongoing debate over the causes of speculative excesses in the securities markets. The common viewpoint is that the more competitive culture and remuneration offered to securities traders, versus traditional bank employees, has prompted more aggressive and risk tolerant people to choose careers in the securities markets. According to this view, it is the self-selection of employees that explains the proneness of tradable securities prices to reach excess. The results of the V Smith experiment suggest that differences in the character of employees may not be the only reason behind the greater volatility of traded securities versus held to maturity loans.

When animal spirits in the securities market were bullish, prices of home mortgages rose (yields declined), which increased Tobin's Q and elicited an increased home construction. And when the collective mood turned sour, prices and home construction nosedived. The locus of speculative excess in financial exchanges is something the housing boom and the prior dot-com boom have in common, since dot-coms were equities traded on the stock exchange and subprime mortgages were packaged into tradable ABS. Keynes was right to maintain that one major cost of organized financial markets was an increase in the indeterminacy and volatility of asset pricing.

Limits of Rationalization

In this chapter I have explained how rational decision-makers could have pushed up the prices of homes and securities backed by home mortgages to unsustainably high levels. Keynes's beauty contest metaphor illustrates that some people may have been aware of it, and yet still participated in the market. In chapter 11 I provide a quote from Citicorp CEO Chuck Prince explaining that his bank was doing just that; playing the game knowing that "when the music stopped"—as eventually it would have to—somebody would be caught out with losses.

Yet, there is another aspect of decision-making during the housing boom that is difficult to rationalize. It is has to do with the contractual structure of ABS. In a typical ABS there is an agent, called the servicer, who is responsible for managing the loans that comprise the ABS. The servicer receives the mortgage payments and distributes them to the holders of ABS tranches. When a borrower fails to pay, the servicer decides how to deal with it. Normally, the decision is whether to restructure the loan in such a way as to forgive some aspect of the borrower's payment obligation—delaying payments, reducing the interest rates, or reducing the principal balance owed on the loan—or to foreclose on the home.

It is a striking fact that servicers have almost never elected to restructure loans, even though there is a great deal of evidence showing that ABS investors would have been made better off by doing so. By contrast, many banks restructured mortgage loans for their borrowers who fell behind on payments. Mian and Sufi cite evidence that the banks were more likely to restructure loans and that their loans outperformed the loans held by ABS.[54] Foreclosure typically costs the lender a nontrivial amount of money. There are the legal costs, the costs of maintaining the home until it is sold, the foregone payments the borrower might have made if the loan was restructured, and the discount at which a foreclosed home usually sells. Moreover, the period after the onset of the financial crisis was the worst time since the Great Depression to be selling a home.

There appear to be three reasons why ABS servicers opted not to restructure delinquent loans. One is that they typically were paid more money to foreclose on a home than to restructure the loan. The second reason is that, in many instances, the servicer either did not have the authority to restructure, or might have become exposed to claims by ABS investors that its restructure caused losses.[55] The third reason is that, in the absence of a delegation of authority to the servicer, the complexity of negotiating a consensus among ABS investors—some of whom may have taken short positions in the ABS, which means they would benefit from a default—was practically impossible.

Banks, by contrast, did not have these conflicts, so they were more likely to restructure when it made sense to do so.[56] The unanswered question is why were ABS servicer contracts structured so as to create a conflict between the interests of the investors and the servicer in the event the loans performed poorly? This flaw in ABS servicer contracts was a huge avoidable error.

What makes this so confounding is that the issue of allocating decision-making power and incentives in future eventualities where things do not go according to plan is an important feature of any financial contract. For example, the mortgages that collateralize the ABS give the lender control over what occurs after the borrower becomes delinquent, and yet the ABS contract structure effectively negates that power and limits the ABS investors to the single option of foreclosure.

Conclusion

In this chapter I have outlined four situations various agents found themselves in during the housing boom that resulted in distinct modes of decision-making. Each mode involves self interested behavior, in the sense that agents were behaving is a reasonable, sensible manner, given the institutional and cognitive constraints they were subjected to. The list may not be exhaustive, but it is sufficient to demonstrate that the majority of decision-makers did not necessarily "go a little nuts" during the housing boom. This does not imply that mistakes we not made; as always, some participants performed better than others. The implication is that, in order to explain the housing boom, it is necessary to work out how rational decision-making interacted with certain structural and institutional features of the US economy to generate a financial crisis that nobody intended. That is the topic of the next chapter.

CHAPTER 7

The Capital Flow Bonanza and the Housing Boom

> Large inflows of capital into the United States and other countries stimulated a reaching for yield, an underpricing of risk, excessive leverage, and the development of complex and opaque financial instruments.
>
> —Ben Bernanke[1]

> Securitization was meant to disperse credit risk to those who were better able to bear it. In practice, securitization appears to have concentrated the risks in the financial intermediary sector itself.
>
> —Hyun Song Shin[2]

> We sit in the mud... and reach for the stars.
>
> —Ivan Turgenev

In the last chapter I explained why the decisions made during the housing boom can be understood as ecologically rational. In this chapter, I shall attempt to explain in detail how those ecologically rational decisions generated an unsustainable boom. To quote Adam Ferguson, the housing boom was "the result of human action, but not the execution of any human design."[3]

The starting point of my explanation is the dramatic growth of the US capital flow bonanza during the housing boom, which was documented in chapter 2. In chapter 4 I explained why the current account deficit was a necessary condition for the boom to occur. In this chapter I will explore the channels through which the capital flow bonanza abetted (and indirectly caused) the explosion in subprime lending that fuelled the housing boom.

Channels of Transmission I—Preliminaries

A current account deficit involves a diversion of income away from the home economy to a foreign country. As can be seen from identity (4.1), starting from a position of full employment income (*Yf*), a shift in expenditure away from domestic goods toward imports, will cause $(X - M)$ to decline, and income (Y) to fall. The first order effect of a shift in demand toward imports is to reduce home economy income. That is the hole in demand created by the current account deficit.

$$Y = (C + I + G) + (X - M). \tag{4.1}$$

The hole can be filled; but only if spending in the home economy by home economy residents, businesses, and government exceeds full employment home economy income (Yf). In terms of identity (4.1), attaining full employment in the presence of a current account deficit requires that

$$(C + I + G) > Yf.\text{[4]} \tag{7.1}$$

The US economy achieved full employment while running record current account deficits during the housing boom. This means the sum of US household, business, and government spending exceeded, respectively, their earnings and tax receipts. How did they achieve this? They did so by borrowing, directly and indirectly, from China and OPEC through the capital flow bonanza. I showed in chapters 2 and 3 that during the housing boom, the current account deficit was recycled into the United States as a capital flow bonanza, and lent to US institutions (primarily the government and GSE's). In this chapter I will explain how the capital flow bonanza provided the means to fill the hole in demand. It did so through two channels. One was by pushing down interest rates and risk and maturity spreads, which interacted with imbalances in financial intermediaries to induce a "reach for yield." The other channel was by crowding out other investors from government-guaranteed debt, which created a safe asset shortage. The combination of these two forces elicited a reaction that propagated an explosion in credit fuelled housing investment and consumer spending.

Channels of Transmission II—the Primary Impact

I explained in chapter 2 how the current account deficit involved a shift in dollar deposits away from the US private sector to Southeast Asia, China, and OPEC. Entities in these countries then typically transferred their dollar deposits to their central banks in exchange for local currency denominated bank deposits. The central banks (or, in the case of OPEC, sovereign wealth funds), in turn, invested their dollar deposits in US government-guaranteed debt. Effectively, there was a shift in dollar deposits from entities with a high propensity to consume (US citizens), to an entity with a zero propensity to consume (foreign central banks and sovereign wealth funds). To gain a very rough idea of the magnitude of the first order impact of this shift, consider that in 2006 the US current account deficit was around \$201 billion[5] and US net private saving was \$776 billion.[6] This implies (at the upper bound) that the capital flow bonanza could have added 26 percent to US domestic private saving.[7] The increase in saving pushed down interest rates. Warnock estimated that foreign purchases of treasuries pushed down yields by 80 basis points.[8] The foreign demand for treasuries and GSE debt crowded out US investors, and forced them into other securities.

Four significant consequences followed from the increased purchases of US government-guaranteed debt by foreign countries and the concomitant crowding out of other investors from long-term risk-free government-guaranteed debt. One was that yields on other long-term debt fell, which meant that the maturity yield spread—the difference in yields between short-term and long-term debt-compressed. These effects were corroborated by Marriuchi and Nier.[9] The compression in maturity yield spread made lending less profitable for banks by reducing the net interest margin earned by banks, which borrow short and lend long. The decline in loan profit margins induced banks to seek ways of generating income by shifting to riskier, higher margin loans and by earning income from sources other than lending.[10]

The second consequence was that the decline in yields created problems for some of the largest institutional investors in the US economy. Low yields threatened the solvency of institutions like Defined Benefit Pension Plans (DBPs) and Life Insurers (LIs) that had long-term payout commitments. They could not meet those commitments if their return on investment fell too low. Low yields also created a problem for investors like hedge funds and long-only bond funds, because low yields made it more difficult for them to meet the return benchmarks they promised their investors. This group is known as bond investors. As a result, they were willing to take on more risk and to increase their leverage (and the leverage of those to whom they lent money and the instruments in which they invested) in order to boost returns. Moreover, the embrace of leverage and shift into riskier investments by bond investors, pushed up the price of risky assets, which had the effect of compressing risk spreads. In this way, the capital flow bonanza caused risk yield spreads to compress.

The third consequence was that the scarcity of government-guaranteed debt posed a problem for another group of investors; the institutional cash pools (defined below) which shunned uninsured bank deposits and sought safe liquid investments. This group suffered from the "safe asset shortage" that Ricardo Cabellaro has written about.

The fourth consequence was that the increase in the value of assets increased household net worth, which elicited an increase in consumption.

Finally, it is notable that the capital flow bonanza had the effect of simultaneously lowering real interest rates while causing asset valuations to rise. While the lower interest rates are consistent with higher asset values, it might appear odd that higher asset valuations failed to elicit enough additional borrowing to push up yields or that initially low interest rates failed to elicit enough additional consumption to cause yields to rise. Higher valuations provide an incentive—by Tobin's Q—to increase investment. Lower borrowing costs provide an incentive to increase current consumption. Borrowing and consumption did increase dramatically, yet the ten year treasury rate barely budged, even after the Fed vigorously raised short-term rates. I shall explain in this chapter, and in chapters 9 and 10, how the sheer magnitude of the capital flow bonanza overwhelmed all other factors and kept interest rates low throughout the housing boom.[11]

What follows is an outline of how the problems created by the capital flow bonanza was solved (or appeared to be solved) in the shadow banking sector (a concept I define below). It was a solution that involved a massive increase in risky residential lending that funded an increase in investment and consumption sufficient to fill the hole in demand created by the current account deficit—that is, until it all unraveled.

Channels of Transmission III—the Shadow Banking Sector

In order to identify the channels through which the capital flow bonanza affected the US economy, it is necessary to understand the structure of the market into which the savings that were crowded out from the government-guaranteed debt market flowed, and the impact the capital flow bonanza had on that market. The crowded out savings, it will be shown, created a shortage of safe assets for a certain group of investors (the institutional cash pools). At the same time, the compression of yields and spreads forced other investors to seek out riskier investment in a reach for yield (the bond investors). The needs of both groups—which were brought on by the capital flow bonanza—were met by the creation of ABS collateralized primarily by subprime mortgages,[12] which were financed by short-term debt. A portion of the ABS paper was purchased by money market funds, which is a type of institutional cash pool. For most of the remainder, a trade was constructed, in which bond investors acquired investment grade rated subprime mortgage ABS and lent them to broker-dealers who conveyed them to institutional cash pools. In this trade broker-dealers acted as matched book money dealers, meaning that the duration and composition of their assets (loans to bond investors collateralized by ABS) exactly matched their liabilities (borrowings from institutional cash pools collateralized by ABS).[13] This is the business of shadow banking. Figure 6.2 shows how the relative size of the shadow banking sector began to far outstrip the commercial banking sector during the housing boom, as finance shifted from held to maturity assets to securitized assets.[14]

Securitizations

Banks issue par on demand deposit and wholesale liabilities, which they use to fund held to maturity loans and other assets. Bank deposits function as money. Some other assets are perceived by the private sector as near-money, to the extent they can be converted into bank deposits or currency quickly, costlessly, and at par. Liabilities of money market funds (called money market NAV shares) fit this definition because they can be converted to bank deposits almost instantaneously.

By issuing short-term liabilities (deposits), and making long-term loans, banks perform what is called "maturity transformation." It is a beneficial, but dangerous, activity. It is beneficial insofar as it provides funding to borrowers who can make profitable use of resources, but who cannot repay on demand[15]; it is dangerous, because the maturity mismatch between deposits and loans subjects the bank to the risk that it will not have the cash on hand to meet a large volume of depositor withdrawals, if they occur all at once (which is a bank run).

In response to the bank runs that occurred in the early 1930s, an independent agency of the US government called the Federal Deposit Insurance Corporation (FDIC) was established to insure bank depositors. Currently, the FDIC insured deposits in member banks up to $250,000.00.[16] Up to that amount, depositors need not worry about the solvency of the bank. But larger depositors have reason to worry. Uninsured bank depositors are effectively the most junior unsecured claimholders on highly leveraged institutions with an asset/liability term mismatch. That is not the most attractive place to be if your main goal is to ensure you can convert your savings into money quickly, costlessly, and, at par.[17]

Large depositors have an incentive to spread their deposits across banks in order to stay below the FDIC insurance threshold at each institution. Between 1990 and 2010, the aggregate amount of money held by institutional cash pools—which are comprised of investors with more than $1 billion in liquid assets—looking for a safe, liquid place to park their funds increased from under $500 billion to over $5 trillion.[18] At the same time, the asset management industry consolidated, so that the money was invested by a smaller group of managers. The increase in the assets under management by institutional cash pools, and the increased concentration of the asset management industry, meant that money managers required more banks over which to spread deposits in order to stay below the FDIC insured limit. Achieving that became more difficult over time since the banking industry became more concentrated. From 1980 to 2010, the number of FDIC insured banks shrank from 15,000 to 8,000. The conjuncture of more funds under management, higher concentration among money managers and fewer banks resulted in too few banks to provide the possibility of insuring all deposits of institutional cash pools (figure 7.1).

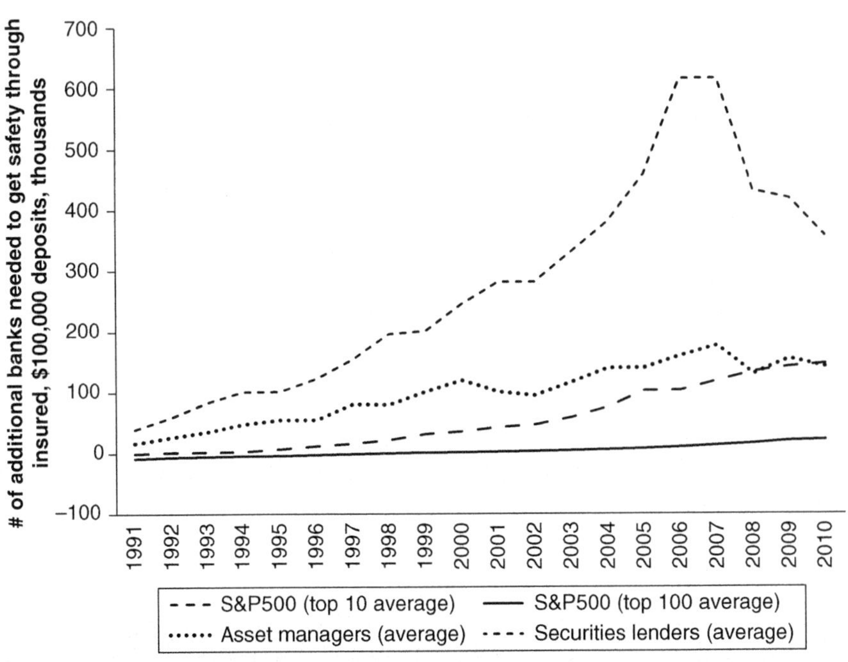

Figure 7.1 Not enough banks to source safety for cash pools.

Source: Zoltan Pozsar, "Institutional Cash Pools and the Triffin Dilemma of the US Banking System." IMF Working Paper # 11/190, 2011, Figure 4, p. 8.

The aversion of institutional cash pools to uninsured deposits constrained the ability of the banking industry to grow its deposit base in response to the increase in the demand for lending that occurred during the housing boom.[19] But it did not prevent banks from using their comparative advantage in originating loans, which were assembled into pools of loans from which securities were created and sold to investors.

There was nothing new about banks originating and then distributing loans. Banks had been originating mortgages and selling some of them off to the GSEs for over a decade. What was different during the housing boom was that banks became sponsors of the ABS into which their subprime loans were placed, and issued guarantees of repayment at par to the investors in the ABS. It was a form of regulatory arbitrage enabling a disguised increase in bank leverage, since the guarantees were off balance sheet and did not require any additional capital.[20] From 2001 to 2008 commercial banks securitized $1.3 trillion of assets—mostly subprime mortgages—on most of which they issued guarantees. Securitization enabled banks to play a decisive role in the issuance of subprime loans during the housing boom, and forced them to absorb a significant share of losses incurred by subprime ABS when prices collapsed and investors fled the securitizations during the financial crisis.[21]

Banks were not the only issuers of ABS. From 2001 to 2006 broker-dealers securitized over $600 billion of subprime mortgages.[22] In addition, $640 billion of CDO, which are actively managed vehicles that invest in subprime mortgages, were issued from 1998 to 2007.[23]

Institutional Cash Pools

ABS issued by US and foreign commercial banks, as well as US broker-dealers, were primarily collateralized by subprime mortgages (see figure 7.2). They were ultimately funded, in part, by institutional cash pools. An institutional cash pool manages assets that are held in bank deposits, or securities that can be converted into bank deposits on very short notice at par value. It is the liquidity the portfolio manager requires to conduct its business.[24]

Institutional cash pools are comprised of four groups. One is foreign exchange investors, who are foreign country institutions that reinvest their dollar deposits into US financial markets. During the housing boom gross capital inflows drove the growth of this group, and it was dominated by Europe. China and OPEC did not play a major role, since the majority of their US investments were in long-term treasuries and GSE debt. The second group is corporate cash reserves, which swelled. Nobody is quite sure what lies behind this growth. One cause of increased corporate cash flow might be that the decline in the cost of IT had reduced the cost of capital investment. Another cause might have arisen from the shift to lower cost Chinese labor in the assembly portion of the supply chain.[25] However, none of these factors account for why corporations did not distribute excess cash to shareholders. The third group is large mutual fund and money market managers. These include retail and institutional money market funds, DBPs LI's hedge funds, bond funds, and wealthy family offices. DBPs grew, as baby boomer workers continued to contribute toward their retirement;

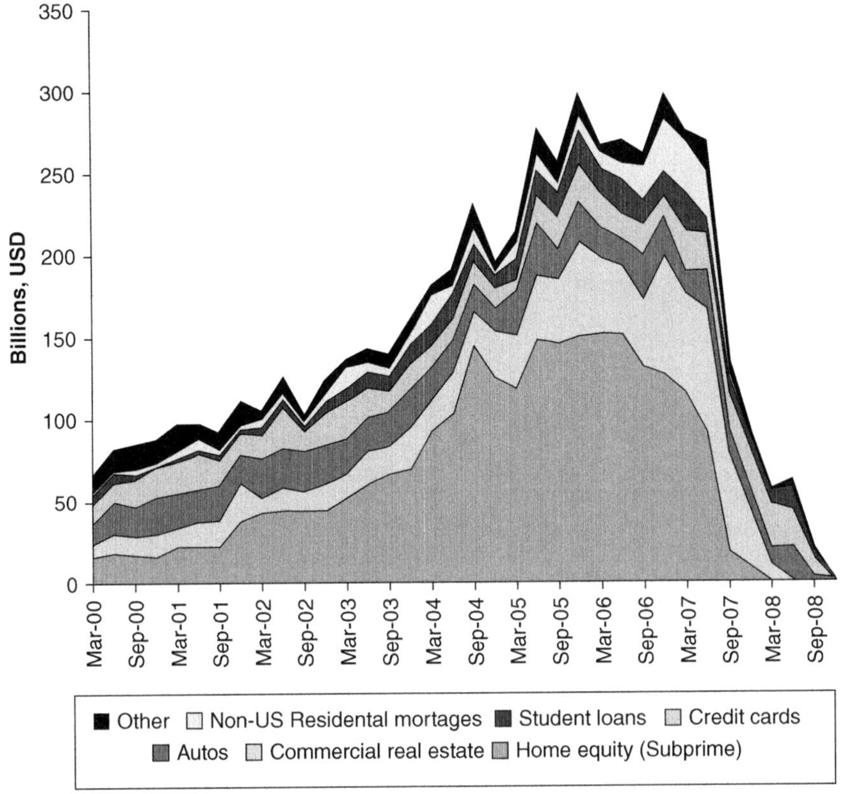

Figure 7.2 Asset-backed securities issuance, 2000–2008.

Source: Tobias Adrian and Hyun Song Shin, "The Changing Nature of Financial Intermediation and the Financial Crisis of 2007–2009," Federal Reserve Bank of New York Staff Report no. 439, 2010, Figure 22 p. 20.

wealthy family offices grew as income and wealth concentration increased dramatically,[26] and other asset management pools grew as the money management industry became more concentrated over time.[27] A fourth category, called securities lenders, is comprised of members of the first three groups and represent the portion of proceeds from securitized loans those parties reinvest in the money market. Figure 7.3 shows that institutional cash pools grew dramatically during the housing boom.

The institutional cash pools were unable to place all their funds in FDIC insured deposits, which was likely their most preferred option. To the extent they placed monies beyond that amount in bank deposits; they were unsecured creditors of banks. They could achieve more security by lending on a collateralized basis, provided there were suitable investments available, in terms of safety and liquidity.

The most desirable nonmoney investment was short-term treasury and GSE debt, which were liquid—in the sense that they could be quickly converted into bank deposits—and had the security of a government guarantee. Alas, this option was limited by an insufficient amount of short-term government-guaranteed

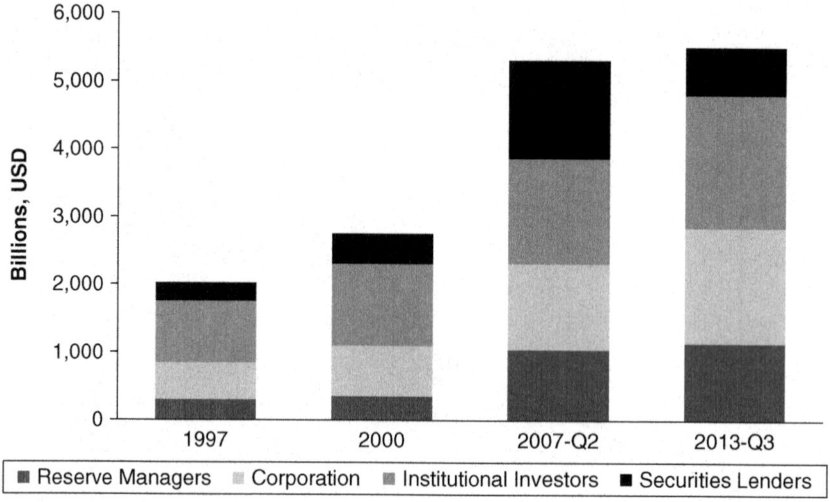

Figure 7.3 Institutional cash pools, 1997–2013.

Source: Zoltan Pozsar, "Shadow Banking: The Money View," Office of Financial Research, US Department of Treasury WP 14, Appendix p. 61, 2014.

paper. Economist Zoltan Pozsar estimated that in 2007 institutional cash pools held around \$3 trillion in funds that were not eligible for FDIC insurance, and there was approximately \$1.5 trillion of government-guaranteed short-term debt (after subtracting out foreign official holdings). This left an excess of at least \$1.5 trillion in funds the institutional cash pools desired to invest outside of banks, if suitable alternatives could be found.[28]

The next best alternative might have been to invest in longer term treasury and GSE debt, provided it was used to collateralized a third-party guaranty of repayment at par in short intervals. This solution was constructed by broker dealers who entered into transactions with institutional cash pools whereby the institutional cash pool paid the dealer money in exchange for a treasury bond, and the broker-dealer promised to repurchase the treasury bond the next day, for the original purchase price plus interest.[29] This is an overnight repo transaction, which, for the sake of expositional convenience, I shall describe as a collateralized lending of money (even though it involves a purchase and sale of an asset). It placed the institutional cash pool in almost as good a positions as if it held an FDIC insured bank deposit. Not quite as good, since the liquidity was not government guaranteed, but the ultimate security was.[30] Alas, there was an insufficiency in the supply of long-term treasuries and GSE debt, due to the large holdings of foreign central banks, most significantly the PBOC.

The mushrooming institutional cash pools were looking for safe, liquid assets in which to invest. Initially, there just weren't enough such assets to go around. That was the safe asset shortage. But a solution was manufactured in the shadow banking sector. Before getting to the solution, I need to describe another group of investors.

Bond Investors

Bond investors are major investors who concentrate their holdings in long-term debt, real estate and corporate equities. Members of this group include DBP's and LI's, who invest to meet actuarially fixed long-term obligations. The other members are long only bond funds and hedge funds, who aim to exceed hurdle returns promised to their investors. Bond investors overlap with institutional cash pools to the extent that the portion of a bond investor's portfolio it retains in short-term liquid securities operates as an institutional cash pool. Bond investors are also intertwined amongst themselves, since LIs and DBPs are major investors in Long-only bond funds and hedge funds. This group invests in securities backed by real economy assets; corporate stocks and bonds, mortgages, ABS, and, sometimes, real estate and other "alternatives."

What is important to know about bond investors for this analysis, is that the decline in long-term interest rates induced by the capital flow bonanza placed them at risk of becoming insolvent and/or losing investors. In response, they were forced to "reach for yield" by investing in riskier investments and/or increasing leverage.

The Role of Broker-Dealers as Matched Book Money Dealers

Traditionally, broker-dealers supported the activities of bond investors by brokering and making markets in government and corporate debt (in addition to which the GSEs sourced and packaged mortgage securities which were sold to bond investors).

Around the year 2000 bond investors started reaching for yield in response to low interest rates. At the same time, institutional cash pools expanded and needed to find alternatives to bank deposits and scarce government-guaranteed debt. A solution emerged that catered to the needs of both parties: commercial banks and broker-dealers packaged loans they originated into ABS backed by real assets and sponsor guarantees, and sold them to bond investors and money market funds. The income streams were divided into tranches and the tranches sold to bond investors and money market funds usually carried an investment grade rating. In order to boost the effective yields of bond investors, broker-dealers intermediated a trade whereby bond investors conveyed their ABS assets to broker-dealers, in a reverse repo transaction in which broker dealers lent money to bond investors short term. Bond investors used the money to engage in transactions—asset purchases, repo lending and derivative trades—that boosted their yields. Concurrently, broker-dealers entered into repo transactions with institutional cash pools whereby broker-dealers conveyed the investment grade ABS collateral to institutional cash pools in exchange for borrowing cash short term. In the end, the institutional cash pools obtained investment grade liquid collateral backed by commercial bank or broker-dealer guarantees. It was a definite improvement over the alternative of holding unsecured, uninsured bank debt.[31]

In conducting this trade, broker-dealers operated as matched book money dealers (i.e., with similar composition and duration of assets and liabilities).[32]

This means they loaned money short term to bond investors, from which they received securities as collateral (reverse repo), while borrowing short-term money from institutional cash pools and conveying the security as collateral (repo).[33] This arrangement worked well for all parties involved. The institutional cash pools received collateral and liquidity (since the broker-dealers are required to repurchase the next day); the bond investors received money to boost their returns by either leveraging their portfolios, engaging in derivatives trades or reinvesting the cash (to which extent they become investment cash pools), and the broker-dealers get to do their thing (brokering and dealing). Zoltan Pozsar described the advantage of the trade for bond investors:

> Matched-book repo is about dealers' role as both massive borrowers and lenders in the secured money market, intermediating between risk-averse cash pools on the one hand and risk seeking, levered fixed income portfolios on the other, with the aim of using cash from the former to provide leverage to the latter to generate returns over a benchmark... for pension funds and other real money accounts that have been struggling with rising asset-liability mismatches since 2000.[34]

Broker-dealers (and some large commercial banks) also operated as matched book derivatives traders. The increased risk taking and leveraging by bond investors created a demand for credit default insurance and interest rate derivatives as part of strategies to mitigate risk and/or to boost profits. Broker-dealers intermediated risk between institutional investors. This activity helped to facilitate the growth of ABS insofar and it enabled investors to lay off a portion of the risk of ABS to credit default swap (CDS) issuers like AIG.[35]

Broker-dealers made another contribution to the growth of subprime ABS. Someone had to retain the "toxic" junior tranche of the securitized assets that could not obtain an acceptable credit rating. This honor was taken up by the Broker-dealers and commercial banks that originated and sponsored the ABS. In addition, those commercial banks and broker-dealers who aggregated mortgage loans into ABS, held portfolios of individual subprime loans (and other loans) as inventory in the process of assembling the ABS.[36] They wanted to play in the arena, and to do so, they had to pay. Yet, they were able to mitigate risk by purchasing CDSs.

One additional element was required to make it all work. Many of the bond and cash pool investors were regulated fiduciaries who were restricted to invest most of their money in highly rated securities. The newly minted securities needed to have the blessing of an investment grade rating. The rating agencies provided their seal of approval on all but the most junior tranches of the ABS. Some say they did so because they believed the diversified pools of loans that comprised the securities mitigated risk; some say they did so because they were handsomely compensated by the sponsoring banks and broker-dealers. It lies beyond the scope of this book to adjudicate that question, except to note that subprime ratings became the principal source of revenue for Standard & Poor's and Moody's.[37]

The shadow banking sector is comprised of the activities described above, which involve originating, selling and intermediating ABS (and other securities[38]) and derivatives between investor cash pools and bond investors.

Understanding an important concept: Shadow banking

Shadow banking (figure 7.4) is the sector where financial intermediation—borrowing from one group in order to lend to, or invest in, another—is carried out by institutions that are not deposit taking banks. The institutions performing the intermediation are called "broker-dealers" (also known as "investment banks"). Economist Zoltan Pozsar has mapped out the ecosystem of the US shadow banking sector. Many things take place in the shadow banking sector, as Pozsar and others have used the concept, but the majority of the balance sheets of broker-dealers are comprised of assets and liabilities that are related to the following activities;

- Intermediation of lending (by institutional cash pools) and borrowing (by bond investors).
- Matched book maturity transformation of securities held by bond investors into overnight repo's issued to institutional cash pools.
- Intermediation of risk by matching derivative exposures between institutional investors.[39]

Pozsar has shown that, in fulfilling these intermediation functions, broker-dealers do not engage in net maturity transformation. The duration of their loans to bond investors is matched by the duration of their borrowings from institutional cash pools (usually overnight), and their risk exposures are matched as well. In this respect broker-dealer intermediation differs from banks, which borrow short and lend long. Banks face two dimensions of risk—maturity mismatch and borrower (and counterparty) exposure, whereas broker-dealers face only the latter dimension of risk in their intermediation activities.[40]

Broker-dealers did, however, take on additional risk in connection with their intermediation activities during the housing boom. They held the unrated "toxic" junior tranches of ABS they originated; they held inventories of subprime mortgage loans used in constructing ABS, and they issued guarantees on debt of ABS they sponsored.[41]

The shadow banking sector grew enormously during the period of the housing boom, which can be seen in the growth of institutional cash pools (figure 7.3). By 2008 the volume of overnight repos' issued by broker-dealers exceeded the demand deposits of the commercial banking system.[42]

Below is a schematic of the shadow banking sector. On the left are the bond investors; on the right are the institutional cash pools and in the middle, mediating between the two are the broker-dealers. Outside the sector are commercial banks and GSEs, who also intermediate in the shadow banking sector: by creating and sponsoring ABS and by intermediating risk.

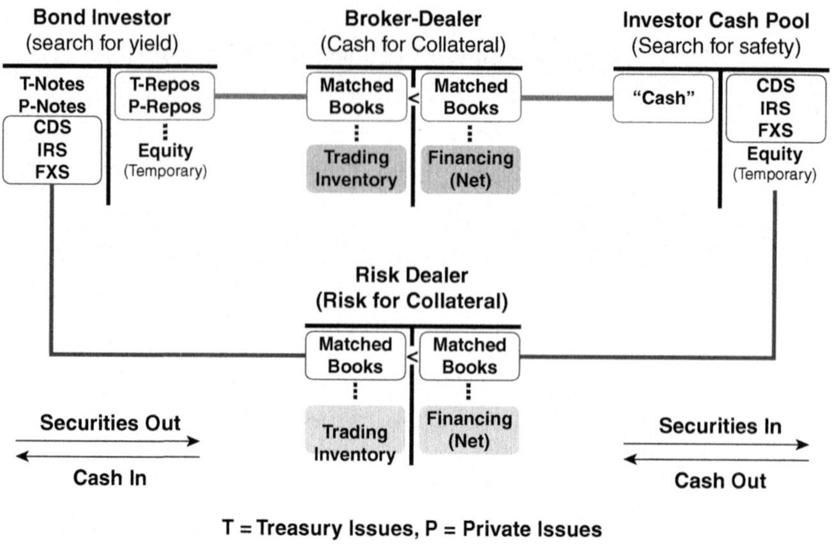

Figure 7.4 Shadow banking diagram.

Source: Adapted from Zoltan Pozsar, "Shadow Banking: The Money View," Office of Financial Research, US Department of Treasury WP 14–04, 2014, Figure 4, p. 56.

Crowding Out and the "Safe Asset" Shortage—the Channel of Transmission

Pozsar's estimated excess of $1.5 trillion in institutional cash pools funds in 2007, after taking account of the availability of short-term government securities and insurable bank deposits, represented the "safe asset" shortage faced by investors. The safe asset shortage was caused by the purchase of government-guaranteed debt by Southeast Asian countries, OPEC and the PBOC. From 2003 through 2007 their cumulative purchases of US government-guaranteed debt nearly matched the safe asset shortage. One channel through which the capital flow bonanza reached the US economy was by crowding out institutional cash pools from the government-guaranteed debt market.[43]

The safe asset shortage created pressure and opportunity to invent alternative near-money substitutes to meet the needs of institutional cash pools. Acharya et al. estimated that commercial banks issued $1.3 trillion in securitized and guaranteed assets during the housing boom. Those ABS (and CDO derived from them) provided the financial raw material which bond investors and money market funds invested in directly, and which broker-dealers accepted as collateral from bond investors in exchange for overnight reverse repo loans and transformed into the near-money "safe assets" demanded by institutional cash pools, which they offered as collateral for overnight repo loans.

The surge in the production of subprime mortgages emerged as a solution to problems and opportunities arising from the impact that the decline in yields and the shortage of government-guaranteed debt had on the balance sheets of, respectively, bond investors and institutional cash pools. In this way, the growth of shadow banking during the housing boom was caused by the capital flow bonanza.

The Link to the Subprime Mortgage Boom

The entire superstructure of lending, borrowing, risk-sharing and intermediating engendered by the conjuncture of the reach for yield and the safe asset shortage (both of which were caused by the capital flow bonanza) required a raw material input. There had to be more real "stuff" to collateralize the securities created to meet the needs of bond investors—for increased yield—and institutional cash pools—for nonbank safe liquid assets. Without it, nothing much would have happened, other than a reshuffling of existing securities. The hole in demand would have remained unfilled and the safe asset shortage would have persisted. The government and corporate sectors did not generate a large enough increase in debt growth to satisfy the appetite. The "stuff" that provided much of the raw material for the ABS and CDO, which filled the hole in demand and sated the appetite of institutional cash pools, was subprime mortgages.

Channels of Transmission IV—Motivations of Subprime Originators, Investors, and Borrowers

In chapter 6 I argued that the principal players in the housing boom behaved in an ecologically rational way. Table 7.1 shows the institutions that were the most exposed to subprime mortgages at the time of the financial crisis. They were all financial institutions; losses were concentrated in the core of the financial system. While I have attributed motives to some of those institutions in the course of describing the functioning of the shadow banking sector in the preceding section, I now provide a more focused analysis of the motivations of the US institutions who became exposed to subprime mortgages during the housing boom. European banks also played a significant role in the subprime mortgage ecosystem; as purchasers of subprime ABS debt and as broker-dealers (through their US subsidiaries). Their motivations lie beyond the scope of this enquiry.

The Insurance and Pensions Channel

Table 7.1 shows that insurance companies were the largest single investor class in subprime mortgages. DBPs were smaller, but they also invested through hedge funds.[44] LIs and DBPs were affected by reduction in safe long-term interest rates induced by the PBOCs concentration of purchases of long-term securities. LIs and DBPs invest an inflow of current funds to meet long-term liabilities. A precipitous decline in interest rates—particularly long-term rates—poses a problem for these investors. They must earn from their existing capital and current inflows of premiums a sufficient return to meet the long-term obligations to which they committed at an earlier date. In the past, when they entered into their long-term obligations, they made an actuarial forecast that they could earn a return on their investments that exceeded some minimum that was required to meet their long-term payout obligations. Yet, long-term interest rates declined throughout the 1990s and the decline accelerated in the early 2000s. The yield on the benchmark constant maturity ten-year US Treasuries declined from 6.7 percent on January 1, 2000, to 3.54 percent on June 1, 2003 (see figure 7.5). The low

Table 7.1 Subprime mortgage exposures, 2008

	Total reported subprime exposure (US$bn)	*Percent of reported exposure*
Insurance companies	319	23
Mutual and pension funds	57	4
US commercial banks	250	18
US broker-dealers	75	5
US GSEs	112	8
US Hedge funds	233	17
Finance companies	95	7
Foreign banks	167	12
Foreign Hedge funds	58	4
Other (rounding)		2
Total	1,368	100

Note: The total for US commercial banks includes $95 billion of mortgage exposures by Household Finance, the US subprime subsidiary of HSBC. Moreover, the calculation assumes that US hedge funds account for four-fifths of all hedge fund exposures to subprime mortgages.

Source: Goldman Sachs. Authors' calculations. Derived from David Greenlaw, Jan Hatzius, Anil K. Kashya, and Hyun Song Shin, "Leveraged Losses :Lessons from the Mortgage Market Meltdown," Proceedings of the US Monetary Policy Forum, 2008, Exhibit 3.8, p. 35. Available at https://research.chicagobooth.edu/igm/docs/USMPF_FINAL_Print.pdf.

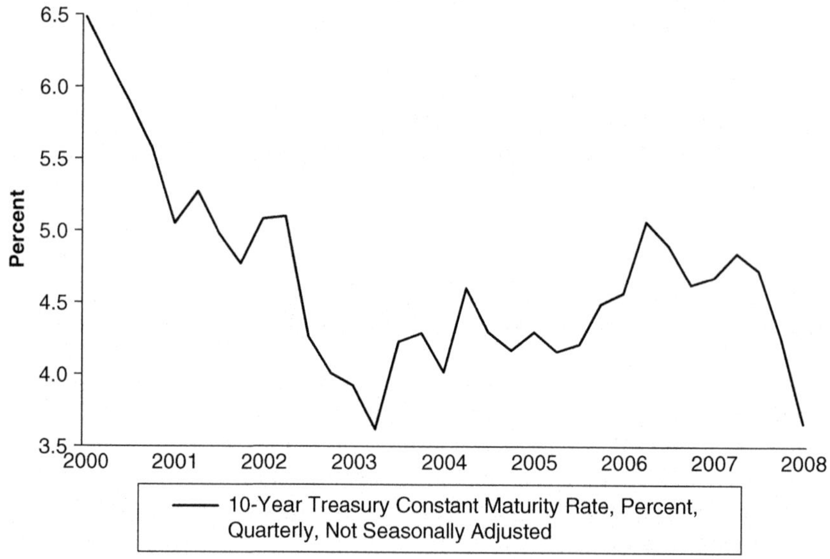

Figure 7.5 Ten-year treasury constant maturity rate, 2000–2008.
Source: Board of Governors of the Federal Reserve System.

rates reached in the early 2000s were below the forecasts made when the bulk of commitments were entered into. The unprecedentedly low rates placed many institutions at risk of insolvency.[45]

By the 2000s, these institutions came to realize that the lower rate environment was permanent, so they had to react. The low rates created pressure for them to "reach for yield" and make riskier investments for the prospect of earning a return adequate to meet their long-term liabilities. In order to avert the threat of insolvency, many of these institutions decided to invest in higher yielding, but riskier assets and to increase their leverage. Zoltan Pozsar noted,

> Underfunded pensions [were] the prime example of rising asset-liability mismatches in the financial ecosystem, and by extension, an ultimate source of reach for yield. Pension funds were one set of institutional investors that following the dot com bubble and subsequent decline in long-term interest rates drove the demand for products (such as levered fixed income and/or credit mutual funds, hedge funds and separate accounts) . . . with a mandate to beat the benchmark and promise equity-like returns with bond-like volatility.[46]

DBPs suffered a sudden reversal of fortune around 2000. Their net worth (measured as the funded ratio) rapidly plummeted into negative territory (figure 7.6) and their return on investment dropped significantly below their assumed returns (figure 7.7). In response DBPs attempted to boost returns by increasing their allocation to risky investments, including shifting allocations to special accounts, hedge funds and subprime mortgage securities. In particular, the weakest 10 percent of US public pension funds massively increased their allocations to risky assets from 2002 to 2008.[47]

Life insurers were constrained by regulation to invest primarily in investment grade debt. In a study focused on the corporate debt market, economists Bo Becker and Victoria Ivashina show that LIs tended to "reach for yield" by purchasing the highest yielding investment grade corporate bonds during the housing boom. The corporate debt favored by LIs was risky, as it had above average credit default spreads

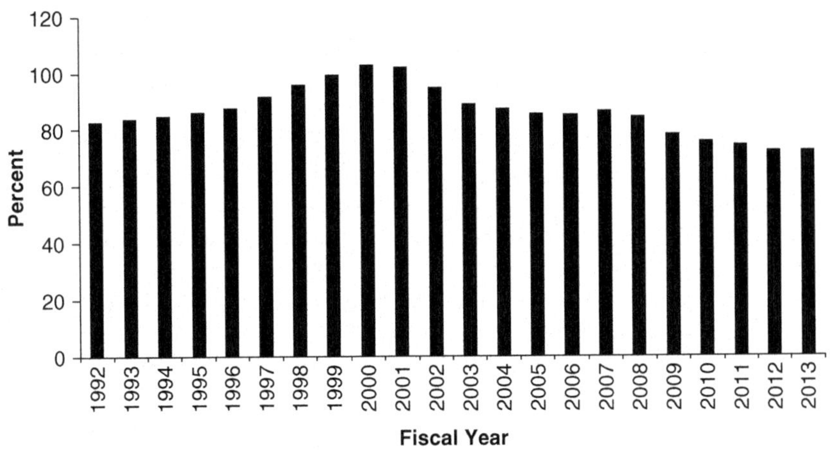

Figure 7.6 Actuarial ratio for public pensions, 1992–2013.

Note: The median discount rate for public pension plans was 8 percent from 1990 to 2011, and 7.75 percent in 2012.

Source: Public Plans Database, 2001–2013. Center for Retirement Research at Boston College, Center for State and Local Government Excellence, and National Association of State Retirement Administrators. http://publicplansdata.org/quick-facts/national/.

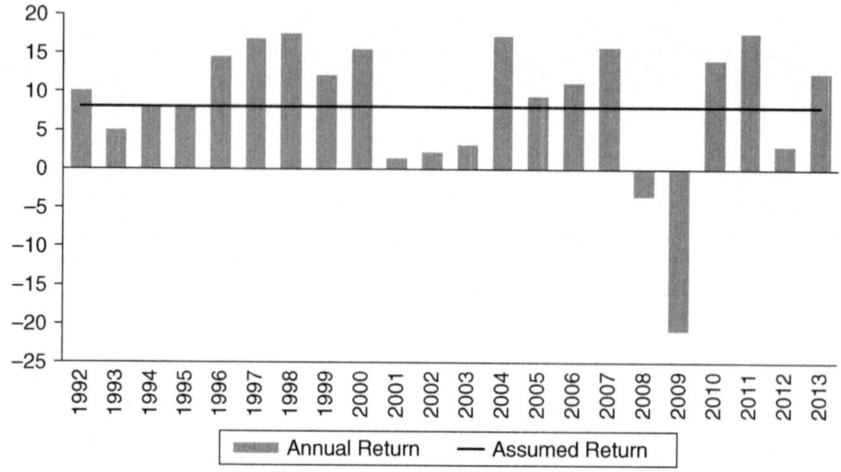

Figure 7.7 Annual return for state and local pensions, 1992–2013.

Source: Ricardo Caballero, "The Shortage of Safe Assets," slide for presentation at Bank of England, 2013, available at http://www.bankofengland.co.uk/research/Documents/ccbs/cew2013/presentation_caballero.pdf.

(for investment grade bonds). Becker and Ivashina also show that thinly capitalized LIs had the highest propensity to reach for yield.[48] LIs and DBPs were among the primary investors in investment grade tranches of subprime ABS and CDOs.[49]

The Bank Channel

Marriuchi and Nier, and Warnock showed that the capital flow bonanza compressed the maturity yield spread.[50] Since banks borrow short and lend long, a compression in the maturity yield spread reduces the net interest margin. Figure 7.8 shows that the net interest margin of large banks contracted throughout the housing boom, declining from a peak of nearly 4 percent to 3.1 percent.[51]

The decline in lending profits created an incentive for commercial banks to look for ways of making profits elsewhere. They did so in two ways. Banks increased mortgage lending, but the deposit growth required to fund the lending was constrained by the aversion of institutional cash pools to bank deposits. The growing demand for securitized assets provided a way for banks to use their loan origination capabilities and balance sheet strength to boost profits without having to grow their deposit base. They did so by selling loans they originated (or "sponsored") into ABS and providing guarantees of ABS debt—commonly referred to as "liquidity puts"—in order to attract investors. The liquidity puts were off balance sheet obligations and did not add to leverage as calculated by regulators. This meant bank were not required to raise capital—which would have diluted earnings—in order to engage in this activity. Moreover, there was no legal limitation on the volume of liquidity puts banks could issue. Economist Viral Acharya and his collaborators studied the characteristics of bank originations of ABS and concluded that they were a form of regulatory arbitrage in which the ultimate risks were retained by the bank sponsors through their guarantees.

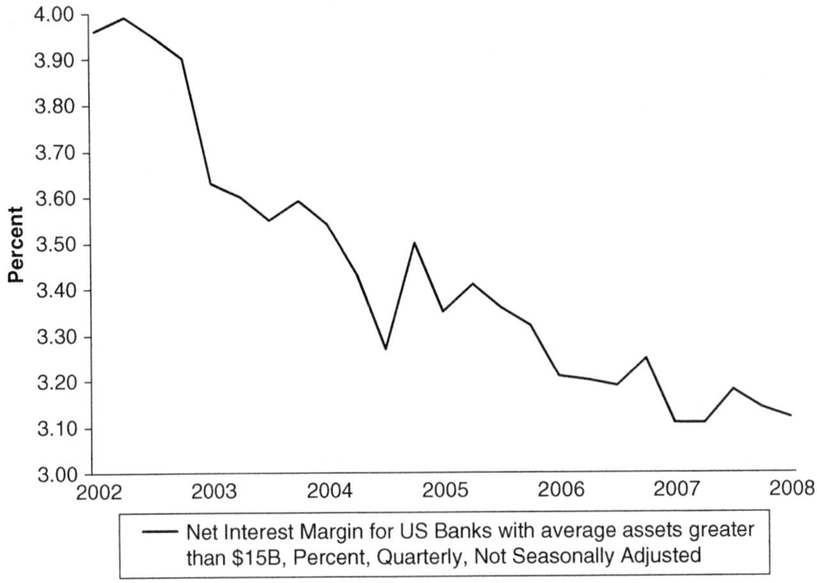

Figure 7.8 Net interest margin for large US banks, 2002–2008.
Source: Federal Financial Institutions Examination Council (US).

> Effectively, banks had used conduits to securitize assets without transferring the risks to outside investors; contrary to the common understandings of securitization as a method for risk transfer . . . banks instead used conduits for regulatory arbitrage.[52]

In addition, banks had to increase their holdings of subprime mortgages in order to engage in the business of ABS creation, since originated mortgages needed to be warehoused until a sufficient number had accumulated to create an ABS for sale. And banks were left holding the unrated junior tranche of cash flow from the ABS, since institutional investors were prevented by regulation from—investing in unrated securities. Finally, the adoption of Basle II capital adequacy rules by bank regulators helped facilitate the business, since it afforded banks wide latitude in setting the risk rating of retained assets. By rating the warehoused subprime mortgages and retained junior ABS tranches as relatively low risk, bank could minimize the capital they were required to set aside to support their holdings. Since bank capital must be held in ultra-safe, low yielding securities—or in zero yielding Fed reserves—banks needed to minimize the risk rating in order to make the business profitable. When the "music stopped" banks that had been engaged in the business of creating ABS suffered massive losses both from calls on their liquidity puts, and from write downs of their holding of subprime mortgages and unrated ABS paper.[53]

Broker-Dealers

Broker-dealer leverage exploded from 20X to 40X during the housing boom (see figure 2.2), but most of the expansion involved matched book intermediation with creditworthy counterparties. Therefore, the increase in broker-dealer leverage per se did not necessarily entail a substantial increase in risk. The primary losses suffered by broker-dealers during the financial crisis arose from the same source of loss for large commercial banks; their retention of warehoused subprime mortgages and unrated subprime mortgage ABS tranches, and the liquidity puts entered into on the ABS they sponsored. Merrill Lynch's 2007 balance sheet gives a sense of the magnitude of subprime mortgage exposure retained on balance sheet (table 5.1). The collapse of Bear Stearns in March 2008 demonstrates the significance of the off-balance sheet exposure to ABS, as it was caused by the losses it suffered on subprime securities Bear purchased in connection with a bailout of two of its sponsored ABS in August 2007.[54]

The GSE Channel

Another major investor in subprime mortgage backed securities were the GSEs: Fannie Mae and Freddie Mac. In chapter 5 I explained that the GSEs lagged behind the mortgage market in their acquisition of risky conforming loans and subprime mortgage securities. This pattern suggests the GSEs were not leaders, but rather were followers, among investors in subprime mortgages.

There is considerable debate over what motivated the GSEs to ultimately ramp up their exposure to higher risk conforming and subprime mortgages. One possible motivation had to do with the greed and pride of the GSE managers; a desire to retain the dominant market shares in all segment of the residential mortgage market. Another possible motivation was to address a risk that the US government might withdraw its implicit guarantee of GSE debt.

The Bush administration expressed concerns about anti-trust implications of the GSEs growing dominance of the home mortgage market and over the accounting scandals at both Fannie and Freddie that came to light in the early 2000s. The administration refused to appoint any board members at either GSE and made clear its desire to see Congress formally revoke the implicit government guarantee of GSE liabilities. In response to this threat, the GSE's intensified their lobbying to Congress and embarked on a highly publicized campaign to purchase more loans issued to low income households. Between 1999 and 2008 the GSEs spent $164 million on lobbying the US Congress.[55] Their appeal to Congress was that the GSEs were providing a social benefit by investing a portion of the excess profits earned from the artificially low borrowing cost afforded by their government guarantee on low income housing, which purely private mortgage lenders would not do.[56] So, while the exact mix of motives may be subject to debate, it is clear that the GSEs had rational, if unseemly, reasons to invest in risky subprime mortgage loans.

The Hedge Fund/Bond Fund Channel

Hedge funds competed with long only bond funds for investors—who included LIs and DBPs—and were generally less restricted in the strategies they could employ to achieve returns. They used leverage and derivatives to boost returns.

The decline in interest rates, risk spreads and volatility during the housing boom induced many hedge funds to reach for yield by taking on additional leverage and risk in order to meet their benchmark return targets.[57] This included significant investment in subprime mortgage ABS. A watershed moment for the movement toward the use of leverage in long only bond fund portfolios occurred in 2003 when Bill Gross, the colorful chairman of the largest bond fund PIMCO, wrote "Holy cow Batman [leveraged bond portfolios] can outperform stocks!"[58] Zoltan Pozsar pointed out,

> While hedge funds and separate accounts are allowed to use leverage liberally—in fact, leverage is the sine qua non of these investment vehicles—it is widely underappreciated that bond mutual funds that are typically thought of as unlevered and long-only also have considerable room to use leverage.[59]

Foreign Hedge Funds and Foreign Banks

At the end of chapter 4 I described a money flow in which US mutual funds lent to European banks, which purchased US ABS and other securities. The analysis here does not extend to the motives of those institutions, except for some cursory observations. A group of German banks, called Landesbanken, that had been subsidized and controlled by federal states, were forced by the EU in the early 2000s to wean themselves off of state guarantees. Their financial position was very weak and they were compelled to use the last dose of state guaranteed funding to reach for yield. One way of doing so was to invest in US subprime ABS and CDO.

The large banks and hedge funds based in Geneva, Paris, and London had a presence in all sectors of US finance, so it is unsurprising that their US subsidiaries were involved in all aspects of financing and investing in subprime mortgage securities.

The Household Channel

Subprime securities required willing borrowers, and moderate income households provided a plentiful source of demand. The areas where credit expanded most during the boom were subprime mortgages for new home acquisition and for "second mortgage" home equity borrowing. I described the characteristics and extent of subprime lending in chapter 5. The typical subprime borrower had lower income, a lower FICO score, a higher debt to income ratio and more recent credit problems than the typical prime mortgage loan borrower; and the loan-to-value ratio was higher for subprime loans than for prime loans (figure 5.2).[60] As a result, subprime loans were riskier for both the lender and the borrower.

I have shown that lenders and investors were motivated to fund subprime mortgage loans, but the incentives of borrowers to take on the additional risk remains to be explained. It is not difficult to think of some compelling reasons. For one, the high LTV ratios enabled millions of people to take a punt on a new home. The low down payment requirements (implied by the higher level of leverage) enabled borrowers to purchase an option on home appreciation for little money down. If home prices rose, they could become wealthy, and if not, they could walk away. A study by economist Amit Seru and his collaborators found that ten percent of non-agency mortgage loans in ABS issued during the housing boom were investor owned, despite being classified as owner-occupied, which suggests that a significant portion of borrowers were pure speculators.[61] Foote showed that over half of the foreclosures in Massachusetts in 2006 and 2007 were on homes in which the LTV at purchase exceeded 95 percent, and over a third were on homes in which the LTV at purchase was over 100 percent![62] The borrowers on these loans put little money down and took a punt. There was nothing manifestly irrational about doing so. For many borrowers it was a "heads I win, tails the lender loses" proposition. For millions of other people, Subprime loans provided an opportunity for home ownership that was otherwise unobtainable. It is understandable that many people were willing to seize a once in a lifetime opportunity, even if they recognized they were taking on considerable risk.

The motives of those people who already owned homes and elected to pull money out in home equity loans, is more difficult to discern. According to Main and Sufi, over half of the increase in homeowner debt during the housing boom came from borrowing against the increased value of their homes.[63] Two features of this type of borrowing have been documented. One is that most home equity borrowing was undertaken by low credit score, low income growth borrowers.[64] The other is that most of the money extracted from home equity loans was used for home improvement and consumption.[65] This behavior seems reckless in hindsight. These borrowers had an equity cushion in their homes; a cushion that could, among other things, provide a source of rainy day money. But they apparently chose to spend it away during good times. It would appear imprudent for them to increase debt when they faced diminishing ability to repay. However, there is a long-standing pattern of people increasing their spending when the value of their homes rise.[66] So, the decision to increase borrowing against home value increases can be seen as ecologically rational in the sense that the behavior produced satisfactory results in the past.

Beginning in 2003 household net worth literally took off (figure 7.9) and by 2006 had increased by over 40 percent. That constituted a huge windfall.[67] With a 40 percent increase in overall wealth and significant gain in home equity, it is understandable that people felt comfortable increasing their consumption. In chapter 9 I shall describe the theory that suggests people tend to spend more when their wealth has increased. Moreover, since home prices had never before (since the Great Depression) declined significantly, households may have felt they were borrowing against an irreversible increase in the value of their home.[68] The possibility that some (maybe very many) home equity borrowers behaved irrationally cannot be ruled out. But I do not think the evidence warrants the conclusion that that was the only possible motive for the majority of borrowers.

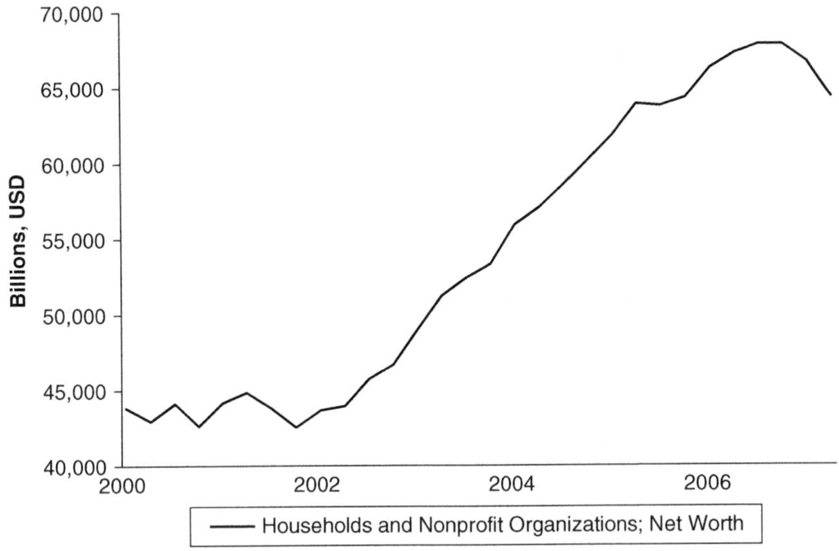

Figure 7.9 Households and nonprofit organizations—net worth level, 2000–2008.
Source: Board of Governors of the Federal Reserve System.

A Summary of How the Current Account Deficit Caused the Housing Boom

To summarize the argument in this chapter so far; the current account deficit created a fundamental disturbance to the US economy by shifting production offshore while sending a huge flow of saving into the US capital market. Most of the capital flow bonanza was invested in US government-guaranteed debt, which pushed down yields and spreads, crowded out other investors and forced them to seek out safe investments elsewhere. Limitations on deposit insurance channeled the crowded out funds into institutional cash pools in the shadow banking sector. These institutional cash pools were seeking safe liquid investments. Meanwhile, the reduction in yields and spreads placed DBPs and LIs at risk of insolvency, and bond funds and hedge funds at risk of underperforming their benchmarks. In response, bond investors "reached for yield" by increasing leverage and allocations to risky assets and by lending securities. Commercial banks and broker-dealers responded to the desire of bond investors to achieve higher yield and institutional cash pools to have more safe liquid securities by manufacturing ABS and CDOs out of subprime mortgages, which could be sold to bond investors and then used as collateral in overnight repo transactions with institutional cash pools that were intermediated by broker-dealers.

Finally, the increased demand for mortgages interacted with willing borrowers to cause increases in home prices, home construction (via the operation of Tobin's Q) and increased consumer spending. The latter two effects filled the "hole in demand" created by the current account deficit and propelled then US economy toward full employment.

The Rationale behind Subprime Mortgages

Why Subprime Mortgage Loans?

I have shown that the lenders who were on the prowl to make riskier loans; the investors who were willing to fund them, and the homeowners who borrowed the loans, all behaved in an ecologically rational manner. But it still needs to be understand why it was subprime loans that were selected to fill the hole in demand. Why was not some other type of asset selected? It was not inevitable that investors would find anything suitable to fill the hole in demand. If they had not found anything, there would have been a contraction in credit and high unemployment. There must have been *something* uniquely compelling about housing, something to pique the interest and win over the seasoned and intelligent managers of financial institutions.

The investment case for subprime mortgages was disarmingly straightforward. If one looked at the past performance of subprime mortgage loans, one would note two prominent features: First, default rates of home loans in different regions of the US did not move together. When defaults were rising in New York, for example, they were not likely to be rising in Los Angeles. This created an opportunity to reduce the risk of investing in home loans by assembling a portfolio of loans spread across all regions of the United States. If assembled in this way, the average fluctuation in defaults would go down; Los Angeles would cancel out New York.[69] Second, while the default on subprime loans was historically higher than prime loans, it was not *that* much higher. What that meant in practice was that, after taking account of the higher default rate and setting the "risk adjusted" interest rate to match the interest rate paid on other securities bearing similar risk ratings, the resultant interest rate was considerably below what banks were able to charge for such loans. These attributes created an opportunity to make a profit from assembling interregional portfolios of subprime loans into securities to sell to investors.

Another factor that encouraged investment in subprime mortgages is that they were preferred by the ratings agencies. This was an important feature because many of the investors were regulated institutions—like money market funds and LIs—who were restricted to investment grade securities. Prior to the housing boom, ABS (and the CDOs that invested in ABS) were collateralized by many other types of assets; including manufactured housing, franchise loans and aircraft leases. The loans on these other types of assets performed poorly during the 2001 recession, but subprime mortgages performed well. As a result, the rating agencies were willing to confer higher credit ratings on subprime mortgage backed ABS and CDOs.[70] By dividing the revenue stream of the subprime ABS into a hierarchy of tranches, it became possible to obtain investment grade ratings on all but the most junior tranche. The investment grade rating enabled regulated investors to purchase the securities. The issuers retained the unrated junior portion, but they felt they were adequately compensated for the risk inherent in the junior tranche by the profit they earned from assembling the securitizations and selling off the senior tranches.

Nevertheless, subprime securities were not the only conceivable investment that could have fulfilled the "reach for yield." The attribute that singled out subprime mortgages as unique among the wide range of securitized assets that were created in the 2000s, was the ability to manufacture investment grade mortgage securities at an industrial scale. This was made possible by the overwhelmingly positive response of borrowers. It was the household mortgage borrowers who provided the crucial ingredient that fuelled the subprime boom.

The Neglect of Keynes's Insights into Uncertainty and Animal Spirits

In the last chapter I explained how the growth of market finance, and the fact that almost all subprime mortgages were financed through ABS, increased the role of animal spirits in determining mortgage prices. I provided theoretical reasons and experimental evidence showing that the movement of loans away from "hold to maturity" bank loans, into tradable securities, increased the possibilities of large and long-lasting deviations from fundamental value, along lines that Keynes had written about.[71]

Keynes's insights into the influence of animal spirits on securities prices has been rediscovered, and embraced by many economists after the financial crisis. It is useful to recall, however, that his ideas on this matter had been long discarded prior to the financial crisis. Economists believed that packaging mortgages together and dividing the resultant income streams into tranches enabled investors to construct portfolios with risk profiles that better matched their preferences and their ability to withstand losses on securities. The diversification of risk enabled by converting mortgages into tradable assets was supposed to make the economy more efficient and more resilient. That lesson was embedded in the canonical models of finance taught in business schools and university economics departments all over the world. Keynes's ideas about animal spirits and herd mentalities were the stuff of legend, surviving only in esoteric tomes on ancient economic thought. Uncertainty was ignored by economists for the same reason Keynes thought it was ignored by investors; it cannot be quantified. At the onset of the financial crisis, in May of 2007, Federal Reserve chairman Ben Bernanke reflected the economists' point of view when he expressed confidence that the shift to market finance and the diversification of risk it presumably promoted, ensured that the spike in defaults of subprime mortgages would not cause disruption to the economy:

> Regulatory changes and other developments have permitted lenders to more easily sell mortgages to financial intermediaries, who in turn pool mortgages and sell the cash flows as structured securities. These securities typically offer various risk profiles and durations to meet the investment strategies of a wide range of investors. The growth of the secondary market has thus given mortgage lenders greater access to the capital markets, lowered transaction costs, *and spread risk more broadly.* [emphases added][72]

Table 7.1 shows Mr. Bernanke to have been profoundly wrong about the impact the shift to market finance had on diversifying risk. Securitization did not disperse subprime mortgage risk. Rather, risk remained concentrated in the financial sector, as Professor Shin noted in the quote at the beginning of this chapter.[73] That concentration of risk is something modern economic theory cannot explain. It would not surprise Keynes, however, to whom it was a predictable result of the herd nature of animal spirits operating in securities markets.

The Collapse of Housing

The Risk Created by Declining Productivity Growth

An important factor that contributed to the risk of financial crisis in the mid-2000s was the toxic combination of increased business and household borrowing during a period when in US productivity growth was in decline and real interest rates were already low.[74]

Real interest rates reflect the return that can be earned on investment, and if rates are low to begin with, adding more investment can only push returns down near zero, where investment is not productive (assuming, of course, that the economy is not experiencing deflation). The combination of declining productivity growth and low interest rates in the 2000s suggests that the United States had a limited capacity to support an increase in investment. To the extent the US economy channeled the capital flow bonanza into increased investment, much of the increase was predestined to turn out to be unprofitable. To the extent that the US economy channeled the capital flow bonanza into household borrowing, the low potential growth rate implied an elevated risk that borrowers would be unable to generate the future earnings required to repay their debt. In the event, the capital flow bonanza was channeled into safe investments, but triggered a rebalancing of portfolios of financial intermediaries that resulted in an increase in lending to households on risky home investments. During the housing boom, leverage and risk were rising as productivity growth was falling—a combination that set the stage for the crisis that followed.

The Devolution of the Housing Market

The implosion of the housing market was very rapid. In 2008 alone, prices declined by nearly 20 percent (and they would decline by another 10 percent thereafter). From 2007 to 2009 the number of mortgages with negative equity shot up from just over 5 percent to 24 percent and an additional 20 percent were near negative equity. Negative equity was concentrated in lower priced homes. Foreclosure is highly correlated with negative equity. Nearly 40 percent of homes with negative equity had ARM mortgages that were originated during the housing boom.[75] These characteristics make it look as if the subprime lending during the housing boom was a colossal error. That is why, as I explained in chapter 5, many analysts have searched for evidence of malfeasance to explain the subprime boom, while others have shrugged their shoulders in disbelief and attributed it to "irrational behavioral tendencies." I, on the other hand, choose to search for rational motives.

The Achilles heel for the subprime home lending turns out not to have been any flaw in the data used to calculate default probabilities, or the analysis of the data; it was what was not in the data. Prior to the onset of the boom, subprime was a small percentage of the housing market and trend home prices had been rising since the end of World War II. The small market share implied that the behavior of subprime borrowers had little influence on home prices, and the trend of rising prices meant that a subprime borrower who was unable to make her payments could usually recoup enough money from the sale of her home to repay her mortgage loan, which dampened the default rate.

The subprime boom was a major innovation that altered the dynamics of the housing market. It involved a dramatic rise in subprime mortgages as a share of total mortgage securities—from 4 percent in 2000 to 25 percent in 2006. Subprime and Alt-A originations rose to 13 percent of total mortgage originations in 2006.[76] The growth in market share increased the influence of subprime borrowers on housing prices. A number of studies have concluded that the wave of foreclosures that began in 2007 was not caused by the uptick in delinquencies, but rather the driving force was the collapse in home prices. Foote provided an illustration of the distinction between delinquencies and foreclosures by showing that in the early 2000s delinquencies in Massachusetts increased by 40 percent, while foreclosures actually fell. In the mid-2006–2007, by contrast, delinquencies again spiked and this time foreclosures did so too (figure 7.10).

The reason foreclosures declined in the early 2000s and rose in the mid-2000s is that Massachusetts home prices appreciated in the early 2000s and plummeted in 2006–2007 (figure 7.11).[77]

This pattern is what one would expect to see. When home prices are rising, delinquent borrowers have an escape valve; they can avoid foreclosure by selling their homes for an amount sufficient to pay off their mortgage. On the other hand, when home prices are declining, delinquent borrowers are likely to allow their homes to go into foreclosure. Punters walk away when the value of their option becomes negative. The equity of highly leveraged homeowners quickly becomes negative when home values decline, which makes it impossible to sell

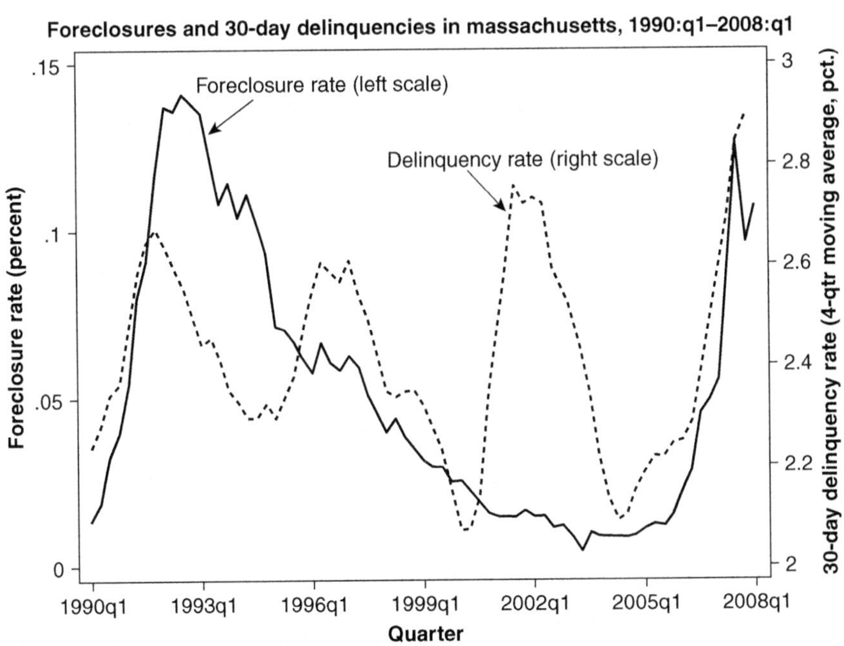

Figure 7.10 MA foreclosures versus defaults, 1990–2008.

Source: Christopher Foot et al. "Subprime Facts: What (We Think) We Know about the Subprime Crisis and What We Don't" Federal Reserve Bank of Boston, Public Policy Discussion Papers No. 08–2, 2008, Figure 6, p. 21.

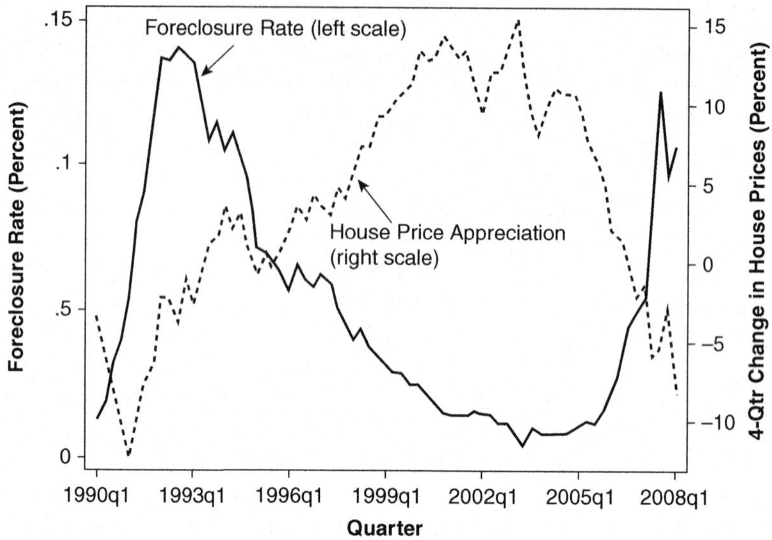

Figure 7.11 MA foreclosures versus home price, 1990–2008.

Source: Christopher Foot et al. "Subprime Facts: What (We Think) We Know about the Subprime Crisis and What We Don't" Federal Reserve Bank of Boston, Public Policy Discussion Papers No. 08-2, 2008, Figure 5, p. 20.

at a price sufficiently high to cover their mortgage obligation. As a result, their best option is to default when they become unable to meet their monthly payments; and foreclosure follows default.

The question of what caused the initial decline in home prices remains. There were two powerful forces interacting in a self-reinforcing way; the physical housing market and the market for mortgage backed securities. The increase in delinquencies and the oversupply of new homes was undoubtedly the precipitating cause, since mortgage values reacted to the state of the physical market. The increase in supply of homes was driven by two forces: the spike in subprime market share, which resulted in an increase in the number of delinquent mortgage borrowers needing to sell their homes, and the construction of new homes, which had increased dramatically. These two forces generated a large supply of vacant homes. The increased supply of homes for sale eventually overwhelmed the increase in demand created by the spread of subprime mortgages, and home prices began to fall (figure 7.12).

The decline in prices wiped out the equity in many highly leveraged homes, which induced punters to walk away. But even before mortgage defaults rose by a significant amount, mortgage security investors became worried—this is where depressed animal spirits come into play—and pushed down the price of mortgage backed securities.[78] Investors became worried about home price declines and defaults by subprime borrowers. As a result, they shunned securities backed by highly leveraged loans and/or high risk borrowers. This fed back to the physical housing market, as it pushed down leverage on new loans and cut off lending to subprime borrowers (figure 7.13). This sent the leverage cycle into reverse gear. John Geanakoplos described the down-phase of the leverage cycle:

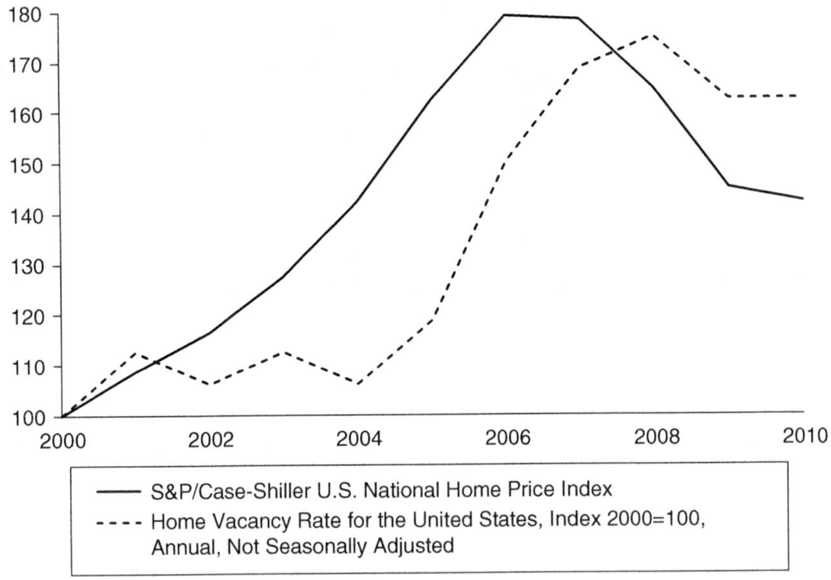

Figure 7.12 Home vacancy rates and home prices, 2000–2010.

Sources: S&P Case Shiller and US Census.

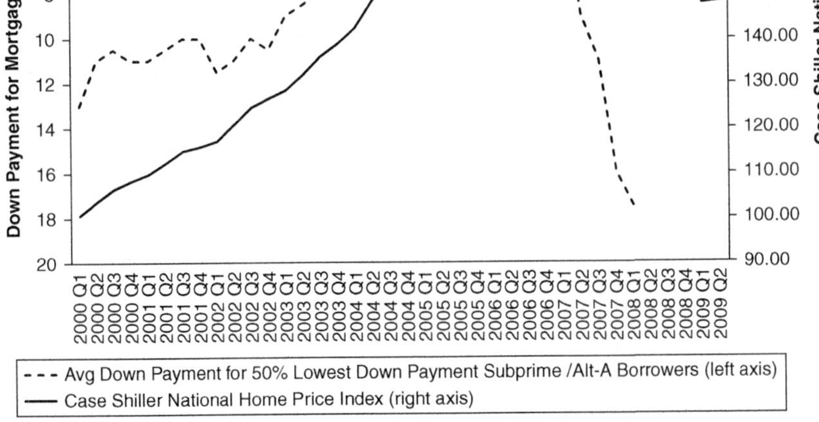

Figure 7.13 Margins offered (down payments required) and housing prices, 2000–2009.

Source: John Geanakoplos, "Leverage, Default, and Forgiveness: Lessons from the American and European Crises," *Journal of Macroeconomics*, Vol. 39 (2014): 313–333, Figure 3, 321.

> The feedback from falling security prices to higher margins on housing loans to lower house prices and the then back to tougher margins on securities and to lower security prices and then back again to housing is what I call "the double leverage cycle."[79]

Conclusion

The advent of subprime mortgage lending on a large scale so altered the characteristics of the housing market as to render prior performance meaningless as a predictor of future performance. *This* is what the market got wrong. Once the market share of subprime loans became significant, the elevated level of delinquencies of subprime borrowers, the reduction in the home equity cushion and the over-expansion of new home construction, created conditions for an excess supply of homes for sale that would cause home prices to plunge throughout the United States. Once prices began to fall, leverage and lending contracted, which created a negative feedback loop between the physical housing market and the mortgage securities market.

Ultimately, it was the toxic interaction between bond investors who were forced by the capital flow bonanza to reach for yield, and institutional cash pools, for whom the capital flow bonanza created a safe asset shortage, which triggered the housing boom and heightened the risk of financial crisis. The chain of reaction set in motion by the capital flow bonanza elevated the probability of financial crisis for two reasons. One reason is that investors took on greater risk to boost returns, and the other reason is that US productivity growth was slowing, which meant that returns on investment were falling.

Yet, it is also important to recognize that the capital flow bonanza did not *require* the United States to increase spending. It is possible the capital flow bonanza could have saturated the US economy with saving; pushed interest rates to their lower bound without generating sufficient amount of investment or consumption to achieve full employment, and left the economy in a low employment liquidity trap. In fact, this is what occurred in the aftermath of the dotcom boom, until the enthusiasm over subprime mortgages sparked another investment led boom. A liquidity trap may also have contributed to the slow recovery after the financial crisis.

CHAPTER 8

The Role of Policy during the Housing Boom

In the long run we are all dead.

—J. M. Keynes

It is the consensus opinion that monetary policy and banking regulation contributed to the boom. The charge lodged against the Fed is that it held the Fed funds rate too low for too long; that its loose monetary policy exacerbated the credit boom. There is a simple answer to this charge. The Fed had no choice but to do so. Its mandate from Congress required it to support employment to the maximum extent possible, subject to maintaining price stability. In the early 2000s, after the dot-com boom had ended, the current account deficit began to grow rapidly, which caused the hole in demand to expand and created deflationary pressure. The recovery from the 2001 recession was slow and tepid. It was dubbed a "jobless" recovery at the time. As late as 2004 Ben Bernanke, then a member of the Fed's board of governors (but not yet it chairman), posed the question:

> Two-and-a-half years into the economic recovery, the pace of job creation in the United States has been distressingly slow. Job losses in manufacturing have been particularly deep, with employment in that sector apparently only now beginning to stabilize after falling by almost 3 million jobs since 2000. Why has the recovery been largely jobless thus far?[1]

The fundamental problem faced by the Fed (whether or not the members of its policymaking Open Market Committee recognized it at the time) was that the large current account deficit presented it with a Faustian bargain; either to induce a deflationary monetary contraction in order to enable the US economy to adjust the terms of trade with China and reduce the trade deficit (since lower prices US goods would be more competitive on world markets), or to acquiesce in the expansion caused by the capital flow bonanza, albeit at the cost of accommodating a potentially destabilizing credit boom.[2] There was no third option, and the Fed would have violated its mandate, and most assuredly provoked intense Congressional opposition, if it had chosen deflation. Chinese mercantilism had placed the United States in a predicament where it could not simultaneously maintain internal balance (full employment) and external balance (equality of exports and imports). Keynes acutely diagnosed the dilemma faced by the Fed nearly a century ago:

> If we are dealing with a closed system, so that there is only the condition of internal equilibrium to fulfill, an appropriate banking policy is always capable of preventing any serious disturbances to the status quo from developing at all . . . But when the condition of external equilibrium must also be fulfilled, then there will be no banking policy capable of avoiding disturbance to the internal system.[3]

The economics profession has been subjected to vituperative criticism for its near unanimous support, at the time, of the Feds' accommodation of the housing boom. There are three things to be said in answer to this criticism. The first is that any verdict on Fed policy must contend with the one unambiguous lesson of the Great Depression: That is was caused by a monetary contraction that precipitated a violent deflation.[4] That was the trauma the central bank had to ensure would never happen again. In 2002, Ben Bernanke delivered a famous speech entitled "Deflation: Making Sure 'It' Doesn't Happen Here,"[5] which was meant to reassure financial markets that the Fed had not lost its vigilance to avoid deflation. During the housing boom, goods prices were barely trending above deflationary levels, so that any attempt to slow growth risked triggering a descent into deflation. The Fed's highest priority was to ensure that did not happen.

The second point is that the Fed had lost its ability to raise interest rates, which meant it lost its ability to rein in credit growth. The Fed set the Fed funds rate very low during the 2001 recession, but when it raised the Fed funds rate, beginning in 2005, long-term rates barely budged, which then chairman Alan Greenspan famously called a "conundrum." The current theory of central banking posits that, in normal conditions, the leverage point for the Fed lies not in its influence over monetary aggregates, but in its influence over interest rates. By setting the Fed funds rate, which is the rate at which the Fed lends to commercial banks, economists believe the Fed can effectively determine both the short-term and long-term interest rates throughout the economy. The idea is that the Fed funds rate determines other safe short-term interest rates, such as LIBOR and three month treasuries[6] and that, by setting expectations as to the future path of the Fed funds rate, the Fed can effectively determine the entire maturity spectrum of interest rates in the economy. It can do so, since arbitrage ensures that a long-term interest rate is equal to the succession of short-term rates that lie between the present and the term of the long rate, with an added amount to cover maturity risk.[7] That is why the Fed's apparent loss of influence over long-term rates in 2005–2006 is so troubling to economists. It appears to contradict their theory.

There are several possible explanations for the Fed's loss control over long-term interest rates. One is the influence of the foreign capital inflows, as documented by Warnock and the Fed economists.[8] Recall that offshore purchases of long term debt accelerated from 2005 to 2007, when the Fed was attempting to push up rates. Another possible explanation for the Fed's loss of influence comes from the changing relationship of money and credit. Broad money—M2 and MZM—and credit have been undergoing a significant decoupling for the past half century. While broad money as a percentage of GDP has remained relatively stable, total nonfinancial sector credit as a percentage of GDP has increased markedly, from under 100 percent of GDP in 1980 to over 1.6 times GDP at the height of the housing boom.[9] While the Fed retains its influence over broad money—from its ability to change the volume of bank deposits through creation of bank reserves and from its regulation of required bank reserve and capital ratios—it has no direct influence over the shadow banking sector, and only indirect influence (through capital regulations) over commercial bank lending that is funded by nondeposit borrowing in the wholesale loan market. Zoltan Pozsar points out that the Fed has been losing influence over liquidity as the shadow banking sector generates near-money substitutes.[10]

The perception that the Fed has lost the ability to control credit, alongside recent research showing a linkage between credit booms and financial crisis, lends credence to the idea that regulators should be given tools to control the expansion of credit.[11] The fundamental appeal of this approach stems from the observation that credit conditions have become more important to macroeconomic performance relative to monetary conditions, and that monetary policy has questionable influence over credit conditions.[12]

The third point in response to criticism of economist's support of Fed policy during the boom is that allowing the housing boom to proceed may actually have been a wise policy choice (to the extent there was any choice) at the time. Even if regulators had tools to control credit expansion during the housing boom, there is a question of whether they should have used those powers to reduce the growth of credit (or leverage). It is not at all clear that they should have. The current account deficit created a hole in demand that was filled by the housing boom. In its absence employment would have been lower. The consequence of restraining credit would have been tantamount to choosing to increase (and perhaps increase drastically) unemployment in exchange for reducing the probability of a future financial crisis (from a low probability to a lower probability).[13] It is not obvious that it would have been a tradeoff worth making. Since the financial crisis, economists have changed their stripes and now universally condemn the housing boom. But they have failed to take account of the consequence of slowing credit in the presence of the large current account deficit. They condemn the bubble in ignorance of the damage their recommendation would have inflicted on laid-off workers.

Regulators are criticized for having failed to pick up on risks in the regulated banking system, particularly those connected to the growth of derivatives and off balance sheet underwriting of mortgage securities. These innovative activities increased the off balance sheet risk exposure that added opacity to bank balance sheets and contributed to the collapse of interbank lending during the crisis. Yet all indicators of risk—VIX, VaR, and the risk yield spreads—reflected a market judgment that risk had materially declined. It is not reasonable to suppose that a regulator would have been able to discern growing risk under these circumstances, or that anyone would have given credence to any counsel to mitigate risk. Nor was it obvious that the housing boom was sending the economy off its rails. If it was obvious, more well-heeled investors would have bet against the boom.[14] Finally, Merrouche and Nier's findings that loose monetary policy and lax regulation cannot account for the expansion in credit or the increase in home prices during the housing boom, undermines the relevance of any criticism of monetary or regulatory policy during the housing boom.

With knowledge of the financial crisis that subsequently occurred, it is easy to issue an indictment against monetary policymakers and financial regulators for their actions (or in-action) during the housing boom. It is much more difficult to prove the charges when placed in the context of their limited knowledge, the tradeoff they faced between current unemployment and future risk of financial crisis, and the evident impotence of the tools at their disposal.

PART III

Accumulation and Secular Stagnation: Identifying the Underlying Malady

In part III, I propose a deep explanation for the patterns of economic volatility and low trend growth that has plagued the United States since the late 1990s. In order to account for these patterns, I introduce the concept of Accumulation, which occurs when some agents save more than they intend to spend later on.

Chapter 9 lays out the theory linking Accumulation to deflation, contraction, and cycles of boom followed by crisis. Chapter 10 explains how the mercantilist policies of Southeast Asia and China prevalent during the housing boom were forms of Accumulation. It also conjectures that the top income earners engage in Accumulation. It then links these forces of Accumulation to the phenomena of secular stagnation that has characterized US economic performance since the late 1990s.

CHAPTER 9

Accumulation and Secular Stagnation: Part I, Theory

> Consumption is the sole end and purpose of all production.
>
> —Adam Smith[1]

> It has also been said, that there is never an indisposition to consume, that the indisposition is to produce. Yet, what is the disposition of those master manufacturers, and merchants who produce very largely and consume sparingly?
>
> —Thomas Robert Malthus[2]

To provide motivation for the theory linking Accumulation to secular stagnation, I review the unexpected breakdown in the transmission of monetary policy that occurred during the late stages of the US housing boom, when long-term interest rates failed to respond to increases in the Fed funds rate. According to the prevailing paradigm of macroeconomics, of which economist Michael Woodford's textbook *Interest and Prices* is considered an authoritative source, the breakdown was not expected to occur, in the sense that the Fed was supposed to be able to set the maturity curve of nominal interest rates by manipulation of the overnight Fed funds rate. Professor Woodford explained that

> determination of the overnight interest rate would also have to imply determination of the equilibrium holding return on longer-lived securities, up to a correction for risk; and so determination of the expected future path of overnight interest rates would essentially determine longer-term interest rates.[3]

It is possible to argue, as I have, that the Fed had lost control of interest rates ever since the current account deficit took off in the late 1990s. But prior to the period when the Fed began to increase the Fed funds rate in 2004, there was no inconsistency between monetary policy—which aimed at low interest rates—and long-term market interest rates (which were low). That was no longer the case after the Fed began to raise the overnight rate.

Greenspan's "Conundrum"—The Dog That Didn't Bark

One of the typical features of business cycles is that interest rates are low at the beginning of the expansion and rise (along with price inflation) throughout the expansion.[4] The increase in rates is driven by competition among entrepreneurs and companies for a limited pool of savings, labor and capital goods, and by households for consumer goods. The expansion phase often ends when the central bank reacts to the inflationary pressure caused by the increase in demand by ratcheting up its policy interest rate. The increase in borrowing costs renders some projects unprofitable and some borrowers unfinanceable, which causes credit, and employment, to contract. The slowdown in credit growth marks the end of the boom. This view has a long and distinguished tradition. Knut Wicksell first propounded it in the late 1800s; F. A. Hayek refined and deepened the theory in the 1930s.[5]

The core of the Wicksell/Hayek theory of business cycles is the proposition that declines in real interest rates (relative to the expected return on investment) start booms.[6] Investment projects take time to complete and require funding in advance of realizing revenue (workers need to be paid every two weeks, etc.). Cheap credit reduces the cost of financing projects, which increases the present value of future earnings. An increase in present value will cause some previously marginal projects to appear profitable. The perception of profitability induces firms to undertake more projects. In our era of consumer borrowing (which largely did not exist in the 1930s), lower interest rates also enhance the borrowing capacity of households and reduce the amount of future consumption that must be forgone to repay the debt incurred by increasing current consumption. These forces cause investment and consumption to move inversely with real interest rates.[7]

Later on, when rates rise, as they will eventually do, the theory predicts some of those previously marginal projects, which were commenced due to the initially low rates, become unprofitable once more, and are abandoned.[8] When projects are abandoned—think of acres of empty lots and houses at the end of the housing boom—workers get laid off and remain unemployed until new projects, requiring additional labor, get launched. In the interim, unemployment swells.[9] The longer the boom goes on, according to this theory, the higher inflation will rise and the deeper will be the recession that follows, since the passage of time increases the volume of projects—all of which take time to complete—that are started and then abandoned in the crash. The waste and unemployment caused by the abandonment of uncompleted projects, along with other inefficiencies induced by inflation, provide compelling reasons for the central bank to put a stop to the boom early on by raising interest rates. A US Fed chairman named William Machesney Martin famously stated that the most vital function of the central bank was to "take away the punch bowl" when the party looked to be getting out of hand, so as to limit the amount of overinvestment and inflation, and thereby reduce the severity of the resultant downturn.

Yet, the housing boom did not match this "typical" fact pattern in one crucial respect. Although real interest rates were low at the onset of the boom and the landscape was littered with abandoned projects at the end of it (which accords with the prediction of Wicksell/Hayek theory) once the boom got under way the key benchmark interest rate (the US government constant maturity ten-year treasury yield) did not rise, as the theory predicts it should have. Instead, the ten-year treasury yield increased only modestly at the end of the boom. In fact, its rise at the end of the expansion that took place during the housing boom was the lowest of any post–World War II boom, even though the Fed raised the Fed funds rate, as it had near the end of all prior expansions.

What happened? It was not the case that the Fed did not try to "take away the punch bowl." It began raising the Fed funds rate in mid-2004, but this time long-term rates did not follow suit (figure 9.1). The Fed lifted its policy rate over the next two years from 1 percent to 5 percent and yet the ten-year treasury yield barely budged. Fed chairman Alan Greenspan was perplexed; this had never happened before. He called the Fed's inability to influence the ten-year treasury yield a "conundrum."[10] Credit and leverage continued to grow and the issuance of subprime mortgages peaked in 2006/07 at the same time as the Fed interest rate hit its peak. Mr. Greenspan correctly dismissed a number of explanations that were

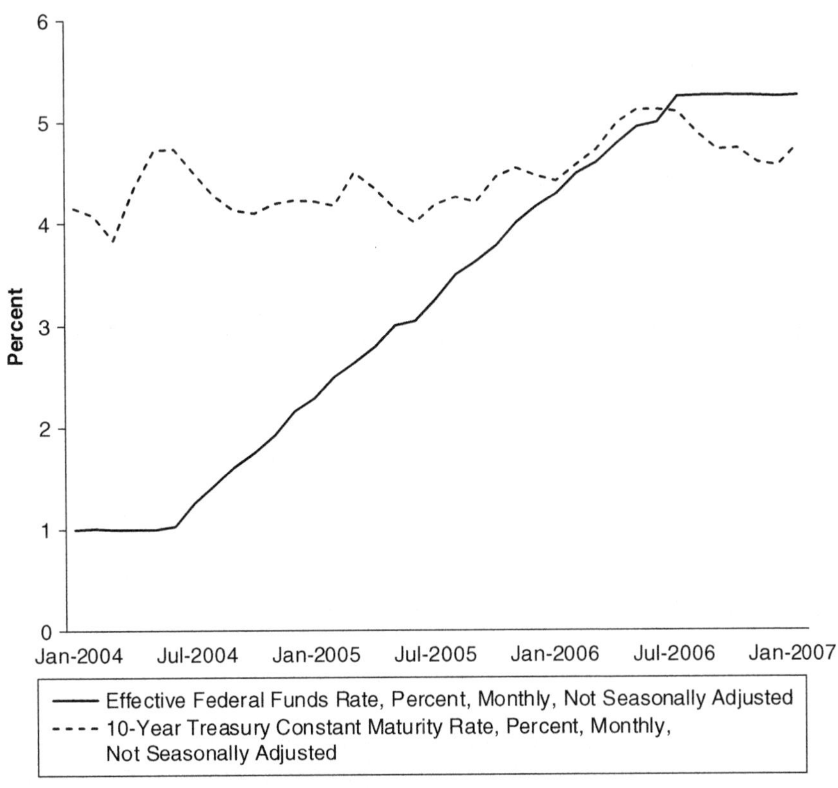

Figure 9.1 Fed funds rate, ten-year treasury yield, 2004–2007.

Source: Board of Governors of the Federal Reserve System.

proposed at the time. He refuted the idea that low inflation expectations had caused long-term equilibrium nominal interest rates to suddenly decline—which might otherwise explain why treasury yields merely treaded water when the Fed funds rate was increased—by noting that inflation expectations had been low for many years prior to the Fed funds rate increase. He refuted the idea that treasury yields failed to rise because the market had already anticipated the rate rise by pointing out that treasury yields did not rise prior to, and therefore in anticipation of, the Fed funds rate increases. Nor, he argued, was it likely that long-term yields failed to react because investors had suddenly become uncertain about the future path of the Fed funds rate. To the contrary, the Fed had begun to provide markets with forward guidance on rates, which meant uncertainty over the future path of interest rates should have been lower than ever before. Economist Axel Leijonhufvud pithily summarized the Fed's impotence: "If you hike the Bank rate 13 or 14 times—I lost count—and the market pays not the slightest attention but leaves the long rate flat, *how powerful are you really?*"[11]

The fact that long-term interest rates did not rise appreciably toward the end of the housing boom is a central riddle that has—inexplicably—gone mostly unrecognized. It was the "dog that didn't bark," and any satisfactory explanation of the causes of the housing boom must account for it. Why did this boom, which preceded the most spectacular crash and the deepest contraction since the Great Depression, meet its end—insofar as interest rates are concerned—with not a bang, but with a whimper?

Defining "Accumulation" and "Secular Stagnation"

I will show that the type of current account deficit that emerged—a product of its large size and its mercantilist origin—introduced a new and historically unprecedented element into the US economy, and that this element may have been magnified by the concurrent reemergence of a significant concentration of income among a small group of US residents. This new element explains the "jobless" recovery from the 2001 recession, the ongoing stagnation in US employment for years after the onset of the financial crisis, and the stagnation in nonhousing US investment spending since the turn of the millennium. The essential idea, whose antecedents trace back to an early-nineteenth-century economist named Thomas Robert Malthus, is that an excess of saving can materialize if people and institutions that accumulate a large share of income have a high propensity to save and do not intend to spend all of their savings in the future. The saving behavior of these groups will cause a deficiency of demand that will either materialize early on, if firms anticipate a shortfall of future demand and curtail their investment plans, or it will occur later on after the investment projects have been completed and the lack of sales cause borrowers to default, triggering a financial crisis.

In this chapter, I articulate the theory that links Accumulation to secular stagnation. In the next chapter, I will explain in detail how this mechanism played out during the US housing boom and its aftermath.

Accumulation and secular stagnation

I define "Accumulation" as an act of saving by someone who does not intend to spend the savings in the future. Such a person or entity is an "accumulator." Secular stagnation has been used in different—though related—ways by different authors. I define "secular stagnation" as a condition in which resources—including labor—are not fully employed, and in which the trend growth rate of the economy is below its potential (i.e., the rate that could be achieved if resources were fully employed). The origin of the linkage between Accumulation and secular stagnation is to be found in Book II of Malthus's *Principles of Political Economy* (1836), where it is stated that "an inordinate passion for accumulation must inevitably lead to a supply of commodities beyond what the structure and habits of such a society will permit to be profitably consumed."[12]

Accumulation and Deflation

Consider an economy initially operating at full employment where all agents behave in accordance with the Permanent Income Hypothesis (which I define in the next chapter), which means they plan to spend all that they save. Suppose some group suddenly decides it is never going to spend (or give away to charity) a portion of its savings. The members of this group are "accumulators," since they desire to accumulate wealth for its own sake, not to spend it. The increase in "permanent" saving—which I have called "Accumulation"—will impact interest rates, employment, and the price level in the following manner.

Assuming the market understands that Accumulation has just shot up, at preexisting interest rates, the increase in Accumulation will reduce the demand for future goods roughly by the amount of the Accumulation, since accumulators have withdrawn that amount from future demand. However, the rise in Accumulation will create an excess supply of saving relative to investment at preexisting interest rates and thereby cause interest rates to decline, which will prompt an increase in borrowing—for investment and consumption. This occurs because the decline in interest rates transfers wealth from savers (among whom are Accumulators) to borrowers (who are, by definition, non-accumulators[13]). The transfer of wealth away from Accumulators will increase demand, possibly by enough to fully offset the decline from Accumulators. But if the increase in Accumulation is large enough, it is possible that interest rates will be pushed to their lower bound (near zero) and spending might still be below the level consistent with full employment. Interest rates cannot fall below zero, provided agents have the option of holding zero yielding money. Therefore, an Accumulation that is large enough to drive interest rates to their lower bound will create a deficiency in demand at preexisting prices. The deficiency in demand will set in motion deflationary forces.

The process of deflation will cause employment to fall for three distinct reasons. One reason is that, at least since the early twentieth century, prices and wages tend to be "sticky"; they do not adjust quickly to reductions in demand. When the decline in spending exceeds the decline in wages and prices, unit sales have to decline.[14] This is so because the decline in spending on goods exceeds the decline in the cost to produce goods. To make this point intuitive, think of a situation where spending falls by 10 percent and goods prices do not change at all. In that case the money spent could purchase no more than 90 percent of the goods that were formerly purchased. A decline in sales will ultimately lead to a decline in employment, since firms would become bankrupt if they indefinitely produce goods they cannot sell. To approach this issue from the other direction, if wages do not change but prices are flexible and decline in reaction to a reduction in demand, the decline in prices will reduce firms' profit margins. This will create an incentive for firms to lay off workers, and if the reduction in price is large enough, firms will operate at a loss. When that occurs firms are forced to lay off workers in order to avoid bankruptcy. There can be many reasons for sticky wages and prices. Economists have been debating the matter for nearly a century. I shall not venture into that debate because for my purpose, what matters is the fact that wages and prices are slow to adjust, not the reasons why.

Nevertheless, prices do eventually decline, even if slowly, when the economy contracts. Many economists contend that unemployment is caused by the inability of wages and prices to adjust rapidly in reaction to a decline in spending. In the earlier example, if all wages and prices declined by 10 percent, full employment could be maintained with workers earning the preexisting real wage and firms earning the preexisting real profit.[15] Yet, this line of reasoning does not take account of the interaction of lower prices with long-term debt that is fixed in nominal money terms. When debt is taken into account, it does not follow that the economy will move toward full employment once wages and prices have declined.

This leads to the second reason that deflation causes employment to fall, which a late-nineteenth-/early-twentieth-century economist named Irving Fisher first articulated. Fisher pointed out that since loans are usually required to be repaid in fixed (let us say) dollar amounts, deflation increases the "real" burden of debt, as borrowers earn less money income but are required to pay a fixed dollar amount on their indebtedness. The attempt to pay off debts as income is falling requires borrowers to reduce their spending out of income by an ever increasing amount, which intensifies the deflationary pressure. This results in a vicious circle, where deflation begets reduced spending to pay off debts, which begets more deflation. Fisher thought this was the primary cause of economic depression. Here is how Fisher described the process of "Debt Deflation" in his celebrated 1933 article entitled "The Debt Deflation Theory of Great Depressions":

> deflation caused by the debt reacts on the debt. Each dollar of debt still unpaid becomes a bigger dollar, and if the over-indebtedness with which we started was great enough, the liquidation of debts cannot keep up with the fall of prices, which it causes. In that case, the liquidation defeats itself. While it diminishes the number of dollars owed, it may not do so as fast as it increases the value of each dollar owed. Then, the very effort of individuals to lessen their burden of debts

> increase it, because of the mass effect of the stampede to liquidate in selling each dollar owed. Then we have the great paradox, which, I submit, is the chief secret of most, if not all, great depressions: the more the debtors pay, the more they owe. The more the economic boat tips, the more it tends to tip. It is not tending to right itself, but is capsizing.[16]

Fisher's insight holds when it is asset prices, rather than goods prices, that deflate. In that case, which occurred during the US financial crisis, the reduction in spending is caused by the effects of deflated asset prices on borrowers and banks. Borrowers are either forced to liquidate unencumbered assets to pay off debts or are denied credit because they lack the collateral (i.e., unencumbered assets of sufficient value) to support new loans. Lenders must write down the value of their loans when collateral values deflate, which depletes their capital and forces them to refrain from new lending.[17] The forced liquidations and contraction in lending cause asset prices to deflate further, which compels borrowers to rein in spending due to the negative wealth effect, the loss of income from liquidated assets, and reduced borrowing possibilities. The process is intensified if lenders become fearful and lower the leverage level at which they are willing to lend against collateral, which causes lending of contract further. In that case the "double leverage cycle" described by Geanakoplos and Fostel in chapter 7 creates additional pressure to reduce asset prices, as possibilities for refinancing or obtaining loans to pay off debts become more constricted.

An increase in Accumulation, or in the market's awareness of it, can spark a decline in asset prices. This occurs because the decline in future demand reduces the estimated future revenue from capital goods. The downward pressure on asset prices links Accumulation to Fisher's insight. The link between Accumulation and asset price declines is an additional channel leading from Accumulation to contraction of output, which is operative even if the monetary authorities successfully avert deflation in goods prices. It is explained in chapters 12 and 13 that this is what occurred in the aftermath of the financial crisis.

For several decades Fisher's idea was dismissed by economists, who reasoned that the repayment of debt merely transferred purchasing power from one group—borrowers—to another group—lenders.[18] Even if, as is often assumed (without foundation), lenders have a lower propensity to spend than do borrowers,[19] a marginal difference in spending propensities is unlikely to account for a the cataclysmic decline in spending required to bring about a depression. And besides, the lenders may turn around and relend the loan repayments to other high spending borrowers. However, there has been a reappraisal and extension of Fisher's idea, which economists now consider a core cause of economic contraction.[20] The fundamental insight is that a decline in asset prices implies a decline in wealth for everyone in the economy, borrowers and lenders alike. When a borrower defaults on her loan payment, as she will do when her nominal income and wealth declines to a point where she is unable to generate sufficient funds from her income or from releveraging or liquidating her assets to pay off the loan, the lender suffers both a decline in cash flow and a decline in the value of its loan collateral. Both variables will force the lender to contract the issuance of new loans, and highly leveraged intermediaries like banks may quickly become insolvent. That is how debt-deflation forces lenders to contract credit just as borrowers are contracting their spending.[21]

The third problem created by deflation, when interest rates are at their lower bound, is that deflation increases real interest rates. The real interest rate on a debt is, roughly, the contract interest rate minus the average rate of inflation during the term of the debt. It represents the rate of discount at which lenders are willing to pay, at the inception of the loan, for the purchasing power commanded by the money at the time interest payments and loan repayment is made. To illustrate this point, consider a one-year loan with a 3 percent yield, payable at maturity. If the price level one year hence is unchanged, the purchasing power at the time of repayment has been discounted at 3 percent. If the price level one year hence is 3 percent higher, the purchasing power at the time of repayment has been discounted at 0 percent, since the purchasing power of the money the lender receives upon repayment is the same as the purchasing power of the money at the inception of the loan. Now suppose the price level one year hence is 3 percent lower. In that case the real interest rate on the 3 percent loan is 6 percent; because the lender is paid 3 percent more money than she lent, and the purchasing power of the money in which she is repaid has increased by 3 percent. The increase in real interest rates will shift wealth back toward Accumulators—who tend to be lenders—which will cause a decline in investment and consumption. That is why deflation is not a cure for a contraction caused by Accumulation, even where debt-deflation is not present.

Finally, Accumulation creates the problem that, even at a lower price level, after the deflationary process has ended, debts are repaid or restructured, and interest rates are low, spending may still be too low to support full employment. If Accumulators are present, there is no evident market adjustment that can restore full employment.[22]

Summary

A significant rise in Accumulation will set in motion forces leading to a decline in nominal interest rates and deflation in goods and asset prices, and the process of deflation will push the economy into contraction. This does not mean a rise in Accumulation will always lead to deflation, just that it will create a force pushing the economy in that direction. There may be other, countervailing forces, including responses by government, that prevent the deflation from occurring. Moreover, since Accumulation reduces future demand, the near-term impact will be affected by whether or not agents correctly anticipate the future shortfall in demand. This underscores that one must be cautions in drawing conclusions without information about the institutional structure of the economy and the expectations of its participants, which can differ by time and place. Accumulation may be reduced by price changes, as when declining interest rates (above zero) shift wealth away from accumulators. In other circumstances, it is possible that market adjustment to Accumulation may push the economy further away from full employment. For example, deflation implies an increase in real interest rates, which shifts income from borrowers to lenders, who are more likely to be Accumulators.

More generally, while there may be price configuration at which Accumulation is eliminated, for the sets of prices at which Accumulation takes place, there is no equilibrium for the economy to hone in on and the economy may move further away from full employment.

How Accumulation Accommodates Booms

Accumulation involves an increase in saving that is not intended to be spent in the future. If it is properly understood by the market, it will cause a reduction in investment and set in motion deflationary forces in asset and goods prices. However, if it is not properly understood that future demand will be reduced, Accumulation can ignite an unsustainable boom in the sense that future goods will be produced for which there will be no demand (or insufficient demand to cover the costs of producing them).[23] The boom is fueled by the availability of an enlarged pool of savings looking for places to invest. With incorrect anticipations, firms fail to recognize that a portion of current saving implies reduced demand in the future and they continue to invest in the false belief that today's savers will be tomorrow's consumers; and households borrow in the expectation of earning higher future wages. However, eventually, when firms discover they cannot sell all of the goods they have produced, their shortfall in sales will cause them to curtail investment, and many firms will default on their debt. Likewise, households will be forced to default on debt when anticipated future earnings fail to materialize. Either way, Accumulation leads to deflation and, if leverage is high, to Fisher's "debt-deflation" spiral, whether or not it is correctly anticipated. I shall explain in the next chapter how the rise in Accumulation was quite possibly the ultimate source of boom and bust dynamics that underlay the dot-com boom and the housing boom.

Accumulation and Say's Law

The idea of Accumulation does not fit comfortably with modern economic theory. Economic models assume individuals intend that they (or their heirs) will spend all the money they earn on consumable "final" goods, which implies they never reach a point of satiation. This is called the "nonsatiation" principle. Macroeconomic models require the nonsatiation principle in order to determine a stable resting point (or trajectory) of the economy, which economists call the "equilibrium" of the economic system.[24] Determining the equilibrium, and its movement in response to changes in the parameters of the model, is the basic concept used by economists to explain and to predict economic phenomena. Accumulation involves a violation of the nonsatiation principle because by definition accumulators do not spend all that they earn.

One way to understand the impact of Accumulation in the context of economic theory is through a relationship called Say's Law.[25] Say's Law states that, in a market economy where the nonsatiation principle holds, any particular final good might be subject to an excess demand or an excess supply at given prices, but the sum of all excess demands and supplies add up to zero. The exposition that follows involves some algebra, which is unavoidable given that my purpose is to place Accumulation in the context of economic models. But this should not deter the reader who is not inclined to follow all the notation and equations. If I have done my job well, she ought to be able to absorb the concept by perusing the paragraphs.

To illustrate Say's Law, I consider an economy where agents (households and firms) live forever (!) and exchange goods over time.[26] These goods include final goods, labor, raw materials, and intermediate capital goods, but do not include money or financial claims, which, according to the nonsatiation principle, agents do not wish to retain (although they may hold them temporarily to facilitate transactions and the timing of consumption). The economy has the following structure. There are I goods in the economy represented by the subscript $i \in \{1,\ldots, i,\ldots,I\}$, each of which may be delivered in the present, or at various future dates. The future dates are represented by the subscript $t\in \{1,\ldots, t\ldots, \infty\}$. Suppose there are h agents, where $h\in (1,\ldots, h\ldots H)$. The price of the ith good, delivered at date t, is given by *Pit*. Let *ehit* represent the hth agent's endowment (e) of the ith good at time t. Let *dh(Pit)* represent the hth agent's demand for units of the ith good at time t, which can be satisfied partially or entirely by the agents' endowment *ehit*. There are prices established in each market and agents use those prices to plan their market transactions.

If an agent plans to purchase the ith good, she must generate the income to pay for it from her transactions in all other goods. Since, according to the nonsatiation principle, she will plan to spend all of her money, it follows that the income she anticipates will be left over from her transactions in all other goods must exactly equal her planned expenditure on the ith good. It cannot be less, or she wouldn't have enough money to make her planned purchase of the ith good; and it cannot be more, or she would be left holding unspent money, which is contrary to the nonsatiation principle. If things work out so that she can purchase and sell the amount she plans for each good at the given set of prices, she will experience no unmet demand and no unsold supply of any good. But even if she is unable to complete all of her planned transactions at the given set of prices, the only reason she would lack the money to purchase all that she planned to purchase of the ith good is if she were unable to generate that amount of money from her sales of other goods.[27] It follows from this line of reasoning that, for any given set of prices, the total planned net expenditure of an agent summed across all goods equals zero.[28] This property is expressed by the budget equation of the hth agent (9.1), and it holds for all combinations of prices across all goods.

Agent's Budget Equation (when nonsatiation holds):

$$\sum_{t=1}^{\infty} \sum_{i=1}^{I} [dh(Pit) - Pit * ehit] = 0, \ \forall \text{Pit}. \tag{9.1}$$

The expression in brackets $[dh(Pit)–Pit*ehit]$ is the hth agent's excess demand for the ith good delivered at time t (referred to as excess supply when it is negative). There are two important things to note about agent i's budget equation. One is that agent I's excess demand for each good need not equal zero. It can be positive or negative, which implies that the ith agent may be a net buyer or seller of the good. The other thing to note is that the budget equation involves agent *I*'s planned purchases and sales at a given set of prices. There is no guarantee that she will be able to carry out all of her planned transactions. She may not be able to do so if there is an excess supply of some goods she plans to sell (in which case she may not be able to sell all that she desires), or an excess demand for goods that she plans to purchase (in which case she may not be able to purchase all that she desires). Say's Law is derived by adding up the budget equations of all agents.

Say's Law:

$$\sum_{t=1}^{\infty} \sum_{i=1}^{I} \sum_{h=1}^{H} [dh(Pit) - Pit * ehit] = 0, \ \forall \text{Pit}. \tag{9.2}$$

The expression $\sum_{h=1}^{H} [dh(Pit) - Pit * ehit]$ is the excess aggregate demand for the *i*th good delivered at time *t*. If it is positive, there is unmet demand for the good. If it is negative, there are unsold supplies of the good. When excess demand for a given good is zero, the market for that good is in equilibrium. When excess demand is zero for every good, the economy is said to be in general equilibrium. Say's Law is derived from individual spending plans at given prices. It applies whether or not the economy is in general equilibrium provided only that the nonsatiation principle holds, which means that each agent plans to spend, over time, all of her income on final goods.

Though it is a static concept, Say's Law lends intuitive support for the idea that markets tend to move toward a position where supply equals demand in all markets (a general equilibrium). One would expect prices to decline for goods experiencing aggregate excess supply, which would induce consumers to purchase more, while leading producers of the given good to reallocate resources to produce goods in excess demand. At the same time, prices would tend to rise for goods experiencing aggregate excess demand, which would induce consumers to purchase less, while leading producers of the given good to reallocate resources to produce more of the good. Since Say's Law implies the aggregate excess supplies are equal to aggregate excess demands, over time this process would dissipate the excess demands and supplies and move the economy toward general equilibrium.[29] Finally, while Say's Law is not a sufficient condition for a general equilibrium to exist, it is a necessary condition.

The Accumulation Challenge to Say's Law

Accumulation was defined earlier as an act of saving by an agent who does not intend to spend her savings in the future. It implies her saving exceeds her demand for future goods. An accumulator's budget equation is therefore negative, since by assumption she plans to purchase less than she earns.[30] Adding up the budget equations for all agents in an economy with accumulator yields a negative sum. This is so because the budget equation of accumulators is negative and the budget equation for all other agents is zero. Therefore, an economy with Accumulation does not obey Say's Law. Say's Law is only an identity if the nonsatiation principle holds. That is why nonsatiation is so important to economists.

Finally, the fact that (9.2) sums to a negative number when there are accumulators in the economy means there is a net excess supply of goods in the economy. There is a greater volume of stuff agents desire to sell (*Pit* * *whit*) than stuff agents desire to purchase (*dh*(*Pit*)). Net excess supply means an economy with accumulators operates below full employment. That is the fundamental source of deflationary pressure exerted by Accumulation. In an economy where net desired supply exceeds net desired demand, employment and prices will tend to fall.

Accumulation and Keynesian Unemployment

Keynes challenged the notion that markets always gravitate toward full employment equilibrium. As I have posited with Accumulation, Keynes described an excess of saving over investment as the cause of deflation and unemployment. There are principally two strands to Keynes's thinking about involuntary unemployment, which is a state where a person willing to work at the prevailing wage for her skill level is unable to find employment. Both strands identify the problem as a failure of the market economy to make the adjustments necessary to restore full employment.

One strand of Keynes's thinking about unemployment, which has been notably revived by Nobel Prize–winning economist Paul Krugman after Japan fell into deflation in the 1990s, has to do with the interaction of depressed animal spirits with the inability of interest rates to drop below zero.[31] A decline in optimism will reduce investment, because investors and entrepreneurs estimate lower potential profits, or are less willing to take on risks. If the economy is operating below full employment when interest rates drop to their lower bound, the deflationary forces described earlier will kick in. It will do so because excess desired saving implies that spending—on final goods and investment—is below income. In this situation the economy is forced to contract until income declines to a level where it is equal to spending. Income must, by definition, be matched by spending. This is the Keynesian liquidity trap. The concept of Accumulation adds nothing to Keynes's story of how the economy operates in a liquidity trap, but there is a crucial difference in the interpretations of what caused the economy to descend into liquidity trap. Both theories attribute the proximate cause to an excess of desired saving over desired investment, resulting from pessimism over future demand. The difference is that Keynes believed the pessimistic projections usually reflected an error, whereas the theory of Accumulation implies that future demand will decline as Accumulation increases.

The distinction between pessimism caused by depressed animal spirits and low expectations caused by accurate forecasts of declining future demand affects how an economy in liquidity trap will respond to fiscal stimulus. The essential difference is that a government generated increase in demand[32] might have the effect of restoring optimism, which in the case of liquidity trap arrived at by depressed animal spirits will kickstart the private sector and enable it to operate at full employment without requiring ongoing stimulus. If the liquidity trap was caused by Accumulation, by contrast, stimulus will be less likely to boost optimism and if it does succeed in doing so, it will lead to an unsustainable boom that will be followed by a crisis of overproduction.

The implication of achieving negative real interest rates—whether through a credible central bank promise to allow the economy to run an inflation rate for an extended period of time after recovery to full employment or by any other means to impose a negative nominal return on cash—is very different depending upon whether the liquidity trap is caused by Accumulation. The prevailing theory is that liquidity trap is caused by a wedge between perceived profit and desired saving at a zero riskless interest rate. A lower rate would increase the volume of profitable investments—by reducing borrowing costs—and would (presumably, but controversially) reduce desired saving. Therefore, it is widely argued, desired saving and investment could be brought into alignment—and full employment restored—at a negative real interest rate. This reasoning does not hold when the liquidity trap is caused by Accumulation. Unless the negative real interest rates transfer a large enough portion of wealth away from accumulators to eliminate their excess saving, the rate reduction will not cure the structural deficiency in demand caused by Accumulation. At most, it will ignite another unsustainable boom.

The other strand in Keynes's thought about unemployment, which has been articulated by Axel Leijonhufvud, has to do with the dynamics of labor market adjustment in the presence of high unemployment.[33] Keynes believed the economy could get stuck in low employment equilibrium because there is no reliable market mechanism to register what an unemployed person would purchase if she were employed and had income to spend. There is no device to coordinate hiring among all firms, and there are few markets for trading future goods. Involuntary unemployment occurs when firms do not perceive there to be sufficient potential demand—generated from the wages paid to new hires and the profits earned from their contribution to output—to justify hiring more workers. If the workers were employed, they would spend their income on current and future goods, but no worker would spend all her income at the firm that hired her. Therefore, even if firms understood the spending habits of workers, no individual firm would have an incentive to hire an additional worker, unless it was otherwise optimistic about the potential for growing its sales.

The paucity of futures markets means most firms cannot book sales in advance and therefore must guess at future demand when setting current production plans, This requires firms to guess at the effects current saving will have on future demand, and the effects that increased employment will have on current and future demand. Keynes made this point in connection with interpreting the impact of current saving on demand:

> An act of individual saving means—so to speak—a decision not to have dinner today. But it does not necessitate a decision to have dinner or to buy a pair of boots a week hence or a year hence or to consume any specified thing at any specified date. Thus it depresses the business of preparing today's dinner without stimulating the business of making ready for some future act of consumption... If saving consisted not merely in abstaining from present consumption but in placing simultaneously a specific order for future consumption, the effect might indeed be different. For in that case the expectation of some future yield from investment would be improved, and the resources released from preparing for present consumption would be turned over to preparing for the future consumption.[34]

The inability to contract for future delivery of goods is an impediment to achieving full employment in a market economy when animal spirits are depressed. It underscores the economy's reliance upon sui generis belief about the future. But Keynes does not doubt the existence of full employment equilibrium. That is the source of his optimism that a government fiscal stimulus can kickstart a movement toward full employment. Where Accumulation is present, the prognosis is more pessimistic. Missing markets and/or liquidity trap may keep the economy away from full employment, but government stimulus will not be sufficient to guide it toward full employment if private spending cannot ultimately be raised. In that case there will not be a full employment equilibrium to hone in on.

Accumulation and Productivity Growth

Productivity is measured as the value of final product produced by some measurable units of labor and capital goods used in the production process. Accumulation reduces the demand for—and therefore the price of—final output. Therefore, Accumulation will reduce the productivity of labor and other capital goods used in production at any given level of output.[35] This means that the decline in productivity growth that gathered pace after the turn of the millennium, which coincided with the growth of Accumulation, may have been (at least partly) caused by Accumulation.

Conclusion

This chapter opened with a review of Greenspan's "conundrum," which provided motivation to propose a theory explaining how Accumulation sets in motion deflationary forces. Chapter 10 will explore the forces of Accumulation that entered the US economy in the 2000s and the role those novel forces had in increasing volatility and moving the US economy toward secular stagnation. It will be seen that Accumulation was the ultimate cause of the housing boom and that the concept can be applied to resolve Greenspan's "conundrum."

CHAPTER 10

Accumulation and Secular Stagnation: Part II, Application

> We may well need, in the years ahead, to think about how we manage an economy in which the zero nominal interest rate is a chronic and systematic inhibitor of economic activity holding our economies back below potential.
>
> —Lawrence Summers[1]

In the last chapter I articulated a theory that relates Accumulation to secular stagnation and employment volatility. In this chapter I explain that foreign mercantilists and people who spend below their income during their lifetime are Accumulators. In so doing, I argue that Accumulation is the ultimate force behind the disruption caused by the capital flow bonanza and the pattern of below trend growth and employment punctuated by booms that the US economy had been subjected to since the late 1990s. Finally, I resolve the mystery of the "dog that didn't bark."

The Current Account Deficit

The Current Account Deficit and Permanent Saving

In chapter 3 it was shown that, beginning in the late 1990s, governments of Asian countries undertook large-scale interventions into the currency market to achieve goals that required they accumulate dollar assets. After the Asian financial crisis, Southeast Asian countries accumulated dollar reserves as a buffer stock to cushion (and to deter) any future run on their currencies. Then, starting in the early 2000s China began to accumulate large volumes of dollar assets as a part of a mercantilist policy to promote exports. In both cases, the policies pursued by the governments required they not spend their foreign reserves, since spending would undo the effects of the intervention. The buffer stocks accumulated in response to the Asian financial crisis were intended only for spending in the event of a run on the domestic currency.[2] China's mercantilist Accumulation had to be retained, and not spent on US goods, for so long as it wished to promote its net exports.[3]

The foreign Accumulation of dollar assets was extremely large. In the 15 years since the onset of the Asian financial crisis, offshore dollar reserves increased by over $1 trillion, while the US current account deficit soared from 1.5 percent of GDP to a peak of nearly 7 percent of GDP in the third quarter of 2006. The common factor between the reaction to the Asian financial crisis and China's mercantilist policy is that, beginning in the late 1990s (as the US trade deficit with Asia took off), its Asian trading partners earned an increasing amount of income from the United States, which they held as savings they never intended to spend. They were engaged in permanent saving.

The US Current Account Deficit as a Source of Accumulation

Adam Smith pointed out that saving is not itself wealth, it is rather an option to acquire the valuable things that comprise wealth. If that option is never exercised, the saver may admire her swelling bank statement, but others will enjoy the goods that the purchasing power of the statement commands. Adam Smith recognized this when he observed that "wealth does not consist in money, or in gold and silver; but in what money purchases, and is valuable only for purchasing."[4] It formed his core argument against the policy of mercantilism, which was then, and still is today, practiced by many countries.

A mercantilist country endeavors to expand its net exports of goods in order to run trade surpluses and accumulate foreign reserves (or gold in Smith's day). There are a number of reasons a country might adopt mercantilist polices. In this book I have identified motivations to deter, or cushion, sudden stops in offshore capital flows and the desire to expand employment by promoting exports. Smith wrote about the desire to accumulate gold, which he derided as an illusory and counterproductive quest to increase wealth. He described the common belief among the mercantilist countries of his time that "a rich country . . . is supposed to be a country abounding in money; and to heap up gold and silver in any country is supposed to be the readiest way to enrich it."[5] Smith argued, to the contrary, that mercantilists do not increase their wealth and their workers labor in vain, if they never plan to spend their export earnings on foreign produced goods:

> To attempt to increase the wealth of any country, either by introducing or by detaining in it an unnecessary quantity of gold and silver, is as absurd as it would be to attempt to increase the good cheer of private families, by obliging them to keep an unnecessary number of kitchen utensils.[6]

He observed that the mercantilist country enables other countries to spend beyond their means, while it frugally spends below its means. It does so by subsidizing its producers at the expense of its consumers:

> Consumption is the sole end and purpose of all production . . . But in the mercantilist system, the interest of the consumer is almost constantly sacrificed to that of the producer; and it seems to consider production, and not consumption, as the ultimate end and object of all industry and commerce.[7]

In this sense, the mercantilist appears to be the unwitting benefactor of the nonmercantilist. Smith argued that those who accused foreign mercantilists of destroying home economy jobs by selling more goods into the home economy than the home economy exports to the mercantilist country, focused on a superficial attribute. The essential underlying matter, according to Smith, is that the mercantilist sends goods to the home economy whilst receiving nothing in return, except for options to buy goods that it does not intend to exercise. Smith was not concerned that the shift in spending in favor of imports from the mercantilists might cause a reduction in home economy employment. He believed that market forces would bring about adjustments in prices, and possibly bring forth monetary substitutes, sufficient to ensure that all resources of the home economy, including labor, would be fully utilized, no matter what its trade balance was. Smith's position issued from his belief that in a market economy, idle resources create profit opportunities for those who can figure out how to employ them to meet unmet desires, and that there is never a shortage of persons eager to make a profit.[8] It is a very compelling argument.

Adam Smith's description of a mercantilist fits my definition of an accumulator—one who does not plan ever to spend all that she has saved. He correctly observed that the accumulator achieves no gain—other than psychic satisfaction—from her abstinence. Yet Smith was, perhaps, too sanguine in his confidence that the nonmercantilist country could readily achieve full employment. Certainly, if the trade imbalance self-corrects, trade cannot be a source of reduced employment in the long run. The market adjustment process described in chapter 3 is a mechanism by which the terms of trade automatically adjust to reestablish balance when large trade deficits and surpluses develop between countries. When exchange rates float, the deficit country currency will depreciate, which will reduce the foreign currency price of its exports and increase the domestic currency price of its imports. This will shift purchases toward the deficit country and thereby shrink the deficit.[9] When the exchange rate is fixed, the surplus country will experience an inflow of foreign reserves[10] and the deficit country may (depending upon whether there is a capital flow bonanza) experience an outflow of reserves. These reserve flows will cause the price level in the surplus country to increase relative to the deficit country. This will alter the terms of trade as before, and shrink the imbalance.[11]

The objective of the mercantilist, as Smith described it, is to build up foreign reserves. In more recent times, the objective of the mercantilist has been to expand output by maintaining positive net exports. The attainment of one goal implies the other and to achieve either goal, the mercantilist must short circuit the market adjustment process in order to prevent its current account surplus from shrinking. In chapter 3 I explained how China blocked the market adjustment process to promote its trade surplus with the United States, by fixing the renminbi-dollar exchange at an artificially low rate, sterilizing the dollar inflows to prevent domestic inflation, and subsidizing exporters. The only other avenue for adjustment would have been US deflation, which was successfully avoided.[12] Adam Smith did not adequately explain how, in an economy running a large current account deficit, where the market adjustment process was blocked, market forces are able to replace the hole in demand caused by the current account deficit.

The essence of the matter lies in the Accumulation of the mercantilist. The very act of withdrawing the surplus it earns from future consumption demand reduces the return on investment. The mercantilist may add to the pool of saving, if it recycles its surplus back into the home economy through a capital flow bonanza, but its act of permanent saving shrinks the size of the market into which any of the products of investment can later on be sold. The mercantilist, by definition, has a negative budget equation.[13] This can be expressed by the identity that defines the relationship, during an interval of time, between a home economy current account deficit and the corresponding buildup in financial claims from foreign economies. Noting that the sum is {Trade balance + Net financial transfers + net return on cross border assets}, the relationship is:

$$\text{Current Account Deficit} \equiv \text{Change in Foreign Net Financial Claims on Home Economy.} \qquad (10.1)$$

A foreign mercantilist runs a current account surplus (which is the mirror image of the current account deficit run by the home economy and reflects a net deficiency in demand for home economy goods and labor) and builds up financial claims in the process. Those claims can be held in the form of money—the currency or central bank reserves of the home economy—or as loans to, or investments in, home economy entities.

A mercantilist does not obey the nonsatiation principle. This is the fundamental reason why mercantilism is a negative sum game for market economies. It creates a reduction in consumption and employment in nonmercantilist countries that is not matched by any increase in employment or consumption in the mercantilist country. One might think the increase in net export boosts employment in the mercantilist country. But in a market economy (assuming nonsatiation obtains), the mercantilist would not require a trade surplus to attain full employment. For this reason, economists from Adam Smith's day to the present time have thought it possible to convince the mercantilist that its policy was self-destructive, in the sense that its abstinence from consumption does not generate any increase in employment.

Smith's argument may not have been persuasive to China in the 2000s, however, which was not a fully market economy. It was a mixed economy plagued by oversaving in its state sector. China might have required a large current account surplus in order to attain full employment in the 2000s. It was shown in chapter 1 that China had a problem of excess saving, which appears to have been generated by nonmarket forces stemming from changes in economic policy that were adopted after the Tiananmen Square protests in 1989. Therefore, China benefitted from its current account surplus insofar as net exports provided a replacement for deficient domestic demand and the capital flow bonanza provided an outlet for its excess saving. More recently, the bilateral trade imbalance has narrowed, so that Chinese mercantilism is not as pressing an issue for the US now, as it was during the housing boom. But the same issue may arise from other mixed economies, which might in future replace China as a low-cost supplier of labor-intensive manufactured goods.

Income Concentration

Income Concentration and Permanent Saving

When a person spends less than the income she has earned, the unspent amount is her savings. That is a familiar concept. She must hold her savings in some asset, and except for stuffing mattresses full of dollar bills, it will usually be lent out, invested in securities, or used to purchase durable assets (like housing, autos, and furniture). That is familiar, too. What may be a somewhat less familiar concept, except to economists, is that people and businesses usually plan to spend most of what they have saved—just later on. The hypothesis is that we want to maximize what we can spend over our lifetime, and to consume as smoothly as possible over time. To achieve this, we borrow (spend more than we earn) when we are young or when we suffer an unexpected temporary decline in income, as from a spell of unemployment, and repay the debts and accumulate savings during our peak earning years, and then spend the remainder during our retirement. It turns out that many of us actually do behave this way, more or less. Nobel Prize–winning economist Milton Friedman first documented this behavior and ascertained the motive that produced it in the 1950s; he called the proposition that people aim to spend all of the income earned over their lifetime as evenly as possible the Permanent Income Hypothesis (PIH).[14] Another Nobel Prize–winning economist, Franco Modigliani, found more evidence and refined the theory[15]; many others have followed in their footsteps and further developed the insight in many ways. Friedman's initial hypothesis has endured the test of time—at least until very recently—and the empirical evidence supporting it makes the PIH one of the most robust theories in economics.

One of the implications of Friedman's theory is that the act of saving normally creates future demand. If we are destined to spend all that we have earned during our lifetime, it follows that we *must* in the future spend what we have saved today (plus the interest our savings have earned in the interim). Today's saver is tomorrow's consumer.[16] In an efficient economy, it will be recognized that today's savers will be tomorrow's customers, which will create an incentive for firms to invest the savings to produce goods for future consumption. Therefore, in an efficient economy every dollar saved will be invested to produce future goods. An increase in saving will not cause employment to decline, because the labor no longer needed to produce current consumption goods will instead be needed to produce an increased amount of future goods.[17] Friedman's finding implies that an increase in the rate of saving out of income cannot, by itself, be a cause for economic contraction. If people behave in accordance with the PIH, there cannot be a recession due to underconsumption, and the concept of underconsumption is meaningless in such a world.[18] So long as agents do not slip their dollars inside their mattresses, and provided the market operates efficiently enough to act on the fact that saving implies future demand, an increase in savings should not affect the level of economic activity; it will just shift the mix of activity away from consumption and toward investment.[19]

One might at this point object that the PIH applies only to individuals (or households) and not to firms or government. This is true, but it does not necessarily alter the conclusion that savings will eventually be spent. Firms ultimately distribute their profits to shareholders, and governments, well the government usually spend everything it collects!

Yet there are important caveats to the theory. Some people do not save. People who live from paycheck to paycheck during their peak earning years are not able to smooth their lifetime spending. Conversely, wealthy people save a great deal and may refrain from spending all that they earn (or inherit) in order to bequeath an estate to their children when they die.[20] In the post–World War II era America became a middle-class society; the distribution of income became concentrated in the middle. What Friedman documented was the behavior of middle-class people who were wealthy enough to smooth their consumption over time, but not so wealthy as to leave large inheritances to their descendants. When the majority of US citizens were middle class (meaning the middle 50 percent of income distribution received the majority of income) these exceptions to the PIH were not significant enough to cause the aggregate outcome to deviate from what Friedman predicted. However, times have changed.[21]

Research by economists Thomas Piketty and Emmanuel Saez indicates that the distribution of income in America has become decidedly less equal in recent decades. The share of income going to the middle 50 percent has declined, while the share of pretax income (including capital gains) going to the top 1 percent earners increased from 10.02 percent in 1980 to 23.5 percent in 2007, on the eve of the financial crisis. The proportionate increase for the top 0.1 percent was even larger; their share increased from 3.41 percent in 1980 to 12.28 percent in 2007. To gain a sense of how dramatic this increase income share is, recall that the size of the trade deficit at its peak in 2006 was just under 7 percent of GDP, which is significantly lower than the increase in the share of income going to the top 1 percent and the top 0.1 percent since 1980 (figure 10.1(a)). Looked at another way, from 1980 to 2007, real income of the top 0.1 percent increased by over $6.4 million, while average real income increased by $19,000 (figure 10.1(b)). The reasons behind the increase in income inequality lie beyond the scope of this book. What concerns this inquiry is how the increased concentration of income may have affected aggregate demand.

The shift in income toward the top raises a vital question as to whether those people "under-consume" their lifetime earnings, or if their consumption follows the PIH.[22] Intuitively, it might seem that people who earn such high incomes would have a tendency to fulfill the common human desire to provide support for their heirs in the form of inheritances, in which event they must by definition spend less than the income earned over their lifetime. There is, however, an important distinction between people who pass on inheritances they received to the next generation and those who create inheritances out of income earned during their lifetime. The former can spend all of the income earned from the inherited assets and still pass them on to their descendants. That behavior is not Accumulation, because such persons are spending all that they earn. The latter persons, by contrast, must spend less than they earn in order to accumulate wealth they can pass on to their descendants. To the extent top income earners save in order to bestow inheritances on their descendants, they engage in permanent

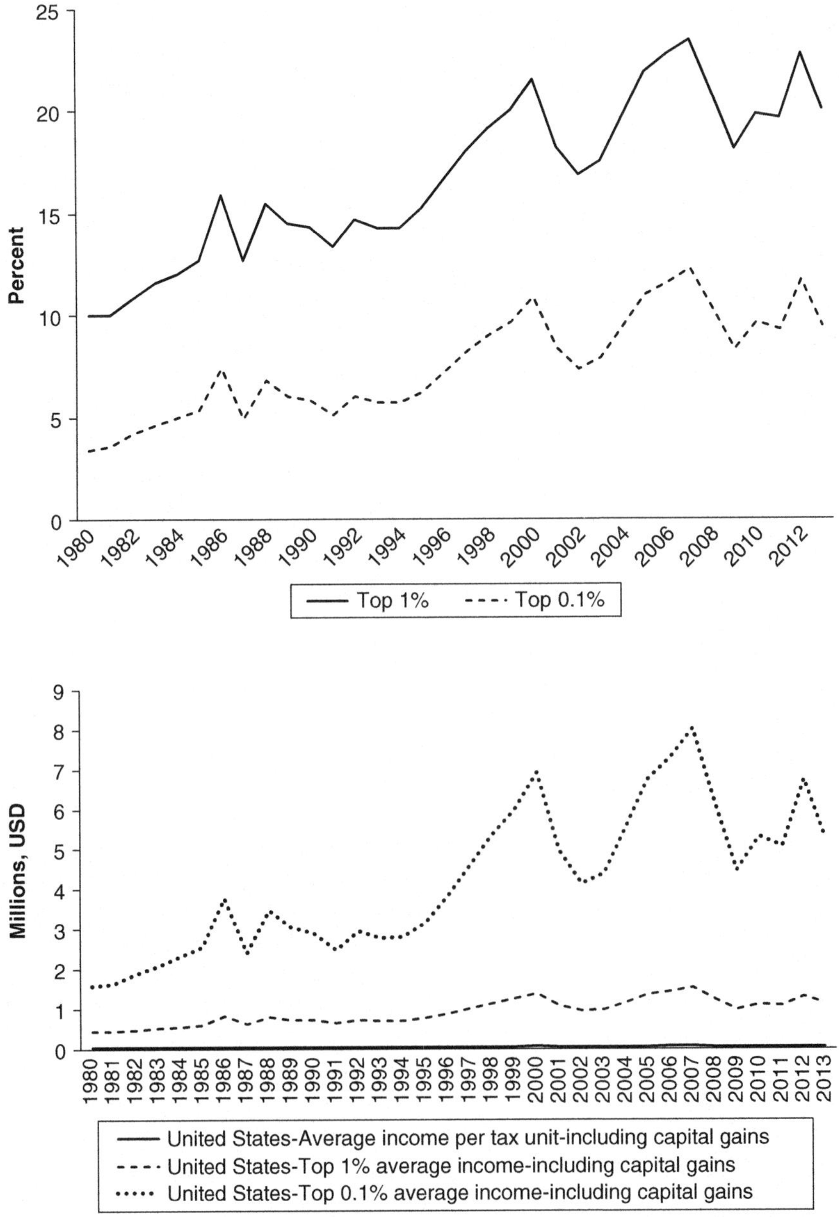

Figure 10.1 (a) Top 1 percent and 0.1 percent income share, including capital gains, 1980–2013. (b) Average, top 1 percent and 0.1 percent income, including capital gains, 1980–2013.

Source: Facundo Alvaredo, Anthony B. Atkinson, Thomas Piketty, and Emmanuel Saez, The World Top Incomes Database, http://topincomes.g-mond.parisschoolofeconomics.eu/ (June 16, 2015).

saving. Piketty and Saez show that most increased wealth in the United States in recent decades has come from wage income, rather than inheritance. This implies that those who leave bequests are likely to have engaged in Accumulation.

Ideally, one would want to have data on lifetime earnings for a large cross-section of the population.[23] Unfortunately, there is no database containing detailed information on the spending habits and earnings of people throughout their lifetimes. The surveys of individual US household earnings and spending collected by the US government[24] do not usually include persons in the top 1 percent of income distribution, which is the relevant group for this discussion. Moreover, there is considerable controversy over what the extant survey data says about the relationship between consumption and income. The raw data shows that savings increase at an increasing rate as income rises, which is not necessarily inconsistent with the PIH, considering that measured income is for a point in time, not for a lifetime. However, the fact that the measured saving increases as income rises does suggest that savings may positively correlate with lifetime earnings, which supports the Accumulation hypotheses. Unfortunately, for this line of reasoning, recent research, which corrects for purported measurement error in the raw data, suggests that consumption rises in line with income, which leaves no room for permanent saving to become larger as income increases.[25]

It is likely that the increase in aggregate measured pretax income inequality at a point in time overstates the increase in inequality of lifetime earnings. One reason is that the increase in measured inequality reflects, at least in part, that lifetime earnings have become more peaked as the number of college graduates has increased. The number of people attending college as undergraduates and graduate students has increased markedly in recent decades, and it is well documented that increased time in school has the effect of concentrating earnings into fewer years, since students spend more time in school. Therefore, trends in education have generated a disproportionate increase in measured income inequality. Another reason that pretax earnings overstate inequality is that it omits the ameliorating effects of progressive taxation and social insurance. The primary beneficiaries of social security, pensions, and Medicare are middle income persons.

The absence of data tracking the lifetime savings behavior of individuals makes it difficult to gauge the extent to which permanent saving among individuals has been increasing. The data that exists pertains to income distribution at a point in time, and does not follow individuals over time. There are, however, two pieces of evidence that lend some support for the thesis that lifetime saving increases at higher levels of income.

One is a study by economists Atif Mian and Amir Sufi that looked at spending patterns at the zip code level during and after the housing boom. They found that high income households adjusted their spending to changes in national income and local housing prices by a lesser amount than lower income households.[26] This lower "marginal propensity to consume" out of changes in income and wealth indicates that high income households do not readily change their spending when their financial circumstances change. This suggests that high income individuals may increase saving as their income rises, and thereby spend below their lifetime earnings. Even so, this result should be taken with a grain of salt, since the comparative stability of spending of high income households to fluctuations in their income and wealth may, or may not, imply its consistency with the PIH. If the affected individuals perceive the increases in income and wealth as permanent, the stability of consumption reflects a higher propensity to save among high earners. However, if they perceive the increase in income as temporary, the stability of consumption may simply reflect that wealthy people have the means to borrow and purchase insurance policies to enable them to smooth their lifetime spending in a manner consistent with the PIH. Since the data do not follow individuals over their lifetime, there is no way to discern which hypothesis is correct.

The second is a study by the IMF, which shows an inverse relationship between the income share of the top 20 percent earners and GDP growth.[27] This is very indirect evidence, but it is consistent with the prediction that an increase in Accumulation slows down GDP growth.

At the end of the day, the lack of data on lifetime earnings and transfers of income through taxation and public goods provision, as well as the inability to discern how individuals view their future earnings prospects, severely limits the degree of confidence with which one can draw conclusions pertaining to lifetime spending behavior from the data on income concentration.[28] Nevertheless, the concentration of income has increased so rapidly, and the amount earned by the top 1 percent and 0.1 percent are so huge that one's intuition (or at least this author's intuition) is that the lifetime earnings of top earners exceeds their lifetime consumption by a margin that is vastly greater than the lower income groups from whom they have accrued a transfer of income share.

On that assumption, the shift in income shares away from the middle to the top had the effect of shifting saving from those who tend to follow the PIH to those who are more likely inclined to accumulate and leave inheritances. Under ordinary circumstances, this ought to show up as an increase in the overall household saving rate, given the assumption that top income earners save at a higher rate that middle income earners. But during the housing boom middle income mortgage debt—which is a form of negative saving—exploded, which means middle income dis-saving might have fully matched the increase in saving generated at the top.[29] Household saving increased dramatically after the housing boom ended, but it has not (to my knowledge) been possible to discern the extent to which this arose from income concentration, and to what extent it is attributable to the debt overhang created by the collapse in home prices, which barred middle income earners from borrowing.

In any event, it is important to realize that Accumulation is not determined by the overall savings rate—which actually declined during the housing boom—but by the amount of permanent saving—which likely increased during the housing boom. From this I draw the (very tentative) conclusion that permanent saving among US households increased during the housing boom.

The Increased Concentration of Income as a Source of Accumulation

People who spend less than they earn over their lifetime are Accumulators. The increase in income share going to top earners raises the prospect that Accumulation has increased. As in the case of mercantilism, Accumulation among the wealthy adds to saving while reducing the return on investment, which creates a savings glut.

An Interaction between the Two Sources of Accumulation

The bilateral current account deficit with China caused income concentration to increase through the effect of offshoring of production, which was motivated by the substitution in favor of lower cost Chinese labor. The effect worked through two channels. One was to push down the wages of the unskilled US industrial workers from whom the substitution was made. Economist David Autor and his colleagues found that Chinese manufactured imports displaced middle income manufacturing employment in the United States in those sectors that competed with China, and the effect was exacerbated by the current account deficit.[30] The other was by increasing the profits of corporations who were able to offshore production. The former reduced the incomes of the middle class, while the latter disproportionately benefitted the wealthy—managers who were compensated with share awards and equity owners. Therefore, shrinking the bilateral current account deficit with China should ameliorate Accumulation by reducing income concentration.[31]

Market Perceptions of Accumulation

An increase in Accumulation implies a reduction in the demand for future goods. As I have explained earlier, the market reaction can fall between two polar extreme cases. In one case, the Accumulation is recognized by all market participants, in which case it will induce an immediate deflationary contraction. At the other end of the spectrum, Accumulation is not recognized, and investment proceeds and the permanent saving is channeled into investment. This leads to a crisis of over-production at a future time, when customers for the produced goods fail to materialize. Reality is likely to fall in between these two extremes, with some believing, and others not believing, that future demand has been reduced.

Accumulation and Secular Stagnation

The recent rise in Accumulation in the United States began in the late 1990s when Asian nations started to accumulate significant dollar reserves, and income concentration accelerated. For several decades prior to that, the United States had incurred current account deficits, and foreign countries had been accumulating dollar assets. Much has been written about the putative benefits of the "exorbitant privilege" accrued by the United States from issuing the world's reserve currency. It has often been commented that lower interest rates and increased consumption subsidized by the rest of the world was "rent" for the use of its currency. In 1971 then US Treasury secretary John Connelly quipped to a gathering of foreign financial officials, "Our dollar, your problem," but that was never the whole story. The chronic current account deficits entailed by the foreign Accumulation of dollars as a reserve asset, reduced aggregate demand in the US economy, while creating a capital flow bonanza. The latter reduced trend growth, while the former increased volatility. This was not a burdensome problem when trade imbalances were relatively small. But it became a major issue when they began to balloon around the turn of the millennium.[32]

By the turn of the century, Accumulation was having a significant effect on the US economy. Labor force participation (as measured by hours of work per household) and the rate of growth of capital per household both began to fall, and median household income growth stagnated (see figure 10.2).[33] This is the reason Ben Bernanke felt the need to calm deflationary fears while puzzling over the tepid job growth in the recovery from the 2001 recession.[34]

Yet, by mid-decade the United States had reattained full employment. In chapter 7 it was explained how this came about. The capital flow bonanza, which reflected excess offshore saving, pushed down interest rate and triggered a "reach for yield" among financial institutions, which expanded the volume of credit. The increased credit was used to finance the housing boom. It was also explained how the excess of borrowing and building amid low and declining productivity growth foredoomed the crisis that followed. In this chapter and in chapter 9 I have delved deeper and identified an ultimate cause; Accumulation was the source of the excess saving, and the cause of the decline in the demand for future goods that eventually brought the boom to its end.

The rise in Accumulation created a tension. It lowered the sustainable level of employment, while at the same time sowing fertile ground for investment and asset price booms. The decline in demand in the US economy caused by the current account deficit and income concentration tended to reduce aggregate demand and employment, while the increase in saving provided fuel for booms

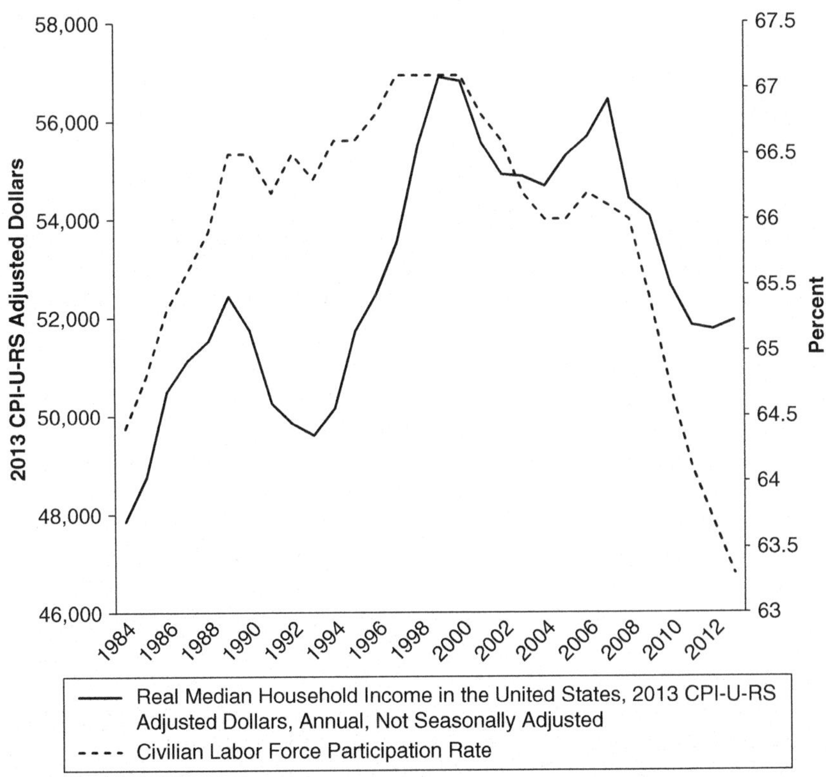

Figure 10.2 Real median household income, labor force participation rate, 1984–2013.
Source: US Bureau of Labor Statistics.

that could temporarily increase spending and employment. Accumulation reduced trend employment over time, while increasing its volatility, as the two opposing forces generated oscillations. Lawrence Summers, former US Treasury secretary and economic advisor to President Obama, has called the latter predicament "secular stagnation."[35]

Professor Summers has placed the issue of secular stagnation at the center of academic and public debate. In so doing, he put forth several possible causes. Investigation of the causes he adumbrated has formed the core research agenda around secular stagnation. Accumulation is related to two of the potential causes he listed—capital flow bonanzas and income concentration. It is worth briefly considering the other potential causes mooted by Professor Summers.

One idea is that declining population growth will lead to a reduction of investment (and employment related to investment), since it implies there will be fewer customers for future goods. This was a core idea of Alvin Hanson's paper on secular stagnation, from which Professor Summers drew inspiration for his revival of the idea.[36] I argued in chapter 9 that if people spend up to their budget constraints and resources are allocated efficiently, so that markets clear, there will be full employment at any rate of population growth (or decline). Intuitively, a declining population moves through the age brackets, so that there will first be a decline in working age population followed by a decline in retirees. In effect, the reduced number of workers will be investing to support their own consumption in future years. Empirical studies of the relations of population and economic growth support this intuition; they have not uncovered any relationship between population decline and declines in per capita GDP.[37]

Another idea is that the decline in the cost of investment goods (i.e., the materials used in production of final goods) enabled all profitable investment prospects to be financed without utilizing all of the available saving. This, it is alleged, created a dearth of opportunity for profitable investment, and an excess of saving over investment. An excess of saving over investment, as I have explained, reflects a reduction in demand, which will generate deflationary forces. There are three problems with this idea. One is that a decline in investment costs enables a greater volume and variety of goods to be produced, which could spur an increase in both investment and consumption. The second is that while (quality adjusted) investment costs have been declining since around 1950 the US investment rate has been stable since that time.[38] The third problem is that a decline in investment opportunities will cause interest rates to decline, which, according to the current macroeconomic paradigm, should stimulate consumption, because lower interest rates reduce the amount of future consumption that must be foregone in order to pay for current consumption.[39]

Therefore, I think the capital flow bonanza and income concentration are the most likely causes of secular stagnation, from the group of potential causes adumbrated by Professor Summers. Insofar as both phenomena are manifestations of Accumulation, it follows that Accumulation is the underlying cause of secular stagnation. It has introduced a chronic weakness into the economy that is occasionally interspersed with unsustainable booms caused by the interaction of low interest rates with institutional structures in the financial sector.

Accumulation and the Safe Asset Shortage

Explaining the Safe Asset Shortage Theory

In chapters 3 and 7 it was explained that the creation of ABS and CDO, mostly backed by subprime mortgages, arose, in part, to meet the growing demand for safe assets in the early 2000s from offshore investors and institutional cash pools. The increase in demand for safe assets reflects, in part, the growth of Accumulation—from foreign governments and from wealthy individuals. Safe assets are securities that have a negligible risk of default. US government guaranteed debt and AAA rated securities comprise the bulk of safe assets. Economists Ricardo Cabellaro and Emmanuel Farhi have developed a model that purports to show that a safe asset shortage contributed to the stagnant growth and increased volatility of the 2000s.[40] According to Cabellaro and Farhi, an excess demand for safe assets has a similar effect to an excess of desired saving in Keynesian theory. The excess demand for safe assets bids up their price (lowering their yield). If the excess demand remains after the yield on safe assets has reached its lower bound, equilibrium can only be restored when the economy has contracted by an amount sufficient to bring about a reduction in saving large enough to eliminate the excess demand for safe assets. According to their model, that is how a safe asset shortage causes secular stagnation.

An excess demand for safe assets at the lower bound of interest rates is similar to the Keynesian liquidity trap discussed in chapter 9, except in one crucial respect. A Keynesian liquidity trap occurs when aggregate desired saving (at full employment) exceeds aggregate investment. A safe asset shortage, by contrast, pertains to demand and supply of a subset of aggregate saving and investment—that involving the demand for, and supply of, safe assets. There may not be an excess demand for safe assets when the economy is in Keynesian liquidity trap and, conversely, there can be a safe asset shortage even when desired saving is equal to investment for all other assets. Whether or not a decline in the yield on safe assets will reduce the demand for safe assets depends upon the responsiveness of the demand for safe assets to changes in interest rates. If the demand is inelastic, it is quite possible that an excess demand (holding constant the supply of safe assets) will cause the interest rate on safe assets to drop to the lower bound without eliminating the excess demand. Chapters 3 and 7 presented evidence that one important group of safe asset investors, Southeast Asian and Chinese central banks, continued to pour money into US government guaranteed securities even as their yields plummeted. Cabellaro and Farhi suggest that, in the absence of an increased supply of safe assets, an excess demand for safe assets at the lower bound interest rates will cause a reduction in aggregate demand, which will create deflationary pressure. During the US housing boom a safe asset shortage was only averted because two related things occurred, which ameliorated the deflationary pressure. One is that institutional investors shifted some of their portfolios out of safe assets in order to reach for yield, thus reducing the demand for safe assets. The other is that the private sector increased the supply of safe assets by manufacturing pseudo-safe assets out of subprime mortgages, which temporarily abated the safe asset shortage. However, by incentivizing the reach for yield and the creation of private sector safe assets, the safe asset shortage generated volatility. After the financial crisis a safe asset shortage was averted even though the pseudo-safe assets were revealed to be unsafe. The supply of government debt increased dramatically and the cash under management of institutional cash pools receded. Yet, the demand for safe assets—by foreign governments and by institutional cash pools—looks set to grow, and the future supply of US government debt—and the solvency of the US government—is uncertain. So, a safe asset shortage may occur in the near future.

It appears that the safe asset shortage model is intertwined with Accumulation and is able to account for the same patterns of below trend growth and volatility. Both theories posit that a chronic imbalance of saving over profitable investment opportunities is the underlying cause of stagnation and volatility.[41] Yet, it will be shown that the theory of Accumulation provides a more convincing and comprehensive explanation of the contractionary forces that cause secular stagnation. The difference is that the safe asset shortage theory does not imply a deficiency in demand. A safe asset shortage may cause a shifting around of money and financial claims without creating a notional excess demand for money and financial claims. Accumulation, by contrast, involves an excess demand for money and financial claims by definition.

Questioning the Dynamics of Adjustment to a Safe Asset Shortage

It is possible to question whether a safe asset shortage will necessarily set off a process of economic contraction even if a reduction in income is required to restore equilibrium. The fundamental reason for skepticism is that an excess demand for safe assets does not imply any reduction in demand. This is so for two reasons.

One reason is that the investors in safe assets must place their money somewhere and they are unlikely to hold any significant amount of currency. Therefore, they will have to find other, less safe, securities in which to invest their money. So long as all of their desired saving gets invested in securities—which may be "unsafe" securities, or "pseudo-safe" securities like subprime ABS and CDO—the excess of desired saving intended for safe assets over the supply of safe assets will not cause any drain on demand. This conclusion stands in marked contrast to the dynamics of adjustment to a Keynesian liquidity trap, which involves an excess of desired *aggregate* saving over *aggregate* investment. When total desired saving exceeds the capacity of the economy to provide suitable projects in which to invest, the economy is forced into contraction because idle savings implies aggregate spending—$C + I + G + (X - M)$—will be below full employment income (Yf). Moreover, since every dollar of income is generated by a dollar of spending, a shortfall of spending relative to full employment income will force income to contract. By contrast, a safe asset shortage, unaccompanied by a Keynesian liquidity trap, may push the economy out of equilibrium, but it is not clear how that will affect employment and income. The safe asset shortage model demonstrates that the new equilibrium is at less than full employment, but it says nothing about whether there are forces that will propel the economy toward that new equilibrium.

The second reason an increase in demand for safe assets may not trigger a decline in demand is that the institutions that demand safe assets do not themselves consume and save; rather, they manage assets on behalf of people who do. The existence of an excess of demand for safe assets by those institutions is unlikely to motivate any individuals to alter spending habits. For example, nobody's spending pattern will be affected by a gap between the targeted and actual returns earned on US long-term government guaranteed debt by Asia, China, and OPEC. Nor will any individual alter her spending pattern because her life insurer, defined benefit pension plan, or bank experiences a decline in returns on investment, at least for so long as they believe the institutions will make good on their obligations to policyholders and depositors.

Perhaps the underlying reason for the cleavage between excess demand by institutional investors for safe assets, on the one hand, and spending behavior by individuals, on the other hand, is that people view the commitments made to them by institutional investors as a "safe asset." For so long as the pay-out commitments by one's insurer, pension plan, money market fund, and bank are not questioned, no change in their investment performance will give reason for any beneficiary to change her plans.

In the context of Cabellaro and Farhi's model, it might be possible to differentiate between two types of safe asset shortages, each with different economic effects. One type of safe asset is the payout commitments of institutional investors to their beneficiaries. If the commitments made by those institutions are backed by government, the government is providing beneficiaries with a safe asset, of which there cannot be a shortage for so long as the (often implicit) government guarantee is believed in. A questioning of the government backstop can create a safe asset shortage, however, which can cause individuals to react by reducing their spending, which will cause the economy to contract. The other type of safe asset shortage involves institutional investor demand for safe assets in the marketplace, which can cause asset bubbles by incentivizing a reach for yield or the creation of pseudo-safe assets, such as subprime mortgage backed ABS and CDO. The effects of safe asset shortages can be decomposed as follows: an excess demand for safe assets by policyholders and depositors can cause stagnation, while a safe asset shortage among institutional cash pools and offshore investors can increase volatility.

This conclusion is tempered by two considerations. One is that an increasing portion of the workforce participates in defined contribution pension plans, or otherwise provide for their own retirement. For this group, a shortage of safe investments and/or a steep decline in yields may cause them to reduce spending in order to achieve a targeted level of retirement wealth. The other consideration is that, to the extent companies are required to increase their contributions to their pension plans in order to maintain solvency when interest rates are low, they will divert into their plans money that otherwise would be available for payouts to shareholders or for investment, which will cause a reduction in spending.

A Case for Increased Government Borrowing

A paradox of Accumulation is that Accumulators save money and desire to earn a return, but their abstinence ensures that aggregate saving cannot earn a positive return. I believe this inability to generate a return is the fundamental source of the safe asset shortage identified by Caballero and Farhi. Many investors desire to earn a safe return on their savings, but if some savers never plan on spending, there will not be enough inherent return on investment to go round.

Caballero has proposed that the US government issue more debt to satiate the demand for safe assets. On its surface, this may appear to be an idea that will create risk for the US taxpayer and which may ultimately undermine the safety of US government debt. But increasing government debt may be less risky than it appears. Caballero's focus is to have the government manufacture additional safe assets in order to alleviate the safe asset shortage. He places a limit at the government's fiscal capacity, which implicitly assumes all investors in government debt will want to be repaid someday (though new investors might be found to replace them).

The presence of Accumulation enables us to go further in this direction. To the extent that the savings really are permanent, and if the interest rate paid on government debt is below the growth rate of the economy, the taxpayer may actually benefit from an increased deficit.[42] If the government transfers the money raised by its debt issuance to non-accumulators, and if the debt is rolled over forever, then it will result in a voluntary transfer of wealth from accumulators to non-accumulators, it will cure the deficiency in demand caused by the Accumulation and it will not crowd out private investment (since the government would be soaking up the excess private saving of accumulators).

Moreover, only government could effectuate this arrangement. Non-accumulators will pay off their debts during their lifetime, in which event the transfer of money from accumulators to non-accumulators (rather than to government) would not increase the lifetime earnings of non-accumulators. Therefore, it will not expand their budget constraint, so it cannot boost aggregate demand. But the transfer of money to government, which itself is infinitely lived (or at least longer lived than any individual), never needs to be repaid. Accumulators looking for a safe return will be willing to lend to a creditworthy government, for as long as it remains creditworthy. In turn, the transfer of those savings to non-accumulators will enlarge their budget constraints. That is how increased government borrowing could, at least in principle, increase spending, employment and trend growth. The risk lies in determining the quantity of savings that are truly permanent (or very long lived). It is a very big risk.[43]

The Dog That Didn't Bark Redux

I am now equipped to answer the question posed at the beginning of chapter 9: why did interest rates not rise at the end of the housing boom? What was different this time is that Accumulation grew throughout the boom. The current account deficit and top income shares soared, which kept interest rates low and created deflationary pressure that remained in place throughout the boom. Chinese purchases of treasuries and GSE debt peaked in 2005–2006, which was the period during which the Fed increased the Fed funds rate.[44] In chapter 2 I presented the results of Merrouche and Nier's study showing that capital flow bonanzas pushed down long-term interest rates in OECD countries in the early 2000s, and Warnock's estimation that offshore purchases of treasuries significantly lowered the yield on ten-year treasuries during that time period (see figure 2.9). The Fed's attempt to stem the tide and lift interest rates was overmatched by these forces.[45] The boom was abetted by a glut of savings, which caused low interest rates and loose credit—something that could trigger a Wicksell/Hayek boom as well—but what ended it was the underlying drain on demand. A dearth of qualified purchasers of the homes produced by the investment undermined the boom.[46]

The dynamics of a boom in an economy suffering from Accumulation can be understood with reference to equation (9.1). At the onset of the boom there was a spontaneous increase in the perceived value of a certain capital asset—homes—which, by increasing perceived wealth (*ehit*), expanded budget constraints and enabled increased expenditure on final goods and homes. It enabled people to offer their homes as collateral to obtain loans from yield-hungry accumulators. The increase in spending by homeowners eliminated the excess supply of final goods and labor. When home prices eventually collapsed—due to an overexpansion of new homes and an leveraging of existing homes—perceived wealth declined, which reduced the volume of supportable demand *(dh(Pit)*.

The forces of Accumulation began to loosen the Fed's influence on monetary conditions before the Fed started to raise rates. The expansion in credit and liquidity during the early stages of the housing boom was generated without any notable expansion in monetary policy. The increase in broad money (M2) grew at trend. Credit expanded without any encouragement from the Fed. A study by economist Daniel Thornton provides direct evidence that the relationship between the Fed funds rate and the ten-year treasury yield deteriorated when the current account deficit began to soar, in the late 1990s. Figure 10.3 shows the results of a regression of changes in the ten-year treasury yield on changes in the Fed funds rate. The regression was estimated using equation (10.2).

$$\Delta\ \textit{10-yr Treasury Yield} = a + \Delta\ \beta \textit{Fed Funds Rate} + \mu. \qquad (10.2)$$

Around 2002 β, the coefficient on the Fed fund rate, actually became negative, which implies the ten-year treasury yield declined in response to increases in the Fed funds rate. The T-statistic became larger (in absolute terms), which indicates the accuracy of the measure of β improved after 2000. But, as Thornton points out, these results are tempered by the fact that R squared, which measures the percentage of variation in the ten-year treasury yield that is explained by variations in the Fed funds rate, was essentially zero from the mid-1990s onward.

Thornton conjectured the deterioration in the relationship between the Fed funds rate and the treasury yield resulted from a Fed policy shift that took place in 1988, long before Greenspan's conundrum. Prior to 1988 the Fed funds rate was set in reaction to the same financial market conditions that affected the ten-year treasury yield, whereas afterward the Fed funds rate was changed less frequently, and sometimes in a direction opposite other market interest rates. I am not going to go into the details of his argument, because it is not relevant to this inquiry, except to note that my proposed explanation is not incompatible with his—it may even be complementary. The increase in Accumulation is an independent cause of the breakdown in the relationship between the Fed funds rate and the ten-year treasury yield. It explains the intensification of the decoupling that took place in the 2000s.

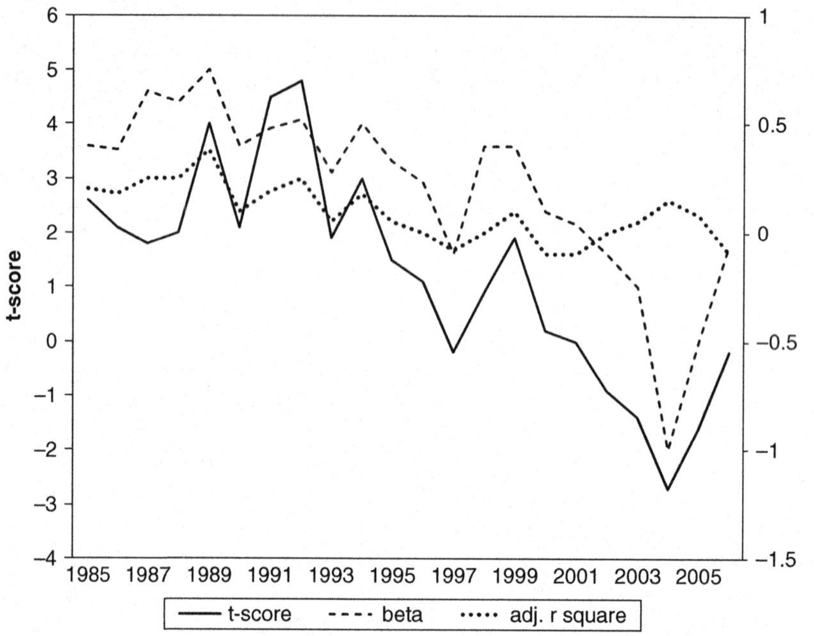

Figure 10.3 Regression tests ten-year treasury yields on Fed funds rate, 1985–2006.

Source: Daniel L. Thornton, "The Unusual Behavior of the Federal Funds Rate and Treasury Yield: A Conundrum or an Instance of Goodhart's Law?" Federal Reserve Bank of Atlanta Mimeo, 2010, Figure 1, p. 55. Data annualized by author.

Conclusion

In past booms, the mistake made by investors was to undertake projects assuming that interest rates and input prices would not increase. Eventually, interest rates would spike, input supplies would run low, and their prices rise, at which point it became necessary to abandon some projects. Hayek's fundamental insight that booms originate from an overestimation of potential profits remains valid; it is just that the nature of the misperception changed. In the housing boom, prices and interest rates remained low, and yet the customers did not materialize. The misjudgment was a failure to recognize that the nature of saving had changed. The Permanent Income Hypotheses had given way to the age of Accumulation.

In the next three chapters, I turn attention to the aftermath of the housing boom. I look into the deflationary process in more detail and examine the other face of Accumulation: when investment languishes because of pessimism over the depth of future demand. I will explain how this aspect helps to account for the "jobless" nature of the recoveries from the recessions that followed the dot-com and housing booms.

PART IV

The Financial Crisis, I: The Meltdown and the Successful Initial Policy Response

In part IV, I explore the channels through which a collapse in the price of subprime mortgage backed securities—caused by unexpectedly large defaults—metastasized into a collapse of credit and securities prices throughout the economy. I then explain how the Fed averted a catastrophe and quelled the panic by flooding the economy with liquidity.

Chapter 11 explains how the leverage built up during the housing boom contributed to the depth of the crisis. It traces the process by which the decline in subprime securities triggered forced sales of other assets and a withdrawal of short-term funding, and how this led to a vicious circle of declines in asset prices, credit, and real activity. Chapter 12 describes the Fed's response, which was to satiate the increased demand for liquidity. By so doing, the Fed prevented the collapse of the banking system and avoided deflation. The bailout of bank creditors, however, increased moral hazard and raises questions about the ethics of protecting the interests of a politically powerful group.

CHAPTER 11

Descent into the Abyss

> In the middle of the journey of our life I found myself astray in a dark wood where the straight road had been lost sight of.
>
> —Dante Alighieri, *Inferno*

The Denouement

On July 9, 2007, Citigroup CEO Chuck Prince made his now infamous pronouncement, which marked the beginning of the denouement of the housing boom. "When the music stops, in terms of liquidity, things will be complicated. But as long as the music is playing, you've got to get up and dance. We're still dancing."[1] Mr. Prince's remarks came at a time some analysts and bankers had begun to express fears that liquidity might drain out of the mortgage market if nascent problems with subprime mortgage delinquencies metastasized into a large wave of defaults. He did not share this pessimism. He reasoned that recent financial innovations had created a more stable, liquid market. "The depth of the pools of liquidity is so much larger than it used to be, so that a disruptive event now needs to be much more disruptive than it used to be." The assessment was not without merit. He pointed to recent buyouts of troubled subprime mortgage lenders by big Wall Street banks and hedge funds as demonstrations that "liquidity rushes in" to fill the gap as solvent players eagerly invested in buying opportunities. Nevertheless, Mr. Prince's assessment turned out to be tragically wrong. Even as he spoke, the market for subprime mortgages was shifting into terminal decline.

Figure 11.1 shows the index of prices of four vintages of AAA rated subprime mortgage backed CDO issued in 2006 and 2007. A subprime CDO is comprised of pools of subprime mortgage backed ABS, which often included liquidity put guarantees from sponsoring banks and broker-dealers. In August 2007, two Bear Stearns sponsored hedge funds dedicated to investing in subprime mortgages became insolvent and narrowly avoided bankruptcy when they were rescued by their sponsor. That marked the beginning of the descent of the subprime CDO and ABS prices. The issuance of mortgage backed securities dried

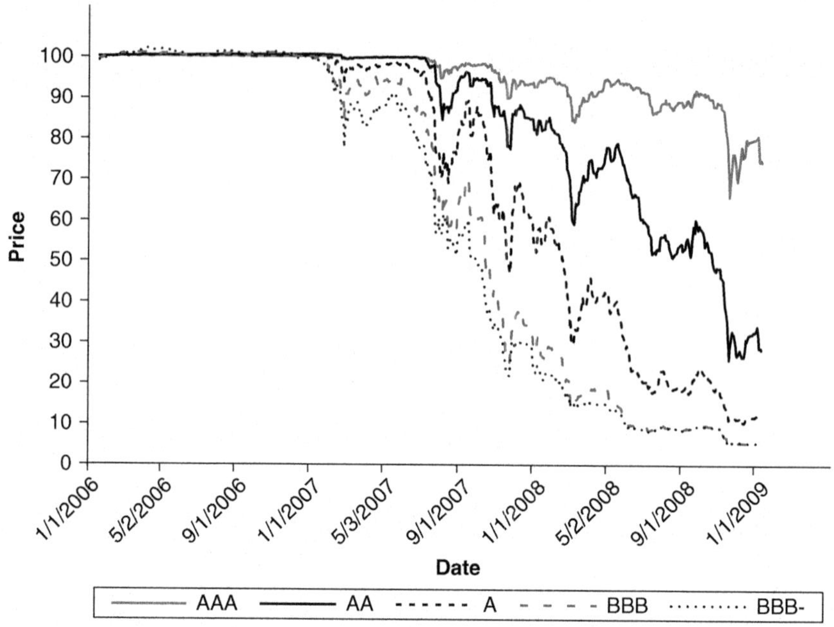

Figure 11.1 Subprime ABX indices by vintage, 2006–2009.

Source: Gerald P. Dwyer, "The Financial Turmoil from 2007 to 2009," Presentation, Federal Reserve Bank of Atlanta, February 2009.

up. Liquidity did not rush in; rather, it fled. Within six months, Bear Stearns was out of existence; and that was before the real trouble emerged.

By March of 2008, when the Fed intervened to orchestrate the rescue of Bear Stearns, the price of subprime CDO and ABS debt was in a free fall that hit rock bottom in September 2008. What next transpired in the housing market was poignantly and poetically captured by Bernard Mandeville's description of an economic crisis brought on by a sudden decline in lending and spending in *The Fable of the Bees* written over 300 years ago:

No honor now could be content,
To live and owe for what was spent,
Liv'ries in Broker's shops are hung;
They part with Coaches for a song;
Sell stately Horses by whole sets;
And Country-Houses to pay debts...
The shew is gone, it thins apace;
And looks with quite another face,
For 'twas not only they that went,
By whom vast sums were yearly spent;
But multitudes that lived on them,
Were daily forced to do the same.
In vain to other trades they'd fly;
All were o'er-stoked accordingly.
The price of Land and Houses falls;

Mirac'lous Palaces whose Walls,
Like those of Thebes, were raised by Play,
Are to be let...
The Building trade is quite destroyed,
Artificers are not employed.[2]

Throughout 2008, subprime mortgage securities prices spiraled downward amid rumors that declines in the value of their holdings of mortgage securities were causing financial distress at Wall Street banks, as well as at those insurance companies who either held or insured the securities. In August of 2008, the Bush administration abruptly reversed course on its prior aversion to guaranteeing GSE liabilities. It issued an explicit government guaranty of all GSE debt in order to enable Fannie Mae and Freddie Mac, who were among the largest holders of subprime mortgage securities, to issue new debt and avoid bankruptcy. Then, in September of 2008, after the bankruptcy of Lehman Brothers and the takeover of insurer AIG, the crisis spread beyond subprime mortgages into almost every other asset class. The stock market plunged, the interbank lending market froze, haircuts in the overnight repo market soared (which meant that less money could be borrowed against collateral of a given value), and the commercial paper market, which supplied blue chip corporations with short-term funding, seized up. GE, the largest and most creditworthy manufacturing corporation in the world, was at risk of not being able to borrow sufficient funds to meet its biweekly payroll. Bank lending virtually shut down.[3]

The financial crisis quickly spread to the "real" economy. In the year following the bankruptcy of Lehman Brothers, US unemployment rate rose from 6.1 percent to 10 percent, US GDP declined by 3 percent, and the decline in trend resulted in an output gap of 6.4 percent.[4] Figure 11.2 is the Fed's measure of the output gap, which is the difference between actual GDP and potential

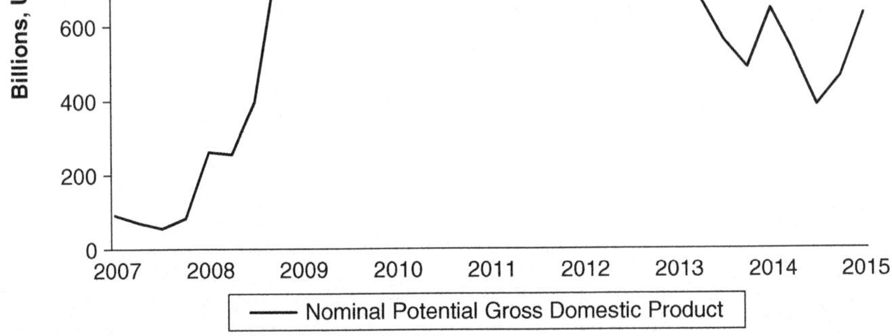

Figure 11.2 Output gap, 2007–2015.

Source: Board of Governors of the Federal Reserve System.

GDP. It shows that in 2008 the United States jumped from full employment to a gap of over $1 trillion. The US economy was launched on a trajectory that appeared frighteningly similar to the Great Depression.

The Amplification of the Subprime Crisis

A signal feature of the financial crisis was that a decline in value of one asset class, subprime mortgage securities, morphed into a generational economic crisis that enveloped almost all asset classes and sent the real economy into a deep recession. The magnitude of losses were staggering; subprime CDO lost 65 percent of their value.[5] Even so, the aggregate value of the decline in subprime mortgage related assets, at the peak of the crisis was an order of magnitude smaller than was the decline in the value of the stock market during the dot-com crash' even though the dot-com crash was mild in comparison to the financial crisis. However, once the virus had spread, the aggregate loss of wealth in the US economy was truly staggering and vastly exceeded the loss of wealth during the dot-com crash. At the nadir of the financial crisis, 25 percent of national wealth had disappeared (figure 11.3). Understanding how this happened is the key to understanding the essence of the financial crisis.

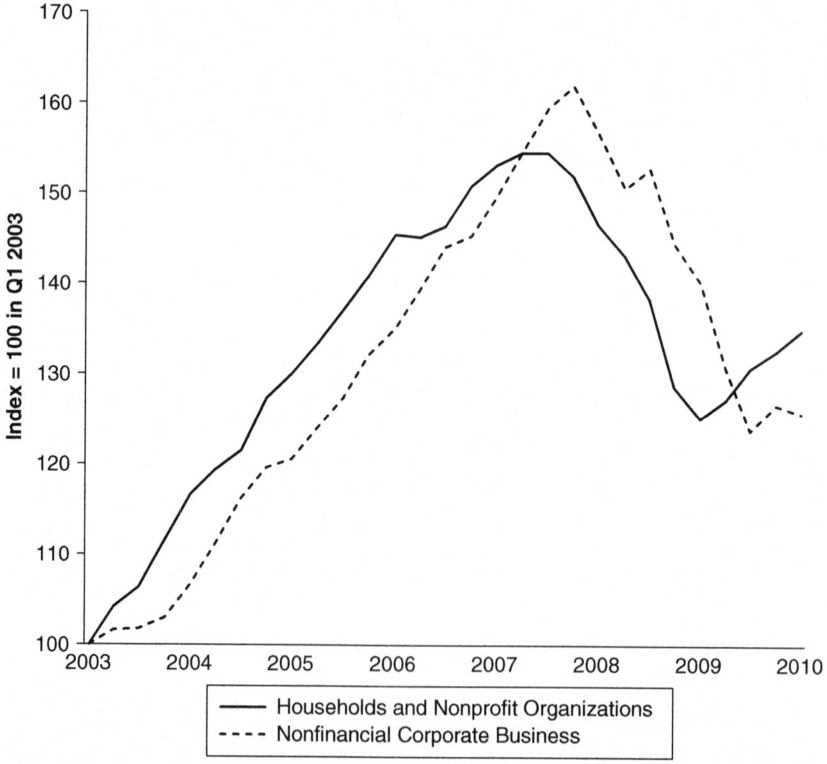

Figure 11.3 Household, corporate net worth, 2003–2010.

Source: Board of Governors of the Federal Reserve System.

I have already pointed out that the buildup of leverage during the boom was neither a necessary nor a sufficient condition for a boom to have occurred: for example, the dot-com boom did not involve an increase in leverage. I will now explain how the high leverage built up during the boom, and its opacity and interconnectedness among large financial institutions, became the crucial factor that transfigured an ordinary recession into the deepest and longest lasting contraction since the Great Depression. To tell the story, I must take a few steps back, into the heady days of the boom.

A Precarious Calm before the Storm

F. A. Hayek defined economic equilibrium as a condition in which "the different plans which the individuals comprising [an economy] have made for action in time are mutually compatible."[6] This concept lies at the core of economic theory. Economists typically assume the economy rapidly adjusts toward equilibrium, subject only to disturbances that force the economy temporarily above or below full employment. The ascendant framework used by macroeconomists requires that agents possess an accurate model of the economy and correctly anticipate the actions of others, so that they formulate mutually consistent plans on the basis of forecasts that correctly predict, at least in a probabilistic sense, what is going to happen in the future. These assumptions, which are bread and butter to economists, will strike most everyone else as patently preposterous. Not only must each of us admit our own ignorance of the structure of the economy and the fate of the future, but economists spend much of their time debating how the economy functions and where it is headed.[7] If the experts cannot agree on what is the "correct" model of the economy, why do they construct models that presume everyone "agrees" on the "correct" model of the economy? Moreover, even if we all individually possessed the correct model, how do each of us know what our fellows are thinking and how they will act? Upon further reflection, however, it can be seen that Hayek's definition of equilibrium does not actually require we all agree, or correctly understand, how the economy works or what our fellows anticipate. It implies instead the less stringent condition that we are able to carry out our plans. "We may very well have a position of equilibrium only because some people have no chance of learning about facts that, if they knew them, would induce them to alter their plans."[8] A financial market can be in a state of equilibrium if profits and securities prices behave as anticipated, even if agents are ignorant of others' beliefs and hold incorrect models of the how the economy works. In this sense, the financial market was in blissfully ignorant equilibrium during the housing boom, even though expectations were unrealistic and ultimately unfulfilled. Most people expected home prices to go on rising indefinitely, and defaults to stay low, and so they did, for a while.[9] During the calm before the storm, mortgage securities performed as anticipated and volatility subsided.

Another feature of economic equilibrium is that financial structure does not affect wealth or the total value of assets, so long as things work out as planned. This means all debts get paid and borrowers and firms pay out—in equity and debt—exactly as expected in each contingent future state of the world. There is a famous proposition in economics, the "Modigliani-Miller" theorem,[10] which demonstrates that, in equilibrium, the financial structure of a firm does not affect the overall value of the firm; the sum of the value of the various components of debt plus the equity is unaffected by how they are configured. The importance of Modigliani-Miller for my analysis is its intuition that financial structure likely does not much affect things so long as the economy is in Hayekian equilibrium. The salient characteristic of a boom is that everyone expects values to rise, and they can continue to do so, for a time, whatever the amount of leverage in the system. So long as the economy remains in equilibrium, a process of self-validating increases in asset values can arise under any financial structure.[11] Modigliani-Miller shows that what the equity dominated dot-com boom of the late 1990s and the debt-laden housing boom of the 2000s had in common was a capital flow bonanza coupled with an expectation of rising values. Leverage was not an essential part of either story.

Things change after the crash hits. Leverage becomes very important in determining the course of events when expectations have been disappointed and plans are revealed to be incompatible. After the blissful spell cast by ignorant equilibrium has been broken, and borrowers default on their loans, we exit the world of Modigliani-Miller, and enter a world where financial structure can exert a significant impact on economic performance. In the financial crisis wealth—as measured by the market price of assets—evaporated. Borrowers suddenly found themselves with smaller resources out of which to finance their obligations, and lenders saw the value of their loan collateral decline.

When leverage is low, the recession will tend to be mild. During the dot-com boom, investors typically received equity shares in exchange for their investments. When values collapsed, investors suffered a decline in wealth and therefore became less able to spend or invest in other ventures, but that was the end of it. The economy temporarily suffered a recession precipitated by the decline in aggregate spending and the layoffs of employees of dot-com firms and related industries. Yet because debt defaults were limited, the ability of banks to extend credit, and the creditworthiness of most individuals and firms, remained unharmed. Banks could still channel credit to promising sectors and firms, and individuals were not constrained by debt burdens they could barely, or not at all, meet. The recession that followed the dot-com boom was relatively short and shallow (though, as pointed out in chapter 8, the labor market was slow to recover until the housing boom began).[12]

When, on the other hand, leverage is high, the crash can trigger a deep recession. During the housing boom debt rose throughout the economy; household mortgage debt, broker-dealer and institutional investor leverage, and broker-dealer and commercial bank off balance sheet liabilities skyrocketed.[13] The high level of household indebtedness reduced the proportion of equity in home value, which shrank the percentage decline in home price that would render the equity negative. Figure 11.4 shows how increasing leverage shrinks equity.

The impact of leverage on the downturn following financial crisis is confirmed by an historical analysis of the sources of severity in recessions following financial crises by Jorda, Schularick, and Taylor. In a pooled sample of 17 countries (which included the United States) covering the period from the end of

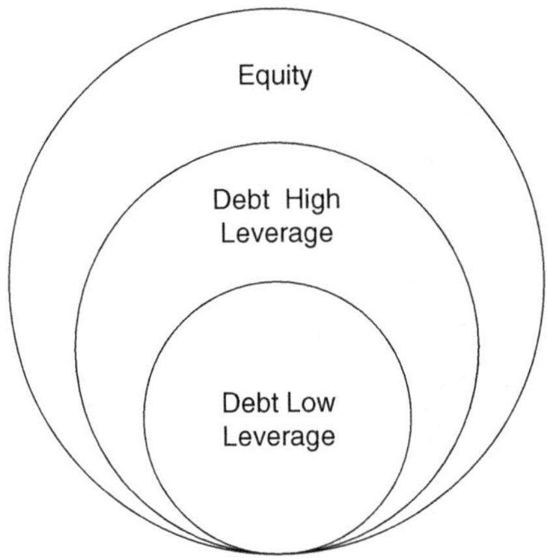

Figure 11.4 Leverage Venn diagram.

World War II to 2012, they found that recessions following asset price bubbles fueled by credit expansion were significantly more severe—in loss of output and duration—compared to recessions following asset price bubbles that were not accompanied by unusual credit expansion. Most significantly, recessions following house price bubbles accompanied by a credit boom were by far the most severe and longest lasting.[14]

Here's a simple example that demonstrates the point: suppose a home has the value of the average new home sold in the United States in 2007—$308,775.00.[15] Now let's consider two scenarios concerning the mortgage on the home. In the "low leverage" scenario, there is a mortgage of $154,387.50 (50 percent LTV[16]) on the home. In the "high leverage" scenario, there is a mortgage of $277,897.50 (90 percent LTV) on the home, which was in the range for subprime mortgages. Now, when the crash hit, home prices fell by 18.5–30 percent on average,[17] which implies that the value of our example home declined to approximately (choosing the midpoint) $273,000.00. At the postcrash price, the low leverage homeowner still has $119,000.00 of positive equity in her home, but the high leverage homeowner has no remaining equity, since the new price of the home is around $6,000.00 below the balance due on her mortgage. She is said to be "underwater" in her home. This is displayed in figure 11.5. Figure 2.1 shows that mortgage debt doubled during the 2003–2007 housing boom. This dramatically increased the number of homeowners who were underwater after home prices collapsed. By 2009 one out of every four residential mortgages in the United States was underwater.[18]

In a similar way, the increased levels of indebtedness and off balance sheet liabilities taken on by banks and broker-dealers to finance their holdings of mortgage related assets reduced the capital cushion with which they could absorb losses in the value of their mortgage related asset holdings. This resulted in the insolvency of almost all large US commercial banks and broker-dealers once the value of mortgages collapsed. In the crisis banks and broker-dealers endured mass withdrawals of short-term funding (called bank runs). Government-backed deposit insurance prevented depositor runs on banks, but short-term wholesale

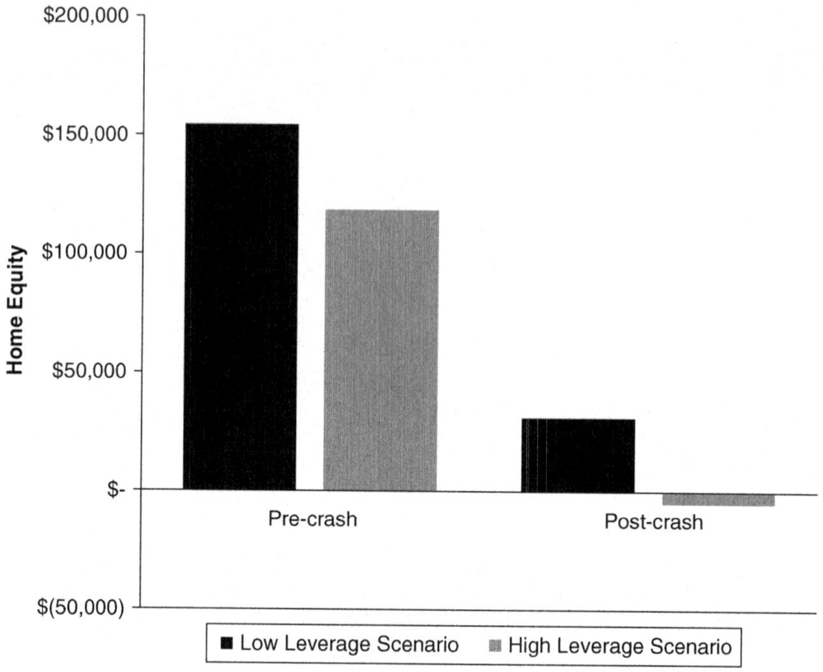

Figure 11.5 Home equity example.

and overnight repo financing dried up and banks and broker-dealers were forced to refinance the ABS they sponsored.

Underwater mortgages forced many households to curtail spending, and diminished mortgage values induced banks to curtail lending. These factors then interacted to propagate the deep recession that followed on the financial crisis. This is how the increased leverage taken on by banks and their homeowner borrowers during the preceding boom deepened the financial crisis and the recession that followed.

Households: Leveraged Losses

Mian and Sufi provide evidence linking the collapse of home prices to the decline in consumer spending. They demonstrate that lower income and lower credit score households accrued a disproportionate share of increased mortgage debt during the housing boom and suffered larger declines in home values after the crash than did other homeowners. This is unsurprising, since subprime loans were targeted at this group and subprime borrowers had the highest default rates.[19] But there was another important factor that came into play after the crash. The equity that subprime borrowers had in their homes, notwithstanding that they were more highly leveraged than other households, was a higher percentage of their net worth than was home equity for wealthier households.[20] As a result, the housing bust hit subprime borrowers hardest in the sense that they suffered the largest proportionate decline in net worth among all homeowners.

Economic theory predicts that subprime borrowers would reduce their spending for two related reasons. The first reason is that home equity lending—which was mostly subprime lending—dried up, so that subprime borrowers no longer had the ability to use their homes as collateral to borrow funds for consumption. Home equity lending had been a major source of borrowing during the boom: from 2002 to 2006, it amounted to over half of the increase in debt for homeowners, around 50 percent of which was used for home improvements or consumption expenditure according to a Federal Reserve survey.[21] By 2008 home equity lending had dried up. The second reason is related to the permanent income hypothesis discussed in chapter 10. Subprime borrowers suffered a large decline in net worth in an environment where most people believed the drop in home values would be long lasting. According to the PIH, a drop in net worth will cause households to reduce consumption.

Mian and Sufi corroborated this proposition in two ways. One was from a database of spending on automobiles, from which they showed that, for a given reduction in home equity, highly leveraged households reduced their spending on automobiles by more than low leveraged households (figure 11.6). The reduction in spending in response to a change in home values is called the "marginal propensity to consume" out of housing wealth. Another form of corroboration was to show that, among counties that experienced large declines in home prices, spending shrunk by more in counties where households had lower net worth (figure 11.7).[22] Consistent with those findings, economists Jonathan

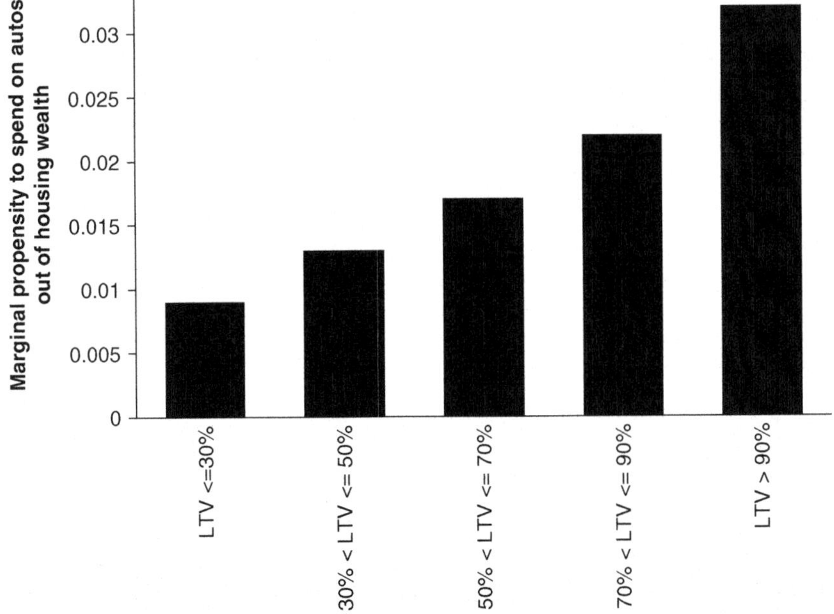

Figure 11.6 MPC based on housing leverage ratio.

Source: Atif Mian and Amir Sufi, *House of Debt* (University of Chicago Press, 2014), Figure 3.3, p. 43.

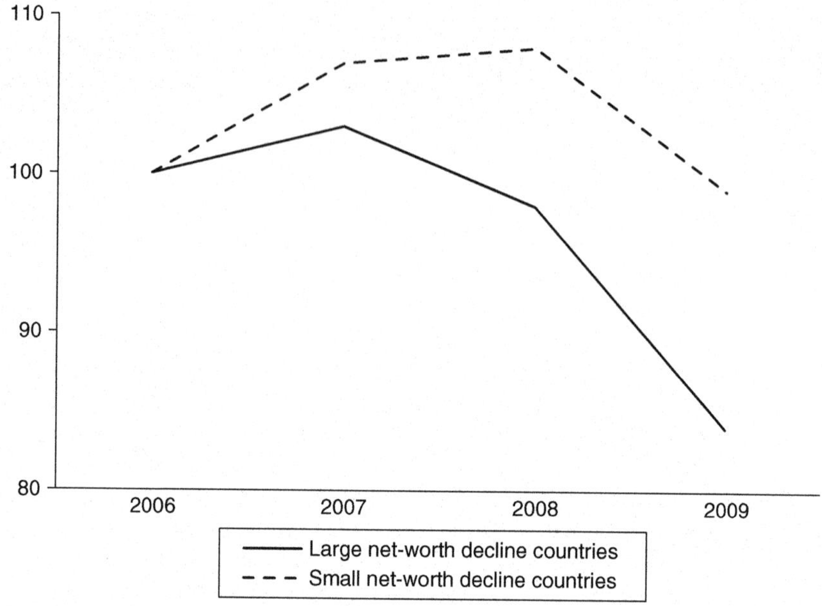

Figure 11.7 Spending in small versus large net worth decline countries.
Source: Atif Mian and Amir Sufi, *House of Debt* (University of Chicago Press, 2014), Figure 3.2, p. 37.

Heathcote and Fabrizio Perri documented that poor US households cut spending after the financial crisis much more sharply (as a percentage of income) than did richer households.[23]

These findings demonstrate the crucial impact that leverage had on constraining spending after the fall in home values. Spending declined most for those households that had become highly leveraged during the boom. This pattern contrasts sharply with the resilience of consumer spending in the aftermath of the bursting of the dot-com bubble. According the Mian and Sufi:

> The bursting of the tech bubble resulted in a huge loss of household wealth but had little effect on household spending, while the bursting of the housing bubble... had a great effect. Why?... tech stocks were owned by very rich households with almost no leverage.[24]

The Meltdown of the Commercial Banking Sector

During the housing boom, banks increased their exposure, both on and off balance sheet, to home mortgages, and financed their operations primarily with short-term debt in the form of demand deposits and wholesale loans. The losses incurred on their mortgage holdings caused the value of bank equity to collapse, as most large banks had become insolvent. Those providing short-term funds to banks (other than insured depositors) became worried about the safety of their investments. This depleted bank capital, which was used to pay off the creditors.

The drain on capital created a liquidity squeeze in the commercial banking system. Here's how it played out.

As the crisis unfolded, bank investors became aware that banks were carrying risks that had not been reported on their financial statements. First, many large banks had engaged in a practice of selling their loans to the ABS they created to hold the loans. The ABS obtained their funding by issuing short-term debt. In many cases, banks guaranteed the repayment of the ABS debt for the ABS they sponsored by issuing liquidity puts,[25] so that when the ABS market imploded, some banks had to step in and fund the ABS to cover the amounts by which outside investors were unwilling to roll-over their ABS debt. The requirement to purchase ABS debt drained more liquidity from banks and revealed that their exposure to subprime mortgages was larger than previously thought. Second, many banks had previously hedged their exposure to mortgage and ABS sponsor guarantee risk by purchasing insurance from apparently well capitalized issuers like AIG and so-called monoline insurers of municipal bond debt. However, when the decline in the value of subprime ABS required AIG to post additional collateral, AIG was unable to meet the requirement and was effectively bankrupt. In the event, the US government bailed out AIG, but several of the other monocline insurers, who had insured around $800 billion of subprime ABS debt, lost their investment grade credit rating and there was questioning of the solvency of those insurers who had not suffered ratings downgrades. In the eyes of the market, ABS default insurance had become worthless.

The revelation of undocumented exposure to ABS and the questionable value of risk hedges came as a shock to bank investors, not only because it showed the potential for loss was far more extensive than had previously been thought, but it undermined trust in the financial information being provided by banks. Suddenly, nobody seemed to know who was bearing the risks associated with mortgage securities. Prior to the financial crisis, banks appeared well capitalized, in large part because risks had been hidden off balance sheet in such places as the liquidity puts issued to backstop the securitizations they sponsored. The dramatic decline in home prices would have inflicted losses on banks in any event, but the revelation of previously undocumented risk, combined with their dependence on short-term debt, placed the banks in a quagmire. The conjuncture of the panicked exit of wholesale lenders and the requirement to fund the liquidity puts drained liquidity from many large banks. This was so because banks found it difficult to sell off assets; nobody was interested in purchasing mortgages and other loans were generally too information intensive for any buyer to be willing to purchase at a reasonable price. This meant banks had to pay off wholesale lenders and ABS investors by drawing down on reserves, which caused some banks to run short of reserves; this led to another problem.

The market for lending reserves between banks collapsed. Not many banks held excess liquidity, and those that did were afraid to lend it out to other banks. One measure of this was the morphing of the spread between three-month LIBOR—the rate at which banks lend reserves to each other—over treasuries of similar duration. In mid-September of 2008, when Lehman went bankrupt and AIG was bailed out, the so-called TED Spread jumped from its historical range of around 50 bps, to 450 bps.[26] The cessation of interbank lending threatened to cause disruption in the payments clearing system. Banks cleared payments between each other by transferring reserves and banks often borrowed reserves from each other to cover temporary shortfalls in reserves. I explain in chapter 12 how it is that almost all payments in the economy involve a transfer of reserves between banks. The risk of a breakdown in the payments clearing system was the financial Armageddon about which Treasury Secretary Paulson and Fed Chairman Bernanke warned Congress in October of 2008.

The predicament faced by banks involved in subprime mortgage lending can be understood by reference to figure 11.8, which is a typical bank balance sheet. The left-hand column is assets, which consist of (mortgage and nonmortgage) loans, other assets and reserves held at the Fed (the bank may hold other assets as well, but I don't want to unnecessarily complicate the explanation). The right-hand column is liabilities, which consist of deposits, short-term wholesale loans, and long-term debt. What remains is equity, or net worth (which I refer to as capital).

The refusal of many short-term wholesale lenders to roll over their debt reduced liabilities (RHS), but the repayment of debt was funded out of reserves—which were applied to the deposit accounts of the creditors and reduced assets by an equal amount (LHS). This did not affect equity, but it did drain reserves.

The requirement to purchase ABS debt pursuant to sponsor guarantees added to assets (LHS), but the reserves (LHS), which were used to pay off the ABS borrowers, reduced assets. Since the value of the ABS debt acquired was less than the debt itself (that is why ABS investors demanded to be repaid) the net effect was to reduce assets. The acquisition of ABS debt drained reserves. The drain on reserves was made worse by the fact that banks in need of reserves were unable to borrow from bank holding excess reserves, since the interbank funding market had shut down (represented by the arrows on the LHS).

The decline in the value of mortgages (LHS) reduced equity (RHS). In the fall of 2008 the decline in mortgage values was large enough to push equity—which was small sliver of total bank assets to begin with—below zero at many banks. Finally, the loss of solvency and liquidity prevented banks from issuing new loans.[27]

		Assets	**Liabilities**
		Mortgages ↓	Equity ↓
		Non-Mortgage Loans	Wholesale Debt ↓
		Other Assets	Long-Term Debt
Other Banks	⇄	Reserves ↓	Deposits
		ABS Assets ↑	

$$\Delta\text{Equity} = \Delta\text{Assets}\downarrow - \Delta\text{Liabilities}\ \{\text{Wholesale Debt}\downarrow, \text{ABS Guarantees}\uparrow\}$$

$$\text{ABS Assets} < \text{ABS Guarantees}$$

$$\Delta\text{Reserve}\downarrow = \Delta\text{Wholesale Debt}\downarrow - \Delta\text{ABS Guarantees}\uparrow$$

Figure 11.8 Bank balance sheet example 1.

The Meltdown of the Shadow Banking Sector

During the housing boom, broker-dealers increased their exposure, both on and off balance sheet, to home mortgages, and financed their operations primarily with overnight repo debt. The losses incurred on their mortgage holdings caused the value of their equity to collapse, rendering most broker-dealers insolvent. Broker-dealers were exposed to the same loss of confidence, and the same loss of funding, as were banks. Unlike banks, however, who were locked into long-term debt, broker-dealers were able to contract their reverse repo loans as their repo funding dried up, which provided funds to repay repo creditors. Broker-dealer leverage contracted rapidly (see figure 6.1). That is a result of the matched book funding of broker-dealers. Nevertheless, broker-dealers suffered a liquidity squeeze. A portion of repo debt was not matched by reverse repos and the requirement to purchase the debt of their sponsored ABS depleted their cash, which forced them to make distress sales of their subprime mortgage related debt and other assets.[28] The predicament faced by broker-dealers can be understood by reference to figure 11.9, which is a typical broker-dealer balance sheet.

In the shadow banking sector, concerns related to subprime losses caused institutional cash pools to pull back from private overnight repo funding, much of which was collateralized by subprime ABS. This, in turn, forced broker-dealers to curtail their matched book overnight securities funding, which transmitted distress to bond investors. Broker-dealers suffered the same type of losses as did commercial banks on the subprime mortgage exposures they retained on balance sheet, and their off balance sheet liquidity puts issued on their sponsored ABS. The need to raise cash to meet these obligations forced broker-dealers and some bond investors into distress sales of securities, which amplified the crisis by pushing down the prices of non-subprime mortgage securities.

The conjuncture of contracting bank and broker-dealer credit, combined with distressed asset sales, triggered a downward spiral of forced liquidations across ever-widening classes of securities, as entities needed to raise cash from whatever assets they could sell at a reasonable price. The forced liquidations quickly

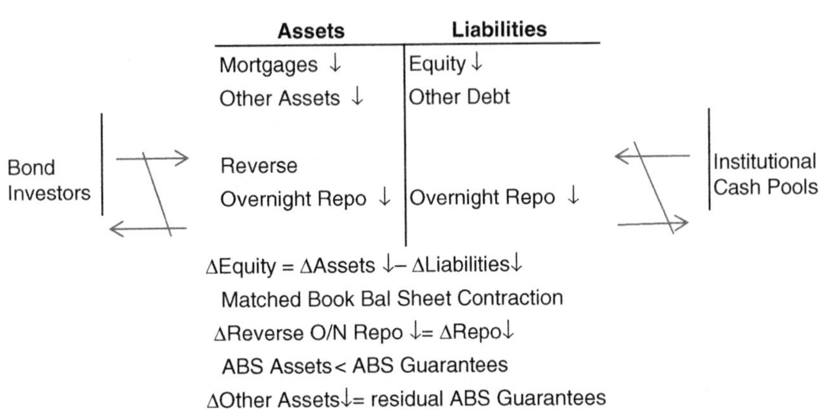

Figure 11.9 Broker-dealer balance sheet example.

spread the losses on subprime mortgages across many other asset classes, which magnified the negative impact of the underperformance of subprime mortgages.

For a time, it appeared that every asset holder wished to liquidate and nobody wished to acquire; which caused securities markets to seize up. That is the environment in which the impact of the collapse in the value of housing related securities spread to other assets. Fed Chairman Ben Bernanke believed that bank and broker-dealer leverage was the crucial ingredient in transmitting losses on subprime securities to other asset classes in the crisis:

> Judged in relation to the size of global financial markets, aggregate exposure to subprime mortgages were quite modest. By way of comparison, it is not especially uncommon for one day's paper losses in global stock markets to exceed the losses on subprime mortgages suffered during the entire crisis, without obvious ill effects on market functioning or on the economy. Thus, losses on subprime mortgages can plausibly account for the massive reaction seen during the crisis only insofar as they interacted with other factors . . . that served to amplify their effects . . . The combination of dependence on wholesale short-term financing; excessive leverage; generally poor risk management; and the gaps and weaknesses in regulatory oversight created an environment in which a powerful, self-reinforcing panic could begin.[29]

Conclusion

The high leverage taken on by households and financial intermediaries during the housing boom reduced the size decline in home prices that could drive home equity below the principal balance due on mortgages. When home values dropped below the balance due on mortgages, homeowner equity was wiped out, which rendered both mortgage borrowers and lenders insolvent. Leverage reduced the ability of the US economy to absorb steep declines in asset prices. It made the reduction in household spending and bank lending more severe, and it caused the distress in housing to be transmitted to other asset classes more quickly. After the events of September 2008, the US economy was on a downward spiral and there did not appear to be any market forces that could break the downward descent.

The collapse of the commercial and shadow banking sectors, the implosion of asset values, and the precipitous fall in employment in the aftermath of the financial crisis elicited an aggressive government policy response to help stabilize the economy. The call for policy action is readily understandable; a market failure is the classic case for intervention. Determining which course of action to follow is more difficult. In the next chapter, I will examine the Fed's attempt to stem the downward spiral.

CHAPTER 12

The Initial Policy Response

> Neither a borrower nor a lender be, For loan oft loses both itself and friend, And borrowing dulls the edge of husbandry.
>
> —William Shakespeare[1]

> If money isn't loosened up, this sucker could go down.
>
> —George W. Bush

The Initial Policy Response

The Desire for Liquidity Reduced Liquidity

After the bankruptcy of Lehman and the takeover of AIG in mid-September 2008, fear began to spread like wildfire. Corporations and households massively increased their demand for liquid assets. Keynes vividly described the motive behind the rush to liquidity that seizes markets in the aftermath of a huge negative shock to expectations:

> Our desire to hold Money as a store of wealth is a barometer of the degree of our distrust of our own calculations and conventions concerning the future. Even though this feeling about Money is itself conventional or instinctive, it operates, so to speak, at a deeper level of our motivations. It takes charge at the moments when the higher, more precarious conventions have weakened. The possession of actual money lulls our sense of disquietude; and the premium which we require to make us part with money is the measure of the degree of our disquietude.[2]

The increase in the "premium which we require to make us part with money" was reflected in a decline in demand for all goods and assets other than money, which created downward pressure on all prices. The panicked rush to acquire liquid assets actually reduced liquidity in the economy. To understand why, I need to explain a bit more about the concept of liquidity. Keynes wrote that one asset is more liquid than another if it is "more certainly realizable at short notice without loss."[3] In normal times, there is a spectrum of liquidity and different assets have greater or lesser degrees of it, money being the most liquid asset. However, during the financial crisis nothing had any attributes of liquidity other than money. Money, in the sense of the most liquid asset on Keynes's spectrum, is ultimately a social construct. An asset is liquid if others will accept it as payment, immediately and without discount (at par). In our times, currency, insured bank deposits, short-term US government guaranteed debt, commercial paper, and money market funds[4] appear to have fulfilled this function. In the shadow banking sector, overnight repos fulfilled the role for institutional cash pools. But after the Prime Fund broke the buck,[5] investors fled repos, money market funds, and the commercial paper market (in which money market funds were an important source of funding), the pool of securities that functioned as money abruptly contracted. As a result, repo haircuts skyrocketed, money market funds tottered on the verge of insolvency, and the issuance of commercial paper issuance plummeted.

Figure 12.1 displays one dimension of the rush to liquidity in the fall of 2008. Treasury yields dropped to zero while yields on investment grade commercial paper soared. The prices of stocks, real estate, and private bonds collapsed and ABS issuance ceased (see figure 7.2). Bank lending contracted (see figure 12.5), which caused the money supply to contract. It did so because loans are a source of liquidity for many borrowers—a loan is a commitment to advance money—and the decline in bank loan volume caused bank deposits to contract (since deposits are extinguished when bank loans are repaid). There were thus several forces acting to reduce liquidity during the crisis. One was the loss of confidence in nonmoney

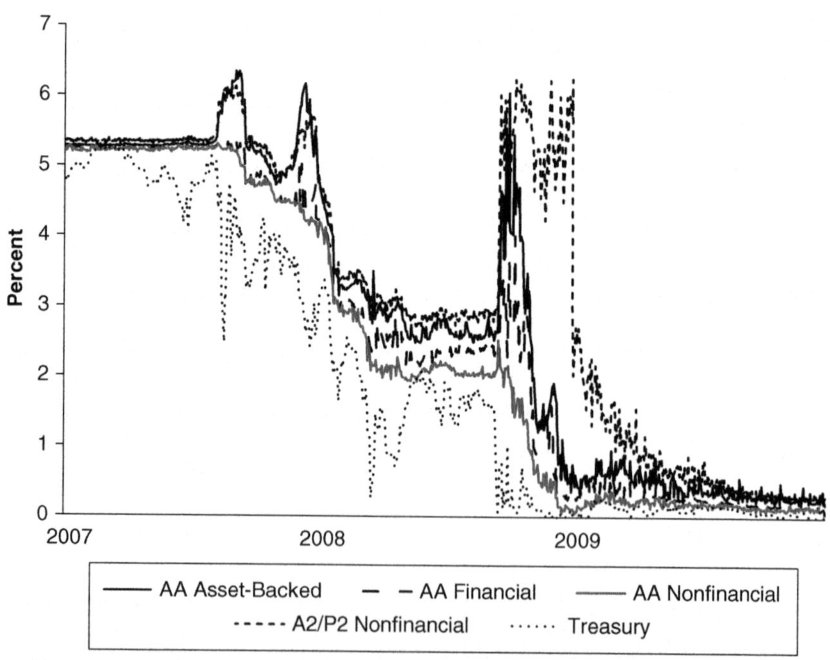

Figure 12.1 Thirty-day commercial paper and treasury rates, 2007–2009.
Source: Board of Governors of the Federal Reserve System.

assets, which rendered then illiquid; another was the loss of confidence in money market funds; another was the contraction of bank loans and the concomitant contraction in bank deposits.

The Fed's Restoration of Liquidity

In response to the deflationary pressure—in order to avert a potentially catastrophic contraction of credit and spending—the Fed undertook a series of unprecedented actions intended to satisfy the increased demand for money.[6] It provided loans to commercial banks (the TAF program); it provided loans to broker-dealers (PDCF and TSLF programs); it provided funding to commercial paper and money markets (the AMLF and CPFF programs); and it funded the acquisition of asset backed securities (the TALF program). The Fed also provided funding to prevent the bankruptcies of two major financial institutions: Bear Sterns[7] and AIG.[8] Within a two-month period, starting from the date Lehman Brothers filed for bankruptcy on September 15, 2008, the Fed's holdings of assets increased from under $700 billion to over $2 trillion. The Fed's acquisition of assets is depicted in figure 12.2.

A by-product of the Fed's programs was to dramatically increase bank reserves (note that bank reserves held by the Fed are a liability to the Fed and an asset to the commercial banks). Here is how that came about. To effect a transfer of money to pay for its purchase of an asset (or to issue a loan) under any of its liquidity programs, the Fed needed to create a deposit balance (the "Deposit Injection," in figure 12.4) at a bank. Once created, the Fed transferred its deposit balance to the party from whom it purchased the asset (or to whom it made the

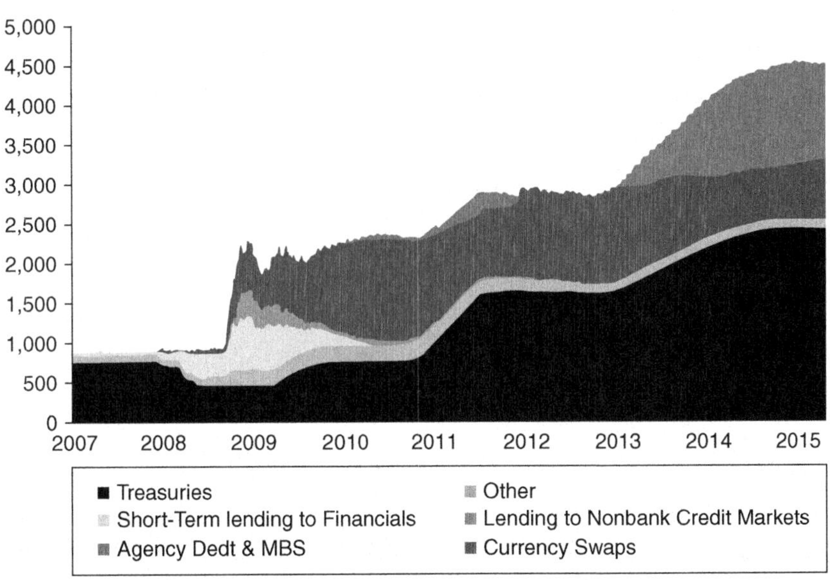

Figure 12.2 Fed assets, 2007–2009.

Source: Federal Reserve Bank of Minneapolis.

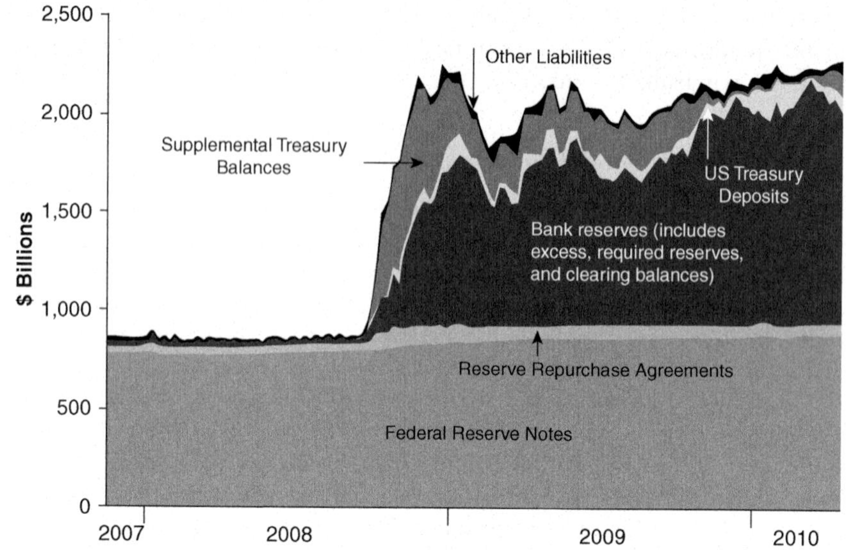

Figure 12.3 Fed liabilities, 2007–2009.
Source: Federal Reserve Bank of Minneapolis.

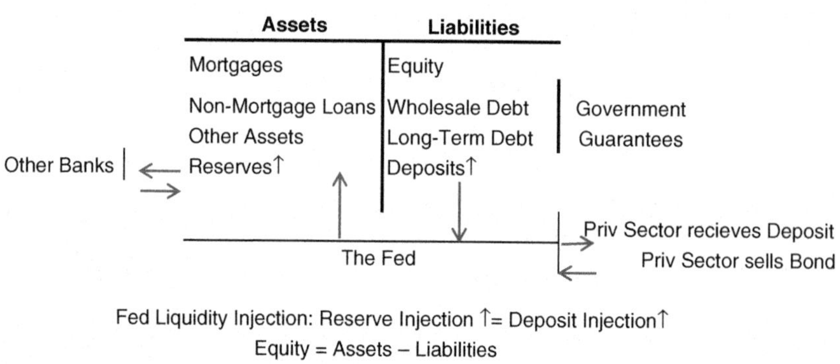

Figure 12.4 Bank balance sheet example 2.

loan) in just the same way the rest of us use our bank deposit account to transfer money. And just like the rest of us, in order to create a deposit balance—which is a liability of the bank—the Fed was required to transfer money into the bank.

But the Fed is able do something none of us can do. We are only able to transfer money in one of two ways; by depositing physical currency into the bank or by transferring a balance from another deposit account (possibly held at a different commercial bank). The Fed has a third option for transferring money; it can create—out of thin air!—a reserve balance at the Fed, which is a deposit account of the bank (the "Reserve Injection," in figure 12.4). Banks count the reserve balance as money because they transfer reserves between themselves in order to settle accounts, and they can require the Fed to convert reserves into currency. Figure 12.4 shows what happened. The Fed simultaneously injected reserves, which is an asset of the bank (the Reserve Injection) and received a deposit account of equal size (the Deposit Injection).

The Fed's programs added liquidity to economy in three ways. First, its injection of reserves—which topped $1 trillion—relieved banks of the need to borrow funds in order to maintain the reserve balances they required to carry out the ordinary business of clearing transfers of deposit balances between banks. It alleviated the threat that the payments system could be disrupted by some banks falling short of the reserves required to clear deposit transfers and not being able to borrow the reserves needed to function. Second, its creation of deposits added money to the economy, which is what the private sector was clamoring for. Third, its use of the added deposits to purchase assets like commercial paper and ABS, or to lend money to parties willing to purchase those assets, restored liquidity to important sectors. In addition to the Fed's liquidity operations, the FDIC and in some instances the US treasury guaranteed new debt issued by banks, which restored their ability to borrow.

To summarize: the Fed was able to lull the disquietude felt by an anxious private sector by injecting liquidity throughout the financial system, which provided financial intermediaries with the funds they required to meet all of their short-term obligation, much of which functioned as money, or near-money, for the non-financial sector. It did so by creating bank deposits—which are a liability of banks and function as money—to enable it to acquire assets and lend money under its liquidity programs. In order to create bank deposits, the Fed delivered assets to banks in the form of reserves at the Fed, which restored liquidity to banks.

The Fed's liquidity operations increased the assets (LHS) and liabilities (RHS) of banks by an equal amount (figure 12.4). For each dollar of deposit the Fed received from a commercial bank, the Fed was required to add a dollar of reserve held by the commercial bank at the Fed. Therefore, the Fed did not increase the net worth of banks. This can be seen by noting that bank net worth (or equity) is equal to assets minus liabilities. The Fed contributed assets—reserves—that exactly equaled the deposit liabilities it received. The fact that bank assets and liabilities both increased by an equal amount meant the difference between them, which is the net worth of the bank, was not altered by the Fed's programs.

If the value of a bank's assets declined below the level of its liabilities during the financial crisis, the bank would have been insolvent and the Fed's liquidity programs would have done nothing (at least directly)[9] to alleviate that problem. The Fed has magical powers to conjure liquidity for the private sector—in the form of bank deposits- and for the banks—in the form of reserves. Yet, because it is constrained to create deposit liabilities and reserves in equal amounts, the Fed cannot increase the net worth of a bank. The Fed is powerful, but it is not omnipotent!

The Implementation of a Lesson Learned

In their monumental study *A Monetary History of the United States 1867–1960*, economists Milton Friedman and Anna Schwartz blamed the Great Depression on the failure of the Fed to provide banks with liquidity when they faced runs. In their estimation, Fed complacency in the early 1930s was the crucial policy error that allowed an unremarkable recession to morph into the Great Depression. A bank run is a situation where panicked depositors rush in at once to withdraw their deposits by demanding the bank pay them currency. Depositors demand currency in a run situation in order to "lull their disquietude" over concerns that their bank may be insolvent. Since banks are highly leveraged and normally hold only a small portion of their assets in the form of currency on hand—the remaining assets being held in the form of loans, securities and reserves at the central bank—a bank can never pay off all depositors during a run. In normal circumstances, the net effect of deposits and withdrawals results in very little need for the bank to pay out currency. When a run occurs, however, the bank needs to receive currency from outside itself to meet the demand for withdrawals.

In the early stages of what became the Great Depression, according to Friedman and Schwartz, the Fed allowed the banking panic to spread by standing aloof (and refusing to lend currency to the banks that needed it) while numerous banks endured runs by their depositors. The rush for liquidity caused liquidity to evaporate; M2 money supply shrunk by over a third. The contraction in money supply reflected the contraction in bank deposits (which is a part of the broad money supply). Deposits contracted because banks defaulted on their deposit obligations, hoarded cash (which reduced the bank money multiplier[10]), and called in loans (which were paid off by transferring cash or bank deposit balances, which—as liabilities of the banks—were extinguished). The monetary contraction induced a drop in aggregate demand, since there was less money in circulation available for transactions. The decline in aggregate demand forced a severe deflation and drop in employment.[11] Friedman and Schwartz explained what happened as follows:

> If deterioration of credit quality or bad banking was the trigger, which it may to some extent have been, the damaging bullet it discharged was the inability of the banking system to acquire additional high-powered money to meet the resulting demands of depositors for currency, without a multiple contraction of deposits... the composition of assets held by banks would hardly have mattered if additional high powered money had been made available from whatever source to meet the demands of depositors for currency without requiring a multiple contraction of deposits and assets. The trigger would have discharged only a blank cartridge. The banks would have been under no necessity to dump their assets. There would have been no major decline in the market prices of the assets and no impairment in the capital accounts of banks.[12]

In a 2002 speech in honor of Milton Friedman's ninetieth birthday, Ben Bernanke, speaking as a member of the board of governors of the US Fed, stated: "I would like to say to Milton and Anna: Regarding the Great Depression. You're right, we did it. We're very sorry. But thanks to you, we won't do it again."[13] In the fall of 2008, Mr. Bernanke had the opportunity to make good on his promise, and he did. While the existence of federal insurance for commercial bank deposits was sufficient to maintain confidence and avert an old fashioned commercial bank run, the issuers of overnight repo loans to broker-dealers, investors in money market funds and short-term wholesale lenders to banks and broker-dealers all panicked and demanded immediate repayment of their loans. Their actions were economically equivalent to a bank run, since they placed financial intermediaries in a position where they faced a demand for withdrawals that exceeded their available funds. The Fed's liquidity programs provided financial intermediaries with sufficient liquidity to meet all their short-term repayment obligations, and thereby successfully quelled the sense of disquietude felt by a panicked multitude and saved the financial system from collapse. In the year following the implementation of the Fed's liquidity programs, repo haircuts contracted; by mid-2009 the Ted Spread shrank back down below 50 bps and the commercial paper market revived.

To illustrate how the Fed prevented a deflationary contraction in the broad money supply consider the following. From September 2008 through January 2010, commercial bank loans declined by approximately $700 billion.[14] Since loans are repaid by extinguishing deposits, this implies a decline of $700 billion in deposits, which is part of the broad money supply (M2).[15] On September 1, 2008, just before the Fed launched its liquidity programs, M2 stood at $7,760.5 billion.[16] Therefore, the decline in deposits induced by the decline in bank lending was about 9 percent of the broad money supply. This means, in the absence of Fed action, the money supply would have contracted by 9 percent. This is even more striking when it is considered that over the 20 years prior to September 1, 2008, M2 grew at around 5 percent per annum.[17] This fact alone demonstrates how dangerous the situation had become. In the absence of action to countervail the decline in deposits, the US economy may indeed have headed into another Great Depression. The monetary contraction was offset by the Fed's creation of over $1 trillion of bank deposits from September 1, 2008, through January 1, 2010.[18] The $700 billion decline in deposits due to the reduction in bank lending and the $1 trillion increase in Fed created deposits implied a net increase of $300 billion in bank deposits. In the event, bank deposits actually increased by $600 billion during that period.[19] Most of the difference is accounted for by the $800 billion exodus from money market funds during the period.[20] Much of the withdrawal from money market funds probably migrated into bank deposits, in order to quell the disquietude of investors.

It is difficult to quarrel with the general thrust of Fed actions to restore liquidity and avert panic in the fall of 2008 (though I shall question details of its implementation later on in this chapter). When faced with the prospect of a financial collapse and destructive deflation it acted to maintain monetary stability. The Fed's performance in 2008 stands in striking contrast to its inaction at the onset of the Great Depression. There are few instances in history where economic scholarship informed economic policy to such beneficial effect. The historical analysis of Milton Friedman and Anna Schwartz and its implementation by the board of governors of the Federal Reserve System may have averted a second Great Depression. This does not mean, however, that monetary policy can accomplish anything more. Friedman harbored a well-known pessimism about the benefits of monetary policy and warned of unintended consequences of policy activism. In his celebrated 1967 presidential address to the American Economics Association, Friedman cautioned, "Experience suggests that the path of wisdom is to use monetary policy explicitly to offset other disturbances only when they offer a 'clear and present danger.'"[21]

The Contraction of Credit

The Three Primary Sources of Credit

Prior to the onset of the financial crisis there were three major sources of credit to households and corporations; ABS, which primarily financed mortgages; banks, which financed most every type of borrowing; and bonds, which were issued by large corporations. After the onset of the financial crisis ABS issuance collapsed (see figure 7.2), bank lending contracted (see figure 12.5), but bond issuance increased (see figure 12.8). Effectively, this meant that only large corporations and the most creditworthy households were able to borrow. It needs to be understood why this particular pattern emerged.

The Fed averted a deflationary disaster, but it was not able to prevent a deep and long lasting recession. The collapse of home values created debt overhangs on banks and homeowners. A debt overhang is a circumstance where the value of assets owned by a firm or a person has precipitously declined while the amount of its debt has not. This matters a lot when the entity is highly leveraged, because a debt overhang shrinks net worth, which reduces the asset value that can be pledged as collateral for loans, and in extremis renders the entity insolvent (i.e., a negative net worth). The Fed was able to use its power to conjure reserves and deposits out of thin air, so to speak, to restore liquidity, but it did not have the power to restore lost wealth; it could not bring insolvent households and banks back to solvency.

While it is readily understandable that bank lending on real estate dried up after the massive defaults on home mortgage loans, the decline in commercial

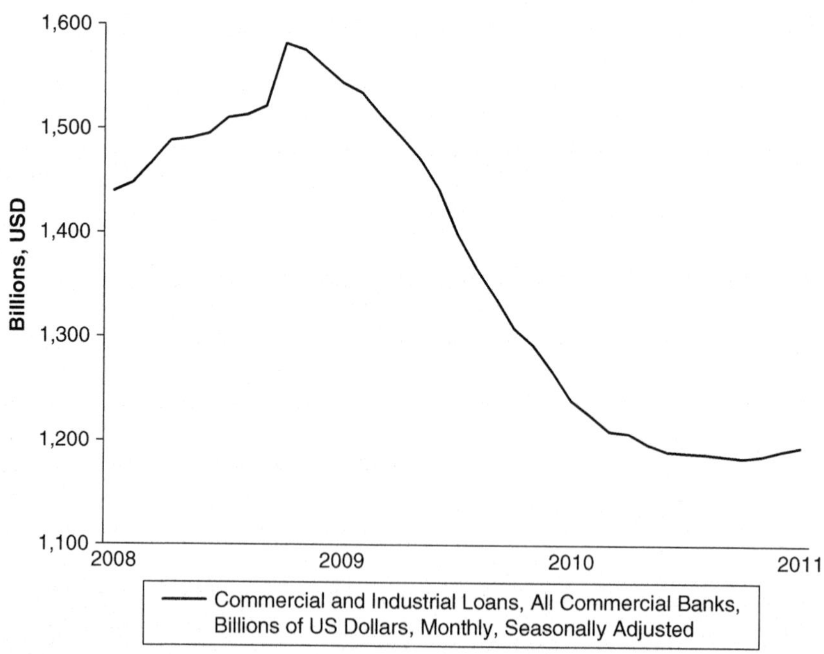

Figure 12.5 Bank C&I loans, 2008–2011.

Source: Board of Governors of the Federal Reserve System.

and industrial lending -which does not involve real estate collateral—means that bank lending dried up for corporate borrowers who did not suffer from the collapse in home values (see figure 12.5). Moreover, the decline in commercial bank lending understates the severity of the pullback in credit for several reasons; many large banks were required to substantially increase lending to support the ABS they sponsored when investors fled and called on banks' guarantees;[22] banks were required to fund lines of credit that had been committed to before the crisis, and the typically long duration of bank debt meant that most existing loans could not be terminated at short notice.

Who Caused Non-Real Estate Bank Lending to Contract—Reluctant Banks or Reluctant Borrowers?

A key question is why bank lending to corporations declined after the onset of the financial crisis. To what extent did the contraction in bank lending result from banks refusal to lend, and to what extent were borrowers reluctant to take on new debt? It might appear that the losses banks incurred on mortgages depleted their capital and prevented them from lending to anyone (figure 12.6).

On the other hand, there is evidence pointing to decline in demand for borrowing from firms. One study found that firms that did not suffer from debt overhangs reduced capital spending by the same amount as did firms that faced debt overhangs,[23] which suggests there was a systemic lack of confidence, and consequent decline in demand for borrowing, irrespective of the creditworthiness

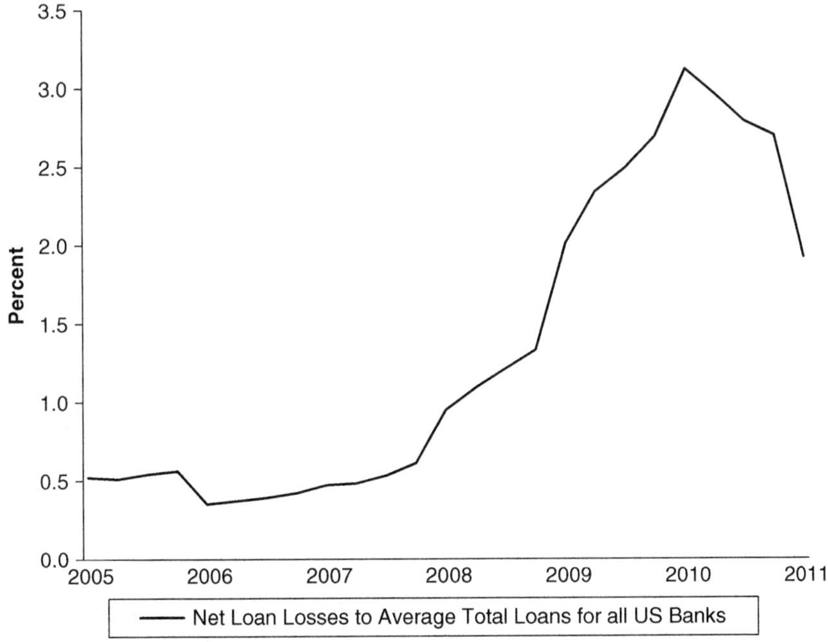

Figure 12.6 Bank loan losses, 2005–2011.
Source: Board of Governors of the Federal Reserve System.

of individual corporations. It is possible, that what motivated corporations to hoard cash after the crisis was a fear of losing access to loans when they needed them (recall that GE nearly went bankrupt in late 2008 when it appeared it might be unable to borrow the money to meet its payroll). Mian and Sufi point to the National Federation of Independent Businesses (NFIB) survey of small businesses, a group that does not have access to the bond market, indicating that credit availability was not a major problem during and after the financial crisis. From 2007 to 2009, the fraction of respondents citing credit as a main concern never rose above 5 percent, whereas the fraction citing poor sales as a problem increased from 10 percent to almost 35 percent.[24]

Yet, there are two pieces of evidence that make a more compelling case that the primary cause of the decline in non-real estate bank lending arose from banks' desire to reduce outstanding loans. One is that corporations with access to the bond market did not curtail borrowing—they offset a reduction in bank borrowing with increased bond issuance—whereas other corporations, who were dependent on banks for credit, borrowed less. The other piece of evidence is that banks increased their loan interest rates even as bank lending declined.

As to the first point, economists Bo Becker and Victoria Ivashina found that after the onset of the financial crisis, when bank credit growth slowed, firms that had previously borrowed from banks and issued bonds tended to shift their financing from bank loans to bonds without appreciably reducing their overall borrowing, whereas firms that were dependent on bank financing alone, experienced declines in borrowing. On the assumption that a firms' desire to borrow, and its change in financial condition during the financial crisis, was independent of whether or not it was able to issue bonds, their result indicates the reduction

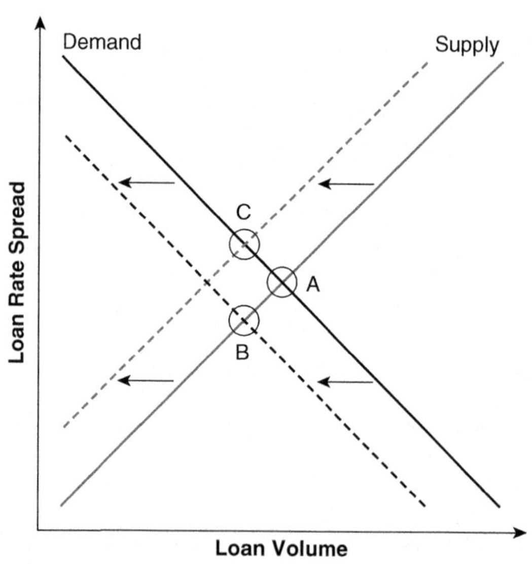

Figure 12.7 Loan rate spread versus loan volume example.

in bank lending resulted from bank's refusal to lend.[25] Figure 12.9 shows that aggregate bond issuance recovered fairly quickly after the crisis.

As to the second point, if the reduction in bank lending was caused by a decline in borrowing demand, one would expect loan rates to fall. If the reduction was caused by a decline in loan supply, one would expect loan rates to rise. The situation can be represented by figure 12.7, which is a textbook supply and demand chart where the upward sloping "supply" curve represents banks' schedule of loans offered at different loan rate spreads, and the downward sloping "demand" curve represents borrowers' schedule of borrowing desired at different loan rate spread.[26]

The initial pre-financial crisis loan volume and loan rate spread is represented by the intersection of the supply and demand curves at point A in figure 12.7. A decline in banks' loan supply is represented by a leftward shift of the supply curve, which moves the intersection to point C, at which the loan volume is lower and the loan rate spread is higher. A decline in borrowers' loan demand is represented by a leftward shift of the demand curve, which moves the intersection to point B, at which the loan volume is lower and the loan rate spread is lower. This elementary exercise enables us to distinguish the cause the decline in loan volume. If it was due to reluctant banks, loan rate spreads would fall. If it was caused by reluctant borrowers, loan rate spreads would rise. All that is required to make the determination is a database of bank loans.

Using a large database on the borrowing activities of medium and large sized public nonfinancial corporations, economists Tobias Adrian and Hyun Song Shin show that the loan rate spread charged on loans to corporate borrowers soared after the onset of the financial crisis, while the volume of bank lending contracted, which is the opposite of what occurred during the preceding boom, when rates fell and loan volume increased due to the fact that during the boom loan demand was high (see figure 12.8).[27] The combination of rising rates and declining volume indicates that banks reduced the supply of loans.[28] It should be noted, however, that bank net interest margins declined after 2010 (and lending continued to decline). I do not think this reflected a sudden reversal of roles, with banks wanting to lend and borrowers becoming reluctant. Rather, the decline in spreads an independent factor; the Fed's policy of purchasing long-term debt. The Fed aimed to reduce long-term interest rates, which compressed the maturity spread and forced down bank net interest margins. I address the Fed's quantitative easing policy in chapter 13.

Why Didn't Excess Reserves Cause Banks to Increase Lending?

One might wonder why banks did not expand lending in response to the massive increase in reserves created by the Fed. As background to exploring this question, it is important to understand that reserves matter to banks for two related reasons. One is that US banks settle accounts between themselves by transferring reserves at the Fed. What this means is that if person A pays $100 to person B by writing a check or presenting a credit card, a balance of $100 is deducted from person A's checking account and transferred into person B's checking account. If

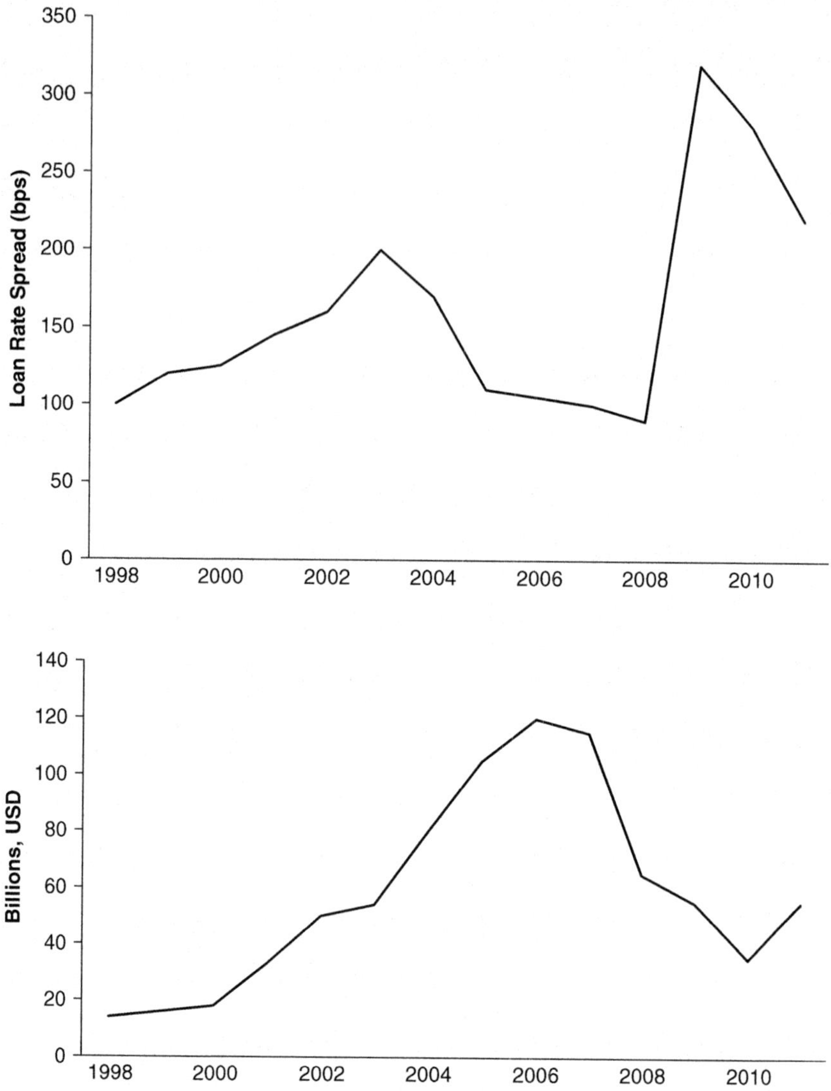

Figure 12.8 (a) Bank loan financing—cost, 1998–2010. (b) Bank loan financing—total amount, 1998–2011.

Source: Tobias Adrian, Paolo Colla, and Hyun Song Shin, "Which Financial Frictions? Parsing the Evidence from the Financial Crisis of 2007–9," Federal Reserve Bank of New York Staff Report No. 528. 2012, Figure 7 p. 19.

persons A and B have accounts at different banks (let us call them Bank A and Bank B, to match up with the persons), then, to effectuate the transfer of the balance between accounts, Bank A will deduct $100 from person A's account and from its reserve balance at the Fed and credit $100 to Bank B's reserve account at the Fed, after which Bank B will credit $100 to person B's account. This is how the vast majority of payments are made nowadays. So, banks need to have reserve balances at the Fed in order for the payments system to function smoothly.

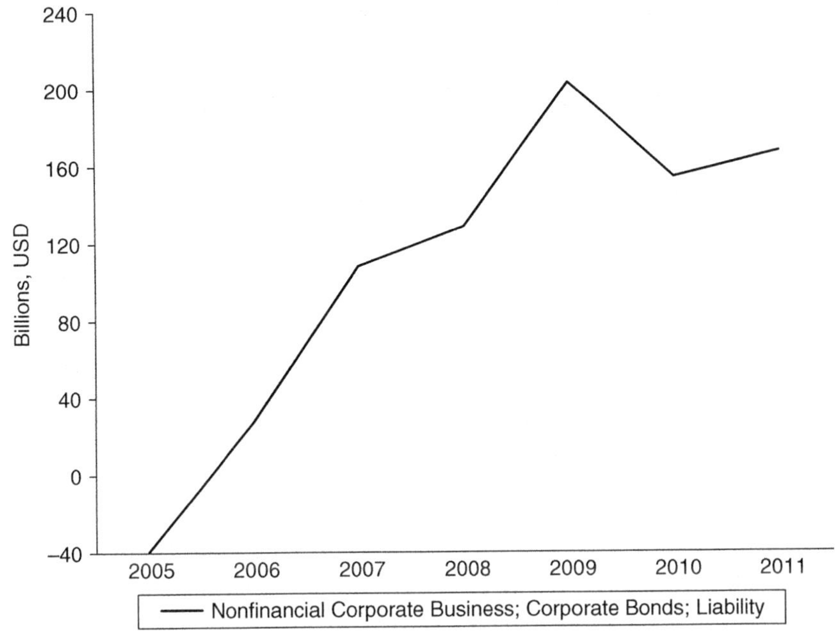

Figure 12.9 Nonfinancial corporation bond issuance, 2005–2011.
Source: Board of Governors of the Federal Reserve System (US). Release: Z.1 Financial Accounts of the United States.

The other reason reserves matter is that they are necessary to enable banks to increase their lending. The way to understand this is to consider what happens when a bank makes a loan. Suppose a bank makes a $100 loan. The bank will not usually hand over currency to its borrower; rather it will create a deposit account for the borrower of $100. Out of thin air, the bank has created an asset—the loan to the borrower—and a liability—the deposit in favor of the borrower. So, the Fed is not the only actor capable of creating money out of thin air; private banks can do so as well! The difference between what happens when a bank expands its balance sheet and when the Fed causes banks to expand can be understood by referring back to figure 12.4. Both types of expansion involve an increase in deposit liabilities. The difference arises from the type of asset that is created. The Fed creates a reserve and the bank creates a loan. One salient difference between a reserve and a loan is that the reserve balance can be transferred between banks to settle accounts (as in the example earlier) whereas a loan cannot usually be transferred to settle accounts.

When a bank issues a loan and creates a deposit, the deposit is likely to be transferred to other banks, as the borrower uses her deposit account to pay expenses. To accommodate the likely outflow of the additional deposit balances, the bank needs to add to its reserves to ensure it has the means to settle the transfer of its deposit liabilities to other banks (a bank must transfer the reserve balance in order to induce the other bank to accept the transfer of its deposit liability), and the Fed mandates that it does so. That is why the Fed ties the minimum reserve requirement to the level of deposits.[30] Therefore, one way the Fed can control lending is by adjusting the formula for required reserves. You might recall from chapter 3 that the PBOC raised reserve requirements in order to slow Chinese money growth as part of its sterilization of dollar inflows. Now you know how it worked; the increase in required reserves forced banks to contract lending in order to reduce the volume of deposits, and the reduction in deposits constituted a contraction in the money supply.

In August 2008, the month before the Lehman bankruptcy and the AIG bailout, Fed required reserve balances at commercial banks was approximately $44 billion, and excess commercial bank reserves at the Fed—which are the volume of reserves held by banks over and above the amount mandated by the Fed—was much smaller, at approximately $1.9 billion. By December 2008 required reserves increased somewhat, to approximately $54 billion,[31] while excess reserves had literally exploded to $767 billion.[32]

It is easy to understand how the Fed's creation of excess reserves solved the liquidity problem for banks. During the crisis, the interbank lending market seized up, and it became impossible for banks to borrow reserves from other banks to meet shortfalls in reserves required either to meet regulatory or transaction requirements. What made the closure of the interbank lending market so dangerous was that it threatened to disrupt the payments system upon which the daily functioning of the economy depends. Creating massive excess reserves solved that problem—at least for the banks that received the reserves—because it eliminated the need to borrow from other banks.[33]

Back to our question: with many hundreds of billions in excess reserves apparently providing capacity to increase lending, what prevented it from happening? Some economists have suggested that banks may have been content to earn the spread between the near zero interest rate on deposits and the 25 bps paid by the Fed on reserves. An individual bank—though not the banking system as a whole—will lose reserves as a result of deposit transfers when it issues loans in the manner described earlier. I do not find this explanation plausible, however, since banks earned a much higher spread on loans; during the financial crisis net interest margins never dropped below 3 percent (300 bps).[34]

The fundamental reason that excess reserves do not automatically lead to increased lending is that lending also requires capital. At its simplest, capital is measured as assets minus liabilities and is equal to equity. That makes sense; the bank needs to be solvent in order to increase lending. At its most complicated, which is what bank regulators allowed before the financial crisis, capital can be computed as an idiosyncratic and funky (and suspect) function of lots of stuff. That is why, after the crisis, regulation has moved back toward defining capital as something closer to equity. Prudent bankers—a concept some may consider to be an oxymoron!—will want to have a capital cushion, to ensure the bank can withstand loan losses and remain solvent. Bank regulations require it (sort of). Anyhow, the excess reserves did not bestow any capital- however one measures capital—since the added reserves (assets) were matched by added deposits (liabilities). Without additional capital the banks were not able to increase lending. For so long as banks suffered from a debt overhang, they lacked the capital to expand credit.

To summarize, banks can create deposits simply by lending. But their ability to lend, assuming they would like to do so, is constrained by two things. One is that capital must exceed some minimum percentage of assets (more or less).

Bank Capital > (X%) Bank Assets. (12.1)

The other constraint faced by banks is that reserves must exceed some minimum percentage of deposits.

Bank Reserves > (Y%) Bank Deposits. (12.2)

The Fed's massive increase in reserves eliminated (12.2) as a constraint on bank lending. The increase in deposits initially issued to the Fed, offset the decline in deposits caused by the reduction in lending. But the depletion in bank capital that occurred during the financial crisis made (12.1) a very binding constraint. However, once banks are recapitalized—as they will eventually be—the Fed's injection of massive excess reserves will have cleared the way for an unlimited expansion in lending, constrained only by the amount of capital banks can raise. The reason is as follows. In aggregate, banks cannot create reserves—only the Fed can. Before the financial crisis, when the banking system had small excess reserves, the Fed could effectively guide the size of bank lending by altering the rate at which it offered to lend reserves. But with massive excess reserves, the Fed has ceded control over the aggregate volume of bank credit to the banks themselves.

The possibility that, when bank capital is fully restored, banks might expand their balance sheets—assets and liabilities—without limit has raised fears that the Fed's liquidity operations have laid the groundwork for a future credit bubble (driven by expansion of loans, LHS of figure 12.2) or a future inflation (driven by expansion of deposits, RHS of figure 12.2).

The Fed is aware of this possibility and Mr. Bernanke has outlined a set of measures the Fed could take to control the growth of bank balance sheets.[35] These measures include increasing interest payments on reserves held at the Fed, which creates an incentive for banks to reduce lending to the private sector and lend to the Fed instead; reverse open market—and reverse repo—operations (selling bonds held by the Fed and retiring the money received), and collecting repayments of bonds currently held by the Fed without any offsetting purchase of replacement bonds, which retires the money paid on those bonds. Yet, each of these actions carries risk. Payment of interest on reserves is a hidden—but very real—tax that will be a drag on the economy.[36] Selling off a significant portion of bond holdings acquired in the financial crisis, or engaging in reverse open market or repo operations—in order to reduce base money—could crowd out funding for new bond issues and thereby reduce credit in the economy. Retiring bond when they come due could take a very long time, since most of the bonds acquired in QE are of long duration. These are all untested propositions, since the Fed has never dealt with the problem of a balance sheet bloated to such a large size. Milton Friedman's warning about the dangers of activist monetary policy remains valid: "we cannot predict at all accurately just what effect a particular monetary action will have on the price level and, equally important, just when it will have that effect."[37]

Did Banks Lack the Capital to Lend after the Financial Crisis?

According to the IMF, US financial institutions suffered $2.1 trillion in losses during the financial crisis, approximately two-thirds of which were shouldered by banks.[38] In April of 2009 the IMF estimated that US banks would have to raise $275 billion in equity to reach the 4 percent of asset amount considered to be a bare minimum requirement, and $500 billion to reach the 6 percent ratio that obtained in the mid-1990s, before banks began to increase their leverage.[39] There is a considerable body of evidence showing that banks did not have an adequate amount of capital to resume lending after the massive losses they suffered on their mortgage loans and other mortgage related holdings in the financial crisis caused their net worth to plummet.

As explained in chapter 11, the conjuncture of unanticipated losses, undisclosed risk and inadequate capital, meant that few people believed in either the asset valuations or the reported capital of banks after September 2008. This is why nobody, including fellow banks, would lend to, or invest in, banks. The banks themselves may have lost contact with the valuation of their own assets, since there was no longer any active securitization market into which loans could be sold, and there was great uncertainly over the solvency of many bank borrowers. This predicament alone would have provided banks with sufficient motivation to pull in their horns and rebuild their capital. Another reason for some banks to hold back on funding was the need to hoard liquidity to deal with the risk of a withdrawal of capital by wholesale lenders, from whom many large banks borrowed on a short-term basis. A refusal by wholesale lenders to roll over their loans would have the same effect as a depositor run. This hypothesis is supported by a study by Victoria Ivashina and David Scharfstein, which documents that during the crisis in the fall of 2008, banks who had a relatively large amount of outstanding wholesale debt, or who had large (relative to their size) contingent funding liabilities (like undrawn lines of credit or ABS liquidity puts) contracted their lending by more than other banks.[40]

The Fed and the US Treasury recognized these problems and attempted to ameliorate them by making a large injection of capital into the banking system. The $700 billion TARP program, established in October of 2008, helped to avert insolvency for many banks by empowering the US Treasury to purchase up to $250 billion of senior preferred shares in banks (which count as capital). TARP may have kept banks solvent, but it did not induce them to lend.[41]

There are several indications that, TARP notwithstanding, doubts about the adequacy of bank capital was long lasting. In 2009 the Fed conducted and published the results of stress tests on the 19 largest US banks, to determine the amount of additional capital they required to withstand certain defined adverse events.[42] Following the stress tests, US banks raised over $205 billion in additional capital. Yet, a government guarantee was required to support the new debt issued by banks. The FDIC insured approximated $600 billion in senior unsecured debt issued by banks under the Temporary Liquidity Guarantee Program, which lasted until 2012.[43] In mid-2010 the IMF reported on its own stress tests of US banks by noting "the system would likely remain under pressure due to expected further losses in the commercial real estate sector" and opined that many banks had insufficient capital to withstand a slowdown in growth.[44] The evidence suggests that concerns over capital adequacy during and after the acute phase of the financial crisis in September of 2008 placed a long-lasting limitation on bank lending. The severe drop in bank equity valuations is evidence that the market believed banks were over-valuing their assets; and it is likely that many bank managers believed it, too.[45]

Was It Necessary to Bail Out Bank Bondholders—or Was It Crony Capitalism?

One of the most controversial aspects of the policy response of the Fed and the US Treasury was the effective bailout of numerous large banks. This became known as the "Too big to fail" policy. TARP, the guaranty of bank and GSE debt, the investment in AIG and the investment and loss guarantee of JP Morgan's purchase of Bear Stearns prompted accusations that the US government used taxpayer money and credit to provide relief to bank bondholders because they were a politically favored constituency. The accusations have merit. First of all, the government spent massive amounts of money to bail out banks and almost nothing to aid struggling homeowners. For example, over 75 percent of TARP funds were extended to banks, while under 2 percent of TARP funds went into mortgage relief.[46] Second, it was not necessary to bail out bank bondholders in order to save the financial system. I shall address this point in detail in chapter 14, but suffice it to say that bank solvency could have been restored by requiring unsecured bondholders to write off (possibly in exchange for equity) a portion of their debt. It could have taken place in, or out, of bankruptcy. If that path was pursued, the debt overhang on bank balance sheets would have been eliminated (because debt would have been extinguished) and bank lending would likely have recovered sooner.[47] In terms of figure 12.4, a conversion of debt into equity would shrink the "Long-Term Debt," which would automatically increase equity by an equal amount. It can be seen by looking at figure 12.4 that the increase in equity depends only on the reduction in debt. It is not affected by how much of the equity is given to bondholders. Requiring bondholders to shoulder their own losses would also have eliminated the moral hazard problems associated with bailing out creditors.

Economists across the political spectrum were in agreement on this point. From Paul Krugman on the left, to Luigi Zingales on the right, proposals were made to recapitalize banks by effectuating a write-down of their unsecured debt obligations. Such action would have avoided the need for a taxpayer bailout and the need to guarantee bank debt. Most importantly, it would enabled banks to expand credit, since the capital constraint, 12.1, would no longer be binding.

There were charges that the bailout was an act of crony capitalism; of the political elite protecting the economic elite.[48] Given the near unanimous disapproval of the bailout by the economics profession, this charge cannot be easily dismissed. The bailout eroded public confidence in the fairness of the US political system. It has given rise to populist movements on the left and the right.

Occupy Wall Street and the Tea Party are bound together by their shared distrust of the US elites; the difference being that one is focused on the economic elites and the other on political elites.

The populist backlash has become a source of gridlock in Congress, as the Tea Party, who suspects governmental elites, endeavors to block further government action on all fronts. The closing of ranks among the financial and political elites to protect the interests of the major financial institutions presents a veritable challenge to the notion that the US is a fair and just society. The integrity of the US political system reached a low point in March 2013 when Attorney General Eric Holder testified to Congress that some banks stood above the law because they were "too-big-to-prosecute." Thomas Hoenig, vice chairman of the FDIC and former president of the Kansas City Fed, is a rare, dissenting member of the policymaking elite. He succinctly expressed the concern created by "Too-big-to fail":

> "It is fundamental to capitalism that markets be allowed to clear in an open, fair manner and that all participants play by the same rules. A situation whereby oligopolies that evolve into institutions that are too big to fail, and are so significant and complex that should they fail the economy fails, is not market economics. To ignore these circumstances is to invite crisis."[49]

One rebuttal is that policymakers were acting under extreme duress in the heat of the crisis and that many considerations are set aside in the fog of war. It was contended-erroneously (see chapter 14)—that bankruptcy would have caused banks to default on short term payment obligations; and it was feared—with good cause—that a failure by systemically important banks to meet immediate obligations to counterparty banks could have triggered a cascade of bank failures by forcing asset write downs at counterparty banks. Yet, the Bear Stearns meltdown in March 2008 should have been a warning. Figure 11.1 shows the ABX.HE index of subprime securities began its descent as far back as far back as August of 2007. There is a legitimate criticism that the Fed and the Treasury should have been better prepared for the storm that hit in September of 2008.

Policy Implication: Capital or Liquidity—Which Is More Important for Financial Stability?

In this chapter and in chapter 11 I have explained how the financial system was injured by both the decline in solvency and liquidity among most important financial intermediaries—banks and broker-dealers. A natural question to ask is; which factor contributed more to the distress? I think the lack of capital was the key factor for the simple reason that the Fed was able to restore liquidity almost immediately, once it set about doing it. Moreover, the liquidity crisis was precipitated by the perception that banks and broker-dealers had become insolvent. Capital, on the other hand, recovered only slowly over time, and the political system lacked the will to effectuate a more speedy recovery. So, it is more important that financial regulations ensure that financial intermediaries maintain adequate capital than that they maintain adequate liquidity. Yet, liquidity does not come cheap. The bloated Fed balance sheet creates inflationary risks for the future.

Conclusion

The collapse of the prices of homes and subprime mortgages spread to many other assets due to the fact that banks, broker-dealers and moderate income homeowners became highly leveraged during the boom. Commercial banks initially curtailed lending due to losses incurred on their retained exposure to subprime mortgages. Broker-dealers initially made distressed sales of their devalued mortgage securities and curtailed matched book lending on subprime mortgage ABS due to the increased haircuts required by their repo lenders. The distress was transmitted to other asset classes and, through feedback effects, triggered a general meltdown of asset prices and a freezing up of credit. The meltdown resulted in a stampede to the most liquid assets—dollars and US government debt—bringing the bank funding and money markets near collapse, an occurrence that would have disrupted the payments system and impaired a significant volume of economic activity. In this way, the collapse of a relatively small corner of the securities market amplified into a major financial crisis. The Fed averted the panic by injecting a massive amount of liquidity in order to satiate the markets' voraciouis demand for money. It worked; the broad money supply did not contract and the liquidity programs restored normal money market functioning and broke the fall in the prices of a wide spectrum of assets.

After the panic had subsided, the central protagonists, homeowners and banks, found themselves saddled with elevated levels of debt relative to asset values. The Fed was able to solve the liquidity shortage, but it could not cure insolvency. The debt overhang dampened household spending and bank lending, and the collapse in the prices of securitized assets caused the shadow banking sector to shrivel up. Bond issuance by large, creditworthy corporations only partially filled the funding gap. These forces reduced aggregate demand and impaired the economy's ability to channel investment to new, profitable areas. The challenge faced by government was to devise policies that would increase employment in the presence of the debt overhang and the structural deficiency in demand generated by the ongoing current account deficit and increasing income concentration. At a more fundamental level, policymakers had to decide whether to address the underlying problems of the current account deficit, income concentration, and the debt overhang, or to purse palliatives to boost employment in the short term while shelving the deeper issues. In the event, they elected to ignore the deep issues and to pursue more traditional, and familiar, monetary and fiscal measures to aid in recovery.

In the next chapter, I will evaluate the results of the fiscal and monetary measures implemented after the financial crisis.

PART V

The Financial Crisis, II: The Limits of Conventional Policy in a Balance Sheet Recession

In part V, which consists of a single chapter, I explain how the decline in asset values during the financial crisis created an overhang of debt on banks and household borrowers, which trapped the economy in a prolonged recession.

The debt overhang rendered banks undercapitalized, which limited their ability to expand credit. It forced households to use their cash flow to pay down debt, rather than to spend. The contraction of credit, and the application of income to pay down debt, muted the effectiveness of conventional monetary and fiscal policy. It did so by limiting the amount by which private sector spending would increase in response to stimulus from either source. It is argued, moreover, that the Fed lacked the ability to provide effective monetary stimulus once interest rates reached their lower bound, and the government was constrained from providing additional fiscal stimulus by concern over the large debt burden already in place, and by Congressional opposition to increased deficit spending.

CHAPTER 13

The Dilemma of Policy in a Balance Sheet Recession

> Who can remember the interest rate Shylock charged Antonio? But everybody remembers the "pound of flesh" that Shylock and Antonio agreed on as collateral.
>
> —John Geanakoplos[1]

> In the four years since financial normalization, the share of adults who are working has not increased at all and GDP has fallen further and further behind potential
>
> —Lawrence Summers[2]

This chapter addresses the fundamental problem faced by policymakers after the financial crisis: how to reverse the decline in employment and stimulate growth. Although US unemployment rate dropped into single digits in 2013 and has continued to fall up to the date of this writing (April 2015), the percentage of employed working age adults, many of whom are not counted as unemployed after suffering long spells of unemployment, remains at an historically low level (see figure 13.1).[3] Unemployment is a personal hardship, and when a sizeable portion of the workforce experiences long spells of unemployment, the depreciation in their skills degrades the productive potential of the entire economy. Therefore, the low rate of employment in the US economy is a major ongoing social and economic problem.

The Aftermath of Financial Crises

Reinhardt and Rogoff document that, over a period of eight centuries around the globe, the contractions in asset prices, employment and output that follow financial crises are usually deep and of long duration. For example, the unemployment rate typically increases by 7 percent during the recession, and takes over 4 years to return to the pre-crisis level.[4] The average decline in asset prices is breathtaking; house prices typically decline by 35 percent and equity prices decline by 56 percent. Real estate prices display more inertia than do other asset

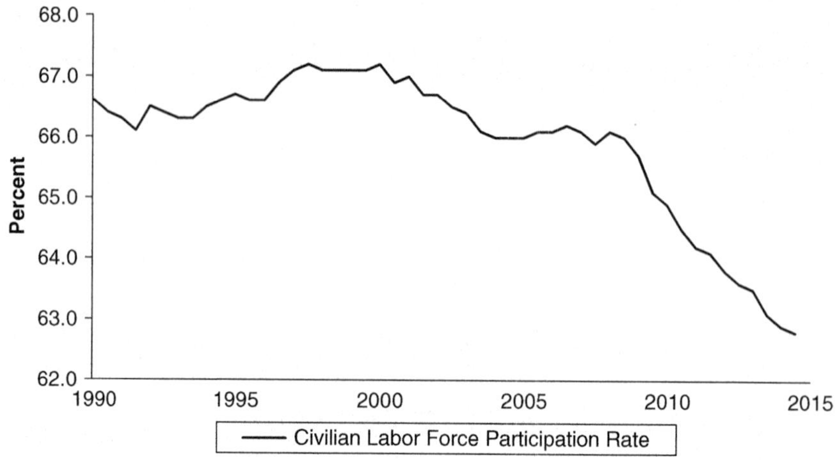

Figure 13.1 Civilian labor force participation rate, 1990–2014.
Source: US Bureau of Labor Statistics.

prices, however. House prices typically take 6 years to recover to pre-crisis levels, whereas equity prices typically take 3.5 years to regain their pre-crisis value.

The fact that home price declines are long lasting has important implications for the recovery from the recent financial crisis. The preceding boom was driven by increased levels of leverage on home mortgages, which reduced the equity cushion in homes. When home prices crashed a high percentage of homes became worth less than their mortgages. In 2009, 24 percent of mortgaged homes were underwater and an additional 20 percent were near negative equity. The slow recovery of home prices (along with the failure to restructure mortgage debt) resulted in nearly 11 percent of mortgaged homes remaining underwater into 2015, and an additional 20 percent of homes near negative equity.[5]

The decline in home prices during and after the financial crisis created a debt overhang in the US economy.[6] A person or firm suffering from a debt overhang will be less able to borrow funds, and more likely to apply its revenues to pay down debt. The implosion of home values during the financial crisis impaired the value of the collateral for many loans, and rendered most banks and many households insolvent. As was explained in the last chapter, the debt overhang on banks and households caused a contraction in bank lending.[7] Banks used their profits and subordinated debt issues to rebuild their capital cushions, and households reduced spending in order to rebuild cash reserves and to pay down debt (figure 13.2). This logic is consistent with the historical finding of Jorda et al. cited in chapter 11, that recessions following the bursting of housing bubbles last considerably longer than recessions following the bursting of equity bubbles.

The contraction in credit and slow recovery took place in spite of massive monetary and fiscal expansion. From 2008 to 2015 the Federal government debt nearly doubled, from 60.6 percent to 101.3 percent of GDP, and the Fed quadrupled its assets (which are matched by increases in the base money supply),

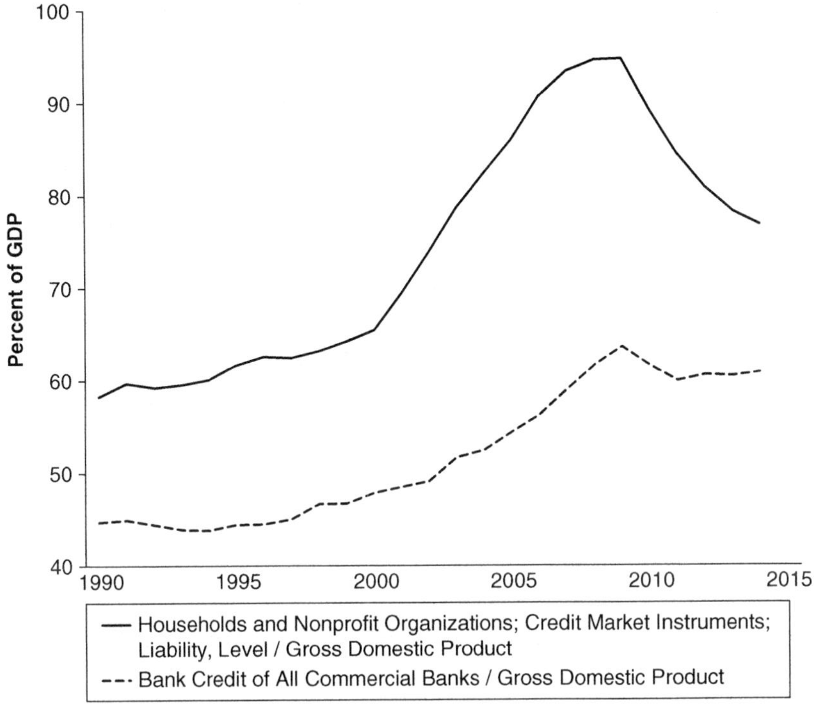

Figure 13.2 Bank and household credit, 1990–2014.
Source: Board of Governors of the Federal Reserve System.

from 60.4 percent of GDP to 250.8 percent of GDP.[8] A so-called balance sheet recession poses unique difficulties for policymakers. Virtually all policy tools are designed to boost spending, but debt overhangs are a formidable impediment to inducing the private sector to increase spending. Eight years after the financial crisis, banks continued to contract credit and households continued to contract borrowing. The channels through which the debt overhang reduced demand in the economy are as follows.

First, households curtailed spending and increased saving, which depressed final goods sales and induced firms to reduce employment, and final goods prices.

Second, the curtailment of household spending, and the uncertainty caused by the financial crisis, induced businesses to slow investment, which led firms to further reduce employment and depressed capital goods prices.

Third, the increase in saving and decline in investment created an excess supply of (nonbank) loanable funds, which caused interest rates to decline to ultra-low levels, for the limited group of borrowers who had access to the bond market.[9]

Fourth, the contraction in bank lending amplified the curtailment in spending and investment by reducing access to credit, and caused bank balance sheets to contract, as the net repayment of loans reduced both assets (loans outstanding) and liabilities (bank deposits used to repay loans).

The combination of anemic spending, credit contraction and ultra-low interest rates reduced the potential effectiveness of both monetary and fiscal policy.

Monetary Policy

The Bank Lending Channel

Most people associate US monetary policy with the Fed funds rate, which is the interest rate the Fed targets to lend reserves overnight to banks. In terms of figure 12.4, the Fed affects bank balance sheets by changing the level of bank reserves. In recent decades the Fed has used the Fed funds rate as its primary monetary policy instrument. The Fed funds rate works through reserves. Prior to the financial crisis, the level of reserves was low enough that banks often needed to borrow reserves to meet daily payment obligations. While banks lend reserves to one another, the banking system as a whole often required to borrow additional reserves. The Fed possessed interest rate pricing power because it was the provider of the marginal additional reserves the banking system needed. By setting a rate at which it offered to lend reserves, the Fed could effectively determine overnight interest rates in the banking system. The Fed funds rate impacted other interest rates by placing a ceiling on the rate banks were willing to pay on deposits. The deposit rate, in turn, placed a floor on other short term rates and, via the lending margin, determined the bank lending rate. The expected future path of the Fed funds rate influenced long term interest rates, since interest arbitrage ensures that long rates are a sequence of expected short rates over time, with a risk premium added on.

The Fed funds rate was an extremely powerful instrument with which to influence the economy. Yet, when the Fed flooded the banking system with reserves during the financial crisis, it lost that power. The reason is that if banks hold massive excess reserves, it matters not at what rate the Fed offers to lend reserves, since no bank will be interested in borrowing.

The Portfolio Channel

The other, less frequently used channel through which the Fed conducts monetary policy is "open market operations". With an open market purchase, the Fed creates reserves and deposits of equal size at banks and uses the deposits to acquire, or lend against, securities from the private sector. This is how the Fed carried out its liquidity operations during the financial crisis (see figure 12.4). This channel increases liquidity into the nonfinancial sector by injecting money—in the form of deposits—in exchange for less liquid securities. In a panicked situation, like the financial crisis, the replacement of money for securities can satisfy the desire for liquidity and stabilize asset prices by eliminating the urge to sell assets for money at fire sale prices.

In quiescent times, when agents are satisfied with the amount of money they initially hold, the increase in liquidity creates an excess balance of money in private sector portfolios which agents will normally want to use to acquire securities or consumer goods. Agents will wish to hold some securities—even risky securities—with attributes that money doesn't have, like earning interest or profits. The desire to purchase securities will bid up the price (and lower the yield) on income producing assets. The lower interest rates will stimulate investment through the Wicksell-Hayek channel (see chapter 10), and the higher asset price will stimulate investment through the Tobin's Q channel (see chapter 2). The increased demand for consumer goods will increase retail employment and, if the demand is expected to last, stimulate investment to meet heightened future demand.

In open market operations, the Fed normally purchases and sells short term treasuries. Figure 12.2 shows that, prior to the financial crisis, treasuries was just about the only asset the Fed held. But when interest rates are very low nobody will mind if their portfolios have fewer treasuries and more money. If treasuries are earning negligible interest, why not hold money instead, which is slightly more convenient anyhow? This does not mean the Fed cannot use open market purchases to induce agents to spend, but it has to purchase securities that are not substitutes for money. The Fed has to purchase securities that pay interest, which implies the securities are either long duration or risky. During the financial crisis the Fed purchased risky securities, but that was in a dire emergency and was a monumental departure from prior operating procedure. Never before had the Fed taken on such risks and never before was the Fed owed money by private sector entities.

But debt overhangs are an additional impediment to the effectiveness of the portfolio channel, no matter what securities are purchased by the Fed. If agents have debt they need to pay down, they may use their increased money balances to pay down debt. If, for example, households used their increased money balances to pay down debt owed to banks, the monetary expansion would be offset by a reduction in bank deposits (and bank loans). This is what economists call a "reflux." So, the portfolio channel is unlikely to spur much spending when interest rates are near zero and many private sector agents are suffering from debt overhangs.

Quantitative Easing

Beginning in late 2009 the Fed ventured beyond the bounds of conventional policy and undertook large-scale purchases of long dated treasuries, GSE bonds and mortgage debt, through purchase programs called quantitative easing or QE for short. Mr. Bernanke explained the objective in terms of the lending channel:

> With unemployment soaring, the economy and job market clearly needed more support. Central banks around the world found themselves in a similar predicament. We asked ourselves, "What do we do now?" . . . Unable to reduce short-term interest rates further, we looked instead for ways to influence longer-term interest rates, which remained well above zero. We reasoned that, as with traditional monetary policy, bringing down longer-term rates should support economic growth and employment by lowering the cost of borrowing to buy homes and cars or to finance capital investments.[10]

But QE is actually the portfolio channel on steroids. Draining a massive amount of securities that are not close substitutes for money out of the private sector in exchange for money, could potentially cause agents to spend down their money balances. The Fed implemented QE by purchasing two classes of bonds; treasuries and mortgage debt. Its purchases of long term treasury bonds reduced the yield on, and supply of, long duration government debt, which forced investors into riskier private sector issues, much as did the PBOCs purchases of treasuries and GSE debt during the housing boom. In addition to lowering borrowing costs, the Fed's purchases of mortgage debt raised the price of mortgage securities which could potentially, through Tobin's Q, spur home construction and reduce the debt overhang on financial institutions who had suffered losses on mortgage securities.[11]

It does not appear that QE worked out as intended. It did not spur an expansion in credit, homebuilding or employment. Meanwhile, pushing yields on long dated bonds to a ultra-low level has rekindled the reach for yield that fuelled demand for subprime ABS during the housing boom. Low rates have also placed an onerous burden on people saving for (or in) their retirement. Finally, there is the question of the unwind: how will the Fed exit QE? As was discussed in chapter 12, further bloating of the Fed's balance sheet might increase doubt over whether it will be able to counter inflationary forces when the current environment of deleveraging and precautionary demand for money ends. Over time the demand for liquidity will recede, banks will be fully recapitalized, animal spirits will revive and the desire to exchange money for goods or other assets will grow. The excess bank reserves will enable a recapitalized banking system to expand credit without limit,[12] and a recapitalized household sector and optimistic firms will generate a demand for credit and increased spending. Bank credit could expand like a coiled spring. That is the source of potential inflationary pressure created by the Fed's monetary expansion.

Michael Woodford, who is perhaps the leading monetary theorist in the world today, has argued that QE is ineffective by itself, unless accompanied by either (a) targeting of credit to specific sectors of the economy, or (b) a credible policy announcement that the Fed will hold rates below the natural rate for an extended time after the economy has reached full employment.[13] In focusing on the specific channels through which credit expansion enters into the economy, and in attempting to foster an expectation of continued long-term low interest rates, Woodford is, in effect, advocating a Hayekian approach (no doubt one that Hayek would disagree with). Even if successful, Woodford's recommended approach would foster the mal-investment criticized by Hayek because the policy involves either using a form of indicative planning to allocate resources to targeted sectors for which there may not be a sustainable market need, or it would induce a general overinvestment by suppressing interest rates. The inflationary bias of setting interest rates below their natural rate would also risk forfeiting the credibility of the Fed's commitment to stable prices.

While Mr. Bernanke asked, "What do we do now?" with the implication that it is preferable to do something rather than nothing, he assumed that QE did not involve significant downside risk. However, it does carry risk. In pursuing

QE the Fed has, perhaps, over-compensated for its passivity during the Great Depression. Sometimes it really is better to do nothing.

Fiscal Policy

The Logic of Keynesian Deficit Spending to Cure Recessions

Fiscal policy relies upon an expansion in the government deficit to finance government spending. In a fully employed economy, an increase in government borrowing to finance increased government spending will "crowd out" private investment. The deficit will affect the allocation of resources between the public and private sector, but not their level of utilization. The reason is that when the economy's resources are fully employed, the only way government can raise its share of spending is to effectuate a diversion of resources from elsewhere. However, during a recession, when the economy is operating below its potential, it is conceivable that government can increase spending (or cause the private sector to increase spending) without diverting resources employed elsewhere. It can do so if it is able to mobilize underemployed resources (which include labor). If it is able to do that, increased government spending can increase total employment and income in the economy.

One possible way to mobilize resources is for the government to finance an increase in spending (or a reduction in tax levies) by issuing bonds. This is called "deficit spending" (I shall refer to it interchangeably as "fiscal expansion") because it requires the government to spend more than it collects in tax revenues, thereby increasing its indebtedness. The basic idea is that if a recession is caused by a decline in absorption or net exports (see identity (4.1)), the spending shortfall can be made up by either increasing government spending (without generating an offsetting decline in private incomes by raising taxes to finance the expenditure), or by reducing taxes to increase the spendable income of the private sector.[14]

Keynes identified two potential salutary effects of deficit spending (assuming spending is positively related to current income[15]). First, the increased spending leads to increased employment; and the new hires add further to spending and so forth, which is the Keynesian multiplier. Second, the portion of the increase in income that is not spent adds to the pool of saving available to purchase the bonds issued by government to finance its deficit. This is the core logic of Keynesian fiscal policy. Keynes's riposte to the "Austerians" in the British Treasury during the Great Depression acerbically summarized this logic: "They [the government] say they cannot spend because they do not have the money, but they have not the money because they will not spend!"[16] Critics of Keynesian fiscal policy discount it as a conjurers trick; a dubious formula to create employment out of thin air. Yet, what usually lies behind this line of criticism, whether or not its proponents are always aware of it, is the belief that there cannot be idle resources in a market economy. There is a respectable area of macroeconomic research called "Real Business Cycle Theory" (RBC) that assumes the economy always to be in equilibrium, so that what appears to be unemployment is actually the result—possibly a depressing result—of preferences interacting with institutions and shocks to the economy. According to RBC, the economy is always operating at full employment in the sense that anyone can get a job if only she is willing to accept the best offer in the marketplace. This is not a crazy idea. Most economists who have studied the issue, for example, agree that the extension of unemployment benefits after the financial crisis increased unemployment by lowering the incentive to find work. Moreover, the recent trend reduction in labor force participation predates the financial crisis. Participation declined during the prior boom, when job vacancies exceeded layoffs by a wide margin, where anyone who sought a job could find one.

There is currently a schism among economists between those who believe there can involuntary unemployment in a market economy (where "involuntary unemployment" means there are unemployed people willing to work at the prevailing wage for their skill level), and those that do not believe this is possible. The former are sometimes referred to as "freshwater" and the latter as "saltwater" economists. That is because many of the leading RBC theorists teach at Midwestern universities and many of the leading (new) Keynesian theorists teach at universities located near the Atlantic coast in New England. It is interesting to note that, until the rise of RBC in the 1980s, all of the major macroeconomists, including those holding opinions as diverse as Hayek, Keynes, and Friedman, believed there was involuntary unemployment in recessions.[17] Their differences arose over how best to alleviate it. I am with them. The distress of people following the onset of the financial crisis, millions of people, affected by breadwinners losing their jobs and their homes, is all too real to be ignored, and I cannot think of it in any other any than an "involuntary" event. So, I will proceed on that assumption.

Many commentators, notable among them *Financial Times* columnist Martin Wolf, former Treasury secretary Lawrence Summers, and Paul Krugman, have advocated for a massive increase in government deficit spending to offset the contractionary impact of the reduction in private sector spending. Mr. Wolf employs a compelling analytical framework to make his point. He partitions the domestic economy into four sectors: government, households, corporations, and foreign trade. Because these sectors comprise the entire economy, the net inflows and outflows of money between them must, as a matter of irrefutable arithmetic sum to zero. This "zero net balance" condition is represented by identity (13.1).

$$\begin{aligned} 0 - &\textit{Government saving} + \textit{household saving} \\ &+ \textit{corporate saving} + \textit{current account deficit}. \end{aligned} \qquad (13.1)$$

After the financial crisis, the household sector reduced its spending in order to pay off its debts; it was spending less than it earned and sending money out to the other sectors. At the same time the corporate sector was investing less than it earned and was sending money to the other sectors, and foreigners were spending less in the United States than they were selling to the United States (i.e., the United States was running a current account deficit) and they too were sending money to other sectors. There remained only the government to absorb the financial outflows from the other sectors, which by definition, it could only achieve by enlarging its deficit.

Mr. Wolf reasons that in the absence of deficit spending, the economy would be forced to contract until income declined by enough to cause a sufficiently large reduction in household and corporate savings to restore the zero net balance condition. Mr. Wolf's framework is complementary to my analysis (see identity 4.3). Where I have argued that the current account deficit created a hole in domestic demand, Mr. Wolf's analysis shows that the US foreign trade sector was running a positive financial balance with the US domestic economy, which implies that foreigners were spending less in the US economy than they were earning from the US economy.

At that level of analysis, I must agree with Mr. Wolf. Moreover, as Mr. Wolf has pointed out, the performance of the economy endogenously determines the government deficit, at least to some extent. The deficit moves inversely to growth, because tax revenues fall and social insurance spending increases during a recession. Therefore, policies that boost growth may conceivably reduce the deficit by reversing those variables. This implies, pace Keynes, that a policy that increases spending will not necessarily cause the deficit to widen—it all depends on how much growth it generates.

The case for fiscal expansion in the face of involuntary unemployment, such as the United States faced after the financial crisis, holds undeniable attraction. However, a number of factors can render fiscal policy ineffective. Some factors are perennial, such as the risks posed by depressed animal spirits and trade leakage. Some are unique to the post financial crisis situation, such as the constraining effects of the private sector debt overhang; the high level of indebtedness of the US government and its unsustainable trajectory, and the effect of Accumulation.

Animal Spirits and Accumulation

Nobel prize–winning economist John Hicks, who created the IS-LM model that forms the analytical foundation of Keynesian economics, described a circumstance where fiscal expansion may not generate employment. He pointed out that, for an increase in the demand of final goods to translate into new hires, businesses must respond by hiring or placing orders to restock inventories.[18] Yet, firms will only hire or restock if they are confident the current increase in demand will persist over time, which requires bullish animal spirits. Here is how Hicks described it:

> Now it would be quite hard to say…that effective demand would determine employment. It is so tempting to say that there can be no output without labor input so that an increase in demand must increase employment (as Keynes effectively did). But the question is not one of the relation between input and output, in general; it is a question of the relation between current demand and current input. For the effect on current input of excess demand or supply in the product market is surely a matter of the way is which the excess is interpreted by decision makers. An excess which is expected to be quite temporary may have no effect on input; it is not only the current excess but the expectation of its future which determines action.[19]

Without optimism, firms will not be willing to enter into the financial commitment required to hire and train new employees or to order new inventory. This applies throughout the supply chain, from retailer to commodity producer.[20] Hicks felt it posed a challenge to the logic of the Keynesian employment multiplier in a recession, when "animal spirits" are at low ebb. If decision makers are pessimistic about the continuation of demand growth after fiscal stimulus expenditures wane, or if they fear that punitive taxation may be on the way, they will refrain from rebuilding inventories. In this case the fiscal expansion will not generate the multiplier effect required to propel the economy back towards full employment. It is something of a paradox for Keynesian analysis that, on the one hand, it attributes the recession to the depressed state of animal spirits while, on the other hand, it prescribes a fiscal expansion that requires some level of positive animal spirits in order to be effective.

However, even with depressed animal spirits, an increase in the government deficit that goes on long enough must eventually boost employment. As inventories are run down toward zero, firms will at some point have no choice but to rebuild their inventories. Even so, if the expansion does not spur a lasting increase in economic activity through a multiplier effect beyond that level necessary to keep things going at a bare minimum level, the employment multiplier will be low and it will be unlikely to generate an increase in tax revenues over time sufficient to repay the debt incurred by government.

The presence of Accumulation creates an ambiguous effect. On the one hand, the increase in permanent saving due the rise of Accumulation creates a rational reason for firms to be pessimistic about the prospects for future demand. On the other hand, an increase in government debt that is matched by Accumulation will be indefinitely sustainable[21]—and it will likely shift income toward non-Accumulators. The problem is to match he growth in government debt to the growth in Accumulation. Nobody has figured out how to accomplish that—yet.

Debt Overhangs

Another reason fiscal expansion may not generate significant employment is that credit constraints may choke off the rebuilding of inventories. Going back to John Hicks's example above, even if businesses wished to increase inventories, they will not be able to do so if they cannot obtain credit. The process of producing goods takes time, and credit is often required to facilitate the building of goods that will be sold (and realize revenue) only after they are completed. If bank lending and securitization markets remain frozen, only the largest corporations, who are able to tap the public bond markets, will have access to the credit necessary to rebuild inventories. In this circumstance, even if animal spirits improve, many businesses will not have access to the credit necessary to act on their optimism and employment will remain stagnant.

The debt overhangs affecting banks and households will prevent household spending from increasing appreciably, which both constrains the multiplier and provides a compelling reason for businesses to remain pessimistic about sales prospects. The structure of the 2009 fiscal stimulus is a good example of the limitation of fiscal policy in a balance sheet recession. The largest component of the 2009 fiscal stimulus was a one off income tax rebate, a significant portion of which recipients saved or used to pay down debt, rather than spend. The use of tax rebates to pay down private debt, in effect, channeled the private savings absorbed by the government deficit back into private savings. Such "round tripping" of private savings had no immediate impact on economic activity, though it may have conferred a longer-term benefit by speeding along the process of household deleveraging.

Trade Leakage

The fiscal multiplier works most effectively in a closed economy (or one with balanced trade) since it operates when agents spend their money in the domestic economy. Expenditures on imported goods do not stimulate domestic hiring since they do not create business for domestic employers. The leakage of demand abroad corresponds to the size of the current account deficit, which remained high after the financial crisis (but has more recently receded).[22] Therefore, the US current account deficit compromised, at least to some extent, the effectiveness of fiscal policy.

Government Debt

While the US government has been able to borrow at negative real interest rates (i.e., it has issued debt with yields below the rate of inflation) during and after the onset of the financial crisis, there is reason to be concerned about the size of the buildup in debt it has accumulated. By the end of 2014 US government debt exceeded 100 percent of GDP. That is a clear danger signal. The only other instance when US debt attained this level was at the end of World War II. That the US economy embarked on a long trajectory of growth after the war, has prompted some analysts to dismiss the notion that the current debt level creates any risk to growth.

This assessment is wrong. In the 30 years following the end of World War II, government debt declined from over 100 percent of GDP to under 25 percent of GDP, due in part to low borrowing costs, solid growth, and mild inflation, but mostly to the effect of the demobilization that took place after the end of World War II, which dramatically reduced government spending. During World War II US government net outlays were above 40 percent of GDP, almost immediately afterward spending dropped to under 15 percent of GDP.[23] In the present situation, by contrast, no major area of government spending is likely to decline. Military spending is unlikely to decrease and current entitlement programs will require the government to spend an increasing amount on Medicare and Social Security in future years. According to the most recent Congressional Budget Office projection, which assumes there will be no major crisis affecting spending, debt service costs or growth, under currently mandated spending commitments, US government spending as a proportion of GDP will rise by nearly a third over the next 25 years and debt will rise from 74 percent of GDP to 108 percent of GDP.[24] These figures are optimistic because they assume the US government will carry out the future spending reductions mandated by the 2011 budget deal that was reached to avert a government shutdown. The CBO projection in the event those cuts are not carried out is truly frightening. It shows spending increasing by over 50 percent and debt rising to 170 percent of GDP by 2040, with spending and debt continuing to accelerate thereafter (see figure 13.3).

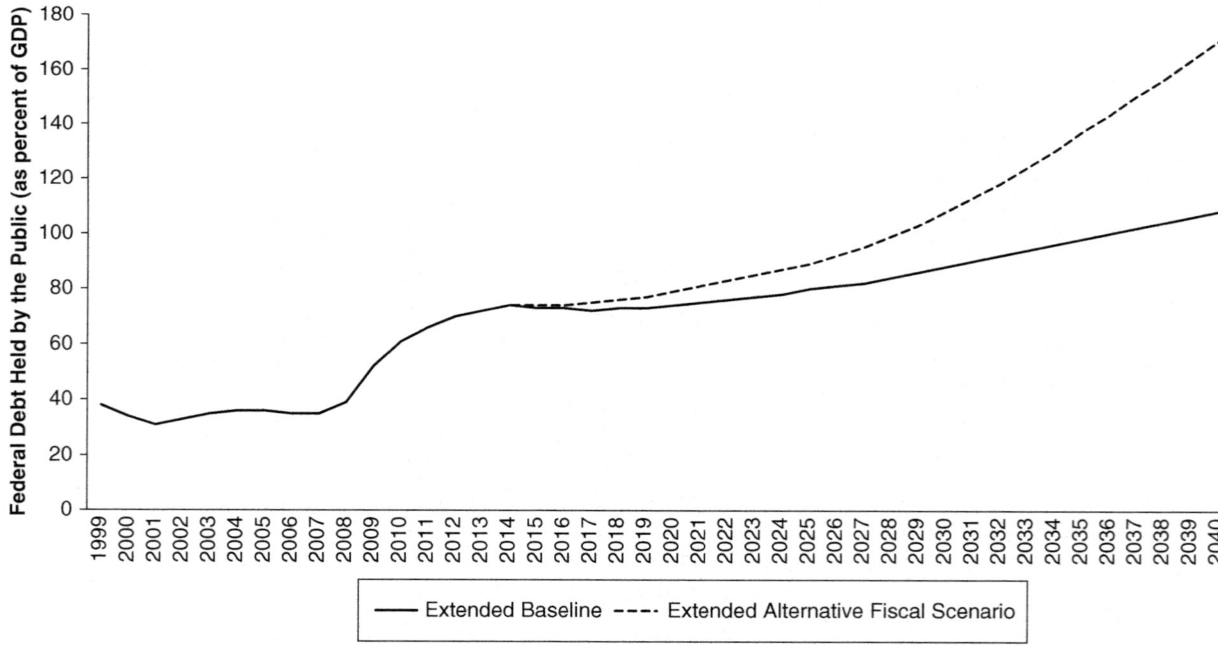

Figure 13.3 CBO 2014 budget outlook.

Notes: This figure shows federal government debt held by the public, which excludes the portion of debt held by the Federal Reserve. That explains the apparent discrepancy between the statement in the text that federal debt exceeded 100 percent of GDP in 2014, and figure 13.3, which shows it to be less than 100 percent. For the amount of total federal debt, see US Office of Management and Budget.

Source: US Congressional Budget Office, July 2014, Long Term Budget Outlook.

It is the trajectory of future spending, more than the current deficit and borrowing requirement, which poses the most significant risk to the US economy. The potential growth in spending and debt is so large there is a risk it will eventually crowd out private investment and thereby lower growth. While the United States is currently able to borrow an unlimited amount of money at near zero interest rates, it is unwise to assume the market will indefinitely fund an enterprise that, under its current operating mandate and tax policy, is going to increase its borrowing without limit. Reinhardt and Rogoff remind that this has been a perennial risk throughout history:

> Perhaps more than anything else, failure to recognize the precariousness and fickleness of confidence . . . is the key factor that gives rise to the this-time-is-different-syndrome. Highly indebted governments, banks or corporations can seem to be merrily rolling along for an extended period, when bang!—confidence collapses, lenders disappear, and a crisis hits.[25]

I explained in chapter 3 how the capital flow bonanza was driven by mercantilist countries that piled into US government guaranteed debt for reasons that were unrelated to the yields offered on the debt. These investors pushed down US government borrowing costs. But the United States cannot count on selling unlimited quantities of its debt indefinitely to mercantilists and other investors, who are likely to weigh the risks/return tradeoff more carefully, may recoil at some point. Reinhardt and Rogoff explain the risk of what could happen: "The basic problem for fiscal policy is that interest rates can turn very quickly but debt ratios cannot."[26] There is a limit to the amount of debt the government can take on before triggering either economic contraction or political instability. Economist John Cochrane summed up the fear very succinctly: "Where is the fiscal limit? I do not know. But there is a fiscal limit, and wherever it is, we are a few trillion dollars closer to it than we were last year, and we will be another few trillion dollars closer next year."[27] There is, finally, an underappreciated dimension of risk associated with large debt. Even if the United States is able to avoid the pitfalls of default or an inflationary monetization of its debt, a large debt burden reduces the flexibility available to respond to future emergencies. It does so by limiting the amount by which spending could be increased. If the United States encounters an emergency sometime in the future on a scale commensurate with World War II or the recent financial crisis, and if it were to respond by increasing debt by a proportionate amount, federal debt would need to increase substantially. There may not be room for it to do so. That is a dangerous position for the United States to be in. One argument for taking steps to reduce debt (as a percentage of GDP) is to rebuild fiscal capacity in readiness for a future crisis.

Time Inconsistency

Advocates of fiscal policy sometimes appeal to Keynes's advice that "the boom, not the slump, is the right time for austerity."[28] There is wisdom in this point of view, but there are also reservations to consider.

One problem with this "jam today" approach is time inconsistency; how can the government be trusted to uphold a self-denying ordinance in the future? The gridlock in Congress reflects this dilemma. Democrats favor spending today, but loathe committing to abstinence in the future. Republicans do not believe in the viability of any such pledge, so they oppose spending today.

Infrastructure Spending

Advocates of fiscal expansion have argued it may be an opportune time for the US government to ramp up spending on badly needed repairs and expansions of infrastructure, which can increase employment while improving the productive potential of the economy. With government able to borrow at negative real interest rates, the net return on investment for the economy may be quite high. The highest value infrastructure improvements are already identified in the plans of the Metropolitan Planning Organizations (MPOs) that set priorities for Federal infrastructure spending. Unfortunately, it is not possible to ramp up infrastructure spending as quickly as it may be needed to spur employment growth. Existing regulations governing environmental review, citizen input and competitive bidding create lead times of years before construction can commence on infrastructure projects. This timing lag is possibly one reason why most of the dollars originally intended to be devoted to infrastructure spending in the 2009 stimulus program shifted to income tax cuts, which, it was hoped, would be spent quickly. Nothing like the WPA of the Great Depression is possible today; our society has become too bureaucratized to allow that to occur.

The Dilemma of Fiscal Policy

The dilemma of fiscal policy can be understood by reference to Martin Wolf's framework of sectoral financial balance. Mr. Wolf notes that when the private sector reduces its desired spending (which is equivalent to increasing its desired savings) at full employment, as it did in response to the debt overhang, the only way to prevent a rise in unemployment (holding the current account balance constant) is for the government to increase its deficit. This can be understood by reference to identity (13.1). An increase in household desired savings, in the absence of a decrease of saving from any other sector, will cause the sum of the sectoral financial balances at full employment to become negative, which represents an excess of aggregate saving over aggregate spending. This condition is not stable. Every dollar of income must be matched, in the aggregate, by a dollar of spending—on consumption or investment.[29] The excess saving will cause the economy to contract until income has declined by an amount sufficient to eliminate the excess saving. Mr. Wolf reasons that an increase in the government budget deficit can soak up the excess private saving at full employment and negate—or reverse—the contraction. Looking at identity (13.1), if the increase in household saving is met by an equivalent decline in government saving, the sectoral balances will sum to zero at full employment and there will be no contractionary forces set in motion.

Mr. Wolf's reasoning is correct, but it does not follow that an increase in the government deficit will *necessarily* cause output to expand. It will not do so if the increase in the government budget deficit is matched by an increase in private saving. This is what happened with the 2009 tax cuts, when households saved most of the increase in their after tax incomes. In that case a decline in government saving was nearly matched by an increase in household saving. If firms are pessimistic or unable to borrow, they may not increase investment in response to an increase in aggregate demand generated by an increase in the government budget deficit. In that event the decline in government saving will be partially offset by an increase corporate saving. In fact, corporate investment spending has grown at an anemic pace since the onset of the financial crisis.[30]

The debt overhang impedes fiscal policy by inducing households to apply extra income to pay down debt and by limiting the access to credit for medium sized and small firms. The constraints may make firms pessimistic about future sales prospects, which act as a further impediment to the effectiveness of fiscal policy. The dilemma for fiscal policy in a balance sheet recession is one of timing between the buildup of public debt and the decline in private debt. The longer it takes the private sector to complete its deleveraging process, or the less effective deficit spending is in promoting growth, the larger is the risk that government debt will balloon to an unsustainable level before private sector spending picks up. If that were to happen, the principle effect of fiscal expansion would be to create a government debt crisis.

Another problem is that fiscal policy has not proven to be effective in the past. That is why governments have relied on monetary policy to maintain full employment. The fact that monetary policy has been made impotent in the aftermath of the financial crisis does not confer potency on fiscal policy. The effectiveness of fiscal policy in the United States and elsewhere since the financial crisis is at present a hotly debated topic on which no consensus has emerged among economists.

Conclusion

I have argued that the combination of the debt overhang and ultra-low interest rates impeded the effectiveness of monetary and fiscal policy after the financial crisis. Moreover, even if monetary stimulus were to increase employment, there is a risk that too much monetary stimulus will generate a dangerous credit expansion or inflationary forces that the Fed will be unable to effectively cope with, or that will require massive taxpayer subsidy to incentivize banks to hold reserves at the Fed. Similarly, even if fiscal stimulus were to increase employment, there is a risk that government debt will balloon too rapidly compared to the pace of private deleveraging, which would increase the risk of a sovereign debt crisis.

Many commentators and policymakers believe there is no choice but to press ahead with monetary and/or fiscal expansion; that the only alternative is to stand by idly while millions remain involuntarily unemployed with no end in sight. I disagree. First, the economy will eventually heal itself as debt is paid down. There is no need to incur excessive risks when a—perhaps very slow—healing process is at work. At the date of this writing, the healing process has progressed quite far. Second, perhaps the most powerful argument against a desperate "Hail Mary" dose of further monetary or fiscal expansion is that it is wrong to think there are no other alternatives. The proximate source of stagnation is the debt overhang and the ultimate and continuing cause of economic malaise is the Accumulation resultant from the large current account deficit and income concentration. It is on these fundamental causes that government should focus its attention

In the next chapter, I look into measures government can undertake to counter the debt overhang and reverse Accumulation in order to facilitate a near term recovery to full employment, and a return to a sustainable growth path.

PART VI

Policy Options: How to Exit the Balance Sheet Recession and End Secular Stagnation

In part VI, which consists of a single chapter, I recommend policies to escape the balance sheet recession, polices to reduce the probability of a recurrence of financial crisis and policies to reverse Accumulation, which is the underlying cause of the maladies that resulted in the financial crisis and the balance sheet recession that followed.

It is possible to exit a balance sheet recession by taking direct action to reduce the indebtedness of banks and households. The can be accomplished equitably by requiring bank bondholders to write down their debt, and by reforming bankruptcy law to empower judges to restructure mortgage debt (as they are already allowed to restructure all other financial contracts).

The probability (and potential severity) of a future financial crisis can be reduced by requiring banks and other financial intermediaries to reduce overall leverage and to limit the size of banks and broker-dealers. The former will ensure intermediaries have capital to withstand declines in collateral values; the latter will limit the systemic damage caused by the failure of a financial intermediary. An additional benefit of limiting concentration in finance is that it will make it a more competitive industry.

Accumulation caused by trade imbalances can, and should, be reduced. To effectuate this, I propose a reconsideration of the "Keynes Plan" presented to the Bretton Woods conference during World War II. It envisions a multilateral system that would promote trade and allow national sovereignty over economic policy, while providing mechanisms to counter large trade imbalances. Measures can be taken to reduce Accumulation due to income concentration without confiscating wealth or damping the beneficial effects of the incentive to create wealth. The application of antitrust law to finance, shortening the duration of software patent protection, and introducing more choice in the provision of education are policies that will likely reduce income concentration while increasing competition and promoting economic growth.

CHAPTER 14

Policy Options

> Give me a one-handed economist! All my economists say, on the one hand... on the other.
>
> —Harry S. Truman

In this chapter I recommend policies and legislation that the US could undertake to address the issues raised in this book, related to the financial crisis and its aftermath. My purview is limited. The recommendations are high level, since a detailed analysis of each policy option lies beyond the scope of this book. Each proposal will meet with resistance from people and organizations who will be negatively impacted. I do not address the likely source of opposition, nor do I propose measures to overcome them. The recommendations are made solely on the basis of their impact on employment and GDP. The reader should understand that the narrowness of my focus does not denote a lack of concern about related issues; quite the contrary. But this book is about the determinants of employment and GDP, and a consideration of other matters is a subject for another book. Each of the following topics is addressed in turn:

- Policies to alleviate the balance sheet recession.
- Policies to restore competition to banking for its own sake and as a means to reduce the likelihood of future financial meltdowns.
- Policies to reduce the Accumulation caused by current account deficits and income concentration that minimize the potential for damage to trade volumes and wealth creation.

Policies to Recover from the Balance Sheet Recession

The balance sheet recession was caused by debt overhangs that emerged out of the financial crisis. Households and banks acted to reduce their debt, and the retrenchment in lending and spending exacerbated the economic contraction. It is conceivable that by the time of this writing (April 2015) a sufficient amount of debt has been paid down and bank capital restored to propel the US economy out of its balance sheet recession. Nevertheless, one should be cautious in declaring victory, as Japan's two decade long struggle with balance sheet problems reminds us.

Deleveraging Banks

Even after many asset prices recovered from the downward spiral of 2008/9, banks have suffered large losses on their mortgage loans. Those losses depleted capital reserves. As I explained in chapter 12, banks cannot expand credit when their capital reserves are too low. Prudent banking practice and regulatory banking rules require that banks rebuild their capital before increasing lending. Fed policy has helped to speed capital replenishment by paying interest on bank deposits at the Fed and by disallowing undercapitalized banks from dissipating capital by paying dividends to shareholders.

The issue of bank recapitalization presents a dilemma. On one hand, requiring banks to build an adequate capital cushion is a prudent precaution against a future financial crisis. On the other hand, the process of rebuilding capital reserves will slow the growth of lending, since a portion of available funds has to be applied to augmenting capital rather than being lent out. The Fed and the international bank regulator, the Bank for International Settlements (BIS), have adopted a middle of the road approach. They have increased minimum capital requirements, but they have given banks several years in which to rebuild their positions, in the hope it will allow banks to issue more loans while the economy is still recovering from the financial crisis.[1] This is a reasonable course of action, given the two competing objective of safety and stimulus. It allows less credit expansion than might otherwise prevail, but it ensures that banks will become safer over time.

However, there is more to the story. In order to prevent bank failures during the financial crisis, the US Treasury and Fed used taxpayer resources to shield the unsecured creditors of large banks from suffering losses. The TARP program enacted by Congress in October 2008 infused $750 billion of additional capital in the form of convertible debt into banks, the Treasury guaranteed unsecured debt of insolvent banks such as Citigroup and the FDIC guaranteed approximately $600 billion in newly issued bank debt.[2] That policy is known as "too-big-to-fail." Protecting a favored class from suffering financial loss is actually a radical policy. In chapter 12 I argued it was inequitable and slowed recovery. In this chapter I shall argue it was unnecessary.

Protecting bondholders was unnecessary because the total amount of unsecured debt of US banks vastly exceeded their capital losses. Banks could have remained in operation if their unsecured debt was reduced to offset the decline in loan losses, which would occur in bankruptcy. Chapter 11 of the Bankruptcy Code was designed to enable a business to regain solvency by allowing it to restructure its financial obligations. Shifting bank losses out of the leveraged banking sector onto bank bondholders who generally had less leverage and less maturity mismatch than banks, would have restored stability to the financial system. Moreover, if the insolvent banks had been allowed to go bankrupt, the unsecured creditors would have shouldered their own losses, which would have avoided the moral hazard problem created by the government bailout. As it is, bank bondholders now have little reason to monitor the behavior of banks, since they have good reason to believe that, in a crunch, the government will likely bail them out again, notwithstanding sanctimonious phrases to the contrary contained in financial reform legislation enacted in response to the financial crisis.

There have been two principal arguments against the efficacy and feasibility of allowing banks to go bankrupt. One objection is that banks would find it difficult to attract outside capital in the future if their bondholders were made to suffer losses. This argument is tantamount to saying the banking is an inherently unprofitable business in which nobody will invest without a guarantee against incurring a loss. If that is true, either the business of banking should be abandoned, or if deemed socially beneficial, it should be socialized and its employees compensated as civil servants. Of course, it is a flawed argument, because banking is usually a profitable business.

The second objection is that a bankruptcy of a large financial institution would have risked a meltdown of the financial system, since the "automatic stay" on payment obligations (effective immediately upon filing bankruptcy) would have caused the overnight payments system to seize up. Policymakers claimed that bondholder bailouts were intended to prevent the possibility of a complete meltdown that might otherwise have occurred if a major financial institution was suddenly unable to meet its payment obligations. This objection holds little water. There are principally three groups with whom banks have short-term payment obligations. One group is depositors, who are not at risk because they are protected (up to a maximum amount) by government backed FDIC insurance. The second group is counterparties to derivative contracts, who are often highly leveraged banks or broker-dealers. A failure to meet payment obligations to this group could place those institutions in jeopardy of becoming insolvent. However, derivatives contract obligations cannot be stayed by a bankruptcy court, so this group may actually benefit from a bankruptcy, to the extent that all other payment obligations are stayed.[3] Moreover, the government could have protected counterparties by intervening in the OTC derivatives market to purchase obligations held by counterparties. If this course was chosen the government would have spent less money than, for example, taking over AIG in order to protect its counterparties.[4] The third group is money market investors, who are wholesale lenders to banks and investors in bank sponsored ABS. A failure to meet timely payment obligations to this group could have serious effects, because money market investors treat their shares as if they were cash.[5] Yet, during the financial crisis the Fed was able to maintain confidence among money market investors by underwriting their risk directly and did not find it necessary to underwrite the entire banking industry in order to accomplish that. Thomas Hoenig debunked the myth that allowing big banks to fail would cause a catastrophe.

> When examining previous financial crises, in other countries as well as in the United States, large institutions have been allowed to fail. Banking authorities have been successful in placing new and more responsible managers and directors in charge and then reprivatizing them.[6]

The only valid objection to allowing large banks to enter into bankruptcy—an objection that was not raised at the time—is that it might cause lending to freeze up during the period in which the bank is being reorganized. This is a serious problem and it underscores the importance of creating viable mechanisms to effectuate speedy bank reorganizations. Post-financial crisis legislation requiring large banks to create credible living wills, which are plans for automatic reorganization in the event of insolvency, should resolve this issue. As noted in chapter 12, however, after the onset of the financial crisis and during the balance sheet recession that followed, the government could have promoted speedy reorganizations among bankrupt banks just as it did with General Motors.[7] If that course were followed the debt overhang on banks would have been eliminated.

Perhaps the strongest argument against the policy of underwriting the risk of bondholders in large banks (so-called too-big-to fail) is the considerable collateral damage such a policy inflicts on the economy. Without the write-down of bank debt, banks remained overleveraged, which constrained lending after the financial crisis and increased the difficulty of attracting additional equity investment. It also reinforced the perception that bonds issued by banks carry a government guaranty, which adds to problems of moral hazard.

To summarize the recommendations made in this section:

1. Financial institutions should be recapitalized to resolve their debt overhangs. The quickest, most direct, and most equitable way to accomplish this is by allowing insolvent institutions to reorganize in a bankruptcy, which will require incumbent bondholders to absorb losses. The risk of systemic meltdown can be alleviated if, during a systemic financial crisis, government intervenes in the derivatives market as a buyer of "last resort" of obligations of insolvent financial institutions and underwrites the risk of money market fund investors.

Deleveraging Underwater Mortgages

In chapter 11 I cited evidence that home mortgage borrowers with negative equity (i.e., value of home less than mortgage) curtailed spending. In chapter 13 I showed that the number of borrowers who are in, or nearly in, negative equity remained elevated into 2015, seven years after the financial crisis. Recovery would occur faster if a way could be found to reduce homeowner debt in the near term. Mortgage restructuring would provide relief to homeowners from the burden of servicing underwater mortgages while reducing foreclosures, which would alleviate the negative effect on neighborhood home values caused by foreclosure sales. Mian and Sufi showed that middle income households would be the primary beneficiaries of mortgage relief, since they suffer from the highest percentage of negative equity in their homes. Moreover, and since this group has a high marginal propensity to consume out of housing wealth, as was discussed in chapter 11, mortgage restructuring would have the beneficial effect of boosting consumption.[8]

Many proposals have been made to implement mortgage restructuring by converting some portion of debt into home equity.[9] The basic idea is that a homeowner saddled with a mortgage balance above the value of the home would be forgiven a portion of her mortgage, enough to bring the loan to value ratio of the debt in line with requirements for new loans. In exchange for this, the lender would be granted, a percentage of proceeds from its future sale. The equity pledge might also be transferred from one owner to the next until the lender recouped all, or some portion, of the amount of loan it forgave. This would reduce onerous debt burdens on households and allow the homeowner to sell her home without going through a foreclosure—since the LTV would be in line with market norms—and thereby restore the functioning of the housing market while relieving the lender of the cost of maintaining and remarketing the home. It would not be a windfall to the homeowner, since a portion of equity earned in the future would be ceded to the lender, but it would give many more families the opportunity to stay in their homes.

The FDIC could incentivize banks, which hold nearly 30 percent of residential mortgages as "hold to maturity" loans, to offer debt for equity swaps by allowing them to count a portion of the equity as capital.[10]

Unfortunately, most of the remaining residential mortgages are held in ABS, which present serious obstacles to restructuring. The fundamental problem is that mortgage servicers are either not empowered to restructure mortgages or they are paid more money if they foreclose on a loan than if they restructure it (see discussion of this issue in chapter 5). This has led to calls for government to intervene to either take over the servicing of delinquent loans, or to forcibly alter servicer contracts to incentivize servicers to restructure loans, possibly with taxpayer funded compensation.[11] This course of action involves the unpalatable feature of requiring the government to invalidate contracts that were entered into voluntarily. It sets a potentially dangerous precedent, in terms of upsetting the expectations that parties have when entering into contracts and in terms of violating property rights.

A more equitable way to solve the problem would be for Congress to amend Chapter 13 of the federal bankruptcy code, to allow Judges to reduce the mortgage debt of bankrupt individuals. This would place mortgage debt on a level footing with all other forms of indebtedness, where it ought to be. Judges already have the authority to "cram down" nonmortgage debt in bankruptcy.

To summarize the recommendations made in this section:

2. Contingent upon a reduction in bank leverage (see recommendation 1) the FDIC should allow banks that offer debt for equity swaps to homeowners with negative equity to count the equity as capital.
3. Chapter 13 of the federal bankruptcy code should be amended to allow bankruptcy judges to restructure residential mortgage obligations.

Policies to Restore Competition to Banking

Limit Concentration in Banking

I explained earlier in this chapter why bailing out large banks was not required to save the financial system from collapse, yet it is what occurred. Regulation should move in the opposite direction. As Thomas Hoenig stated:

> I think [too big to fail banks] should be broken up. And in doing so, I think you'll make the financial system itself more stable. I think you will make it more competitive, and I think you will have long-run benefits over our current system, which leads to bailouts when crises occur.[12]

The current banking oligopoly is prone to rent seeking behavior. Incumbent banks raise barriers to entry—sometimes through government regulation—to keep out would-be competitors in order to hold their customers captive, so they can overcharge them. A competitive financial market, on the other hand, would possess all the virtues of competition in other markets. It would compel banks to reduce cost; to cater to customer preferences, and to innovate. In order to have competition, however, there must be competitors; the more the better. There is a well-established correlation between the number of firms in a market and the rate of increase in Total Factor Productivity (TFP), which is the portion of value added that is not accounted for by investment.[13] Another benefit of a less concentrated banking industry is that it would alleviate the safe asset shortage faced by institutional cash pools by increasing the number banks in which they could hold insured deposits. Figure 7.1 shows that the number of banks required to provide insured deposit coverage to institutional cash pools has been rising as the number of banks in existence has been declining. Placing a limit of bank size, somewhere in the range of midsized banks—around $50 billion in assets—and eliminating the too-big-to-fail cost of capital subsidy would cause the number of banks to increase.

Some have argued that banking is a natural oligopoly. They reason that banking concentration increased after barriers to interstate banking were dismantled in the 1990s because large banks are able to operate more profitably than small banks. They warn that efforts to impose limits on bank size will constrain the economies of scale which enable large banks to deliver services to large nonfinancial businesses at reduced cost. These arguments do not stand up to scrutiny. Economists have concluded that big banks exist to take advantage of the "too-big-to-fail" government guarantee, which reduces the cost of their debt. Big banks are no more profitable than small banks and, absent the taxpayer subsidy, fewer of them would be around.[14]

Nor can it be maintained that a banking oligopoly makes the financial system more stable. In a past era, when there was less interconnection between banks and other parts of the financial system, there was an argument to be made that large banks helped to stabilize the financial system in times of crises. Milton Friedman and Anna Schwartz described how JP Morgan and other banking oligarch's organized self-regulating syndicates that provided liquidity to struggling banks before the creation of the Federal Reserve System.[15] But financial interconnectedness has so magnified the adverse consequences of a failure of a large bank today, that the potential systemic danger posed by large banks far outweighs any perceived benefits.[16]

Economists have pointed out two ways in which a reduction in concentration can be achieved; An upper limit to bank assets or a graduated capital requirement. There are pros and cons to both approaches. The Fed has chosen the latter route.[17] It probably matters less which approach is taken than that one of them be implemented.

Finally, the need to limit concentration and to promote competition extends beyond commercial banking, and applies to all financial intermediaries, including broker-dealers, money market funds, and insurance providers.

To summarize the recommendations made in this section:

4. Large commercial banks, broker-dealers, and money market funds should be broken up into smaller units to end the "too-big-to-fail" conundrum. It is less risky to allow a small bank to go bankrupt than it is a large one, and a competitive banking industry will be more innovative and provide services at lower cost than the current oligopoly. There are a variety of ways to pursue this goal. The Fed's approach of increasing capital requirements on large banks is acceptable if the size of capital charges is large enough so that only those banks that can achieve significant economies of scale remain large. The capital charges should be extended to large broker-dealers and money market funds.

Extend the Scope of Financial Regulation, Increase Capital Requirements and Deregulate Banking

The underlying premise that has guided postfinancial crisis regulation is that the greed of bankers and the avarice of borrowers fueled the housing boom, and that an intensification of regulation is required to rein in the tendency toward irresponsible lending and borrowing. Much of the Dodd-Frank legislation is aimed at this inappropriate target. On the contrary, I do not believe there is any sound argument for increasing the regulation of banking activity.

There is no compelling argument that regulators can improve upon the lending decisions, risk evaluation, or any other aspect of bank operations. In this respect, banking is no different from any other industry. For banking to make the maximal contribution to the welfare of society, the banking industry should operate as free of governmental interference as possible. What we should desire from banking is what we want from other industries: innovation, risk taking, and competition to provide more satisfaction at lower cost to its customers. There are those who desire banks to operate like regulated utilities—safe and boring. I profoundly disagree. I think banks should be dynamic and competitive so they continue to improve our economic well-being. There is nothing wrong with creative destruction, so long as it does not destroy the whole economy.

Yet, there are features of banking that create systemic risk to the entire economy which mark banking as different from other industries; the difference arises from two unique features of banking. One is the composition of bank balance sheets. Banks issue short-term liabilities to funds long(er)-term loans. A bank is always vulnerable to a run on its liabilities, since it is never in a position to liquidate its loans at short notice (unless it is prepared to suffer large losses). In addition, the increased involvement of banks in issuing and trading derivatives has added another dimension to liquidity risk. Derivative contracts often require a party to increase collateral in the event some variable specified in the contract—current trading price, credit rating of the bank, or credit rating of the underlying insured exposure—goes against the bank. An unusually large withdrawal of deposits, an inability to refinance short-term debt or a large collateral call on derivatives contracts, can render a bank unable to meet its financial obligations.[18] These events are economically identical to old-fashioned depositor bank runs.

The other feature of banking that creates systemic risk is that banks interact with many other sectors of the economy; through its operation of the payments network, through the fact that deposits function as money, and because of the ubiquity of bank lending. As a consequence, a disruption of the banking system may trigger disruptions throughout the economy. For example, if several sizeable banks experience large cash calls at the same time, the liquidity drain can cause the payments system to seize up and economywide credit issuance to contract.

Money market funds and broker-dealers similarly interact with many other sectors of the economy and the short-term claims issued by those institutions—overnight repos and NAVs—function as money substitutes (claims convertible to money on demand, at par). Therefore, a disruption of large money market funds and broker-dealers will cause disruption throughout the economy.

The need for banking regulation (including regulation of broker-dealers and money market funds), over and above the regulation of other industries, therefore, is to mitigate the risk of a systemic shutdown of the payments system and a contraction in liquidity, and credit issuance. Banking policy should aim to ensure the stability and functioning of the payments system and maintenance of liquidity in all future states of the world, and to prevent a severe contraction in credit in all (or most) future states of the world.[19] In order to carry out its economic function, the banking system needs to be insured against a systemic loss of liquidity (which would shut down the payments system and credit) and a systemic loss of capital (which would shut down credit).[20]

The classic prescription to mitigate the risk of widespread loss of liquidity was promulgated over a century ago by Walter Bagehot, a late-nineteenth-century British journalist. Bagehot advocated for the central bank to provide loans to illiquid but solvent banks to enable them to meet their depositor obligations. Those shadow banking institutions that issue money-like claims—broker-dealers and money market funds—should be granted regular access to Fed liquidity as well(as they were on an emergency basis during the financial crisis). A loss of liquidity in the shadow banking sector poses the same systemic risk to the financial system as does the illiquidity of the commercial banking sector. In exchange for being included in the liquidity safety net, shadow banking institutions should be subjected to Fed oversight. They should be subjected to Fed rules on capital, reserves, and transparency.

Banks (including broker-dealers and money market funds) also need to hold a sufficient amount of capital to avoid insolvency during crises, in order to continue operating and to extend credit. The risk of bank insolvency will be minimized if banks are required to hold a sufficiently high level of capital. The risk of a credit contraction will be minimized if, in addition, bank regulators have the discretion to temporarily reduce required capital during systemic crises (with the requirement to reimpose them gradually over time, after the crisis has passed). The ability to adjust bank capital levels during crisis events should be the primary macro-prudential tool for bank regulators.[21]

Tier 1 Capital is the broadest definition of bank capital used by regulators.

$$\textit{Tier 1 Capital} = \textit{Equity} + \textit{Reserves} - \textit{intangible assets}. \tag{14.1}$$

After the financial crisis the Fed adopted a broad definition of assets that includes net off-balance sheet derivatives exposures.

$$\begin{aligned}\textit{Adjusted Assets} = {} & \textit{Balance sheet assets} \\ & + \textit{net derivatives exposure} - \textit{intangible assets}.\end{aligned} \tag{14.2}$$

The Bank Leverage Ratio is given by:

$$\textit{Leverage Ratio} = \textit{Tier 1 Capital/Adjusted Assets}. \tag{14.3}$$

I discussed the concept of bank capital in chapter 12. Capital provides the cushion that enables banks to absorb losses and remain solvent. Prior to the financial crisis, bank regulations set minimum capital requirements for risk weighted assets. Crucially, derivatives exposures were not counted as assets and balance sheet assets were weighted by thier risks (as calculated by banks). This enabled "creative" banks to reduce their capital requirement as they expanded the size of their balance sheets.

A simple and comprehensive bank capital requirement should replace (or at least supplement) "risk weighted" capital requirements. The financial crisis has reacquainted us with Keynes's insight about the uncertainty of the future—especially the so-called tails of the distribution of potential outcomes. All of the models used by banks and regulators to calibrate risk completely failed to predict the crisis. Therefore, it would seem the utmost of folly, and a betrayal of much of what has been learned from the crisis, to carry on with "risk weighted" capital requirements as the primary tool of capital regulation. It is not possible to know, ex ante, with precision what activities carry the most risk for the future.[22] Therefore, it is preferable that banks (and broker-dealers and money market funds) be required to meet a simple overall maximum leverage ratio. All contingent liabilities, including off balance sheet net negative derivative and repo exposures, should be subtracted from assets in the calculation of leverage. Fortunately, that is what the Fed has done.[23] One might take issue with the maximum level chosen; the items included in capital and the manner in which derivative exposures are calculated, but the fact that US bank regulations now include an overall maximum level of leverage predicated on an un-weighted valuation of all on and off balance sheet exposures, is a giant leap forward in the setting of standards to ensure bank solvency.[24]

Those who complain that reduced leverage will increase the cost of capital to banks—and thereby to bank borrowers—even if they are correct, are in effect pointing out that removal of the taxpayer subsidy will shift costs formerly borne by the taxpayer onto the parties who directly benefit from the transactions, which is precisely as it should be! Moreover, there is no evidence that constraints on leverage will cause economic activity to slow. Growth soared in the decades after World War II, when bank leverage was much lower than it is today. There has been no correlation between bank leverage and growth in US history.[25]

Nevertheless, there are some parts of the Dodd-Frank legislation that deserve to remain in place. One is the requirement that large banks have living wills to ensure they can become insolvent without disruption to the payments system or the provision of credit. Living wills compel banks to compartmentalize their financial and operational structure so as to allow the components that are vital to the operation of the economy to continue functioning. Effectively, living wills—if properly enforced—will make debt forgiveness automatic when a bank becomes insolvent. The compartmentalization of the functions will also reduce economies of scope, which might cause large banks to voluntarily shed functions and shrink their size.

Other elements of the Dodd-Frank legislation that deserve to remain in place include those provisions that improve the transparency of traded assets such as derivatives, which is important for enabling regulators, investors and counterparties to discern the contingent liabilities of banks. It was shown in chapter 11 that the opacity of bank contingent liabilities contributed to the seizing up of the inter-bank loan market during the financial crisis, which banks rely upon to fund their daily cash needs. The Dodd-Frank provision that requires OTC derivatives to be moved onto exchanges is very desirable. Moving derivatives onto exchanges will improve liquidity, because products are more standardized; it will improve transparency, because the exchanges can be made to report positions, and it will enable banks to net out their positions, which will make it easier to restructure or to liquidate financial institutions in the event they become insolvent.[26] The complexity of the OTC derivatives market increased the difficulty of unwinding positions, which contributed to the decision of policymakers during the financial crisis to avoid bank failures at all costs

But those parts of Dodd-Frank that involve regulation of the internal operations of banks and their interactions with customers should be repealed. If the banking industry is made more competitive by breaking up the behemoth banks, intrusive regulation merely adds cost and complexity and detracts from the benefits of competition.

To summarize the recommendations made in this section:

5. Banks, broker-dealers, and money market funds should be subjected to overall (un-weighted) leverage limitations that include all on and off balance sheet exposures. Regulators should have the discretion to relax capital requirements temporarily during and after systemic crises.
6. The Fed should be given authority and responsibility to provide liquidity to broker-dealers and money market funds.

7. The Fed should be given authority and responsibility to regulate broker-dealers and money market funds, including capital, reserves, and transparency of accounts.
8. Derivative contracts should be standardized, moved onto exchanges, made transparent and each institution's exposures netted out.
9. Systemically important financial institutions should have regulator approved living wills and should be required to hold a greater portion of their assets as regulatory capital.
10. Contingent upon big banks, broker-dealers, and money market funds being broken up into smaller units and their capital requirements being increased, the breadth and extent of regulation of their operations should be relaxed.

Policies to Reduce Current Account Deficits and Income Concentration

The Dilemma of Trade

Trade policy is a difficult issue to deal with. For one thing, it involves relations between countries whose interests and objectives may clash. A central theme of this book is that the bilateral trade imbalance between China and the United States helped China by providing an outlet for its excess saving and harmed the United States by inducing an unsustainable housing boom. Another difficulty is that while trade per se increases wealth, the trade imbalances and large capital flows (whether or not accompanied by imbalances) that often accompany open trade promote instability.

From an economic point of view, trade between countries is identical to trade within countries. Whether or not Los Angeles and New York are in the same country has no bearing on the benefit each receives from trade with the other. The same applies to Shanghai and Detroit. The economic case for trade is the same as the argument in favor of markets. Adam Smith's insight that the market creates wealth by promoting a division of labor (echoed by David Ricardo's law of comparative advantage), F. A. Hayek's insight that the market creates wealth by coordinating the use of knowledge held by disparate individuals, Joseph Schumpeter's insight that market competition creates wealth by rewarding innovation, and Robert Lucas's insight that knowledge spillovers from trade are a primary pathway for poor economies to take off have convinced almost all economists that trade enhances the wealth of individuals and countries. As a policy to promote long-run growth, the argument for trade is persuasive—the more, the freer, the better. Throughout history there has been a strong correlation between openness to trade and growth.[27]

Free international trade—in goods, services, and capital—is self-regulating, at least in theory. It contains feedback mechanisms that automatically rein in large trade imbalances. In a floating exchange rate world, the currencies of surplus countries will appreciate, which will cause a shift toward imports.[28] In a fixed exchange rate world, the increase in exports will cause inflation in surplus countries, which is equivalent to an appreciation in the real exchange rate.[29] The remaining imbalances that persist are efficient. They reflect differences in investment opportunities, with capital flowing into places that offer the prospect of high returns.

The problem is that in practice, open trade has not always been self-regulating. One problem is that free capital flows can generate financial instability. The disruptions caused by sudden stops in money flows to small open economies, like the Southeast Asian countries in 1997, were exacerbated by the conjuncture of large short-term capital flows and highly leveraged US dollar borrowings.[30] Figure 2.7 shows that international capital mobility and financial crises are closely related. The growth of capital mobility from the mid-nineteenth century to the early 1930s was associated with a historically unprecedented increase in financial instability. From World War II to around 1980 there was open trade in goods and services among developed countries, but very limited capital mobility and almost no financial crises. Following the financial liberalization that began in the 1980s, the specter of financial crises reemerged. Notably, however, world GDP growth did not much improve in the period after financial liberalization. It therefore appears that placing restrictions on the movement of capital and debt across borders can reduce financial instability without impeding growth. In light of these arguments, the IMF has recently relaxed its opposition to countries placing restrictions on the flow of capital across their borders.[31]

Another problem is that large trade imbalances can cause economic instability, particularly in deficit countries. In chapter 2 I referred to Reinhardt and Rogoff's findings that throughout history capital flow bonanzas have sowed the seeds of financial crises. Often, persistent large trade imbalances are caused by government interventions that impede the self-regulating feedback of the market. In the 1930s, most currencies were exchangeable for gold at a fixed price and counties settled international payments by transferring gold. The United States ran a large current account surplus and hoarded the gold inflows it received as payment for goods sold overseas. There was no capital flow bonanza sent to the deficit countries. They were forced to contract their money supply. In the absence of intervention, the gold inflow would have caused the US money supply to increase, which would have put inflationary pressure on prices. The combination rising US prices and falling foreign prices would have caused demand to shift away from US goods in favor of foreign goods, which would have reversed the imbalance. But the Fed chose to fight inflation and sterilized the gold inflow (much as the PBOC did in the 2000s). The restriction on US monetary growth inflicted deflationary pressure in both the United States and Europe and contributed to the Great Depression. In this book I have explained how China's interventions to promote net exports caused a massive trade imbalance with the United States that, through the channel of a capital flow bonanza, stoked an unsustainable housing boom. It follows that reducing trade imbalances would reduce instability.

Resetting US Trade Priorities

Since World War II, when the United States took leadership of international economic affairs, it has promoted free trade. The observations in this section—indeed the argument of this book—suggest the United States should adopt a more nuanced approach to trade. The benefits of trade perceived by Adam Smith et al. are correct, but short-term capital movements, large cross-border indebtedness, and trade imbalances can promote instability. The Asian financial crisis and the US (and global) financial crisis were each precipitated by one or more of these factors. The United States also needs to come to terms with two other recent changes in the international economic landscape. It has a limited ability to influence the internal economic policies of other countries and a diminished ability to direct the policies of international bodies involved in the regulation and management of international trade. Keynes grappled with these issues in contemplating the design of a postwar international economic order. I think it would be wise to look again to his ideas as a guidepost to a resetting of US trade priorities.

The Keynes Plan

The underlying premise of the so-called Keynes Plan[32] is that trade should be encouraged while trade imbalances should be minimized. Keynes believed US trade surpluses in the interwar years were a major contributor to deflation and the resultant unemployment in Europe. The impact of US surpluses in the late 1920s and early 1930s was even more injurious to other countries than was China's surpluses in the 2000s; a fact that should temper the urge to castigate China. Keynes thought it vitally important to design a system that would avoid a reoccurrence of those turbulent times.

> a country finding itself in a creditor position *against the rest of the world as a whole* should enter into an arrangement not to allow this credit balance to exercise a contractionist pressure against world economy and, by repercussion, against the economy of the creditor country itself.[33]

Keynes believed a durable framework for international trade would allow individual countries to retain sovereignty over their internal economic arrangements. The aim should be to encourage balanced trade, so as to prevent surplus countries from transmitting deflation (or, in our day of international capital mobility, a capital flow bonanza), while also preventing deficit countries from accumulating unmanageable debt. This would be accomplished by "putting some part of the responsibility for adjustment on the creditor country as well as on the debtor."[34] He stated the principle as follows:

> We need a system possessed of an internal stabilizing mechanism, by which pressure is exercised on any country whose balance of payments with rest of the world is departing from equilibrium in either direction, so as to prevent movements which must create for its neighbors an equal but opposite want of balance.

In order to implement this system, countries that ran large trade deficits or surpluses would be required to make adjustments.

> It is not contemplated that either the debit or the credit balance of an individual country ought to exceed a certain maximum—let us say its *quota*. In the case of

> debit balances this maximum had been made a rigid one, and, indeed, countermeasures are called for long before the maximum is reached. In the case of credit balances no rigid maximum has been proposed. For the appropriate provision might be to require the eventual cancellation or compulsory investment of persistent...credit balances accumulating in excess of a member's quota.[35]

Keynes recommended the creation of a customs union through which countries would process their trade and hold credit balances, and the creation of an international currency he called "Bancor." He proposed that trade and financial flows would channel through the customs union, which would act as a bank for countries, holding national debits and credits denominated in Bancor and settling transactions in Bancor. Keynes was concerned with controlling the proliferation of speculative "hot money" capital flows, which were to be limited through the allocation of credit in the customs union. This concern has contemporary resonance, given the destabilizing impact of the "sudden stop" reversal of capital flows into Southeast Asian countries during the Asian financial crisis of 1997 and the ballooning of international debt during the 2000s.[36]

The Keynes Plan would not be dominated by any individual country. The currency for international transactions would be truly non-national, and the operation of the system would be relatively impersonal.

> The plan must operate not only to the general advantage but also to the individual advantage of each of the participants, and must not require a special economic or financial sacrifice form certain countries. No participant must be asked to do or offer anything which is not to his own long-term interest.

Alas, the Keynes Plan was not adopted, and international trade remained crisis free for four decades after Bretton Woods. This was probably due to a combination of the preeminent position the United States held in the international economy, which enabled it to enforce stability (except when it abdicated, as in the early 1970s) and limitations on cross-border capital flows. But that period of stability has now passed, and it is time to reconsider what Keynes proposed as a possible blueprint for a new world trading architecture.

To summarize the recommendations made in this section: The "Keynes Plan" outlines a framework for preventing the buildup of large trade imbalances and large accumulations of reversible short-term capital flows. It outlines an architecture that cannot be dominated by any one country and any one currency. It is a good starting point for developing a new international trading order that will reduce the risk of financial crisis without damping the volume of trade

11. Enact internationally enforceable penalties against any country that operates with a current account balance that exceeds some percentage of its GDP.
12. Enact internationally enforceable limitations on, or discouragement of, short-term capital flows between countries, possibly in the form of a cross-border capital transactions tax.

Causes and Consequences of Income Concentration

In chapter 10 I argued that the increasing concentration of income may have created deflationary pressure by increasing permanent saving, which is a form of Accumulation. The question is, what can and what should be done to alleviate the deflationary pressure caused by Accumulation by top earners? Any approach to this issue requires caution. First, there is no evidentiary basis to conclude that increasing income concentration has led to an increase in permanent saving; any such conclusion is based upon a measure of intuition. Second, not much is known about the underlying forces that have generated the increased income concentration in recent decades. If, for example, the increased earnings at the top is the result of forces connected to globalization and technological change that have rewarded the people most responsible to creating value with enormously higher wages, then an attempt to reduce their incomes that either loosens their control of assets or their incentives to work, could negatively impact productivity and lower incomes for everyone else. Finally, there is a lack of unambiguous evidence of the extent of the growth of inequality in lifetime earnings.

The problem of income (and wealth) concentration—if indeed it is a problem—may self-heal. Keynes expressed the view that when the pool of accumulated capital grew very large, as it would if wealth became concentrated and was perpetually reinvested, its interaction with the declining marginal productivity of capital would push the rate to return on capital down to a level that rendered it impossible for wealthy people to live solely off of the interest earned on their saving. Low returns would force them to spend a portion of their accumulated saving in order to maintain their lifestyles. This deaccumulation of saving implies an increase in spending out of current income and thereby a reduction in Accumulation. Keynes described the process this way:

> The demand for capital is strictly limited in the sense that it would not be difficult to increase the stock of capital up to a point where its marginal efficiency has fallen to a very low figure... it would mean the euthanasia of the rentier, and, consequently, the euthanasia of the cumulative oppressive power of the capitalist to exploit the scarcity-value of capital... I see, therefore, the rentier aspect of capitalism as a transitional phase which will disappear when it has done its work.[37]

The fact that the primary source of income inequality in the United States today is not inherited capital, but labor income, has two features relevant to this analysis. One is that, unlike Keynes's landed gentry, the Accumulation is not primarily from inherited property, but from high wages, and there are new high wage earners born into each generation. Recent research by Raj Chetty and his collaborators at the Harvard *Equality of Opportunity Project* concludes that intergenerational earnings mobility in the United States has not diminished over time, and that each new generation produces a large crop of high earners from backgrounds of modest wealth.[38] If the distributional structure of the economy remains as it is today, it will produce an inexhaustible supply of new rentiers over time, in which event capital may be more widely owned, and not all owners of capital will necessarily be extremely wealthy. A lower concentration of passive capital income will result in an increased aggregate propensity to consume out of capital income. The second feature is that, because inequality is driven by wage income, rather than capital income, any attempt to meaningfully reduce income concentration will require a reduction in the after-tax remuneration of workers—as opposed to the earnings of passive wealth-holders—which can discourage the incentive of the most productive individuals to work.

In light of the incompleteness of our knowledge of causes of income concentration; the relation of income concentration to Accumulation and the consequences of actions designed to reduce concentration, it seems prudent to limit focus to policies that will unambiguously enhance market performance while at the same time reduce income concentration. The following policies would reduce income concentration without damping incentives to create wealth or violating property rights.

Market Friendly Policies to Reduce Income Concentration

Banks should be encouraged to swap residential debt for equity (proposal 2) and bankruptcy law should be reformed to enable judges to restructure mortgage debt (proposal 3).[39] These reforms will increase the wealth of and disposable income of middle income households, and it will encourage them to increase consumption.

Monopolies and oligopolies should be eliminated through extending the scope and vigorously enforcing anti-trust laws (proposal 4). This will reduce excess profits (and earnings of top executives) while improving market performance by increasing competition. The outsized pay of executives in the commercial and shadow banking industries is a source of income concentration that is promoted by US government policies that subsidize the largest firms in the industry while allowing it to become ever more concentrated. As discussed earlier, a breakup of large financial institutions will make the industry more competitive and, by eliminating the "too-big-to-fail" problem, enhance the credibility of the commitment to refrain from future bailouts of bank investors and managers. The increase in industry competition will reduce income concentration by shrinking the pool of excess profits out of which owners and financial executives are compensated. In 2012 the average compensation of an employee in the financial sector was more than triple the average compensation in the US economy.[40] At least some portion of this wage gap is likely attributable to the fact that banking is subsidized oligopoly.

Reform the patent law to shorten the time span of the applicability of patents, and to reduce the scope in order to reduce the monopoly position conferred by patents. Software is a product that can be produced by a relatively small team and reproduced at close to zero marginal cost. As a result, successful software patents have conferred enormous wealth on a small number of people—anecdotally, to a greater extent than most other products. The ever present caution in this area is that some level of patent protection is necessary to maintain the incentive to invest in the invention of new software and other products. It should be kept in mind, however, that while shrinking income concentration by increasing competition and reducing monopoly rent is both equitable and efficient, there is no justification to regulate the level of return on capital or pay in the financial services or software industries (or in any other industry). A certain portion of the elevated returns and pay are related to the superior productivity of industry participants, and reflect their marginal contribution to the creation of value. Compensation at these levels confers a benefit on society, and any attempt to curb it would likely result in a decline in overall economic performance. Limiting profit and wages in competitive industries would also unjustly deprive individuals of their right to retain what they have earned from voluntary transactions with counterparties who have wide choices of whom to do business with. Moreover, there is no way, other than through market interactions that generate actual compensation, to infer how much value an individual has contributed, or to design the incentive contracts to elicit maximal productivity. What is alone desirable is to eliminate the quasi-monopoly rent extracted by managers and owners of businesses in highly concentrated industries and to eliminate the discouragement of innovation due to the reduced pressure of competition and/or barriers to entry erected by incumbents.

Another area where it is possible to reduce income concentration while enhancing overall economic performance would be to improve access to and quality of, education, since wage differentials tied to years of schooling have continued to widen. Ideally, this could be accomplished with less, rather than more, government involvement. Education could be made more competitive and more accessible if vouchers were provided to student at all levels. That way, students would have the means to attend school, and schools would have to compete to attract students.[41]

An expansion of Charter schools and vouchers at the K-12 level would open up more choices for students from moderate and low income households whose parents cannot afford to pay for a private education, and it would increase competition for their patronage. There is every reason to believe that competition in schooling will elicit superior innovation and outcomes, just as it has done so in all other areas of human endeavor. Vouchers that contribute a portion of university tuition can make higher education more affordable, while requiring that a portion of tuition must be shouldered by the student ensures she has "skin in the game," so that only committed students will take advantage of the opportunity. It is useful to remember that the GI Bill, which made a university education possible for many returning solders after World War II is generally regarded as a success. So why not build on it?

To summarize the recommendations made in this section (not previously made):

13. Reform patent law to reduce the time span of the applicability of patents, and contract their scope.
14. Improve access to, and quality of, education by expanding charter schools and vouchers at the K-12 level, and by expanding offers of co-pay for university level education.

Policy Contingencies

Some of the policy recommendations are contingent upon the prior implementation of other policies.

Banking deregulation (proposal 10) is predicated on breaking up big banks (proposal 4) and the establishment of un-weighted maximum leverage levels (proposal 5). This is because de-regulating too-big-to-fail banks would heighten the risk of a systemic financial crisis.

Maximum leverage ratios (proposal 5) better ensure bank solvency, but they impede banks from expanding credit to fill a hole in demand created by a current account deficit. Therefore, it is important to implement polices to reduce the current account deficit (proposals 11 and 13).

Conclusion

Perhaps the first lesson of this book is that when external equilibrium is disturbed by mercantilist policies pursued by governments of large trading countries, it will disturb the internal equilibrium of countries placed in deficit by the mercantilist policies. It short circuits market feedback mechanisms that would otherwise place a brake on economically unsustainable activities; it reduces trend growth and increases volatility. Governments of deficit countries have no good policy options, short of acting to balance trade. Their most vexatious dilemma concerns credit expansion. A high rate of credit expansion can alleviate unemployment, but the increase in leverage it entails increases the risk of financial crisis.

The second lesson is that mercantilism is a species belonging to the genus of Accumulation, which includes any behavior whereby what is earned, exceeds what is planned to be spent. That is why the increased income concentration of recent decades may—but at the current state of knowledge it must be admitted many not—produce the same maladies as mercantilism. The third lesson is that a boom enabled by the excess saving from Accumulation can inflict long-term damage by causing mal-investment and debt overhangs. The fourth lesson is that the damage is exacerbated by the existence of financial oligopolies and policies that protect creditors of financial institutions.

Finally, if the arguments and explanations provided in this book have merit, Accumulation ought to become a subject of public policy discussion, research and reform.

Notes

Preface

1. A capital flow bonanza is the reinvestment into a country running a large current account deficit (say, over several percentage points of GDP) of monies from its trading partners that is roughly equal to the current account deficit. In other words, a capital flow bonanza is an inflow of foreign investment equal to the size of a country's current account deficit, when the deficit is large. See definition of "capital flow bonanza" in chapter 2, pp. 23–26.
2. I define "Accumulation" as an act of saving by someone who does not intend to spend the savings in the future. Such a person is an "accumulator."
3. I define "secular stagnation" as a condition in which resources—including labor—are not fully employed, and in which the trend growth rate of the economy is below its potential (i.e., the rate that could be achieved if resources were fully employed). See chapters 9 and 10 for a discussion of this concept.
4. I knew about the damage sudden stop reversals of currency flows had inflicted on Southeast Asian economies during the Asian financial crisis of 1997, after those countries had grown dependant on capital flow bonanzas. But I did not then (and I do not now) think the United States is at risk of anything like that occurring.
5. Carmen and Vincent Reinhardt provide evidence that capital flow bonanzas have increased economic volatility during the past several decades. See Carmen M. Reinhardt and Vincent R. Reinhardt, *Capital Flow Bonanzas: An Encompassing View of the Past and the Present*, in Jeffrey Frankel and Francesco Giavazzi (eds.), *NBER International Seminar in Macroeconomics 2008* (Chicago: University of Chicago Press).
6. Kenneth Rogoff and Carmen Reinhardt, *This Time Is Different: Eight Centuries of Financial Folly* (Princeton University Press, 2009).
7. Ironically, it was Hayek who developed a business cycle theory, and the first concept of equilibrium, that requires consistency of future plans among agents in the economy and accurate of forecasts of the future. Meanwhile, Keynes lamented the loss of "local" knowledge that occurs when the locus of investment shifts from illiquid investment in firms to liquid speculation on financial exchanges.
8. It should be noted that several large commercial banks participated in the shadow banking sector through their broker-dealer subsidiaries.

1 The Metamorphosis of China's Trade Policy

1. "Conversation between President Nixon and the Ambassador to the Republic of China (McConaughy): Washington, June 30, 1971, 12:18–12:35 pm," FRUS 17, 351–352.
2. Jonathan D. Spence, *The Search for Modern China* (W.W. Norton & Company, 1999), p. 122.

3. J. L. Cranmer-Byng (ed.), *An Embassy to China: Lord Macartney's Journal, 1793–1794* (London, 1962), p. 340.
4. Zhao Ziyang, *Prisoner of the State, the Secret Journal of Zhao Ziyang* (Simon and Schuster, 2009), p. 97.
5. Ibid., p. 137.
6. Ibid., p. 102.
7. Ibid., p. 107.
8. Ibid.
9. Ibid., p. 149.
10. Yasheng Huang, *Capitalism with Chinese Characteristics: Entrepreneurship and the State* (Cambridge University Press, 2008).
11. Ibid., p. 110.
12. For an analysis of China's economic policies in the 1990s, see Yiping Huang and Kunyu Tao, *Causes of and Remedies for the People's Republic of China's External Imbalances: The Role of Factor Market Distortions* (Asian Development Bank Institute WP No. 279 April 2011); and Dennis Tao Yang, "Aggregate Savings and External Imbalances in China," *Journal of Economic Perspectives*, Vol. 26, Number 4 (2012): 125–146.
13. Source World Bank Data, available at http://data.worldbank.org/indicator/NY.GDP.MKTP.KD.ZG?page=1.
14. Ben S. Bernanke, "The Chinese Economy: Progress and Challenges," Speech at the Chinese Academy of Social Sciences, Beijing, China December 15, 2006. Available at http://www.federalreserve.gov/newsevents/speech/Bernanke20061215a.htm.
15. Fabrice Defever and Alejandro Riano, *China's Pure Export Subsidies* (Centre for Economic Performance Discussion Paper No 1182, London School of Economics and Political Science, 2012).
16. Ibid.
17. Barry Naughton, *The Chinese Economy: Transitions and Growth* (Cambridge, MA: MIT Press, 2007).
18. "In 2005, when the central government felt it should avoid over-heating the economy, the National Development and Reform Commission issued a directive to impose controls against overinvestment with a list of 'prohibited industries'—industries that should avoid further expansion. The heavy industries that had undergone dramatic expansion incapacity topped that list." Yang, "Aggregate Savings and External Imbalances in China," 139.
19. See Rudolph Bems, Robert C. Johnson, and Kei-Mu Yi, "Vertical Linkages and the Collapse of Global Trade," *American Economic Review Papers & Proceedings*, Vol. 101 (2011): 308–312.
20. The cost of transport and the ability to coordinate activities across vast distances have also been factors in shaping supply chains. The growth of international trade is, in part, a consequence of the dramatic reduction in transport and communications costs over the past several decades. For an empirical analysis of the complex role of transport costs in international trade in recent decades, see David Hummels, "Transportation Costs and International Trade in the Second Era of Globalization," *Journal of Economic Perspectives*, Vol. 21, No. 3 (2007): 131–154.
21. A model of this tradeoff is developed by Se-Jik Kim and Hyun Song Shin, *Working Capital, Trade and Macro Fluctuations* (2013), available at http://www.princeton.edu/~hsshin/www/working_capital.pdf.
22. This is an application of F. A. Hayek's theory that production processes involve a tradeoff between time and cost—the longer the period of production, the lower the unit cost. For this reason lower interest rates induce longer production chains. See F. A. Hayek, *Prices and Production* (New York: August M. Kelly, 1931). The concept was originally developed by Eugen Bohm-Bewerk. For a modern exposition, see John Hicks, *Capital and Time* (Oxford, UK: Clarendon Press, 1987).

23. Source: Data on World exports/GDP available at WTO, April 10, 2013, Press Release Chart 3; Data on China exports/GDP available at https://www.wto.org/english/news_e/pres13_e/pr688_e.htm; and OECD sta Extracts database, available at http://stats.oecd.org/Index.aspx?DataSetCode=TISP#.
24. Hu Jintao, speech at the *18th National Congress of the Chinese Communist Party* (2012).
25. Adam Smith, *The Wealth of Nations*, Modern Library Edition (Random House Inc., 1994 [1776]), p. 694. The passage quoted in the text occurs in the context of qualifications to the definition as stated. Smith's concept of mercantilism involved running surpluses in the trade of *final* goods. In order to achieve that end, mercantilists will often restrict exportation of capital goods (or intellectual property) that might aid foreigners in developing competing final goods. Likewise, the mercantilists will promote the importation of capital goods that improve the competitiveness of its exports of final goods. The ultimate goal, however, is the same as stated in the text—to run "an advantageous balance of trade."
26. US Department of the Treasury, *Report on Foreign Portfolio Holdings if US Securities*, which is updated periodically. Also note that many economists believe these figures are understated by as much as 18 percent, since they do not include holdings of China's main Sovereign Wealth Fund, China Investment Corporation, and those held by state banks. See Brad Setser and Arpena Paudney, *China's $1.7Trillion Bet: China's External Portfolio and Dollar Reserves* (Council on Foreign Relations, 2009).

2 The Current Account Deficit and the Housing Boom

1. In this boom, I refer to the acceleration in subprime mortgage origination in 2003 as the start, and the March 2007 Federal Reserve rescue of Bear Stearns as marking the end of the housing boom and the onset of the financial crisis. These markers are, admittedly, subjective, but they are not implausible, and they more or less conform with the dates cited—explicitly or implicitly—by most writers on the subject. Among other things, the ABX index of subprime mortgage backed securities plummeted in March of 2007 and the issuance of new mortgage backed securities came to a standstill.
2. It is often said that bankers were greedy for money and willing to lure unsuspecting borrowers into taking on loans they could not afford, while borrowers coveted an upgrade in lifestyle and were willing to lie on loan applications to attain it.
3. *The Financial Crisis Inquiry Report*, Final Report of the National Commission on the Causes of the Financial and Economic Crisis in the United States, January 2011, http://www.gpo.gov/fdsys/pkg/GPO-FCIC/pdf/GPO-FCIC.pdf.
4. Ibid., p. XIX.
5. Gary Gorton, *The Subprime Panic*, Yale ICF Working Paper No. 08–25, 2008, pp. 2–4.
6. http://newsbusters.org/blogs/tom-blumer/2009/02/19/rant-ages-cnbcs-rick-santelli-goes-studio-hosts-invoke-mob-rule-downplay.
7. Frank Rich, "The Other Plot to Wreck America," *The New York Times*, January 9, 2010. http://www.nytimes.com/2010/01/10/opinion/10rich.html?_r=0.
8. Minsky did not live to experience the financial crisis. He died many years earlier, in 1996.
9. The "Greenspan Put" refers to the concept of at "put option" whereby an investor acquires the right to sell a security to another party at a preagreed-upon price. The "put" effectively sets a minimum price for the security. The term in the text denotes the perception that Fed policy ensured a minimum price for all securities.
10. In 2004 commercial banks and broker-dealers were allowed by their regulators to use their proprietary VaR models to establish the risk rating of their portfolios. Basel II allowed banks to use VaR and SEC Rule 17 CFR Parts 200 and 240 allowed Broker-dealers to use VaR.

11. For a good nontechnical explanation of the relationship between VIX and VaR, see Thomas Coleman, *What Is the Link Between VIX and VaR?* (2013), http://cloSoutheastmountain.com/2013/09/what-is-the-link-between-vix-and-var/.
12. Ana Fostel and John Geanakoplos, "Leverage Cycles and the Anxious Economy," *American Economic Review*, Vol. 98, Number 4 (2008): 1211–1244. The theory works in reverse when perceived risk of loss increases. Then, lenders reduce the allowed leverage on loans, which drains funds available to speculators and causes asset prices to fall, which increases losses. Also note that Geanakoplos arrived at his insight independently of Minsky. He developed the "leverage cycle" theory from reflecting on his experiences as a Wall Street mortgage bond analyst.
13. Moritz Schularick and Alan M. Taylor, "Credit Booms Gone Bust: Monetary Policy, Leverage Cycles, and Financial Crises, 1870–2008," *American Economic Review*, Vol. 102, Number 2 (2012); and Oscar Jordà, Mortiz Schularick, and Alan M. Taylor, *Financial Crises, Credit Booms, and External Imbalances: 140 Years of Lessons*, IMF Annual Research Conference, 2010.
14. Schularick and Taylor, "Credit Booms Gone Bust"; emphasis in the original.
15. Oscar Jordà, Mortiz Schularick, and Alan M. Taylor, *The Great Mortgaging: Housing Finance, Crises and Business Cycles*, National Bureau of Economic Research Working Paper 20501, 2014.
16. Ibid.
17. Ibid.
18. John Geanakoplos, et al., "Getting at Systemic Risk via an Agent-Based Model of the Housing Market," *American Economic Review: Papers and Proceedings*, Vol. 102, Number 3 (2012): 53–58.
19. Ibid., Figure 2, p. 56.
20. The measure includes liabilities from all sources—public, corporate, and household. Also note that the definitions apply to bilateral relationships between countries.
21. Which is why the foreign exchange transaction flowed through the PBOC. It offered to pay a higher price for dollars than could be got on the open market.
22. Measured in Yuan.
23. Measured in dollars. Note that, since the exchange rate established by the PBOC overvalued the dollar, the value of renminbi expansion would have exceeded the value of the dollar contraction. This reflects a transfer of wealth from China to the United States.
24. Since the PBOC does not report the composition of its assets, economists must infer, from indirect information, the size of PBOC holdings of US debt. See US Department of the Treasury, *Report on Foreign Portfolio Holdings of US Securities*, which is issued annually.
25. The definition of capital flow bonanza used in this book is equivalent to the definition given in Reinhardt and Reinhardt, where a threshold size (relative to GDP) to qualify is proposed. They define the capital flow bonanza as "reserve accumulation less the current account balance which will be positive when the country runs a current account deficit. In terms of the discussion in the text, note that (i) the volume of US bank lending is constrained (or was constrained before the financial crisis—see chapter 12 to understand why this ceased to hold after the financial crisis) by the volume of Fed reserves held by banks and (ii) the money supply (M2, M3, MZM) is partially determined by the volume of bank deposits. To the extent the PBOC retains its Fed reserves (which would count as a loss of reserves in the US banking system), the result is a contraction in US money supply and credit. This is so because the transfer of Fed reserves to the PBOC requires the extinguishment of a deposit of equal size at the bank that transferred the reserve. Therefore, the difference between the capital flow bonanza and the current account deficit is "reserve accumulation," which is the amount of US bank reserves that foreigners choose to retain.

    See Carmen M. Reinhardt and Vincent R. Reinhardt, "Capital Flow Bonanzas: An Encompassing View of the Past and Present," in *NBER International Seminar in Macroeconomics 2008*, ed. Jeffrey Frankel and Francesco Giavazzi (University of Chicago Press for the National bureau of Economic Research, 2008), pp. 1–54.

26. In 2006 the US current account deficit was $811.5 billion (source: US Bureau of Economic Analysis, US International Transactions Accounts Data, Table 1. US International Transactions), and the issuance of subprime and Alt-A mortgages was $815 billion (source: derived from Gorton, *The Subprime Panic*, Table 3, p. 4).
27. Dissenting Statement of Keith Hennessy et al., to Financial Crisis Inquiry Report of the Financial Inquiry Commission of the United States Government, pp. 417–418.
28. See figure 11.1.
29. Ibid.
30. Carmen Reinhardt and Kenneth Rogoff, *This Time Is Different: Eight Centuries of Financial Folly* (Princeton University Press, 2009), Table 1.2, p. 11.
31. Note that Schularick and Taylor argue that, in the correlation between money growth and financial crises in the pre–World War II data for developed countries, money growth may have proxied for credit growth, since bank credit and money were closely correlated prior to World War II. See Schularick and Taylor, "Credit Booms Gone Bust."
32. A "bank run" of depositor withdrawals is the classic example. In the recent financial crisis, deposit insurance forestalled depositor runs, but overnight repo and wholesale funding became subject to runs. I ignore the possibility of "sunspot" runs, which are not occasioned by a decline in bank solvency, but induce illiquidity.
33. For empirical evidence that banks fund fluctuations in assets by adjusting liabilities (as opposed to equity), see Tobias Adrian and Hyun Song Shin, "Procyclical Leverage and Value—at-Risk," *Review of Financial Studies*, Vol. 27, Number 2 (2014): 373–403.
34. I address the role of international capital mobility, as a matter independent of capital as a possible cause of the US housing boom, in the final section of this chapter 4.
35. Reinhardt and Rogoff, p. 157. It must be acknowledged, however, that the historical evidence linking financial crisis to capital flow bonanzas is much less pronounced for advanced economies like the United States. For an analysis of correlations between capital flow bonanzas and financial crises prior to the recent financial crisis, see Carmen M. Reinhardt and Vincent R. Reinhardt, "Capital Flow Bonanzas: An Encompassing View of the Past and Present," in *NBER International Seminar on Macroeconomics 2008*, ed. Jeffrey Frankel and Christopher Pissarides (University of Chicago Press, 2009), Chapter 1, pp. 9–62.
36. Reinhardt and Rogoff, *This Time Is Different*, pp. 216–217. Jordà et al. reach a similar conclusion using more formal statistical methods: "the correlation between credit growth and current accounts has grown much tighter in recent decades. In a globalized economy with free capital mobility credit cycles and capital flows have the potential to reinforce each other more strongly than before. The historical data clearly suggest that high rates of credit growth coupled with widening imbalances pose stability risks that policy makers should not ignore." Jordà et al., *Financial Crises, Credit Booms, and External Imbalances*.
37. Reinhardt and Rogoff, *This Time Is Different*, p. 207
38. A potential pitfall of historical studies of macroeconomic variables is the temptation to overanalyze the data in search of correlations. It is always possible to fit any finite set of data into some pattern, if only one tortures the data enough. This is a possible criticism of (an aspect of) the pathbreaking empirical investigations of Jordà, Schularick, and Taylor. They employ so many statistical tests to measure different possible patterns in the macroeconomic data (and one suspects they ran tests additional to those they report) that it seems they are almost bound to find some pattern in the data. The overanalysis of the data should temper our confidence that the correlations have any real-world meaning, or that they can be used to forecast the future evolution of the system. That is why event studies, which have the disadvantage of fewer data points, carry

the advantage of enabling the researcher to identify more reliable causal relationships between economic variables and real-world outcomes.

39. Concurrent with US housing boom, from 2003 to 2007, several countries on the coastal periphery of Europe—notably Portugal, Ireland, and Spain—experienced massive booms in housing construction and prices.
40. Ouarda Merrouche and Erland Nier, *What Caused the Global Financial Crisis? Evidence of the Drivers of Financial Imbalances 1999–2007*, IMF Working Paper 10/265, 2010.
41. The comments on the transmission mechanisms linking current account deficits to measures of domestic financial conditions that follow go beyond the results in Merrouche and Nier, which document the correlations between the variables without examining the underlying transmission mechanisms. The comments on transmission mechanisms are supported by other evidence discussed in this book.
42. US Federal Reserve Board.
43. See Jordà et al., *The Great Mortgaging.*
44. This is part of the conventional view as well.
45. Ouarda Merrouche and Erland W. Nier "The Global Financial Crisis—What Caused the Build-Up?" http://www.voxeu.org/article/global-financial-crisis-what-caused-build.
46. Ibid., p. 29; emphasis in the original.
47. Francis E. Warnock and Veronica Cacdac Warnock, "International Capital Flows and US Interest Rates," *Journal of International Money and Finance*, Vol. 28 (2009): 903–919.
48. By 2011, China had become the largest owner of US Treasuries.
49. Warnock and Warnock, "International capital flows," 903–919, 904. The authors attribute the foreign accumulation of US government bonds during the mid-2000s to East Asia (which include China): "our analysis suggests that East Asian accumulation is responsible for about two-thirds of our estimated impact" (905 and 918).
50. See US Department of the Treasury, *Report on Foreign Portfolio Holdings of US Securities*, available at http://www.treasury.gov/resource-center/data-chart-center/tic/Pages/fpis.aspx; and discussion in chapter 3.
51. Daniel O. Beltran, Maxwell Kretchmer, Jaime Marquez, and Charles P. Thomas, *Foreign Holdings of U.S. Treasuries and U.S. Treasury Yields* Board of Governors of the Federal Reserve System International Finance Discussion Papers Number 1041, 2012, p. 16. Available at http://www.federalreserve.gov/pubs/ifdp/2012/1041/ifdp1041.pdf.
52. Oscar Jordà, Mortiz Schularick, and Alan M. Taylor, "Betting the House," National Bureau of Economic Research Working Paper 20771, 2014.
53. Ibid.
54. Ibid.
55. Maurice Obstfeld and Kenneth Rogoff, "Global Imbalances and the Financial Crisis: Products of Common Causes," Federal Reserve Bank of San Francisco Asia Economic Policy Conference, October 18–20, 2009, p. 26.
56. See Niall Ferguson and Mortiz Schularick, "Chimarica and Global Asset Markets," *International Finance*, Vol. 10, Number 3 (2007).
57. Another factor that boosted reported profits was the 1998 reduction in capital gains tax rates, which caused many corporations to shift shareholder payouts from dividends (which are deducted from profits) to share buybacks (which are not deducted from profits).
58. Reinhardt and Rogoff, *This Time Is Different*, p. 172.
59. Ibid.
60. Ibid., pp. 213–214.
61. Ibid., p. 213.
62. Douglas L. Campbell, "Relative Prices, Hysteresis, and the Decline of American Manufacturing," Job Market Paper UC Davis, April 14, 2014.
63. David Autor, David Dorn, and Gordon H. Hanson, "The China Syndrome: Local Labor Market Effects of Import Competition in the United States," *American Economic Review*, Vol. 103, Number 6 (2013): 2121.

3 Mercantilism and the Current Account Deficit

1. Ben S. Bernanke, "Global Imbalances: Links to Economic and Financial Stability," Speech at Banque de France Financial stability Review Launch Event, February 18, 2011. Available at http://www.federalreserve.gov/newsevents/speech/bernanke 20110218a.htm.
2. Ben S. Bernanke, "The Global Savings Glut and the U.S. Current Account Deficit," Speech at the Sandbridge Lecture, Virgina Association of Economists, March 10, 2005, available at http://www.federalreserve.gov/boarddocs/speeches/2005/200503102/.
3. Ben S. Bernanke, "The Global Saving Glut and the US Current Account Deficit," Homer Jones Lecture, St. Louis, MO, April 14, 2005, available at http://www.federal-reSoutheastrve.gov/boarddocs/speeches/2005/200503102/.
4. Ibid., p. 8.
5. Although US corporate earnings continued to surge into the decade of the 2000s, only a small proportion of net foreign capital inflows were invested in US corporate equities after the dot-com crash. Thus US equities cannot have been a motivating factor in the capital inflows into the United States. For example, China's holdings of US equities in 2006, at the height of the housing boom, were less than 1 percent of its holdings of US securities.See Wayne M. Morrison and Marc Labonte, "China's Holdings of US Securities: Implications for the US Economy," CRS Report for Congress RL34314, 2008, p. 6.
6. Obstfeld and Rogoff, "Global Imbalances and the Financial Crisis p. 13.
7. Gross investment, as a percent of GDP, remained flat. Net investment declined, due to the impact of increased depreciation charges, which were caused by the shift in investment from long-lived assets—such as plants—to short-lived assets—such as computers.
8. Though many have tried to obscure the inescapable conclusions, anyone looking at the graph can plainly see it. For an example of a denial, see, for example, Menzie D. Chinn and Barry Eichengreen, "A Forensic Analysis of Global Imbalances," 2013, available at http://www.ssc.wisc.edu/~mchinn/CEI_GI.pdf.
9. Note this does not imply that households borrowed directly from foreigners—in most instances they did not do so. It will be seen in chapter 7 that the capital flow bonanza was invested in US government-guaranteed debt, which set off a chain reaction that ended in mortgages issued to US households from primarily US institutions.
10. See Christopher D. Carroll, Misuzu Otsuka, and Jirka Slacalek, "How Large Is the Housing Wealth Effect? A New Approach," National Bureau of Economic Research Working Paper No. 12746, 2006.
11. However, these countries comprised a minority of the gross capital flow into the United States. See figure 3.6.
12. Ricardo Caballero, Interview with Ricardo Caballero, *The Region*, July 2011 Issue, Federal Reserve Bank of Minneapolis, p. 3. Available at https://www.minneapolisfed.org/publications/the-region/issues/6-2011.
13. Following Caballero, I interpret "safe-assets" to be those that reliably guarantee to pay out in all future circumstances. US government-guaranteed debt tops the list, followed closely by AAA rated Municipal and privately issued bonds.
14. Ibid., p. 4 Note that Caballero is saying that the ABS backed by subprime mortgages really weren't "safe assets," even in their design, since they were destined to default in at least one future state of the economy—when there was a synchronous national downturn in the housing market.
15. Ibid.
16. There were also some European banks who invested heavily in subprime ABS, including recently deregulated and undercapitalized German Landesbanken.
17. Stephanie E. Curcuru, et al., "On Return Differentials," 2012, http://faculty.darden.virginia.edu/warnockf/papers/OnReturnsDifferentials.pdf.

18. China's State Administration of Foreign Exchange (SAFE), *FAQ's on Foreign Exchange Reserves,* July 20, 2010.
19. The Southeast Asian countries to which I refer in the text are Indonesia, Malaysia, Philippines, Singapore, South Korea, and Thailand. These are the countries that suffered sudden stops in capital flows and huge exchange rate depreciation in 1997.
20. Consistent with Adam Smith's description of the motives of mercantilists, China promoted the importation of raw materials and capital goods necessary to build its internal infrastructure and to become integrated into global supply chains. As a result, China ran large current account deficits with commodities suppliers like Brazil and Australia.
21. Wayne M. Morrison and Marc Laboute, "China's Currency Policy: An Analysis of the Economic Issues," Congressional Research Service RS21625, 2013, p. Summary.
22. Ibid. Note that China's relatively higher rate of productivity growth meant that its effective labor cost advantage increased throughout the decade of the 2000s.
23. BEA data on Balance of Goods and Services.
24. US Department of the Treasury, "Report on Foreign Portfolio Holdings of US Securities." After the financial crisis, China liquidated the majority of its holdings in GSE debt and transferred it into Treasuries.
25. Ibid. Many experts believe China holds US Securities through intermediaries not identified with China.
26. Wayne M. Morrison and Marc Labonte, "China's Holdings of U.S. Securities: Implications for the US Economy," Congressional Research Service RL3414, 2013, Summary page.
27. The economist reader will note I am assuming the Marshall-Lerner conditions obtain. The condition is that after the currency depreciation, the sum of changes in export sales and import purchases is positive, measured in terms of the home country currency. Often, the trade deficit will initially increase after depreciation, as it takes time for the reduction in purchases of imports and the increases sales of exports to take place. The determinant of whether the Marshall-Lerner condition holds depends upon the elasticity of substitution of imports and exports. Formally, the condition is that the sum of the long run price elasticity of imports and exports is greater than 1. Since most goods traded between the United States and China could be produced in either country (or elsewhere) the goods are substitutable. Therefore, it is highly likely that Marshall-Lerner holds in the case of US-China trade.
28. Obstfeld and Rogoff, "Global Imbalances and the Financial Crisis: Products of Common Causes," p. 19.
29. China could have forced a deflation in the United States had it elected to hold Fed reserves—which would have drained money out of the US economy—rather that recycling the dollars accumulated by its current account surplus into investments in the US economy. This is an important point, because it underscores that current account deficits are not automatically matched by capital flow bonanzas. That occurs only if the surplus country elects to invest in the deficit country.
30. Ben Bernanke described what would occur if the PBOC stopped sterilizing China's dollar inflows. "Increases in the domestic money supply will result unless the central bank offsets the effects of these purchases on the money supply by selling bonds to investors, primarily commercial banks, in exchange for RMB—a procedure commonly referred to as 'sterilization.' If dollar purchases by the central bank were not routinely sterilized, the money supply might increase more than desired, possibly leading to an overheating of the economy and inflation." Bernanke, "The Chinese Economy: Progress and Challenges."
31. Gian Maria Milesi-Ferretti, "Fundamentals at Odds? The U.S. CURRENT ACCOUNT DEFICIT and the Dollar," IMF WP 08–260, 2008.
32. Ibid., p. 9. See also Douglas L. Campbell, "Relative Prices, Hysteresis, and the Decline of American Manufacturing," Job Market Paper UC Davis, April 14, 2014, for an

explanation of the problem with the Fed's real exchange rate index measure and a proposed replacement measure of relative unit labor costs.

33. By "independent cause" I mean the current account deficit that arose during the housing boom was independent of both US government policy and US economic conditions.

4 The Current Account Deficit: A Necessary Condition for the Housing Boom

1. Isaac Newton, *Principia Mathematica* (1687).
2. Cf. the excerpt from the Financial Crisis Inquiry Report quoted in chapter 2.
3. Single family housing starts increased from 1.2 million in 2000 to 1.8 million in 2005. Residential construction increased from \$347 billion in 2000 to \$617 billion in 2006 (the peak in spending normally follows on the peak in starts). Source: US Bureau of the Census, *Privately Owned Housing Starts: 1-Unit Structures*; and US Bureau of the Census, *Total Private Construction Spending: Residential.*
4. Insofar as the increase in housing investment caused GDP to rise, the measured increase in residential construction as a proportion of GDP understates the magnitude of its rise. Source of residential construction to total gross investment data: US Bureau of Economic Analysis, *Gross Private Domestic Investment*; and US Bureau of the Census, *Total Private Construction Spending: Residential.*
5. Residential construction was also boosted by the availability of mortgage financing, even in markets that did no experience significant home price increases. See Atif Mian and Amir Sufi, *House of Debt* (University of Chicago Press, 2014).
6. Note that, in order to capture all elements of the current account balance in the term $(X-M)$, I assume all payments related to investments are captured in the spending on "investments."
7. I state identity (4.1)–(4.3) as "identities" because they express logical relationships that are always true whatever the situation.
8. The relationships in identities (4.1)–(4.3) are in terms of "real" home economy values, which means they are indexed to some base year home economy price level.
9. Home economy consumption, investment, and government spending represent spending on, or investment in, home economy produced goods and services by home economy economic agents.
10. All variables represent "real" magnitudes, that is, gross magnitudes divided by an index of home economy prices.
11. Price inflation is not incompatible with a current account deficit; it will occur when $Yf < C + I + G + (X - M)$. If the economy overheats by enough, inflation will be kindled in the presence of a deficit, as occurred in the 1970s in the United States.
12. Identity (4.3) also shows that a government surplus can finance an investment boom, but it is so unusual for a government to operate with a surplus that I ignore that possibility.
13. Whether the Chinese boom will end in a bust remains an open question.
14. Bernanke, "The Chinese Economy: Progress and Challenges.
15. Ibid.
16. Note that I do not identify a reduction in the government deficit $(T-G)$ as a possible relief valve. The reason is that any increase in taxes would divert saving, so that the deficit reduction would likely be matched by (at least some) reduction in saving.
17. Ibid.
18. Viral V. Acharya, Phillipp Schnable, and Gustavo Suarez, "Securitization without Risk Transfer," *Journal of Financial Economics*, Vol. 107 (2013): 515–536.
19. Notably by Claudio Borio, chief economist at the Bank for International Settlements.
20. Claudio Borio and Piti Disyatit, "Global Imbalances and the Financial Crisis: Link or No Link?" Bank for International Settlements Working Paper No 346, May 2011, Graph 6, p. 14.

21. The causal path identified by researchers so far runs from the United States outward to other countries. Ibid., and Valentina Bruno and Hyun Song Shin, "Cross Border Banking and Global Liquidity," NBER Working Paper No. 19038, 2014.
22. Ben S. Bernanke, et al., "International Capital Flows and the Returns to Safe Assets in the United States, 2003–2007," Board of Governors of the Federal Reserve system, International Financial Discussion Papers Number 1014, February 2011.
23. Hyun Song Shin, "Global Banking Glut and Loan Risk Premium," Mundell-Fleming Lecture, IMF, 2012.
24. Hyun Song Shin, *Global Savings Glut or Global Banking Glut?*, 2011. Voxeu.org, http://www.voxeu.org/article/global-savings-glut-or-global-banking-glut.

5 A Review of Explanations for the Housing Boom

1. A FICO is a measure related to the probability that a person will repay a loan. It is derived from data on the payment and transactions history of a person. Most banks report such data to the company that publishes FICO scores. A person's FICO score usually forms part of the credit evaluation of a potential borrower for a loan.
2. See Gary Gorton, "The Panic of 2007," Paper delivered at the Federal Reserve Bank of Kansas City Jackson Hole Conference, August 2008, p. 8, for a matrix of characteristics of different mortgage categories.
3. In keeping with common practice, I count Alt-A mortgages as "subprime." Alt-A borrowers had FICO scores lying between subprime and prime borrowers, typically in the range of 640–730.
4. See figure 2.1; and Dwight Jaffee and John M. Quigley, "The Future of the Government Sponsored Enterprises: The Role for Government in the US Mortgage Market," Chapter 8 in *Housing and the Financial Crisis*, ed. Edward L. Glaeser and Todd Sinai, National Bureau of Economic Research, 2013, Table 8.1, p. 367.
5. The descriptions and data in this section are from Gorton, "The Panic of 2007."
6. The proportion of all mortgages that were securitized increased from 55 percent in 2000 to 63 percent in 2010. See Jaffee and Quigley, "The Future of the Government Sponsored Enterprises Table 8.1, p. 367.
7. See ibid., Table 8.3, p. 376.
8. CDO divvyed up cash flow into tranches and securities called CDO squared were constructed from CDO tranches.
9. For subprime volumes I count ARMs as subprime and I use the estimates in ibid.; Gorton, "The Panic of 2007"; and Gerald P. Dwyer and Paula Tkac, "The Financial Crisis in Fixed Income Markets," Federal Reserve Bank of Atlanta Working Paper, 2009, 20. For CDO volumes I refer to Larry Cordell, Yilin Huang, and Meredith Williams, "Collateral Damage: Sizing and Assessing the Subprime CDO Crisis," Federal Reserve Bank of Philadelphia Working Paper No. 11–30/R, 2012.
10. See Eric Arentsen, David C. Mauer, Brian Rosenlund, Harold H. Zhang, and Feng Zhao, "Subprime Mortgage Defaults and Credit Default Swaps," *Journal of Finance*, Vol. 70, Number 2 (April 2015): 689–731, http://finance.eller.arizona.edu/documents/seminars/2012-13/DMauer.Subprime09-12.pdf.
11. An exasperated Paul Krugman wrote that "of AAA backed subprime-mortgage-backed securities issued in 2006, 93 percent—93 percent!—have now been downgraded to junk status." See Paul Krugman, "Berating the Raters," *New York Times*, April 25, 2009. Available at http://www.nytimes.com/2010/04/26/opinion/26krugman.html?_r=0.
12. Originators are the parties that arrange for issuance of the mortgage loan to the borrower. They interact directly with the borrower. Originators are typically mortgage brokers and commercial banks. Sponsors are the entities that aggregate the loans into

pools and create the securities that are sold to investors. Sponsors are typically GSE's, commercial banks and broker-dealer investment banks.

13. In some instances the intermediary was another department within the entity that originated the mortgage.
14. Typically, the intermediaries would retain the most junior tranche, which is derisively referred to as "toxic waste."
15. The Goldman employee who carried out the Abacus transaction, Fabrice Tourre, was convicted of securities fraud in 2013, for misleading investors in the Abacus deal.
16. Christopher L. Foote, Kristopher S. Gerardi, and Paul S. Willen, "Why Did So Many People Make So Many Ex Post Bad Decisions? The Causes of the Foreclosure Crisis," Federal Reserve Bank of Boston, Public Policy Discussion Papers No. 12–2, 2012, p. 16.
17. Ibid., p. 28.
18. Ibid.
19. Ibid., p. 19.
20. One finding that raises the possibility that some parties were harmed by asymmetric information is that subprime MBS securities, on which credit default swaps (CDS) had been issued at inception, were more likely to default. It is possible that loan originators knew of this pattern and that investors and CDS issuers did not. The study found that CDS coverage is associated with an increased probability of loan delinquency of 3.2–5.4 percent. This result suggests that originators and investors may have been less concerned about credit quality on securitizations for which default insurance was available, which is rational. The higher delinquency rate does not, however, imply that CDS issuers were victimized by asymmetric information, since they had access to the same information as the other parties. CDS issuers may have knowingly issued policies on riskier pools of mortgages because investors were willing to adequately compensate them (in their opinion, at the time) for policies written on riskier pools. See Arentsen et al., "Subprime Mortgage Defaults and Credit Default Swaps."
21. Depositors were also indifferent to bank policy, since deposits—up to some maximum amount—were effectively guaranteed by the government through the FDIC insurance guarantee.
22. If the bonds were not insured by the US government and investors believed that managers were taking on too much risk, they would sell off their bond holdings, which would cause bond prices to drop and capital market access to be impaired. Managers would then have an incentive to restore confidence by paring back risk.
23. Charles Calomiris and Steven Haber, *Fragile by Design: The Political Origins of Banking Crises and Scarce Credit* (Princeton University Press, 2014); and Raghram Rajan, "Bankers have been sold short by market distortions" *Financial Times*, June 2, 2010.
24. Sumit Agarwal, Effi Benmelech, Nittai Bergman, and Amit Seru, "Did the Community Reinvestment Act (CRA) Lead to Risky Lending?" National Bureau of Economic Research NBER Working Paper No. 18609, 2012.
25. Calomiris and Haber, *Fragile by Design*.
26. See Jaffee and Quigley, "The Future of the Government Sponsored Enterprises," Figure 8.2, p. 370, and Figure 8.4, p. 371.
27. A conforming loan is a mortgage sold to investors with a guaranty from one of the GSEs. Subprime mortgages (including Alt-A) were nonconforming, in that they were not guaranteed by a GSE. However, the GSEs purchased nonconforming subprime mortgage backed securities for their own account.
28. Ibid., Table 8.3, p. 376 and Table 8.4, p. 378.
29. Ibid., p. 377.
30. Financial Crisis Inquiry Commission Report, p. xxvi.
31. It is not universally true that all explanations that assert "irrational exuberance" waive any analysis of the underlying cause of the behavior. There are some researchers, like

George Akerlof and Robert Shiller, who are attempting to apply insights from the field of psychology to account for the behavior.

32. One might contend that the rate of increase in "real" home prices, that is, home price appreciation minus CPI inflation, which was unprecedentedly high during the housing boom, should have been a warning signal of possible risk of overheating (see figure 2.2). This is not necessarily correct. The relevant basis of comparison is the discounted value of projected real price appreciation over the useful life of the home, which is difficult to discern, since homes last for many decades (sometimes centuries). The real rate of appreciation over a short interval of time is not very informative.
33. N. Gregory Mankiw and David N. Weil, *United States Regional Science and Urban Economics*, Vol. 19 (1989): 235–258. Available at http://www.econ.brown.edu/faculty/David_Weil/Mankiw%20Weil%20Baby%20Boom%20and%20Housing%20Market.pdf.
34. Atif Mian and Amir Sufi, *House of Debt* (University of Chicago Press, 2014).
35. Ibid., p. 83.
36. Christopher Foote et al., "Subprime Facts: What (We Think) We Know about the Subprime Crisis and What We Don't," Federal Reserve Bank of Boston, Public Policy Discussion Papers No. 08–2, 2008, Table 3, p. 14.
37. Ibid., p. 79.
38. "Relative" earnings refers to the earnings growth of subprime borrowers versus median income growth. The relative earnings of subprime borrowers was in decline due to a shift in income distribution to top earners. See the discussion in chapter 11 for more on this point.
39. Mian and Sufi, *House of Debt*, p. 90.
40. In 2006, 17.7% of MBS issued, and 13% outstanding, were Alt-A. See Gorton "The Panic of 2007," p. 9.
41. Foote et al., "Why Did So Many People Make So Many Ex Post Bad Decisions?," demonstrate that, at the time of the financial crisis, mortgage originators retained exposure to loans in amounts that substantially exceeded the Dodd-Frank requirements. See p. 37.
42. Ibid., Table 3, p. 14.
43. Ibid., pp. 5–8.

6 Decision-Making during the Housing Boom

1. Martin Wolf, *The Shifts and the Shocks* (New York: Penguin Press, 2014), p. 146.
2. Adam Ferguson, *An Essay on the History of Civil Society*, 5th ed. T. Cadell (London, 1782). Available at http://oll.libertyfund.org/titles/1428.
3. Adam Smith, *The Wealth of Nations* Modern Library Edition (Random House Inc., 1994 [1776]), Modern Library Edition, p. 15.
4. Sigmund Freud, *A Difficulty in the Path of Psycho-Analysis*, vol. 17, Complete Works, Standard edn, eds. James Strachey and Anna Freud (1955 [1917]).
5. A reader of Smith's *Theory of Moral Sentiments* might justifiably conclude that Smith believed man was swayed by little else than emotion! Even in the *Wealth of Nations*, Smith did not impose any constraints on either the scope of what people regarded as their "interests" or on the rules they employed for making decisions. All that is required for the feedback loop to drive the economy toward equating supply with demand in each market is that people do not act in a grossly inconsistent manner. Nevertheless, Smith has been unjustly associated with the narrow view of human motivation I describe as the "Smithian premise." For that reason I hesitate to use it, except that it has become the most recognizable statement of the "narrow" view of human nature implied by the maximization premise that forms the core of modern neoclassical economics.

6. Rogoff and Reinhardt, *This Time Is Different.*
7. Schularick and Taylor, "Credit Booms Gone Bust.
8. Robert J. Shiller and George Akerlof, *Animal Spirits: How Human Psychology Drives the Economy and Why It Matters for Global Capitalism* (Princeton University Press, 2009).
9. See Vernon L. Smith, "Constructivist and Ecological Rationality," Nobel Prize Lecture, 2002, pp. 502–561. Available at http://www.nobelprize.org/nobel_prizes/economic-sciences/laureates/2002/smith-lecture.pdf.
10. "We must constantly adjust our lives, our thoughts and our emotions, in order to live simultaneously within different kinds of orders according to different rules." F. A. Hayek, *The Fatal Conceit* (Chicago: University of Chicago Press, 1988), p. 18.
11. The reaction of contractually constrained investors to low yields and the compression of the maturity curve is discussed in more detail in chapter 7.
12. Vernon Smith wrote that decision-making often gets delegated to "autonomic, neuropsychological systems that enable people to function effectively without always calling upon the brain's scarcest resource—attention are reasoning circuitry." Smith, "Constructivist and Ecological Rationality," p. 507.
13. Ibid.
14. In chapter 10 I explain how the current account deficit is part of a broader phenomenon that includes the increase in income concentration, which is also a novel event.
15. F. A. Hayek, "The Use of Knowledge in Society," *The American Economic Review*, Vol. XXXV (1945): 519–520.
16. A person's "cognitive purview" might encompass a wide area of geography, but it will necessarily be limited to a very small slice of events within that extended geography. This does not just reflect ignorance per se, but also the advantages of specialization.
17. Ibid., 528.
18. Hayek was agnostic on where those distortions came from. In his early work on trade cycles, he conjectured that, after a period of economic stability, market competition and the profit motive would cause banks to underprice risk and offer loans at unsustainably low rates. In this sense, Hayek anticipated the theory of an endogenous market generated credit cycle later developed by Hyman Minsky. In later works, Hayek cited polices of central banks as a cause of unsustainably low interest rates.
19. Hayek thought the error was that the increasing competition for resources would eventually bid up interest rates and leave some investment projects—which took time to develop—stranded because the higher rates would make them unprofitable. Some have pointed to the excess inventory of abandoned homes at the end of the housing boom as evidence of a Hayekian process, but this similarity is superficial, since interest rates did not go up. See the discussion of this point in chapter 10.
20. F. A. Hayek, *Monetary Theory and the Trade Cycle* (Jonathan Cape, 1933), pp. 123–124.
21. Title XI of FIRREA created the Appraisal Subcommittee (ASC) of the Federal Financial Institutions Examination Council (FFIEC) to oversee and monitor appraisal standards.
22. Andrew G. Haldane, *On Microscopes and Telescopes* Bank of England speech, March 27, 2015, available at http://www.bankofengland.co.uk/publications/Documents/speeches/2015/speech812.pdf.
23. See Gorton, "The Panic of 2007."
24. See the discussion of Atif and Mian's findings in chapter 12.
25. I do not mean to imply that all participants were equally knowledgeable of circumstances in the housing market. There were some well-known examples of investors who knew (or believed) that subprime ABS prices had become overpriced. At the beginning of the housing boom there were no market instruments that they could trade to express their views. By early 2006, the introduction of the ABX.HE subprime index

and the creation of a market for shorting individual ABS made it possible to short subprime mortgages. In the event, many investors moved to do so. Most notable were John Paulson and Goldman Sachs. Their shorting activity may have had a material effect in precipitating the downturn in subprime securities prices that followed a year later.

26. Lehman Brothers, *US ABS Weekly Outlook*, US Securitized Products (April 11, 2005).
27. This brings to mind the distinction drawn by former US secretary of defense Donald Rumsfeld, "There are known knowns. These are things we know that we know. There are known unknowns. That is to say, there are things that we know we don't know. But there are also unknown unknowns. These are things we don't know we don't know." Mr. Rumsfeld has been unjustly pilloried in some quarters for the linguistic awkwardness of the passage. That is unfortunate, because he articulated a profound insight into the nature of uncertainty.
28. J. M. Keynes, *The General Theory of Employment, Interest and Money* (Macmillan Press, Ltd., 1973 [1936]), p. 152.
29. The term "uncertainty" as used here was originally coined by an economist named Frank H. Knight, who developed a similar concept at around the same time as Keynes.
30. People will also seek to hold cash and other liquid securities (those that can be converted into cash on short notice at par value) to retain flexibility in the face of uncertainty. This "liquidity preference" is a central pillar in Keynes monetary theory (in the General Theory) and of his explanation of investor preference for tradable securities over illiquid investments in individual firms. Keynes's liquidity preference theory is discussed in chapter 12.
31. Keynes, *The General Theory of Employment, Interest and Money*, p. 148.
32. The data for figure 6.1 is the asset weighted average of Bank of America, Citibank, JP Morgan, Bear Stearns, Goldman Sachs, Lehman Brothers, Merrill Lynch, and Morgan Stanley.
33. Keynes, *The General Theory of Employment, Interest and Money*, p. 148; emphasis in the original.
34. Ibid., p. 161.
35. Ibid., pp. 154–155.
36. J. M. Keynes, "The General Theory of Employment," *The Quarterly Journal of Economics* (February 1937): 213–214; emphasis added.
37. Ibid., 214.
38. Keynes's insight here has been confirmed empirically by Nobel Prize—winning economist Eugene Fama, who a leading proponent of the Efficient Market Theory. Fama has demonstrated, in both theory and in measured performance of money managers, the futility of attempting to systematically outperform the market. The most successful investor in recent decades, Warren Buffett, has endorsed the Efficient Market view, even though he might seem like an outlier to the theory, since he has consistently outperformed the market. Buffett contends that his outperformance arises not from any superior ability to predict the future performance of the economy or the market, but from his superior insight into a few industries to which he has devoted a lifetime of study. As he describes it, he has made his fortune, in large part, by (i) ignoring any alleged informational content of financial market prices, instead relying upon his intimate knowledge of the very few companies and markets where he possesses a cognitive advantage; and (ii) ignoring the liquidity offered by tradable securities markets, instead holding long-term positions in the securities he purchases. Buffett uses financial exchanges merely to access the securities he has decided to invest in based on his local knowledge.
39. Of course, Tobin hadn't written about his "Q" when Keynes was alive, but Keynes used the concept that Tobin was later to codify. See the description of Tobin's Q in chapter 4.

40. Hyman Minsky, *Stabilizing an Unstable Economy* (Yale University Press, 1986).
41. A reduction in interest rates, or the yield on a security, increases the price of the security.
42. Fostel and Geanakoplos, "Leverage Cycles and the Anxious Economy."
43. The Leverage Cycle process is self-reinforcing on the way down, when bad news sets off deleveraging, as I shall explain in chapter 7.
44. The sentiment that complacency leads to doom was forcefully stated in recent times by former Intel chairman Andrew Grove, "Success breeds complacency. Complacency breeds failure. Only the paranoid survive."
45. See ibid and Keynes, The General Theory of Employment, Interest and Money, Chapter 12.
46. Keynes mused that "the spectacle of modern investment markets has sometimes moved me towards the conclusion that to make the purchase of an investment permanent and indissoluble, like marriage, except by reason of death or other grave cause, might be a useful remedy for our contemporary evils. For this would force the investor to direct his mind to the long-term prospects and to those only." But he backed away from the idea out of concern that it would deter investment, at least so long as investors had the opportunity to hoard their money or lend it out. See Keynes, *The General Theory of Employment, Interest and Money*, p. 160.
47. The issue of whether loans held to maturity by banks should be "marked-to-market" was hotly debated during the financial crisis. The argument was that, at least for those loans that traded in financial markets, banks should use the price set in the financial market in valuing the loans. Banks argued that prices set in financial markets reflect volatility and other factors that are unrelated to the intrinsic value of the loans. Critics argued that price discovery in the financial market is the only reliable indicator of intrinsic value. Ultimately, (US) banks were not required to mark-to-market the loans they intended to hold to maturity.
48. Ibid., p. 156.
49. For the model described in the text, and for references to other models, see Franklin Allen, Stephen Morris, and Hyun Song Shin, "Beauty Contests and Iterated Expectations in Asset Markets", *The Review of Financial Studies*, Vol. 19, Number 3 (2006).
50. See John Dickhaut, Shengle Lin, David Porter, and Vernon Smith, "Commodity Durability, Trader Specialization, and Market Performance," *Proceedings of the National Academy of Science*, Vol. 109 (2012): 1425–1430.
51. Equilibrium in these experiments was defined as the single price at which all potential mutual gains from transacting between subjects would take place.
52. Ibid.
53. Another result of the V Smith experiment is that an increase in liquidity into the market—represented by an increased cash endowment—results in an increase in price dispersion under both scenarios.

    This is not prima facie consistent with the behavior of the housing market prior to the crisis, where volatility decreased as liquidity increased. Yet, the spike in home prices above equilibrium does indicate that speculative excess—a feature of the deviation (from equilibrium) in the V Smith experiment—was enabled by the increase in liquidity.
54. Mian and Sufi, *House of Debt*, pp. 137–139.
55. According to Mian and Sufi, "Research suggests that up to 40 percent of private-label MBS contained some restrictions limiting the servicer's ability to modify mortgages in the securitization pool" (ibid., p. 138).
56. Mian and Sufi cite studies showing that "delinquent mortgages were more likely to end up in foreclosure if they were held in a securitization pool rather than on the balance sheet of an individual bank" (ibid., p. 139).

7 The Capital Flow Bonanza and the Housing Boom

1. Ben S. Bernanke, "Stabilizing the Financial Markets and the Economy," Speech at the Economic Club of New York, October 15, 2008.
2. Hyun Song Shin, "Financial Intermediation and the Post-Crisis Financial System," Paper delivered to the 8th BIS Annual Conference, June 25–26, 2009, p. 1.
3. Ferguson, *An Essay on the History of Civil Society.*
4. Where (C) is home economy consumption; (I) is home economy investment; (G) is home economy government spending; (X) is exports and (M) is imports.
5. Source: OECD.
6. Source: US Bureau of Economic Analysis.
7. This is an overestimate since (i) the US private sector had a positive marginal propensity to save out of income, which implies that some of the $201 billion would have added to domestic saving in the hypothetical circumstance that trade was balanced; and (ii) the capital flow bonanza probably induced a decline in US savings.
8. Warnock and Warnock, "International Capital Flows and US Interest Rates." As was mentioned in chapter 3, Warnock's estimate did not include 2006 and 2007, when the capital flow bonanza peaked. The impact of foreign purchases on interest rates in those years was likely higher than 80 bps. Also, as figure 3.4 shows, the primary offshore investors in US government-guaranteed debt were the developing nations and OPEC with whom the US ran bilateral current account deficits which directly links the capital flow bonanza to US interest rates.
9. Ouarda Merrouche and Erland Nier, "What Caused the Global Financial Crisis?.
10. Broker-dealers massively increased leverage during the housing boom, but there is a debate as the reasons why. Economists Tobias Adrian and Hyun Song Shin have produced evidence that broker-dealers manage their balance sheets by targeting VaR (see figure 6.1). In chapter 2 I showed that volatility, which is the key input into VaR models, declined precipitously during the housing boom. Adrian and Shin argue that broker-dealers expanded their balance sheets during the housing boom by financing an increase in lending with increased borrowing (as opposed to equity) to increase earnings, in the belief that they were not thereby adding to risk. When VaR skyrocketed during the financial crisis, broker-dealers deleveraged to maintain the targeted VaR. This can be seen in figure 6.1. It is also possible that, at least for a time (before the crisis) a feedback loop developed whereby increased leverage lowered volatility by pumping more credit into the market. The other possibility is that the increased leverage of broker-dealers was a by-product of their role as matched book money dealers. Pozsar has argued that as the shadow banking sector expanded—due to forces that were independent of to the actions of broker-dealers—the demand for matched book funding increased. According to Pozsar, the increased leverage on the balance sheets of broker-dealers during the housing boom was a by-product of the increased volume of matched book dealing demanded by bond investors and institutional cash pools. See Tobias Adrian and Hyun Song Shin, "Financial Intermediary Leverage and Value—at-Risk," Federal Reserve Bank of New York Staff Reports, 2012, Number 338; and Zoltan Pozsar, "Shadow Banking: The Money View," Office of Financial Research, US Department of Treasury Working Paper 14–04, 2014.
11. For a general theory of the concurrence of asset price booms driven by a low cost of capital, see Ricardo J. Caballero, Emmanuel Farhi, and Mohamad L Hammour, "Speculative Growth: Hints from the US Economy," *American Economic Review*, Vol. 96, Number 4 (2006): 1159–1192. The authors cite instances where capital costs are lowered by an increase in the supply of credit, due to capital flow bonanzas or procyclical fiscal surpluses, or to a reduction in the demand for credit resultant from improvements in the productivity of capital, and those same forces drive up asset prices. In my review of monetary policy during the housing boom in chapter 8, I shall

reflect one theme from this paper; that it is not always a good idea to prick an asset price bubble, even one that might crash later on.

12. There were assets called collateralized debt obligations (CDO), which were comprised of investments in various subprime ABS. CDO were themselves leveraged, so they magnified the leverage of the underlying ABS. By order of magnitude, there were around $1.8 trillion of subprime ABS and $640 CDO issued during the US housing boom. CDO filled a similar, but riskier, investment niche as ABS. In the text, for notational convenience, I refer to both assets as ABS, unless there is a reason to distinguish between them. For data on ABS issuance, see Viral V. Acharya, Phillipp Schnable, and Gustavo Suarez, "Securitization without Risk Transfer," *Journal of Financial Economics*, Vol. 107 (2013): 515–536. For data on CDO issuance, see Cordell et al., "Collateral Damage: Sizing and Assessing the Subprime CDO Crisis."
13. I do not mean to suggest that overall broker-dealer assets and liabilities were mirror images. Borrowing and rehypothecating ABS comprised a significant portion of their balance sheets, but there were other assets and liabilities. Notably, broker-dealers were required to warehouse subprime mortgages, to retain the junior tranches of the subprime backed ABS and CDO, and to issue liquidity puts to buyers of the ABS and CDO they issued. They also engaged in businesses that were unrelated to trading ABS. However, as Pozsar has noted, it was the collapse in value of the subprime mortgage related assets, and the call on the liquidity puts issued on subprime ABS and CDO, rather than assets and liabilities related to matched book money and risk dealing, that caused the insolvency of broker-dealers in the financial crisis.
14. Note, however, that commercial banks were major participants in shadow banking through their issuance of ABS See Acharya et al., "Securitization without Risk Transfer."
15. A more general statement—and perhaps a more accurate one given the shift in bank assets toward consumer and residential mortgage lending over the past 100 years—is that banks intermediate between those who have excess liquidity at a point in time (depositors and wholesale lenders), and those who have a deficit of liquidity at that same point in time (borrowers). For evidence of the shift in the composition in bank assets over time toward residential mortgages, see Jordà et al., "The Great Mortgaging. For a theoretical discussion of the origins and functions of financial intermediation, see John Moore and Nobuhiro Kiyotaki, "Evil Is the Root of All Money," Clarendon lecture #1, 2001.
16. Prior to 2008, the insured amount of US commercial bank deposits was $100,000.00. The FDIC is funded by insurance payments from member banks, but the public perceives that the FDIC's obligations are backed by the federal government.
17. At the end of 2013, US banks had $3 trillion of demand deposits, of which 46 percent were insured; and $7.2 trillion of time deposits (deposits which cannot be withdrawn immediately on demand), of which 83 percent were insured. See Pozsar, "Shadow Banking," Charts 1 and 2. The text refers to the universe of institutional cash pools with over $1 billion of funds under management.
18. Zoltan Pozsar, "Institutional Cash Pools and the Triffin Dilemma of the US Banking System," IMF Working Paper # 11/190, 2011, pp. 8–9.
19. A crucial point to note here is that while banks create deposits when they lend—in which respect bank deposits are sui generis—the aversion of a major class of investors from holding bank deposits created a countervailing movement of lending into the shadow banking sector, which reduced bank lending and hence bank deposits.
20. The banks sold their mortgages into the ABS, for which they received payment from the ABS investors. However, the guarantees issued by the banks left them financially responsible for losses incurred by investors who had purchased the ABS. Off balance sheet liabilities are sometimes referred to as incognito leverage since the increased leverage is real but concealed.

21. See Acharya et al., "Securitization without Risk Transfer."
22. Derived by subtracting the approximate $1.3 billion of subprime securities issued by commercial banks (2001–2008) from the $1.8 trillion of subprime mortgage backed securities issued from 2001 to 2006 as listed in Gorton, "The Panic of 2007."
23. Cordell et al., "Collateral Damage: Sizing and Assessing the Subprime CDO Crisis."
24. The names and definitions of the investor groups in this chapter follow Pozsar, "Shadow Banking."
25. See the discussion in chapter 2.
26. The extent of the increased concentration of wealth is the subject of debate. See the discussion in chapter 10.
27. Pozsar, "Institutional Cash Pools," Figure A2, p. 26, for graph depicting the growth of dollar billionaires. See figure 10.1 for a graph of the increased income shares of the top 1 percent earners.
28. Ibid., Figure 8, p. 10. I say "at least" because there were other investors competing to purchase short-term government-guaranteed debt.
29. Broker-dealers often matched the repo with the institutional cash pool with a reverse repo with a bond investor, as shall be explained later.
30. And, of course, there was a maturity risk, as the price of the long-term bond could decline significantly during a short interval of time if long-term interest rates increased.
31. See Pozsar, "Institutional Cash Pools."
32. See Pozsar, Zoltan (2015) *A Macro View of Shadow Banking* Draft (as of January 31, 2015), available from SSRN, at http://papers.ssrn.com/sol3/papers.cfm?abstract_id=2558945, where Pozsar provides evidence that broker-dealers have functioned as matched book money dealers in the repo market, intermediating between bond investors and institutional cash pools.
33. There are a variety of structures under which these transactions occur, including repo, reverse repo, tri-party repo, term repo, and security lending. What matters for the argument in the text is that they all involve the same basic structure of payment and collateralization. Also note that the description of broker-dealers as matched book money lenders within the shadow banking sector is at odds with the usual description in which broker-dealers use the overnight funds raised by repo borrowing to finance holdings longer term securities. For a discussion, see Pozsar, *A Macro View of Shadow Banking.*
34. Ibid., p. 3.
35. A CDS is contract in which the issuer agrees to pay the counterparty a sum of money to cover a decline in the value of some asset. In the case of subprime mortgages, the asset way typically an index of subprime ABS, like the ABX.HE index. Since movements in the price of the subprime indices were correlated with movements in many subprime mortgages, a broker-dealer or bank could hedge the risk on its holdings of unrated subprime ABS debt and subprime mortgage inventories by purchasing a CDS. Similarly a bond investor could mitigate the risk of its subprime securities holdings by purchasing a CDS. CDS were introduced for the first time in 2005, at the height of the housing boom. See ISDA Market Survey—Annual data, available at http://www.isda.org/statistics/pdf/ISDA-Market-Survey-annual-data.pdf.
36. See the "Whole Loans" category (and the massive losses incurred) on Merrill Lynch's 2007 balance sheet in table 5.1. As is shown, commercial banks also have a motive to hold subprime mortgage securities for income.
37. In order to secure the ratings, many securities were required to have guarantees from a sponsor, who was typically a bank, a broker-dealer or (in the case of "conforming" mortgages) a GSE.
38. Government bonds were (and are) a major source of collateral for intermediation in the shadow banking sector.

39. In addition to the activities mentioned in the text, broker-dealers fund long-term assets and provide services to clients such as wealth management (where they act as institutional cash pools), hedge fund lending and servicing, advice on mergers and acquisitions and securities brokerage.
40. Broker-dealers also engage in borrowing short and lending long, as do commercial banks, but these "money market funding of capital market lending" activities lie outside of shadow banking as I have defined it. Pozsar has provided a more general statement of the uses of cash by financial intermediaries:"These three uses of cash—loan based lending, money dealing, and money market funding of capital market lending—can be found on the balance sheets of banks, dealers, money funds, and other investors to varying degrees. Banks do all three, dealers do both money dealing and money market funding of capital market lending, money funds do exclusively money dealing while other investors do exclusively money market funding of capital market lending" (Pozsar, "Shadow Banking," p. 34).
41. Commercial banks took on the same exposures in connection with their origination and sponsorship of ABS.
42. See Pozsar, "Shadow Banking," Chart 1, p. 19.
43. From 2003 to the end of 2007, China's cumulative trade surplus with the United States was $1.24 trillion (source: US Bureau of Economic Analysis). Many experts believe that almost the entire surplus was invested in US government-guaranteed debt.
44. Therefore, LIs and DBPs were the beneficial owners of some portion of Hedge Funds' holdings of subprime mortgage securities.
45. There was some offsetting compensation from the increase in the value of their securities holdings that occurred as a result of the plunge in interest rates (since lower interest rates imply lower discount rates applied to future earnings of their capital assets).
46. Pozsar, *A Macro View of Shadow Banking*, p. 20. In the same paper (p. 29) Pozsar elaborates further on the impact the low yields on riskless securities had on shifting pension fund investment strategies:"One reason behind the shift in finance away from funding real economy transactions and toward funding financial economy transactions (the rise of securities financing—as evident from the increased provision of working capital to asset managers as opposed to traders and manufacturers) may be increased demand for the underwriting of equity –like returns with bond- like volatility for pension funds and other real money accounts amidst a proliferation of structural asset—liability mismatches. Asset managers use securities financing and derivatives as techniques to bridge the gap between rosy return expectations and the realities of a down—drift in yields on safe, long-term assets." It is at once understandable why pension funds reached for yield, and why the attempt was founded on an illusion; there is no way to "manufacture" yields that are above safe rates without incurring more risk.
47. Ricardo Caballero, "The Shortage of Safe Assets," Speech at the Bank of England, May 2013, slides. Available at http://www.bankofengland.co.uk/research/Documents/ccbs/cew2013/presentation_caballero.pdf.
48. Bo Becker and Victoria Ivashina, "Reaching for Yield in the Bond Market, Harvard Business School WP 12–103, 2013, Figure 3, p. 35.
49. During the 2000s LIs and DBPs also increased their allocations to hedge funds and long only bond funds, and these funds began to engage in leveraging their portfolios through securities lending and derivatives transactions in an effort to boost returns. For evidence of increased leverage in DBP portfolios, see Figure 3 in Pozsar, *A Macro View of Shadow Banking*.
50. I do not analyze the motives for German Landesbak investments in subprime securities in what follows. These institutions had rational motives to reach for yield, as they were recently privatized with insufficient capital. However, their motives were not related in any way to the US capital flow bonanza.

51. US commercial bank net interest margins had been declining since the mid-1990s, but that does not negate the fact that the continued decline into the 2000s reduced loan profit margins to ultra low levels.
52. See Acharya et al., "Securitization without Risk Transfer," p. 516. Most of the ABS created by banks were funded with short-term paper, which is why banks were forced to pay off investors when the market fell into panic in 2008. Acharya et al. note that commercial bank issuance of ABS accelerated in 2004 after bank regulators decided not to impose capital requirements for off-balance sheet guarantees. See Figure 2, p. 518, of the paper.
53. Another form of regulatory arbitrage engaged in by banks was to sell off their subprime loans into ABS, and then turn around and invest in investment grade ABS tranches. The investment grade rating reduced the amount of capital a bank was required to set aside (according to Basle II) as compared to what would have been required if the bank held underlying loans.
54. Bear Stearns did not issue liquidity puts on the ABS issued by its subsidiaries, but was compelled to act as if it had in order to maintain its "franchise value," or so it believed at the time. One Wall Street analyst described it this way: "If [Bear Stearns] walked away from it, investors would have lost all their money and lenders would have had lost all their money... If they did that to everyone in the financial community, the financial community would have shut them down." As reported in the *New York Times*, June 23, 2007, "$3.2 Billion Move by Bear Stearns to Rescue Fund," Julie Creswell and Vikas Bajaj.
55. *Financial Crisis Inquiry Commission Report*, p. xxvi.
56. Or, at least with respect to the portion of profit left over after paying outsized managerial compensation.
57. See Pozsar, *A Macro View of Shadow Banking*.
58. Bill Gross, "Imagine," PIMCO Investment Outlook, December 2003. For evidence of increased leverage in DBP portfolios.
59. Pozsar, *A Macro View of Shadow Banking*, p. 13.
60. See Gary Gorton, "The Subprime Panic," Table 1, p. 3, for a matrix of characteristics of different mortgage categories.
61. Tomasz Piskorski, Amit Seru, and James Witkin, "Asset Quality Misrepresentation by Financial Intermediaries: Evidence from RMBS Market," Working Paper Columbia Business School, Columbia University, February 12, 2103.
62. Foot "Subprime Facts", Table 4, p. 34.
63. Mian and Sufi, *House of Debt* p. 87.
64. Mian and Sufi state: "The results are quite remarkable. For high credit-score homeowners, the effect of house price on borrowing during the 2002–2006 period was small. In contrast, the effect was enormous for low credit-score borrowers" (p. 88).
65. While there is no conclusive evidence showing the disposition of spending out of home equity proceeds, one survey supports the assertion in the text. See Glenn Canner, Karen Dynan, and Wayne Passmore, "Mortgage Refinancing in 2001 and Early 2002," Federal Reserve Bulletin 88, no. 12, 2002, pp. 469–481.
66. Christpher D. Carroll, Misuzu Otsuka, and Jirka Slacalek, "How Large Is the Housing Wealth Effect? A New Approach," National Bureau of Economic Research Working Paper No. 12746, 2006.
67. Housing was a component of the increase in wealth, but the largest component was the increase in the value of corporate securities. The increase in the value of corporate equities accompanied an historic increase in corporate profits (figure 2.10). The increase in home values extended to all segments of the housing market, and therefore benefitted middle income homeowners. The benefits of the rise in the value of corporate securities was probably skewed toward wealthy people, although pension plans were significant owners of corporate securities and their beneficiaries were primarily

middle income people. In any event, a 40 percent increase in overall wealth and significant gain in home equity make it understandable that people would be inclined to increase consumption.

68. Something I find difficult to rationalize, however, is the reason why household debt service relative to income rose steeply during the boom, from 5.9 percent to 7.2 percent. Perhaps the increase applied to punters, who could just walk away if thing didn't work out. More research is required to answer that question. Federal Reserve Economic Data (FRED), "Mortgage Debt Service Payments as a Percent of Disposable Personal Income," http://research.stlouisfed.org/fred2/series/MDSP.
69. The benefits of geographic diversification of mortgages was nothing new; it had been incorporated into mortgage backed securities since the 1980s.
70. See Jian Hu, "Assessing the Credit Risk of CDO's Backed by Structured Finance Securities: Rating Analysts' Challenges and Solutions," *Journal of structured Finance* (Fall 2007): 43–59.
71. One could, with justification, counter that Keynes's concept of uncertainty, interpreted in its most literal and extreme form, renders the idea of "fundamental value" meaningless, since the stochastic process generating future performance is unknown. I shall not go there, as it would open up a line of enquiry that would take up more space than is available in this book.
72. Ben S. Bernanke, "The Subprime Mortgage Market," Speech at the Federal Reserve Bank of Chicago, May 17, 2007; emphasis added.
73. See Shin epigraph at beginning of this chapter.
74. See figures 3.1 and 3.2.
75. George R. Carter, III, "Housing Units With Negative Equity, 1997 to 2009," *Cityscape: A Journal of Policy Development and Research*, Vol. 14, Number 1 (2015); and Core Logic Q3 2009 Media Alert, available at http://www.recharts.com/reports/FACLNERQ32009/FACLNERQ32009.pdf.
76. See Gorton, "The Panic of 2007," p. 9.
77. In addition, Massachusetts home sales were growing in the early 2000s and declining in the mid-2000s. See Christopher Foot et al. "Subprime Facts: What (We Think) We Know about the Subprime Crisis and What We Don't," Figure 1, p. 8.
78. There is no mystery why mortgage securities prices nosedived ahead of large declines in physical home prices. It is well known that real estate prices react sluggishly compared to tradable securities prices to new information. The difference in reaction speed arises from the fact the securities trade continuously and are highly liquid—so their prices quickly incorporate the latest information, while housed trade infrequently and it takes time for new information to be incorporated into prices. John Geanakoplos has pointed to another possible explanation for the timing of the decline in mortgage securities prices; the introduction of credit default swaps on mortgage securities in 2005/2006, which provided a way for pessimists to register their beliefs—by purchasing CDS contracts. The increase in CDS prices pushed down the prices of the mortgage securities they insured. Another cause of the decline in subprime securities prices may have been that the introduction of the ABX.HE index of subprime mortgage securities in 2006 disseminated information that had hitherto not been widely known, and thereby helped to facilitate the spread of the bad news about subprime mortgage performance.
79. John Geanakoplos, "Leverage, Default, and Forgiveness: Lessons from the American and European Crises," *Journal of Macroeconomics*, Vol. 39 (2014): 313–333, 319.

8 The Role of Policy during the Housing Boom

1. Ben Bernanke, "Trade and Jobs," Federal Reserve Board, 2004. While Bernanke maintained that the current account deficit could not have been the cause of slow job growth, he may have been misled in similar way that subprime investors were misled.

He looked at past correlations between trade and jobs and saw none. But the size of the US current account deficit was just then reaching unprecedented heights, which might have produced effects that were different than in the past. By 2005, when he delivered his "global savings glut" speech, Bernanke had begun to see the current account deficit as an important factor in US economic performance.

2. The possibility of altering the terms of trade with China by deflation presumes that China would not react by devaluing its currency further, or by increasing export subsidies. That is an unrealistic premise. China would likely have acted to protect its export market share, which would make deflation a futile policy no matter what its effect on employment.
3. J. M. Keynes, *A Treatise on Money*, Vol. I, *The Pure Theory of Money* (Harcourt Brace and Company, 1930), p. 349.
4. Two giants of postwar monetary economics, Milton Friedman and Robert Mundell, who differed on almost everything, agreed on this point, though they attributed different causes of the 1930's deflation. Freidman thought it arose from Fed's failure to provide liquidity to banks when they faced depositor runs; Mundell argued that it was caused by the Fed's sterilization of gold inflows. For Friedman's argument, see Milton Friedman and Anna Jacobson Schwartz, *A Monetary History of the United States 1867–1960* (Princeton University Press, 1963), Chapter 7. For Mundell's point of view, see his Nobel Prize lecture, available at http://www.nobelprize.org/nobel_prizes/economic-sciences/laureates/1999/mundell-lecture.pdf. However, it should be noted that Schularick and Taylor's statistical analysis of the influence of credit and money suggests it was actually the contraction in credit, which was then highly correlated with money, that marked the Great Depression This interpretation is consistent with the analyses of the Great Depression made by Irving Fisher and Ben Bernanke that I reference in explaining the causes of the financial crisis later on in this book. Economist Claudio Borio and his colleagues at the Bank for International Settlements have produced evidence that questions whether deflation in wages and goods prices cause contraction in real output. Yet, the monetary policy implication is the same, whether it is a contraction in wages and goods prices or credit that is to be avoided. In both instances the mandate would be to keep interest rates low. See Claudio Borio et al., "The Costs of Deflations: A Historical Perspective," *BIS Quarterly Review* (March 2015): 31–54.
5. Ben S. Bernanke, "Deflation: Making Sure 'It' Doesn't Happen Here," Speech before the National Economists Club, 2012, available at http://www.federalreserve.gov/BOARDDOCS/Speeches/2002/20021121/default.htm.
6. I am, of course, assuming the Fed sets the Fed funds rate on the basis of criteria that are independent of the other short-term rates. If this were not so, if the Fed merely followed the path of market rates in setting its own interest rate, then it would not be exerting any influence over market interest rates. It is an open question as to what determines Fed policy at any given time.
7. See quote from Michael Woodford in chapter 9, p. 133.
8. Warnock and Warnock, "International Capital Flows and US Interest Rates."
9. See Schularick and Taylor, "Credit Booms Gone Bust: and Bank for International Settlements (for data on total nonfinancial sector credit).
10. Although the Fed still retains its unique ability to manufacture liquidity when the private sector has run short—as it demonstrated during the financial crisis. There is another reason why the Fed may lose influence over interest rates in the future. It is based on the observation that financial market innovations are creating more product differentiation in assets. Since differentiated products are not perfect substitutes, the effects of a change in the price (interest rate) on any one asset will have a muted effect on the price of other assets, and the influence will decrease as the holders of the different assets become more segmented.

11. Schularick and Taylor, "Credit Booms Gone Bust."
12. The research on credit booms and financial crises was reviewed in chapter 2. Economists call the idea that in order to achieve an optimum outcome, the number of policy instruments must at least equal the number of policy targets the "Tinbergen Rule."
13. While Jordà et al. (in *"Financial Crises, Credit Booms, and External Imbalances",; "The Great Mortgaging",;* and "Betting the House," have demonstrated that above trend credit expansion has predictive power for subsequent financial crises (and more predictive power than monetary aggregates), the linkage is still weak. Their regression models show statistical significance, but explain very little of the variation in the data (low R2). Their Receiver Operating Characteristics analysis similarly shows predictive power, but at a low level. Their Area Under Receiver Operating Characteristics Curve is generally below 0.7, which is considered to be relatively uninformative by the standards of other sciences. They acknowledge the limited predictive power of credit booms: "The model can therefore be judged to have predictive power versus and coin toss, although it is far from a perfect classifier" (Schularick and Taylor, "Credit Booms Gone Bust"). Moreover, their analysis presumes stability over time in the underlying relationships between credit and financial crises; but this may not hold as the economy evolves over time. These considerations cast doubt on the efficacy of following a policy of pricking credit bubbles, especially when accompanied by large current account deficits. The correct policy response should be to reduce the current account deficit. In that case, the employment reducing impact of shrinking credit will be offset by the employment enhancing effect of increasing net exports. How to effectuate such a policy is another matter.
14. One possible answer to this question is that it was not until 2006 that financial instruments allowing contrarian investors to bet on a downturn in home prices had come into widespread use. Contracts based on credit default swaps and the ABX index of subprime mortgages grew exponentially beginning in 2006. As I explained in chapter 7, it is conceivable that the proliferation of these instruments were integral in bringing down the prices of mortgage-backed securities, with knock-on effects on home prices.

9 Accumulation and Secular Stagnation: Part I, Theory

1. Adam Smith, *The Wealth of Nations* Modern Library Edition (Random House Inc., 1994 [1776]), Modern Library Edition, p. 715
2. Thomas Robert Malthus, *Principles of Political Economy* 2nd edn reprinted by Augustus M. Kelley (New York, 1964 [1836]), p. 322.
3. Michael Woodford, *Interest and Prices: Foundations of a Theory of Monetary Policy* (Princeton University Press, 2003), p. 37.
4. The preceding sentence should be interpreted as referring to nominal rates of interest and inflation relative to trend. Therefore, a given rate of interest or inflation could be low, if trend rates of interest or inflation were high; or high, if trend rates of interest or inflation were low.
5. See Knut Wicksell, *Interest and Prices* (London Macmillan Ltd., 1936); F. A. Hayek, *Monetary Theory and the Trade Cycle* (London Jonathan Cape Ltd., 1933); and F. A. Hayek, *Prices and Production* (New York: August M. Kelly, 1967).
6. If animal spirits are elevated at the start of a boom—and it is almost inconceivable that a boom could commence in the absence of elevated animal spirits—then it might require no more than a small decline in interest rates to spark an expansion. Another variable not discussed in the text is that risk spreads will typically compress at the beginning of a boom—another dimension of elevated optimism—which represents a reduction in borrowing costs.

7. The effect of interest rates on consumption is a core driver of economic fluctuations of the contemporary "New Keynesian" models of the economy, which posits that sluggish adjustments of wages and prices to exogenous shocks to the underlying conditions of supply and demand in sectors of the economy can be offset by central bank adjustment of nominal interest rates. For example, a shock that causes income to contract can be offset by a reduction in nominal interest rates, since (1) sluggish wage/price adjustment ensures the nominal reduction will be a real reduction (at least for some time), and (2) the reduction in real interest rates will induce consumers to increase current spending, by reducing the amount of future consumption that must be foregone to indulge in an increase in current consumption. Thus, the impact of interest rates on economic activity in New Keynesian models is quite similar to their effects in the Wicksell/Hayek model. See Richard Clarida, Jordi Gali, and Mark Gertler, "The Science of Monetary Policy: A New Keynesian Perspective," *Journal of Economic Literature*, Vol. XXXVII (December 1999): 1661–1707.
8. This is an oversimplification of Hayek's theory. He argued that lower interest rates increase the profitability of more time consuming production processes, and therefore induce a lengthening of many production processes. In Chapter 1 I discuss a recent application of this theory to the location of offshore production. The profitability of a production process is more sensitive to a change in interest rates the more time consuming is the process. Therefore, the lengthening of production processes that take place during the boom magnifies the negative impact on profits of the rise in interest rates at the end of the boom. This increases the volume of projects that must be abandoned, and thereby deepens the recession that follows.
9. The dynamics of the Wicksell/Hayek theory fits the data on labor market behavior. When the economy goes into recession, layoffs rise relative to job vacancies. When it recovers, vacancies rise relative to layoffs.
10. Mr. Greenspan made that remark in his February 17, 2005, testimony before the US Senate Committee on Banking, Housing and Urban Affairs.
11. Axel Leijonhufvud, *So Far from Ricardo, So Close to Wicksell*, Paper given at the 2007 Jornadas Monetarias y Bancarias, Central Bank of Argentina, June 4–5, 2007, session on "Trade-off between Monetary and Financial Stability," p. 6, emphasis in the original. http://www-ceel.economia.unitn.it/staff/leijonhufvud/files/axel4.pdf.
12. Malthus, *Principles of Political Economy*, 2nd edition, p. 325.
13. A more general statement would allow for the possibility that among borrowers are people who are accumulators. This might occur with young persons borrowing to pay for schooling and so on, who will nevertheless earn more in their lifetime than they plan to spend.
14. Assuming a constant markup of goods prices overproduction costs.
15. Real wages and profits refer to the purchasing power of the nominal—money—wage and profit. If all prices declined by 10 percent, then a worker earning 10 percent less wages could purchase exactly the same bundle of goods as she could before the reduction in spending.
16. I. Fisher, "The Debt-Deflation Theory of Great Depressions," *Econometrica* (1933).
17. The reason why a reduction in loan collateral values force banks to reduce lending is explained in chapter 12.
18. "[Fisher's] diagnosis led him to urge President Roosevelt to subordinate exchange-rate considerations for the need for reflation, advice that (ultimately) FDR followed. Fisher's idea was less influential in academic circles, though, because of the counterargument that debt-deflation represented no more than a redistribution from one group (debtors) to another (creditors). Absent implausibly large differences in marginal spending propensities among the groups, it was suggested, pure redistributions should have no significant macroeconomic effects." Ben S. Bernanke, "The Macroeconomics

of the Great Depression: A Comparative Approach," *Journal of Money, Credit, and Banking*, Vol. 27, Number 1 (February 1995): 17.

19. There are no grounds to assert, prima facie, in a fractional reserve banking system, that borrowers have higher propensities than depositors. It may be the other way round! The liquidity transformation performed by banks enables high spenders to temporarily deposit unspent funds. The deposits, as is well understood, are then re-lent to borrowers for longer duration.
20. Ben Bernanke led the reappraisal of Fisher's idea and emphasized the balance sheet channel of propagating distress into the economy. See Ben S. Bernanke, "Nonmonetary Effects of the Financial Crisis in Propagation of the Great Depression," *American Economic Review*, Vol. 73 (June 1983): 257–276. Richard Koo has become the leading contemporary advocate of the debt-deflation theory, which he has relabeled "balance sheet recession." See Richard Koo, *Escape from Balance Sheet Recession and the QE Trap: A Hazardous Road for the World Economy* (John Wiley, 2014).
21. Several additional costs flow from the contraction in lending, including the costs of reorganizing bankrupt borrowers and banks, and the decline in new ventures or the expansion of existing ones. As an example, Ricardo Caballero and his colleagues showed how, in Japan in the 1990s, banks continued lending to zombie borrowers, with dim prospects for profitable investment, in order to avoid the realization of the loan losses on their accounting books. Channeling loans to zombie borrowers diverted the flow of savings away from productive investments and deterred entry into the industries occupied by the subsidized zombies. Both effects reduced economic growth and job creation. See Ricardo J. Caballero, Takeo Hoshi, and Anil K. Kashyap, "Zombie Lending and Depressed Restructuring in Japan," *American Economic Review*, Vol. 98, Number 5 (2008): 1943–1977.
22. It is tempting to conjecture that the decline in wealth engendered by Accumulation will cure it. That is what Keynes believed. But it is also possible that a decline in wealth will motivate Accumulators to reduce spending further, in order to maintain their targeted bequests. It all depends on motives, about which economic theory has nothing at all to say; and upon which empirical studies have not—to this author's knowledge—shed light.
23. Note that an increase in Accumulation does not have to be accompanied by an increase in aggregate saving. For example, Accumulation can be increased by an increase in accumulators' share of existing savings. Furthermore, since a shift in a fixed pool of saving toward Accumulators implies an absolute decline in the demand for future goods, a continuation of the preexisting level of investment will constitute an unsustainable boom.
24. All that is required to establish that all income is spent is to assume that agents will always desire at least one more increment of some good. If that is so, people will always want to spend whatever extra money they have to acquire more of that good. In order to ensure that equilibrium exists, economic models include this assumption.
25. Named after its progenitor, Jean Baptiste Say, an early-nineteenth-century French economist. Note that, in my book *Accumulation and Secular Stagnation: A Malthusian Approach to Understanding a Contemporary Malaise* (Palgrave Pivot, 2016), I use the term "Say's Principle" to describe the same concept when the budget equation includes money and financial claims. For an explanation of the historical origins of the two concepts, see Robert Clower and Axel Leijohnhufvud, "Say's Principle, What It Means and Doesn't Mean," *Intermountain Economic Review*, Fall 1973, reprinted in Axel Leijonhufvud, *Information and Coordination: Essays in Macroeconomic Theory* (Oxford University Press, 1981), chapter 5, pp. 79–102.
26. Note that the same reasoning applies when the economy lasts for a finite period of time and/or when people live finite lives, but children are born over time and people internalize the welfare of their progeny. This is called an "overlapping generations" model; in it parents and their progeny form dynasties that behave in a similar way to infinitely lived individuals.

27. If the nonsatiation principle holds, she will never find herself holding excess money, since by assumption she will ultimately spend all that she has.
28. This does not preclude the act of saving. At any time (*t*) an agent may consume less than she earns. But if she plans to consume all her income over her lifetime, her budget equation will be zero.
29. In equilibrium, all goods markets clear, but that does not mean there is no saving. At any point in time, some agents may save, while others borrow to spend on final goods or production of future goods. General equilibrium implies that every dollar saved by one agent is matched by a dollar borrowed by another agent. The importance of this condition will become apparent in the discussion of Keynesian unemployment that follows.
30. It is possible to restate the issue in such a way that Say's Law continues to apply in the presence of Accumulation. This can be done by adding a market for wealth accumulation (money and financial claims). With this addition, the budget equation of the Accumulator will be zero. But since Accumulation implies the market for wealth will be in chronic excess demand, the economy will not attain equilibrium. The economist reader will note that if it is assumed agents have utility functions and preferences are convex, the inclusion of wealth in the utility function implies that the rate of time preference between current and future consumption exceeds the interest rate. This means consumption is below the level that would obtain in the absence of a preference for wealth accumulation.
31. See Paul Krugman, "It's Baaack: Japan's Slump and the Return of the Liquidity Trap," *Brookings Papers on Economic Activity*, Brookings Institution, Vol. 2 (1998): 137–204.
32. The concept of stimulating demand includes Krugman's suggestion of credibly setting a future inflation target. See ibid., 137–204.
33. See Axel Leijonhufvud, *The Wicksell Connection: Variations on a Theme* in *Information and Coordination: Essays on Macroeconomic Theory* (Oxford University Press, 1981), pp. 131–203.
34. J. M. Keynes, *The General Theory of Employment, Interest and Money* (The Macmillan Press, Ltd., 1973 [1936]), pp. 210–211.
35. This does not imply that Accumulation will reduce actual productivity. If Accumulation reduces employment, the smaller workforce may be more productive, which will increase actual productivity.

10 Accumulation and Secular Stagnation: Part II, Application

1. Lawrence Summers, IMF Fourteenth Annual Research Conference in Honor of Stanley Fischer, November 8, 2013.
2. And its existence was to lend credibility to its exchange regime so as to deter the possibility of any future run on its currency in which it would need to be spent.
3. It should also be noted that in the decade of the 2000s, Southeast Asian countries were forced to manage their exchange rates in order to prevent an appreciation relative to the RMB, since they desired to remain competitive as input suppliers to China's assembly of manufactured goods. This provided an additional reason for them to maintain a dollar exchange rate that resulted in current account surpluses with the United States.
4. Adam Smith, *The Wealth of Nations* Modern Library Edition (Random House Inc., 1994), p. 466.
5. Ibid., p. 456.
6. Ibid., p. 468.
7. Ibid., p. 715.
8. Many (most?) economists still believe that sustainable full employment can be achieved even if a country imports more than it exports (i.e., runs a current account deficit).

Greg Mankiw, a prominent contemporary economist, recently wrote, "Politicians and pundits often recoil at imports because they destroy domestic jobs, while they applaud exports because they create jobs. Economists respond that full employment is possible with any pattern of trade" (N. Gregory Mankiw, "Economists Actually Agree on This: The Wisdom of Free Trade," *New York Times*, April 24, 2015).Some time ago, I published the same sentiment: "the US has achieved full employment with stable average compensation levels in the face of the huge expansion in the effective worldwide low-cost labor supply, thus proving that a flexible domestic labor market will achieve equilibrium regardless of the external financial balance" (Daniel J. Aronoff, "US Has a Stake in Keeping China Stable," *Financial Times*, March 17, 2006). I have since come to realize that the full employment achieved during the US housing boom was unstable. This book reflects that change in my point of view.

9. The economist reader will note I am assuming the Marshall-Lerner conditions obtain. The condition is that after the currency depreciation, the sum of changes in export sales and import purchases is positive, measured in terms of the domestic currency. Often, the trade deficit will initially increase after depreciation, as it takes time for the reduction in purchases of imports and the increased sales of exports, to take place. The determinant of whether the Marshall-Lerner condition holds depends upon the elasticity of substitution of imports and exports. Formally, the condition is that the sum of the long-run price elasticities of imports and exports is greater than 1. For example, depreciation against the currency of an oil producer might well result in an increase in the trade deficit, since the price elasticity of the demand for oil is very low. Economists continue to debate whether the Marshall-Lerner condition ultimately holds in most circumstances.
10. In Smith's day, when most currencies were fixed to gold, the country running a surplus would accumulate gold.
11. As before, assuming the Marshall-Lerner conditions obtain.
12. I say "successfully avoided" because deflation might have caused severe economic contraction, as was explained in chapter 9.
13. See definition of budget equation (9.1) in chapter 9.
14. Milton Friedman, *A Theory of the Consumption Function* (Princeton University Press, 2008 [1957]).
15. See Albert Ando and Franco Modigliani, "The 'Life-Cycle' Hypothesis of Saving: Aggregate Implications and Tests," *American Economic Review*, Vol. 53, Number 1 (1963): 55–84.
16. And today's customers, insofar as they purchase durable assets.
17. A more concise statement is that the demand for labor will shift from the distribution and servicing of current consumption goods to capital goods production. Employment and wages will not necessarily be the same in the two states, but there is no prima facie way to determine how a shift to increased saving will affect the demand for labor in the short run, or over time.
18. The economist reader will recognize this as a restatement of Say's Law; that there will be demand—either as a capital good or a consumption good—for everything that is produced.
19. As was discussed in chapter 9, a central insight of Keynes is precisely that decentralized markets, where savers and investors are separated, sometimes do not "work out" that saving implies future demand. When that happens, according to Keynes, deficient demand causes income to decline until saving has shrunk to a volume that equals investment. That was Keynes's seminal refutation of Say's Law. I shall take a related, but slightly different tack in this chapter. The underlying logic of my point is rooted in Keynes. See Axel Leijonhufvud, "The Wicksell Connection: Variations on a Theme," in *Information and Coordination* (Oxford University Press, 1981), pp. 131–203, and the discussion in chapter 9.
20. I am also ignoring the effects of constraints that might prevent young people from borrowing. I think I am justified in doing so, since Friedman made a convincing case for

the PIH in the 1950s, when the possibilities for borrowing were more restricted than they would become in the decades that followed.

21. For data on the evolution of US incomes over time, see Facundo Alvaredo, Anthony B. Atkinson, Thomas Piketty, and Emmanuel Saez, The World Top Incomes Database, http://topincomes.g-mond.parisschoolofeconomics.eu/.
22. It is possible that a shift in income shares to top earners who obey the PIH will increase gross saving, since the increase in earnings will cause them to save more in the peak earning years in order to increase consumption after retirement. But these same people will increase borrowing when they are young, so that the increase in saving by peak earners will be matched by increased consumption of nonpeak earners leaving aggregate consumption unaffected (assuming a few additional "ceteris paribus" conditions). In the text I focus on the changes wrought when the top earners *do not* obey the PIH and leave large inheritances.
23. Friedman, Modigliani, and others who studied savings behavior deduced aggregate consequences of their hypotheses and compared it against aggregate data, but they have not ever been able to track behavior of individuals over their lifetimes. The PIH predicted that aggregate consumption would respond very sluggishly—if at all—to changes in aggregate income; a prediction that was at odds with the prevailing Keynesian theory of the consumption function. The aggregate data—much of which had only recently been collected by governments—showed the PIH to be a better predictor of aggregate consumption behavior compared to the Keynesian theory. Consumption did not move in tandem with income. This robust observation was in direct conflict with the Keynesian theory, and was in direct conformance with the PIH. It is much more difficult to differentiate between the PIH and the theory of Accumulation I propose based solely on aggregate economic data. This is so because there are possible explanations of, for example, secular stagnation that are compatible with both, or neither one, of the two hypotheses.
24. The US Census Bureau conducts an annual survey of the earnings and spending of a sample of households called the Consumer Expenditure Survey ("CEX"). The CEX follows households for a maximum of two years (see the CEX website at http://www.bls.gov/cex/ for a description of the CEX). Another survey, the PSID, follows middle and lower income households, and can be found at https://psidonline.isr.umich.edu/.
25. See Orazio Attanasio, Erik Hurst, and Luigi Pistaferri, "The Evolution of Income, Consumption, and Leisure Inequality in the US, 1980–2010," National Bureau of Economic Research Working Paper No. 17982, 2012.
26. See discussion of Mian and Sufi's studies in chapter 11.
27. "Causes and Consequences of Income Inequality: A Global Perspective," IMF, June 2015, available at http://www.imf.org/external/pubs/ft/sdn/2015/sdn1513.pdf.
28. Another feature that complicates the analysis of the linkage between income concentration and Accumulation is the finding that the wealth-to-income ratio has increased in recent decades, though to a lesser extent in the United States compared to other developed countries. An increase in the wealth-to-income ratio can accommodate both an increase in consumption *and* an accumulation of wealth. When the growth of wealth is generated by a rise in the capitalized value of assets, rather than income, an increase in consumption—even if it is a small fraction of the increase in wealth—will reduce Accumulation, since it will reduce the amount of income that is intended never to be spent. This is so because Accumulation is measured as the extent by which income exceeds consumption, not the extent by which wealth exceeds consumption. See Thomas Piketty and Gabriel Zucman, "Capital Is Back: Wealth-Income Ratios in Rich Countries 1700–2010," *The Quarterly Journal of Economics* (2014): 1255–1310.
29. It is also possible that the increase in asset values during the housing boom, which increased household wealth (see figure 11.3), induced people at all income levels to reduce saving.

30. "Rising imports cause higher unemployment, lower labor force participation, and reduced wages in local labor markets that house import-competing manufacturing industries" (see Autor et al., "The China Syndrome: Local Labor Market Effects of Import Competition in the United States," p. 2121).
31. This conclusion is tempered by the fact that US consumers benefitted from the lower prices paid for Chinese imports. One might argue that gross imports from China reduced US middle class incomes, but this leaves out possible gains from exports to China. I am not aware of any persuasive evidence bearing on this issue.
32. It was perceived as a problem in the 1980s, when the current account deficit ballooned. At that time Japan and Germany were the principal sources of the current account deficit. The Plaza Accord of 1985, which was prompted by US concerns, led to a coordinated depreciation of the dollar that reduced the current account deficit.
33. See Robert E. Hall, "Secular Stagnation," National Bureau of Economic Research, 2014.
34. Ben S. Bernanke, "Deflation: Making Sure 'It' Doesn't Happen Here," Speech before the National Economists Club, 2002, available at http://www.federalreserve.gov/BOARDDOCS/Speeches/2002/20021121/default.htm.
35. See Lawrence Summer's address at the IMF economic forum, November 8, 2013. http://larrysummers.com/imf-fourteenth-annual-research-conference-in-honor-of-stanley-fischer/. Paul Krugman stated a version of the secular stagnation thesis two years earlier in his blog. My idea that the current account deficit is a form of Accumulation was inspired, in part, by Krugman's post. But he dismissed the notion that income inequality could be a source of underconsumption based on the fact that household savings had not increased. He assumed that underconsumption—or permanent saving—implied that the overall savings rate must increase. I part company with Krugman on that point, because—as I stated earlier in this chapter—I think it is possible that an increase in permanent saving among top earners can be matched by an increase in borrowing (negative saving) by the middle class, in which event Accumulation would have increased even if aggregate saving had not. I conjecture that this is what occurred during the housing boom (see Paul Krugman, "The Return of Secular Stagnation," *New York Times*, November 8, 2011, available at http://krugman.blogs.nytimes.com/2011/11/08/the-return-of-secular-stagnation/?_r=0).
36. Alvin H. Hansen, "Economic Progress and Declining Population Growth," *American Economic Review*, Vol. XXIX, Number 1, Part 1 (1939): 1–15.
37. See Barry Eichengreen, *Secular Stagnation: The Long View*, 2015, AEA Web. It is certainly possible that if workers and investors are taxed to support retirees, their incentive to work and to invest will be damped. That is a problem the United States will potentially face in the future if it does not reduce Medicare and Social Security payout commitments from current levels. But during the 2000s the United States reduced taxes on income and investment earnings, and so it was not a concern at the time.
38. Professor Summers has mooted two other ideas that are not considered in the text. One is that high costs of financial intermediation deter investment. While that does not seem to have been operative during the housing boom, when financial intermediation expanded, Professor Summer may be correct in supposing that this factor lowers the trend rate of investment, by reducing the net return on investment. The other has to do with the reduced tax incentive to invest at lower interest rates (due to the tax deductibility of interest). Professor Summers may be right about this factor, but it doesn't address the more fundamental issue of what has caused the decline in interest rates.
39. The macroeconomic paradigm may, of course, be wrong in certain instances. For example, during the financial crisis people reduced their spending as a precaution in response to the fear and uncertainty propagated by the crisis, in spite of negative, real, riskless interest rates. On the other hand, people nearing retirement might actually increase saving in response to lower interest rates, in order to meet their retirement saving target.

There is a heightened possibility this might have occurred after the financial crisis, which reduced the wealth of aging of baby boomers. This type of reaction would exacerbate the contraction in activity caused by a reduction in profitable investment opportunities.

40. See Ricardo J. Caballero and Emmanuel Farhi, "On the Role of Safe Asset Shortages in Secular Stagnation," in *Secular Stagnation: Facts, Causes and Cures* (London, UK: CEPR Press, 2014), Chapter 9, pp. 111–123; and Ricardo J. Caballero and Emmanuel Farhi, "The Safety Trap," NBER Working Paper No. 19927, 2014.
41. Although perhaps a key distinction is that the safe asset theory posits that an excess of saving cannot be cured by an increase in investment generally, but requires an increase in safe assets, which normally can only be produced in volume by government. The safe assets manufactured by the private sector during the housing boom were, it turns out, not safe at all.
42. An interest bill on the debt that is below the growth rate of the economy ensures that non-accumulator borrowers are paying back less than the returns generated by the borrowed funds—which ensures they benefit from the transfer. It is possible that non-accumulators could benefit even if the interest bill exceeded the growth rate, but it would require a fully articulated model to work out the conditions under which that result would obtain.
43. For a note of caution on increased US government debt, see the section on government debt in chapter 13.
44. For Chinese purchases of Treasuries, see US Department of the Treasury, "Report on Foreign Portfolio Holdings of US Securities," available at http://www.treasury.gov/resource-center/data-chart-center/tic/Pages/fpis.aspx. For the current account deficit, see figure 2.6.
45. I explained in chapter 8 how credit and money had been decoupling for some time prior to the housing boom, which reduced the influence of monetary policy in any event.
46. Mr. Greenspan's failure to understand the source of his conundrum arose from his dismissal of the idea that capital inflows were pushing down long term interest rates. His contention that "it is difficult to attribute the long-term interest rate declines of the last nine months to glacially increasing globalization" misses out on the dramatic increase in the capital flow bonanza that was then taking place and its channeling into long-term securities. Mr. Greenspan was led astray by his failure to recognize that the capital flow bonanza was compressing the maturity yield curve. He was not alone in misreading the evidence at the time.

11 Descent into the Abyss

1. Michiyo Nakamoto and David Wighton, "Citicorp Chief Stays Bullish on Buy-Outs," *Financial Times*, July 9, 2007.
2. Bernard Mandeville, *The Fable of the Bees* (1714). In Mandeville's poem, the cause of the contraction in borrowing and spending is a sudden bout of frugality among borrowers, whereas the contraction in borrowing during the US financial crisis resulted from a reduction in lenders' willingness to extend credit.
3. Banks were forced to increase lending in two instances: they were required to fund precommitted unused lines of credit, and they were required to fund the liquidity puts issued to investors in the ABS they sponsored as conduits for mortgages they originated.
4. The estimate of potential output is the Congressional Budget Office projection.
5. Between 1999 and 2007 there were \$641 billion of publicly traded subprime CDOs issued, of which an estimated \$420 billion was written off after the financial crisis. See Cordell et al., "Collateral Damage: Sizing and Assessing the Subprime CDO Crisis."

6. F. A. Hayek, "Economics and Knowledge," in *Individualism and Economic Order* (University of Chicago Press, 1948 [1937]), pp. 33–57.
7. See the discussion of Keynes and Hayek in chapter 4.
8. Ibid.
9. Hayek's elaboration of the condition for equilibrium fits the housing boom very well:

   > It appears that the concept of equilibrium merely means that the foresight of the different members of the society is in a special sense correct. It must be correct in the sense that every person's plan is based on the expectation of just those actions of other people which those other people intend to perform and that all these plans are based on expectations of the same set of external facts, so that under certain conditions nobody will have any reason to change his plans....nor need foresight for this purpose be perfect in the sense that it need extend into the indefinite future or that everybody must foresee everything correctly. We should rather say that equilibrium will last so long as the anticipations prove correct and that they need to be correct only on those points which are relevant for the decisions of the individuals. (Ibid.)

10. See Merton H. Miller, "The Modigliani-Miller Propositions after Thirty Years," *Journal of Economic Perspectives*, Vol. 2, Number 4 (1988): 99–120.
11. This is not meant as a disagreement with the leverage cycle theory of Fostel and Geanakoplos. As I explained in chapter 2 and in chapter 7, the leverage cycle is a compelling explanation for the dynamics of the US housing boom. My intention here is to point out that it is not the only possible mechanism capable of generating a boom.
12. This raises an interesting policy question. Since an asset price bubble involving low leverage is unlikely to lead to a financial crisis, should policymakers be concerned only about bubbles that involve high levels of leverage?
13. See figures 2.2, 2.3, and 7.2.
14. Oscar Jorda, Moritz Schularick, and Alam M. Taylor, *Leveraged Bubbles*, 2015, Mimeo available at http://conference.nber.org/confer/2015/EASE15/Jorda_Schularick_Taylor.pdf.
15. "Average Sales Price for New Houses Sold in the United States," US Bureau of the Census.
16. LTV is an acronym for "loan-to-value" ratio.
17. The Case Shiller national home price index (HPI) fell by approximately 30 percent from its peak in Q1 2006 to its trough in Q2 2009. The FHA HPI declined by approximately 18.5 percent from its peak in Q1 2007 to Q2 2012.
18. http://www.corelogic.com/about-us/news/new-corelogic-data-shows-23-percent-of-borrowers-underwater-with-$750-billion-dollars-of-negative-equity.aspx.
19. See discussion of subprime mortgages in chapter 4.
20. Mian and Sufi define wealthy households as those in the top 20 percent of wealth.
21. As reported in Mian and Sufi, *House of Debt* pp. 87–88.
22. "Home equity" is the value of the home minus the mortgage debt.
23. Jonathan Heathcote and Fabrizio Perri, *Wealth and Volatility* (FRB Minneapolis Mimeo, 2015).
24. Mian and Sufi, *House of Debt*, p. 43.
25. In some cases banks issued legally binding guarantees while in other cases banks felt compelled to act as a guarantor in order to maintain credibility with their investors who had funded their ABS.
26. Federal Reserve Bank of St. Louis, "TED Spread", retrieved from FRED, Federal Reserve Bank of St. Louis https://research.stlouisfed.org/fred2/series/TEDRATE/.
27. It is important to note that the decline in commercial bank lending was tempered by requirements to fund unused lines of credit and to fund the off balance sheet ABS on which they had issued liquidity puts when these entities were unable to refinance the short term ABCP used to fund their holdings.

28. According to Zoltan Pozsar, approximately 20 percent of broker-dealer repo debt was not matched by short term (mostly reverse repo) assets. See Zoltan Pozsar, *A Macro View of Shadow Banking*.
29. Ben S. Bernanke, "Some Reflections on the crisis and the Policy Response," speech at the Russell Sage Foundation, New York, April 13, 2012.

12 The Initial Policy Response

1. Hamlet, Polonius, Act 1, Scene 3.
2. Keynes, "The General Theory of Employment," p. 216.
3. J. M. Keynes, *Treatise on Money* (1931).
4. Investopedia defines "money market funds" as an investment whose objective is to earn interest for shareholders while maintaining a net asset value (NAV) of $1 per share, which is the par value per share. A money market fund's portfolio is comprised of short-term (less than one year) securities representing high-quality, liquid debt and monetary instruments. Investors can purchase shares of money market funds through mutual funds, brokerage firms, and banks. Available at http://www.investopedia.com/terms/m/money-marketfund.asp#ixzz3dFp79nwh.
5. The Prime Fund was a large retail money market fund that lost considerable value when Lehmann went into bankruptcy in September 2008. The term "break the buck" refers to a breaking of the implicit promise that money market fund investors will always be able to liquidate their holdings immediately, at least at par (i.e., receive back at least the amount they invested).
6. The Fed also cut the Fed funds rate to zero, but marginally reducing the overnight bank borrowing rate was not a very significant event when the entire credit system had seized up.
7. The Bear Sterns funding took place in March 2008, six months prior to the full flowering of the crisis.
8. For an excellent summary of Fed Liquidity programs implemented in the fall of 2008, see Neil Willardson and LuAnne Pederson, "Federal Reserve Liquidity Programs: An Update," Federal Reserve Bank of Minneapolis, June 2010, available at https://www.minneapolisfed.org/publications/the-region/federal-reserve-liquidity-programs-an-update.
9. It is possible that, to the extent the Fed's liquidity programs caused asset prices to rebound, the Fed's liquidity programs could have indirectly increased the net worth of banks. In fact, this was one goal of the programs.
10. The bank money multiplier is the factor by which the sum of currency and deposits exceed "high powered" money created by the central bank. It is determined by the percentage of each loan against which the bank desires holds currency or reserves. When banks desire to increase that percentage—which is what I refer to as hoarding in the text—and if there is no increase in currency or reserves in the economy, the banking system will be forced to contract its loans. Finally, since loans are repaid in the form of currency or deposits, to the extent loans are repaid by the borrower transferring its deposit balance to the bank, the result is a contraction in deposits.
11. Subsequent research by Ben Bernanke established an additional Fisherian "debt-deflation" channel that was operative in the Great Depression, which showed the contraction in bank lending, caused by a decline in collateral values, to have been an independent source of contraction in economic activity. More recently Oscar et al., *Financial Crises, Credit Booms, and External Imbalance* showed that credit and money moved hand-in-hand during the Great Depression. These findings indicate that the asset deflation channel identified by Bernanke may have had more effect than the goods deflation channel identified by Friedman and Schwartz in causing the economic downturn (although note that Friedman and Schwartz identify a secondary asset deflation

channel in the quote in the text). See Ben S. Bernanke, "The Macroeconomics of the Great Depression: A Comparative Approach," *Journal of Money, Credit, and Banking*, Vol. 27, Number 1 (1994).

12. Milton Friedman and Anna Jacobson Schwartz, *A Monetary History of the United States, 1867–1960* (Princeton University Press, 1963), pp. 356–357.
13. Ben S. Bernanke, "On Milton Friedman's Ninetieth Birthday," Remarks at the Conference to Honor Milton Friedman, University of Chicago, November 8, 2002.
14. Board of Governors of the Federal Reserve System (US), *Loans and Leases in Bank Credit, All Commercial Banks*, retrieved from FRED, Federal Reserve Bank of St. Louis https://research.stlouisfed.org/fred2/series/TOTLL/.
15. M2 consists of (1) currency outside the US Treasury, Federal Reserve Banks, and the vaults of depository institutions; (2) traveler's checks of nonbank issuers; (3) demand deposits; (4) other checkable deposits (OCDs), which consist primarily of negotiable order of withdrawal (NOW) accounts at depository institutions and credit union share draft accounts; (5) savings deposits (which include money market deposit accounts, or MMDAs); (6) small-denomination time deposits (time deposits in amounts of less than $100,000); and (7) balances in retail money market mutual funds (MMMFs).
16. Board of Governors of the Federal Reserve System (US), *M2 Money Stock* [M2], retrieved from FRED, Federal Reserve Bank of St. Louis https://research.stlouisfed.org/fred2/series/M2/.
17. Ibid.
18. Federal Reserve Bank of St. Louis, *Excess Reserves of Depository Institutions*, retrieved from FRED, Federal Reserve Bank of St. Louis https://research.stlouisfed.org/fred2/series/EXCSRESNS/.
19. Board of Governors of the Federal Reserve System (US), *Deposits, All Commercial Banks*, retrieved from FRED, Federal Reserve Bank of St. Louis https://research.stlouisfed.org/fred2/series/DPSACBM027SBOG/.
20. Board of Governors of the Federal Reserve System (US), *Money Market Mutual Funds; Total Financial Assets, Level*, retrieved from FRED, Federal Reserve Bank of St. Louis https://research.stlouisfed.org/fred2/series/MMMFFAQ027S/.
21. Milton Friedman, "The Role of Monetary Policy," *The American Economic Review*, Vol. 58 (1968): 1–17.
22. Bank loans to ABS made as a result of their liquidity puts were counted as commercial loans, not real estate loans.
23. Kathleen Kahle and Renee Stultz, "Access to Capital, Investment, and the Financial Crisis," *Journal of Financial Economics*, Vol. 110 Issue 2 (2013): 280–299.
24. Mian and Sufi, *House of Debt*, p. 128. These authors also site the decline in banks' cost of short-term borrowing after the onset of the financial crisis as evidence that banks were not financially constrained. But that is not a valid inference, since bank debt was de facto guaranteed by the government after the crisis which meant that borrowing costs did not reflect the creditworthiness of banks. Moreover, as I argued in chapter 11 and in this chapter, the constraint on bank lending came from a deficiency of capital, and such a deficiency was not resolved by the lower debt costs afforded by the implicit government guarantee.
25. Becker Bo and Victoria Ivashina, "Cyclicality of Credit Supply: Firm Level Evidence," Working Paper 10–107 Harvard Business School, August 23, 2011.
26. The loan rate spread is the amount over its cost of funds a bank charges on a loan. The reason for using the spread, rather than the interest rate, is to adjust for changes in general market interest rates. What is captured here is the change in loan rates relative to other rates in the economy.
27. Tobias Adrian, Paolo Colla, and Hyun Song Shin, "Which Financial Frictions? Parsing the Evidence from the Financial Crisis of 2007–9," Federal Reserve Bank of New York Staff Report No. 528, 2012. The authors also show that bond interest rate spreads

and volumes rose during the post-financial crisis period, which is consistent with an increase in demand by bond borrowers who faced reduced bank loan supply. For description of the data and methodology, see paper.

28. After 2010 bank loan interest rates and net interest margins declined. This does not necessarily indicate a decline in the demand for borrowing. Rather, it coincided with the QE programs of the Fed which were designed to reduce long-term interest rates (see discussion in chapter 13). It may be that QE had the effect of compressing bank net interest margins and reducing the interest rates on all long-term loans. In addition, bank borrowers who had the option of issuing bonds at lower rates likely forced banks to reduce rates in order to compete with bond rates. The cause of this pattern, however, remains an open question for me.
29. For an explanation of reserve requirements, see http://www.federalreserve.gov/monetarypolicy/reservereq.htm.
30. Required reserves increased because the deposit base of banks had increased somewhat due to the Fed's creation of deposits. See later in this chapter for a discussion of the behavior of deposits during the financial crisis.
31. Excess reserve data obtained from Federal Reserve Bank of St. Louis, *Excess Reserves of Depository Institutions*, retrieved from FRED, Federal Reserve Bank of St. Louis https://research.stlouisfed.org/fred2/series/EXCSRESNS/. Required reserve data obtained from Board of Governors of the Federal Reserve System (US), *Required Reserves of Depository Institutions*, retrieved from FRED, Federal Reserve Bank of St. Louis https://research.stlouisfed.org/fred2/series/REQRESNS/.
32. The other Fed bank lending programs implemented at the same time ensured that all banks had access to adequate reserves.
33. Federal Financial Institutions Examination Council (US), *Net Interest Margin for all U.S. Banks*, retrieved from FRED, Federal Reserve Bank of St. Louis https://research.stlouisfed.org/fred2/series/USNIM/.
34. Ben S. Bernanke, "The Crisis and the Policy Response," 2009, available at http://www.federalreserve.gov/newsevents/speech/bernanke20090113a.htm.
35. Payment of interest on bank reserves is also a subsidy to banks, which the public will not like.
36. Friedman, "The Role of Monetary Policy," p. 15.
37. The other third of losses incurred during the financial crisis were absorbed by US hedge funds, insurance companies, and pension funds. IMF Global Financial Stability Report, April 2009.
38. IMF Global Financial Stability Report, April 2009, Table 1.4.
39. Victoria Ivashina and David Scharfstein, "Bank Lending during the Financial Crisis of 2008," *Journal of Financial Economics*, Vol. 97 (2010): 319–338.
40. There are many possible reasons for this, including continued uncertainty over asset values. One possible additional reason is that bank shareholders may have wanted to avoid suffering a dilution in ownership percentage that would occur if the conversion right of TARP investment was ever exercised. The best way to ensure that did not occur would have been to hold on to the cash injection from TARP, continue to game the capital adequacy rules to show adequate capital, and then eventually pay back the TARP money at the end of the loan term.
41. "The Supervisory Capital Assessment Program: Overview of Results," Board of Governors of the Federal Reserve (May 7, 2008). Available at http://www.federalreserve.gov/newsevents/press/bcreg/bcreg20090507a1.pdf.
42. The TLGP lasted from October 2008 to December 31, 2012. The maximum outstanding guaranteed debt at a point in time was just under $350 billion. See "Temporary Liquidity Guarantee Program," at https://www.fdic.gov/regulations/resources/TLGP/.
43. "United States: Financial System Stability Assessment," July 9, 2010, IMF, available at http://www.imf.org/external/pubs/ft/scr/2010/cr10247.pdf.

44. As noted in footnote 24, bank debt yields and CDS spreads did not reflect market perceptions of bank solvency since the government was effectively guaranteeing bank debt.
45. Office of the Special Inspector General for the Troubled Asset Relief Program, "Quarterly Report to Congress," April 24, 2013. Available at http://www.sigtarp.gov/Quarterly%20Reports/April_24_2013_Report_to_Congress.pdf.
46. The architects of the bailouts, like former Treasury Secretary Tim Geithner, defend their actions, in part, by pointing out that the government loans were all paid back—with interest. The implication is that taxpayer actually made money. But that defense skirts two vital issues. One is that the alternatives proposed by economists would have caused an immediate recapitalization of banks, which would likely have speeded recovery. That would have conferred more benefit on the public than the interest earned on government loans to banks. The other is the unfairness of extending loans to a preferred group that excluded the vast majority of US citizens and businesses that were also in need of financial relief during the crisis. Nevertheless, I must acknowledge that while I disagree with Mr. Geithner's policies, I have no evidence to suspect his motives. He appears to me to have been acting honorably in the public interest, as he perceived it to be.
47. Simon Johnson, a former chief economist at the IMF, is a prominent proponent of the view that the US government acted to protect powerful bankers and bank investors from incurring losses, while neglecting the interests of the majority of US citizens. See Simon Johnson, "The Quiet Coup," *The Atlantic*, May 2009. Available at http://www.theatlantic.com/magazine/archive/2009/05/the-quiet-coup/307364/.
48. Thomas M. Hoenig, Speech at National Association for Business Economics 30th Annual Economic Policy Conference, Arlington VA, February 24, 2014.

13 The Dilemma of Policy in a Balance Sheet Recession

1. John Geanakoplos, "Leverage, Default, and Forgiveness,"p. 319.
2. Lawrence Summers, *IMF Fourteenth Annual Research Conference in Honor of Stanley Fischer*, November 8, 2013.
3. Labor force participation grew steadily from the 1960s to the late 1990s, as a result of the entry of women into the workforce. The current level of labor force participation is above the levels of the 1950s, but the comparison is not "apples to apples," since a large majority of women did not consider wage employment prior to recent decades.
4. Reinhardt and Rogoff, *This Time Is Different*, p. 224.
5. Sources: 2009 data from Carter, "Housing Units with Negative Equity, 1997 to 2009," date from *Corelogic* Equity Report Fourth Quarter 2014.
6. Since the prices of equities and bonds recovered fairly rapidly from their steep declines during the financial crisis, they did not contribute to the long lasting debt overhang. Home prices, and the prices of nonprime residential mortgage securities, on the other hand, remained depressed for many years after the financial crisis.
7. See figure 12.5.
8. Federal Reserve Board
9. There are several forces that pulled interest rates down. I have explored the depressive impact of Accumulation and the capital flow bonanza earlier in this book. What is implied in the text is that the debt overhang would be sufficient to produce this effect even in the absence of other causes. Also, note that effective interest rates for borrowers suffering from a debt overhang, or damaged credit scores inflicted by distress experienced in the financial crisis, rose to infinity; they could not get a loan at any interest rate.
10. Ben Bernanke Speech, October 1, 2012.
11. The Fed's commitment to purchase mortgage ABS also had the effect of reducing the perceived risk of investing in those securities.
12. Provided that banks are able to raise the additional capital required to support an expansion in lending.

13. Michael Woodford, "Methods of Policy Accommodation at the Interest-Rate Lower Bound," *Federal Reserve Bank of Kansas City Conference at Jackson Hole WY*, 2013.
14. The economist will recognize that I have ignored Ricardian Equivalence, which contends that taxpayers will factor in an increase in future tax liabilities required to repay the government bonds, which will reduce future after-tax incomes, and increase their current saving to provision for the future liability. The increase in current saving will exactly offset the increase in private sector income created by the government spending. In response to this line of reasoning are arguments that (1) people do not tend to act in so farsighted a manner; (2) individual taxpayers do not actually know what portion of the future tax bill they will be liable for; and most importantly (3) if the increase in government deficit spending generates a sufficiently large increase in total income, the deficit spending will be repaid out of future tax revenues without having to raise tax rates.
15. The reason for this caveat is that the PIH implies that changes in income that are perceived as temporary will not induce changes in spending; only changes in income that are perceived as long lasting will alter spending. Economists have been debating the determinants of spending for decades, without forming a consensus.
16. John Maynard Keynes, *Collected Writings* (1937).
17. In the past, recessions were commonly thought of as events where workers were involuntarily unemployed.
18. Note that in a service business the analogue to ordering more inventories is to hire and train more workers.
19. John R. Hicks, "IS-LM: An Explanation," *Journal of Post Keynesian Economics*, Vol. 3 Number 2 (1980–1): 139–154.
20. It applies to service providers as well.
21. Provided the interest paid on government debt is below the growth rate of the economy. See the discussion of this point in chapter 9.
22. By the end of 2013, the US current account deficit had declined to under 2 percent of GDP.
23. Source: Federal Net Outlays as Percent of Gross Domestic Product (FYONGDA188S) was first constructed by the Federal Reserve Bank of St. Louis in January 2013. It is calculated using Federal Net Outlays (FYONET) and Gross Domestic Product (GDPA).
24. In 2014 noninterest US government spending was 20.4 percent of GDP. The projection for 2040 is 26 percent of GDP. See "The 2014 Long Term Budget Outlook," Congressional Budget office, available at https://www.cbo.gov/publication/45471.
25. Reinhardt and Rogoff, *This Time is Different*, p. XXXVIIII.
26. Carmen Reinhardt and Kenneth Rogoff, "Reinhardt and Rogoff: Responding to Our Critics," *New York Times*, April 25, 2013.
27. John R. Cochrane, "Understanding Policy in the Great Recession: Some Unpleasant Fiscal Arithmetic," *European Economic Review* (2010).
28. Keynes, *Collected Writings*.
29. The condition that income = consumption + investment follows from the fact that if income exceeded total spending, then income would have to contract, since spending is the source of income. Conversely, the idea that spending exceeds income is nonsensical.
30. Mr. Wolf also argues that reducing the government budget deficit in a balance sheet recession is contractionary. He is almost certainly correct. The only scenario where private spending would be stimulated by a reduction in the government budget deficit is if (1) it is interpreted as an indicator that future deficits will be lower and (2) there are firms or households who are currently holding back on spending because they fear future deficits. But (1) will only hold if future entitlement commitments are reduced, and I am not aware of evidence that (2) describes the motives of a large group of savers.

14 Policy Options

1. For the Fed's current (as of April 2015) bank capital rules, see *Federal Registrar*, Vol. 78, Number 198 pp. 62018–62291, available at http://www.gpo.gov/fdsys/pkg/FR-2013-10-11/pdf/2013-21653.pdf.
2. See discussion in chapter 12.
3. A bankruptcy filing may allow the counterparty to a derivative contract to close out the contract by forcing the bankrupt entity to immediately pay the market value of the contract, to the extent it implies a payment is owed to the counterparty. Such a demand could increase the financial stress on the bankrupt party, but it would not cause stress for the counterparty, unless the bankrupt party was unable to meet its obligation to pay. The inability to meet its payment obligation would be a problem whether or not the party filed bankruptcy, and terminating the derivatives contract is an option, not an obligation, accorded to the counterparty after a bankruptcy filing.
4. In September 2008 insurance company AIG, a large issuer of CDS on subprime mortgage securities, was unable to meet collateral requirements on approximately $411 billion of CDS it had issued on super senior tranches of ABS, approximately $55.1 billion of which were on subprime mortgage securities. The increased collateral requirements resulted from downgrades in the credit ratings of AIG and the subprime ABS on which it issued CDS. In order to avoid a default on AIG's obligations, and to keep AIG out of bankruptcy, the US government pumped a total of $185 billion dollars of taxpayer money into AIG, beginning in September of 2008. The justification for the bailout was a concern that an AIG default on its CDS would, by forcing its counter-parties to write down the value of their ABS holdings, render many of them insolvent.

   AIG's subprime exposure was at most $55.1 billion and that hugely overstates the amount of outside money that would have been necessary to cover those obligations, even in the extremely unlikely case that *the entire* underwritten subprime ABS defaulted and failed to pay out any money. AIG had assets of sufficient value to cover most, if not all, of any forecasted shortfall. Moreover, mark-to-market accounting rules had already forced AIG's counterparties to write off a substantial portion of the face value of their CDS. For example, one of AIG's counterparties the US government expressed concern over was Goldman Sachs. Goldman had already written off (i.e., taken losses) on approximately half the face value of the AIG subprime mortgage CDS obligations it held, and Goldman remained in business. Therefore, AIG needed to pay at most half it outstanding subprime obligations to prevent a meltdown. That takes the maximum amount required to cover AIG's counterparty obligation down to $22.55 billion.

   It can be argued that if AIG itself offered less than full value to settle its CDS obligations it might have led to protracted negotiations during which time AIG's counterparties would have been forced to further write down the value of the AIG obligations. Negotiating haircuts on debt and collateral obligations with numerous counterparties might have been a time consuming process. In September of 2008, days after the Lehman bankruptcy, with markets in turmoil, there was no time to spare. Therefore, renegotiation of contracts was probably not a viable solution to resolving the ticking time bomb of AIG's derivative obligations. Goldman and other counterparties were on the financial brink, and further significant write-down may have rendered them insolvent.

   Yet, the problem could have been resolved if the government had offered to purchase AIG's credit default swaps directly from AIG's counterparties. Rather than buying most of the company and taking on all its obligations (which went beyond its derivatives obligations), the government could have simply announced that it stood ready to purchase the CDS claims on AIG for the value then placed on them by counterparties—approximately half of face value. This would not have been an unprecedented move. The Fed made a market in repo-debt, providing liquidity to repo dealers, so why not do the same for OTC debt? It would have restored confidence in the OTC derivatives markets without preventing insolvent companies from liquidating or reorganizing in bankruptcy. After acquiring its subprime CDS obligations—which would have cost at most 12 percent of what it invested in AIG—the US government could have elected to do one of two things. It could have held on to the claims until markets calmed and resold them into the market. Or it could have pursued collection from AIG, possibly forcing it into bankruptcy. Either course could have been pursued without igniting any risk of systemic meltdown.

This argument applies to every other large financial institution. Taxpayer-funded bailouts were not required to prevent financial meltdown. FDIC insurance for deposit taking banks and the Fed injection of bank reserves described in chapter 12 ensured the continued operation of the payments system—which is carried out by those institutions—and direct intervention in the OTC derivatives market alongside guarantees to money market fund investors could have stemmed the tide of panic without requiring the wholesale bailout of large financial institutions.

5. Recall from chapter 12 that when loans from the Prime Fund to Lehman looked as if they would incur losses due to Lehman's bankruptcy filing, investors fled money market fund until the Fed stepped in a guaranteed performance.
6. Thomas Hoenig, "Too Big Has Failed," Speech delivered on March 6, 2009. Available at http://www.federalreservehistory.org/Media/Material/People/127-36.
7. Former Fed governor Randall Kroszner pointed to precedent where the US government to nullified a clause in debt contracts that has become onerous. During the Great Depression, when the United States went off the gold standard, the dollar price of gold soared, which caused distress to borrowers on loans that had repayment tied to the value of gold. To alleviate borrower distress, the US government repudiated gold indexation clauses on all private contracts. At the time, gold indexation clauses appeared in almost all long-term debt contracts. Kroszner showed that the cancellation of debt led to an increase in asset values. See Randall Kroszner, *Is It Better to Forgive Than to Receive? Repudiation of the Gold Indexation Clause in Long-Term Debt during the Great Depression* (University of Chicago, 1998).
8. See figures 11.5 and 11.6.
9. See Mian and Sufi, *House of Debt*, chapter 10, pp. 135–142, and the notes for references to many proposals for mortgage relief.
10. See Jaffee and Quigley, "The Future of the Government Sponsored Enterprises: The Role for Government in the US Mortgage Market," Chapter 8, Table 8.2, p. 369. I refer to the 2010 data.
11. See the discussion and notes to chapter 10 of Mian and Sufi, *House of Debt*.
12. Thomas Hoenig interview as reported in Shahien Nasiripor, "Top Fed Official Wants to break Up Megabanks, Stop Fed from Guaranteeing Wall Street's Profits," *Huff Post Business*, June 2, 2010. Available at http://www.huffingtonpost.com/2010/04/02/top-fed-official-wants-to_n_521842.html.
13. See, for example, Arnold C. Herberger, "A Vision of the Growth Process," *American Economic Review*, Vol. 88, Number 1 (1998): 1–32.
14. For an example of recent research on the topic of "too-big-to-fail," which shows a negative correlation between the market to book value ration and the relative size of a bank, which indicates that size is actually value destroying, see Asli Demirguc-Kunt and Harry Huizinga, "Are Banks Too Big to Fail or Too Big to Save? International Evidence from Equity Prices and CDS Spreads," *Journal of Banking & Finance*, Vol. 37, Issue 3 (March 2013): 875–894.
15. Milton Friedman and Anna Jacobson Schwartz, *A Monetary History of the United States, 1867–1960* (Princeton University Press, 1963).
16. Some economists have argued that a group of small banks that engage in the same practices will pose the same systemic risk as a large bank. That might be correct, however, it is a limiting condition—banks will not necessarily replicate each other and such arguments overlook the other benefits of competition.

17. For a discussion of the Fed's approach, see Jeremy Stein, *Regulating Large Financial Institutions*, 2013, comments at the "Rethinking Macro Policy II" conference of the IMF.
18. FDIC insurance on deposits, up to a limit of $250,000.00, mitigates the risk of depositor runs. But the volume of uninsured time deposits and short-term wholesale loans comprise a sizeable portion of liabilities of large banks, and are vulnerable to runs.
19. The reason for protecting the payments system in *all* future states of the world is because a malfunctioning of that system would be catastrophic. The reason for tolerance of future states where credit might contract is in recognition of the potential existence of a risk-reward tradeoff between an efficient credit system and a stable credit system. A temporary collapse of credit is not catastrophic and it may be worthwhile taking some risk in order to promote the financing of risky ventures that increase trend growth.
20. This does not mean the individual banks should be insured against these risks. On the contrary, in a competitive market it is normal that individual banks would frequently fail.
21. The design of rules allowing adjustment of bank capital in systemic crisis can be accomplished in other ways as well. Some proposal have addressed the incentive issues in a more nuanced way. See, for example Ricardo Caballero, "Sudden Financial Arrest," Mundell-Fleming Lecture delivered at the Tenth Jacques Polak Annual Research Conference, IMF, 2009.
22. This does not imply that there are no guideposts to evaluate risk. Without such guideposts, all planning for future activity would be useless. Rather, the idea (as Keynes described it; see discussion in chapter 6) is that there are certain types of social and economic activities who's outcomes become difficult to define in terms of probabilities the further out into the future one tries to forecast.
23. See "Regulatory Capital Rules: Regulatory Capital, Revisions to the Supplementary Leverage Ratio," *Federal Register*, Vol. 79, Number 187 (September 26, 2014): 57725–57751.
24. The Dodd-Frank requirement that systemically important financial institutions be required to hold more capital is equivalent to my recommendation for leverage limits.
25. Some critics of a simple leverage rule make the risible claim that such a rule might induce banks to take on more risk. They argue that a reduction in leverage will reduce expected equity returns—while ignoring that it would also reduce the risk of loss—and thereby induce managers to take on more risk in order to maintain returns at preexisting levels. They also claim that a leverage rule that does not discriminate between the relative risks of different activities will incentivize bankers to increase lending to riskier areas. But have we not recently experienced the consequences of the high leverage, risk-based leverage rules they advocate? Surely, the financial crisis should have put an end to the nonsensical argument that high leverage will cause banks to take on less risk.
26. It is vitally important that derivatives contracts allowing traders to short position be included in the set of standardized contracts. Shorting provides a mechanism for contrarians to express their views and counter the tendency for asset prices to become over-valued when animal spirits are high. I mentioned in chapter 7 that the inability of housing contrarians to short housing securities prior to late 2005—when AIG expanded its issuance of CDS on subprime ABS and shorting contracts were initiated for the ABX.HE subprime index—may have resulted in home prices and home construction increasing more than would have been the case if the infrastructure for shorting was in place at an earlier date.
27. To be fair, economists have occasionally withheld unfettered support for free trade. Economists have, on occasion, recommended that home economies offer subsidies to attract global industries with large economies of scale, since these natural oligopolies earn large profits out of which they can confer benefit on the home economy in excess of the subsidies offered. Likewise, economists have sometimes recommended that less developed economies offer subsidies to attract investment that can effectuate a transfer of knowledge of advanced technologies into the home economy through the training and experience

gained by its workforce. Also, trade can adversely affect certain groups. Notably, the shift in labor intensive manufacturing from the United States to China in the 2000s reduced the wages of unskilled US workers, while enriching the 1 percent who own shares in corporations that have profited from the decline in costs. But set against the gains from trade, as economist have measured them, these are caveats; exceptions that prove the rule.

28. Correspondingly, the currencies of deficit countries will depreciate, which promotes exports.
29. Correspondingly, the deficit countries will experience deflation, which will effectuate depreciation in their real exchange rate, just as in the flexible exchange rate regime.
30. Recently the IMF backed off from its long standing support for open capital flows and opined that capital account restrictions may be desirable in some instances.
31. See "The Liberalization and Management of Capital Flows—An Institutional View," IMF, November 14, 2002, available at http://www.imf.org/external/np/pp/eng/2012/111412.pdf.
32. J. M. Keynes, "Proposal for an International Clearing Union," *The International Monetary Fund 1945–1965 Volume III: Documents* (1969 [1943]), pp. 19–36, available at http://imsreform.imf.org/reserve/pdf/keynesplan.pdf.
33. Ibid., p. 27; emphasis in the original.
34. Ibid., p. 28.
35. Ibid., p. 25.
36. Even though capital mobility is not yet an issue with China, since it currently maintains a relatively closed capital account, it will become an issue over time as China's capital account eventually opens up.
37. Keynes, *The General Theory*, pp. 376–377.
38. Raj Chetty, Nathaniel Henderson, Patrick Kline, and Emmanuel Saez, "Is the United States Still a Land of Opportunity? Recent Trends in Intergenerational Mobility," *American Economic Review: Papers and Proceedings*, Vol. 104, Number 5 (2014): 141–147.
39. David Autor, David Dorn, and Gordon H. Hanson, "The China Syndrome: Local Labor Market Effects of Import Competition in the United States," *American Economic Review*, Vol. 103, Number 6 (2013): 2121–2168.
40. US Census Bureau 2012 Statistical Abstract of the United States, available at http://www.census.gov/compendia/statab/cats/labor_force_employment_earnings/compensation_wages_and_earnings.html.
41. One large obstacle to comprehensive education reform is that K-12 education is primarily financed at the state and local level and operates under state law.

Index

Page numbers in italics refer to tables and figures.

CPSIA information can be obtained
at www.ICGtesting.com
Printed in the USA
LVOW01*1005210116
471647LV00017B/166/P

9 781137 553683